D1207170

Analytical Skills
for Community
Organization
Practice

Analytical Skills for Community Organization Practice

Donna Hardina

COLUMBIA UNIVERSITY PRESS
New York

Columbia University Press
Publishers Since 1893
New York   Chichester, West Sussex

Library of Congress Cataloging-in-Publication Data

Hardina, Donna
　Analytical skills for community organization practice / Donna Hardina.
　　p.　cm.
　Includes bibliographical references and index.
　ISBN 0-231-12180-6 (alk. paper)
　　1. Community organization.　2. Evaluation research (Social action
　programs).　I. Title.
HM766.H37 2002
361.2′5—dc21   2001058378

Casebound editions of Columbia University Press books are printed on
permanent and durable acid-free paper.

Printed in the United States of America

c　10　9　8　7　6　5　4　3　2　1

Contents

Acknowledgments

■ I would like to thank the following friends and colleagues for reviewing sections of the book and for their support during the writing process: Richard Salsgiver, Alice Johnson, John McNutt, Jane Yamaguchi, Serge Lee, and Jane Middleton. Betty Garcia and Jackie Mondros contributed helpful comments about the contents of the manuscript. I would also like to acknowledge the following friends and mentors: Dr. George Hemmens (University of Illinois–Chicago) and Dean Richard Ford (California State University, Fresno, deceased).

I am very grateful to my editor, John Michel, for his help and support. Thanks to Paul Schmitz for his diligent efforts at proofing the early drafts and checking Web addresses. Wei (William) Dai, MSW, conducted much of the original Internet research for this book. I would also like to thank Sherrill Clark and the California Social Work Education Center (CAL-SWEC) for funding the curriculum project that led to the development of this book.

I would also like to thank the following community groups and organizations that assisted my professional development and provided me with a wealth of material for this book: the Hyde Park Kenwood Community Conference, the Hyde Park Tenants Organization, the Illinois Hunger Coalition, the Independent Voters of Illinois—Independent Precinct Organization (IVI-IPO), Metro Ministries (Fresno, CA), the Fresno County Medi-Cal Outreach Project, the Hmong Suicide Prevention Task Force, the Association for Community Organization and Social Administration (ACOSA), and the political campaigns of Toni Preckwinkle (Chicago City Council alderwoman) and Emily Carasco (Windsor, Ontario, candidate for Parliament).

Last, but certainly not least, I want to thank my MSW graduate students in formal organization and community practice courses. You have inspired me!

Preface

■ This book is intended as a guide to advanced community organization at the graduate level. It includes information on technical and analytical skills that are often used in practice but are seldom discussed in community organization courses devoted to case studies, theories, or "action" projects. Some of these skills are taught in field practicum, but practicing organizers often develop them in response to situational demands of the job.

I found that a master's degree in social work and a Ph.D. from a public policy program did not prepare me to conduct demographic analysis, research legislation, or develop funding proposals. Consequently, this book is intended to help community organization students gain the skills they are likely to need in practice. It also contains three chapters on practice models and theories to help students link theories to specific aspects of practice.

I have organized the text around five basic assumptions:

- Organizers must be cognizant of basic theories and models of practice and be prepared to apply them to a variety of practice situations.
- The organizer must be able to use his or her research and analytical skills to conduct an assessment of the situation at hand, the issue involved, the power resources associated with the target and action systems, and probable outcomes.

- Theories, research data, and "practice wisdom" must be combined for the effective development of community intervention plans.
- Computer technology and the Internet provide the organizer with a valuable source of information that can be used for assessment and analysis. It can also be utilized to establish linkages with constituents, colleagues, and decision makers.
- The organizer should use process and outcome evaluation methods; intervention plans should contain evaluation criteria and clear outcome goals.
- Intended beneficiaries as well as organization members and participants in organizing campaigns must be fully informed of the consequences of taking action and must be involved in both intervention planning and evaluation.

In this book, I use the term constituents to describe members, beneficiaries, and others who participate in organizing efforts. Mondros and Wilson (1994) define constituents as those people for whom the organization speaks. Consequently, while an organization's constituency contains both leaders and dues-paying members, it also includes people who benefit from any intervention planned by the organization.

Using Computer Technology

Throughout the book, you will find references to specific types of computer and Internet technology. The following terms and definitions are used:

E-mail. E-mail provides a vehicle for computer users who are connected to the Internet to send mail electronically (Giffords, 1998; McNutt, 2000). This mode of communication is less expensive than sending messages via regular mail. Participants must subscribe to an Internet service provider (ISP). Most large employers (universities, corporations, and government) provide Internet services to their workers. Individuals and small nonprofit organizations are typically charged a monthly fee ($10–$20 per month) for Internet service from private ISPs.

LISTSERVs. A LISTSERV is a device that provides a mechanism through which a large number of users can receive the same E-mail message at once (Giffords, 1998; Grant & Grobman, 1998; McNutt, 2000). Each individual subscriber can send the same message to all other subscribers. To subscribe to the LISTSERV, a participant simply by sending an E-mail and asking to become a member. Most LISTSERVs do not require members to pay a fee. However, members can be required to adhere to certain rules of behavior (for example, no racist or sexist messages or rude comments).

LISTSERVs usually focus on a specific topic and allow members to engage in detailed discussion about the issue. Participants may receive literally hundreds of messages from members over the course of a week, or they may choose to subscribe to a digest service that summarizes the individual messages contributed to the list. LISTSERVs work best when a list administrator or facilitator takes responsibility for processing subscriptions and making sure members follow the rules of protocol.

Chat Rooms. Chat rooms are live conversations that take place during a predesignated time by sending text to a specific "window" or location (Giffords, 1998; Grant & Grobman, 1998). Readers can access your typed words just after you type them. Consequently, you are able to "chat" in real time with other correspondents. A facilitator imposes order and decides when individuals are allowed to "talk." This is essential because chat rooms often contain multiple users. Chat rooms can be used in community practice for meetings or to allow individuals to network.

Bulletin Boards. Electronic bulletin boards allow users to post messages regarding a topic of concern for others to read. Bulletin boards are available on Web sites maintained by organizations. Unlike chat rooms, bulletin boards allow people who are not online at the same time to communicate with one another (Giffords, 1998).

World Wide Web. The Web allows individuals and organizations to post information on pages or sites using a type of document called hypertext (Giffords, 1998). Most computer manufacturers install Web page creation software on their computers' hard drives (in addition to other types of software). Posting information on the Web is a low-cost way of publishing information and making it accessible to the public. To use the Web, each computer user must have a navigator or browser program on his or her computer.

Search Engine. The various ISPs provide a selection of search engines that allow users to access information on the Web related to a variety of topics or to locate individuals and organizations. The most commonly used search engines are Alta Vista, Excite, Infoseek, and Yahoo. The search engine determines what information you will be able to find on the Web (Giffords, 1998).

Web Site and Computer Resources Listed in This Book

This book provides an extensive listing of Web sites for community organization practice. Be aware that Web addresses often change rapidly. Most of the addresses listed in the book were confirmed as close as possible to the time of publication; however, some of these addresses may have changed or fallen into disuse. Consequently, if the address provided here doesn't open the Web site you want, try entering the name of the organization or site into your search engine.

Note also that the Web sites listed here are not exhaustive. Since this textbook pertains exclusively to one field of practice—community organization—some major social work sites (for example, the Social Work Access Network) are not included here. Sites listed are those evaluated as useful for organizers. Readers are encouraged to search for additional sites. Many of the sites listed are related to liberal or progressive politics, but some tilt to the political mainstream.

Many sites maintained by small progressive organizations are not listed here. The list of Web sites barely scratches the surface in terms of its coverage of diversity issues. However, a number of major organizations that represent the interests of women, people of color, older people, persons with disabilities, and gay men, lesbians, and bisexual and transgendered people are listed in the text (for example, the American Association of Retired People, the National Association for the Advancement of Colored People, the National Organization of Women, the Mexican American Legal Defense Fund, and the Human Rights Campaign). The reader should search these sites for links to other organizations that are similar.

As more information becomes available on the Internet, some sources are beginning to charge money for access to their sites (Giffords, 1998). Before using Web sites that charge for information, try to carefully evaluate the product. In addition, you should be aware that most Web sites require you to furnish personal information such as addresses and phone numbers when you register as a member or a customer. Assess whether you want to provide such information. Particularly of concern is the use of credit card information to purchase products on the Web. If you choose to purchase services on the Internet, please make sure that the provider uses a secure server so that unauthorized persons do not gain access to your credit card number (Johnston, 1999).

Although the author has made every attempt to screen the sites listed here, a listing in this text does not indicate endorsement, especially in terms of those sites that charge for their services.

References

Giffords, E. (1998). Social work on the Internet: An introduction. *Social Work, 43*(3), 243–51.

Grant, G., & Grobman, L. (1998). *The social worker's Internet handbook.* Harrisburg, PA: White Hat Communications.

Johnston, M. (1999). *The fundraiser's guide to the Internet.* New York: John Wiley & Sons.

McNutt, J. (2000). Organizing cyberspace: Strategies for teaching about community practice and technology. *Journal of Community Practice, 7*(1), 95–109.

Mondros, J., & Wilson, S. (1994). *Organizing for power and empowerment.* New York: Columbia University Press.

Analytical Skills
for Community
Organization
Practice

1 Introduction to Community Organization Skills

■ Community organizers use a wide variety of intervention strategies to promote social change. Social workers who engage in community practice often take on a variety of roles: They can coordinate community outreach efforts, linking people to services. They work in the constituency offices of elected political leaders. They are employed as social services planners for government agencies. They are social activists working to organize protests for groups such as ACT-UP or consumer boycotts for the National Council of La Raza. Organizers are also employed by interest groups to lobby for legislation or to analyze data to document the impact of government policies.

Community organizers use a great variety of skills to promote social change. Some of these skills are interpersonal, involving the art of motivating people to participate in organizing efforts or to alter the course of decision making by government and social institutions. Other skills are analytical in nature. They involve the collection and interpretation of data by the organizer. Analysis is necessary to ensure that the best and most effective social change strategies are used. The curriculum policy statement of the Council of Social Work Education (CSWE) (1994) specifies that social work students, regardless of practice specialization, must have instruction that "strengthen[s] the student's understanding and appreciation of a scientific, analytic approach to knowledge for the delivery and evaluation of practice" (p. 5). The purpose of this book is to provide community organizers and social work students with a guide that promotes the use of analytical skills in practice.

Most community organization textbooks focus almost exclusively on the organizer's interpersonal skills (Kahn, 1991; Mondros & Wilson, 1994; Rivera & Erlich, 1998; Tropman, 1997). The text introduces the community organization student to a wide variety of analytical tools and decision-making frameworks that can be used for assessment, intervention planning, and evaluation.

This book also includes an introduction to using the Internet for community organization research. The World Wide Web contains a great variety of resources for researching social problems, government policies, legislation, and political campaign funding. Computer networking greatly increases the organizer's access to information. It also gives members of constituency groups an opportunity to increase linkages with each other as well as a vehicle with which to contact decision makers.

Skills for Community Organization Practice

Analytical skills for community practice can be developed in field placements, through action assignments, or in the classroom (Johnson, 1996). Students can find it difficult to develop a consistent set of skills in the field due to diversity in the types of macro field settings available to them. Students can be placed in unions, election campaigns, social planning organizations (such as the United Way), or traditional community organizations. The role of the organizer can differ substantially across settings. Weil and Gamble (1995) have identified at least eight models of community practice.

The great variety of practice settings available to community organization students often makes skills instruction in the classroom difficult. However, a review of the literature on teaching community organization practice (Austin, 1986; Fisher, 1995; Halseth, 1993; Karger & Reitmeir, 1983; Rivera & Erlich, 1998) suggests a number of analytical or technical skills that students should acquire:

- Budgeting
- Grant writing
- Information gathering and processing
- Legislative research
- Needs assessment
- Participatory action research
- Political analysis
- Population forecasting and social indicator analysis
- Power analysis

- Program development and planning
- Resource development

These skills can be used across practice settings, interventions, and situations. Analytical methods help the practitioner identify community problems, plan interventions, and conduct evaluations.

Community Organization Practice and the Problem-Solving Model

This book is organized to help the student or practitioner use the problem-solving model to resolve community problems. The problem-solving model (also known by planners as the rational model) has the following components:

- Problem identification
- Assessment (NEEDS)
- Goal setting
- Implementation
- Evaluation

Social workers in clinical and policy practice also use the problem-solving process to plan and conduct interventions. Gilbert and Terrell (1998) have added two additional components to this model that require specific community organization skills.

1. Inform the community about the problem.
2. Build public support and legitimacy for the action to be taken (pp. 248–49).

In addition to presenting content on community organization values and theories, this book focuses primarily on five stages in the problem-solving model: problem identification, needs assessment, goal setting, implementation, and evaluation. The book also includes material on new computer technologies (primarily E-mail and the World Wide Web) used to inform the public about community problems, influence decision makers, and organize constituency groups. The use of the Internet to conduct assessment and analysis is also described.

Values and Ethics

Before an organizer can identify community problems, he or she must have a thorough knowledge of the values and ethics associated with community practice. Although organizers often share common views about social justice and the empowerment of oppressed populations, the ethical implications of the various strategies and tactics the organizer uses are seldom discussed (Mondros & Wilson, 1994). While the organizer may use in-depth research and analysis to identify effective strategies, his or her personal values also influence these decisions. Seldom are intervention plans "value free."

The code of ethics of the National Association of Social Workers (NASW) provides a framework for making practice-related choices. The code identifies specific aspects of a social worker's responsibility to society, clients, colleagues, and employers. All social workers are required to "advocate for living conditions conducive to the fulfillment of basic human needs and should promote social, economic, political, and cultural values and institutions that are compatible with the realization of social justice" (NASW code, standard 6.01; see Reamer, 1998, p. 283). CSWE, the organization that sets accreditation standards for social work education programs, also defines the purpose of social work as the "alleviation of poverty and oppression" (CSWE, 1994, p. 2). CSWE also specifies that social workers are to "empower" disadvantaged populations (see box, "Council on Social Work Education Curriculum Policy Statement").

Empowerment through Community Organization: Acquiring the Power to Fight Oppression

The purpose of community organization practice is to empower members of oppressed groups. Empowerment can be defined as "the psychological state—a sense of competence, control, and entitlement—that allows one to pursue concrete activities aimed at becoming powerful" (Mondros & Wilson, 1994, p. 5). Empowerment also refers to the process through which people maintain control over their own lives and communities (Staples, 1990). An individual becomes empowered when his or her self-esteem is increased. At the intrapersonal level, empowerment comes through the construction of knowledge and analysis of social problems acquired through shared experience. Within communities, empowerment occurs when social-change strategies are used to acquire goods, services, decision-making authority, and other resources. This in turn helps group members gain control over their environment (Hardina, 1996; Labonte, 1990).

Oppression is "the assumption that one group in our society [the dominant culture] successfully maximizes its life changes by minimizing those of another" (Moreau, 1990, p. 53). Oppressed groups are typically excluded from participation in government decision making and economic or educational opportunities. Oppression is most often based on the characteristics of individuals and groups. This book will use the acronym CRAASH, outlined in the following list, to describe the various forms of oppression. Specific types of oppression can include (but are not limited to):

C	Classism	Oppression directed at people of another social class (most often the poor)
R	Racism	Oppression directed at people of another race or ethnic group
A	Ableism	Oppression directed at people with disabilities
A	Ageism	Oppression directed at older people
S	Sexism	Oppression directed at people of another gender (most often against women)
H	Heterosexism	Oppression directed at people who are gay, lesbian, bisexual, or transgendered (LGBT)

Linking Theory and Practice

Successful community organization practice requires that the social worker be able to use theoretical frameworks to make appropriate practice deci-

---

Council on Social Work Education Curriculum Policy Statement for Master's Degree Programs in Social Work Education

M4.0 Purpose of Social Work

The profession of social work is committed to the enhancement of human well-being and the alleviation of poverty and oppression. The social work profession receives its sanction from public and private auspices and is the primary profession in the provision of social services. Within its general scope of concern, professional social work is practiced in a wide variety of settings and has four related purposes.

M4.1.1 The promotion, restoration, maintenance, and enhancement of the social functioning of individuals, families, groups, organizations, and communities by helping them to accomplish tasks, prevent and alleviate distress, and use resources.

M4.1.2 The planning, formulation, and implementation of social policies, services, resources, and programs needed to meet basic human needs and support the development of human capacities.

M4.1.3 The pursuit of policies, services, resources, and programs through organizational or administrative advocacy and social or political action to empower groups at risk and to promote social and economic justice.

M4.1.4 The development and testing of professional knowledge and skill are related to these purposes.

Source: Council on Social Work Education, 1994.

---

sions. The concept of praxis, the term Freire (1970) assigned to the merging of theory and experience, is an important component in community organization practice. It is expected that the social worker will use his or her own experience to choose theories and skills that are appropriate to a variety of situations. In time, experience will lead the organizer to develop a personal framework for practice as well as knowledge about what works and what doesn't work in practice situations. One of the basic premises of this book is that the beginning practitioner must have a basic knowledge of current and emerging practice theories to select the appropriate practice skills for any situation. Consequently, the first few chapters in this book provide a theoretical overview for community organization practice. Succeeding chapters describe theories pertinent to specific analytical skills.

The easiest way for a community organizer to use theories in day-to-day situations is to rely on practice models. Models incorporate a specific theoretical framework and offer a prescription for how to intervene in specific practice situations. In community organization, the organizer uses models of practice to determine the degree to which he or she assumes control of the social change effort, the types of strategies and tactics used, and specific social work roles inherent in the change process. Models of community organization practice also describe the relationship between the organizer and the target system (i.e., the person or organization to be changed). Models also contain specific value statements about the relationship between the organizer and members of the action system (the constituents or partners in the social change effort).

This book introduces the reader to what Rothman (1995) has identified as the three primary models of community organization practice: social action, social planning, and locality (or community) development. Social action involves organizing and participating in activities intended to influence social change: legislative lobbying, electoral politics, unions, public education campaigns, and protest demonstrations. Community organizers work with a constituency group (usually people traditionally excluded from participation in the larger society). The group then targets government or community institutions in order to influence decision making or redistribute power or other resources. Social planning involves the use of technical skills by one or more experts to examine a variety of program options, choose the best available plan, and implement programs or services. Locality development focuses on bringing all groups in a community together to reach a consensus about community problems and their resolution.

Three emerging models are also examined: the transformative model, feminist organizing, and multicultural practice (Freire, 1970; Hyde, 1994; Rivera & Erlich, 1998). These last three models provide the organizer with a vehicle for making practice responsive to the needs of diverse populations. Freire (1970) developed transformative organizing methods with the primary intention of increasing literacy among low-income peoples in Brazil.

The student participants developed literacy skills and acquired knowledge about how the political structure influenced their lives, and the educator gained information about the participants' traditions and values. The educator also gained knowledge about the oppression the participants experienced. A central component of Freire's work is the development of critical consciousness, defined as

> . . . the process through which personal and political factors interact with each other and one's work, as well as how values, ideas, and practice skills are influenced by social forces and, in turn, influence them. (Rivera & Erlich, p. 7)

Multicultural organizing is heavily influenced by Freire's (1970) work. In addition to the development of a critical consciousness, Gutierrez and Alvarez (2000) describe a number of skills that are useful in working with members of underrepresented communities.

1. Familiarity with the customs, values, and language of members of the constituency group
2. Awareness of one's own cultural biases
3. Ability to empower constituents to make decisions that affect their lives

Another model of practice, feminist organizing, also requires that the organizer work in partnership with constituents to produce change (Hyde, 1994; Weil, 1986). Members of feminist organizations share decision-making power; engage in consciousness raising about oppression; and take action, grounded in feminist principles, to produce social change (Weil & Gamble, 1995).

Assessment Skills

Though many of the skills used in transformative, multicultural, and feminist practice are interpersonal in nature, the organizer must find appropriate ways to acquire information about the values and cultural practices of constituency communities. This textbook gives the reader a description of the research skills needed to become an "active learner" who can exchange information about cultural values with members of diverse groups (Freire, 1970). In addition to presenting traditional quantitative models for community-based needs assessment, sections of this book describe approaches to research that involve members of the constituency group as participants in the research process: ethnographic, feminist, and participatory action research. These methods require the researcher to recognize that community residents and members of groups outside the dominant culture are the best experts about their own lives, values, and experiences. Using participatory research models requires that research incorporate specific value assumptions about the role of the community organizer, the mission of social work practice, and the involvement of constituents in the community organizing process.

This book contains information on assessment tools that organizers can use to document community needs and analyze community decision-making structures and power dynamics. The ability to facilitate political, social, and economic change is essential for any social worker but is especially important for organizers. Consequently, organizers can use analytical skills to analyze legislative processes, the content of policies and legislation, political power, and the electoral process. These chapters contain specific assessment tools and information about using the Internet to conduct power-related research.

Goal Setting and Program Implementation

Once the organizer, in conjunction with constituents, completes a thorough assessment of community needs and power dynamics, he or she must establish intervention goals. This process requires that partners in the intervention process agree on action outcomes and program plans. Effective interventions require clear linkages between theories, practice models, goals, interventions, and proposed outcomes. Consequently, this book describes techniques to identify appropriate strategies and tactics that are central to the development of any social change–oriented intervention plan.

To ensure that organizing efforts are not confined to one-time, crisis-related interventions, organizers must form social change–oriented organizations to sustain their efforts. To this end, the textbook also outlines the skills necessary to sustain any organizing effort: organizational development and maintenance. Organizers should know how to plan programs, set organizational goals, identify appropriate funding sources, write fundable proposals, and raise money from donations or special events. They should also be able to construct program budgets and monitor expenditures.

Evaluation

Organizers should also act to evaluate program outcomes and processes. Although many foundation and government funding sources require that community-based organizations keep careful records of program outcomes, evaluation of practice has evolved into a distinct field of practice. New methods have emerged that require the involvement of organization constituents and staff in a process of self-evaluation. Empowerment-oriented evaluation is used to promote a continuous change that includes program monitoring, process evaluation, and outcome assessment in community-based or social action organizations. Consequently, it becomes a tool for program development, motivation of volunteers, staff performance assessment, and program growth and renewal.

Organization of the Book

This book is organized in a way that explicates the use of the problem-solving model. The remaining fourteen chapters are organized into four distinct sections:

- Concepts and Theories for Practice
- Problem Identification and Assessment
- Goal Setting and Implementation
- Evaluation

Chapters 2 through 5 examine concepts and theories that guide community practice. Without knowledge of concepts and theories, the organizer cannot identify problems, make assessments, set goals, implement programs, or evaluate practice. In chapter 2, basic value assumptions associated with community practice are identified. The relationship between these values and the NASW code of ethics is described. The material in this chapter is also intended to help the reader develop a personal framework for making practice decisions that may involve ethical choices. Chapter 3 offers an overview of theories that guide community practice. Social work practice often relies on systems or ecological theories to bridge the gap between clinical and community practice; community organization also borrows heavily from theories derived from sociology and political science to explain conflicts among competing groups in society. These theories also help explain how coalitions and social movements develop in response to political oppression or public concern for people or entities that are not represented in the political process (e.g., children, the environment, and animals).

Chapter 4 identifies models of practice including community development, social planning, social action, feminist organizing, transformative practice, and multicultural organizing. Each intervention model is linked to the theoretical literature on social forces, interest groups, and social movements. Also described are the appropriate situations in which the organizer should use these models and the likely outcomes associated with each.

Organizers primarily practice their craft in neighborhoods and communities. Chapter 5 provides an overview of the theoretical literature on community that moves beyond the traditional conceptualization of the geographic community to focus on communities of people defined by race, culture, social class, common problems, and the formation of a collective identity. This chapter also describes the rules of inclusion and exclusion that determine the degree to which individuals participate in the life of the community.

The second section of the book, chapters 6 to 9, focuses on specific analytical tools used for problem identification and needs assessment—the first two steps in the problem-solving model. Chapter 6 describes methods used to involve community residents in problem identification. This chapter also contains a description of research methods typically used to assess community problems.

A detailed assessment of communities is never complete without an analysis of power. Chapter 7 contains an overview of the theoretical literature on power in communities. Analytical techniques that can be used to assess the power of individuals, policy makers, interest groups, and social movements are described. Chapters 8 and 9 contain information about analytical techniques related to two specific types of social action: lobbying and electoral politics. Although most social workers will not be employed in organizations primarily devoted to these activities, most social change initiatives require that the organizer participate in efforts to influence legislation. Consequently, it is important for the organizer to know whether individual legislators will be reelected and what interest groups contribute to their campaigns. Chapter 8 presents descriptive information about how to analyze the content of legislation and monitor the status of new legislation as it moves through Congress or the state legislature. In chapter 9, methods used to predict the outcome of political races or identify likely voters are described. Both chapters contain detailed information about how to use the Internet to conduct power analysis.

The third section of the book examines techniques for setting goals and developing intervention plans. Chapter 10 describes strategies and tactics that the organizer should incorporate into an intervention plan to help the organization and constituency group acquire power. Strategy choice is determined by a combination of the organizer's preferences and values, the model of practice chosen in response to the situation at hand, and the preferences of the constituents involved in the intervention. Chapter 11 presents procedures that can be used to plan programs and services or build organizations. Each of these chapters contains an overview of the intervention-planning literature and describes specific analytical procedures. Frameworks for making planning decisions are also provided.

The fourth section of this book contains information that pertains to the implementation stage of the problem-solving process. Once a program is planned, the organizer needs to find the resources to operate it. Chapter 12 includes an examination of the various types of funding available for community intervention and describes the impact of various types of funding (such as government, foundation, corporate, and individual donations) on community-based social action agencies. The chapter also lists Internet resources that can help organizers identify appropriate funding sources. A step-by-step process for developing grant proposals is also included. Chapter 13 describes procedures for constructing and analyzing budget information. This chapter also provides information on Internet sites that an organizer can use to monitor the budgets of government agencies.

The last section of this book pertains to evaluation of practice. Chapter 14 examines evaluation as the final stage in the problem-solving process. As in clinical practice, the organizer must be able to document whether the social change initiative has been effective. If such an effort has not been effective, the organizer will do one of the following:

1. Adopt new strategies and tactics to increase effectiveness
2. Examine the organizing process in order to document barriers to success

In this chapter, qualitative methods, used to examine the organization process, and quantitative methods, used to examine effectiveness, are described. Research methods that organizers can use to involve constituency group members in the evaluation process are also examined.

Chapter 15, the book's conclusion, contains an evaluation of the implications of computer technology for organizing in the new millennium—both an assessment of current computer applications and a prediction of how technology will be used in the future. The use of E-mail to contact constituents and decision makers and the creation of Web pages to transmit information have important implications. The new technology has great potential for increasing linkages among organizations and neighborhood residents and to increase community access to both decision makers and the decision-making process (Grant & Grobman, 1998; Tropman, 1997). Unless computer applications are used cautiously, however, they can increase divisions between those with power and those who have comparatively little voice in social, economic, or political decision making.

Summary

Analytical skills for community practice are applicable to a variety of practice settings and situations. The community organizer must be prepared to be an active learner, finding out about the customs and values of the diverse populations involved in the organizing effort. The organizer must also be prepared to document community needs and evaluate the outcomes of interventions. To generate financial resources and carry out interventions, the organizer must be able to construct and monitor budgets, write grant proposals, and identify appropriate funding sources. To implement successful community change efforts, the organizer must be able to analyze community power dynamics, identify influential interest groups, and monitor the status of pending legislation. Access to the Internet allows the organizer almost unlimited opportunity to conduct much of the analysis needed for community practice.

■ QUESTIONS FOR CLASS DISCUSSION

1. How are the analytical skills needed by the community organizer similar to those skills used in clinical or policy practice?
2. Describe the role of the community organizer in a variety of organizational positions:

   Activist
   Program planner
   Grassroots organizer
   Community development specialist
   Political campaign manager
   Which of the skills described on pages 2–3 could be used in each of these job positions?

3. Describe how the values identified in the NASW code of ethics or the CSWE curriculum statement pertain to community organization practice. Give specific examples.
4. Give examples of oppression exhibited toward members of the demographic groups listed in the CRAASH typology on page 5. Give examples based on your own experiences or situations that you have observed.

References

Austin, M. (1986). Community organization and social administration: Partnership or irrelevance. *Administration in Social Work, 10*(3), 27–39.

Council on Social Work Education (1994). *Curriculum policy statement for master's degree programs in social work education* [On-line]. Available: http://www.cswe.org/mswcps.htm

Fisher, R. (1995). Political social work. *Journal of Social Work Education, 3*, 194–204.

Freire, P. (1970). *Pedagogy of the oppressed.* New York: Continuum Books.

Gilbert, N., & Terrell, P. (1998). *Dimensions of social welfare policy* (4th ed.). Needham Heights, MA: Allyn & Bacon.

Grant, G., & Grobman, L. (1998). *The social worker's Internet handbook.* Harrisburg, PA: White Hat Communications.

Gutierrez, L., & Alvarez, A. (2000). *Educating students for multicultural community practice. Journal of Community Practice, 7*(1), 39–56.

Halseth, J. (1993). Infusing feminist analysis into education for policy, planning, and administration. In T. Mizrahi & J. Morrison (Eds.), *Community organization and social administration* (pp. 225–41). New York: Haworth.

Hardina, D. (1996, Spring). Barriers to consumer empowerment: Implications for health and social services planning in Ontario. *Canadian Review of Social Policy, 37,* 1–19.

Hyde, C. (1994). Commitment to social change: Voices from the feminist movement. *Journal of Community Practice, 1*(2), 23–44.

Johnson, A. (1996). The revitalization of community practice: Characteristics, competencies, and curricula for community-based services. *Journal of Community Practice, 5*(3), 37–62.

Kahn, S. (1991). *Organizing: A guide for grassroots leaders.* Washington, DC: National Association of Social Workers Press.

Karger, H., & Reitmeir, A. (1983). Community organization for the 1980s: Toward developing new skills based within a political framework. *Social Development Issues, 7*(2), 50–61.

Labonte, R. (1990). Empowerment: Notes on professional and community dimensions. *Canadian Review of Social Policy, 26,* 64–75.

Mondros, J., & Wilson, S. (1994). *Organizing for power and empowerment.* New York: Columbia University Press.

Moreau, M. (1990). Empowerment through advocacy and consciousness raising. *Journal of Sociology and Social Welfare, 17*(2), 53–67.

Reamer, F. (1998). *Ethical standards in social work.* Washington, DC: National Association of Social Workers.

Rivera, F., & Erlich, J. (1998). *Community organizing in a diverse society* (3d ed.). Boston: Allyn & Bacon.

Rothman, J. (1995). Approaches to community intervention. In F. Cox, J. Erlich, J. Rothman, & J. Tropman (Eds.), *Strategies of community organization* (5th ed., pp. 26–63). Itasca, IL: F. E. Peacock.

Staples, L. (1990). Powerful ideas about empowerment. *Administration in Social Work, 14*(2), 29–42.

Tropman, J. (1997). *Successful community leadership: A skills guide for volunteers and professionals.* Washington, DC: National Association of Social Workers Press.

Weil, M. (1986). Women, community, and organizing. In N. Van Den Bergh & L. Cooper (Eds.), *Feminist visions for social work* (pp. 187–210). Silver Spring, MD: National Association of Social Workers.

Weil, M., & Gamble D. (1995). Community practice models. In R. L. Edwards (Ed.), *Encyclopedia of Social Work* (19th ed., pp. 577–94). Washington, DC: National Association of Social Workers.

PART ONE

Concepts and Theories for Practice

2 Values and Ethics

■ This chapter discusses basic values inherent in community practice. It describes similarities and differences between those values inherent in models of community practice and the values identified in the National Association of Social Workers (NASW) code of ethics. The ethical mandates inherent in the NASW code are examined, and an exploration is made as to how these mandates do or do not pertain to community organization. Ethical dilemmas that community organizers encounter are identified. The last section of this chapter presents decision tools that the organizer can use when facing complex ethical decisions.

Basic Values in Community Practice

Social work is built around a value base that makes it distinct from other professions. One primary concept that unites all fields of social work practice is a commitment to social justice (Reamer, 1999). However, community organization practice can be viewed as a unique form requiring an ethical code and a theoretical framework that commit the organizer to the struggle for changes in social structure that improve economic conditions and civil rights for members of marginalized groups (Rivera & Erlich, 1998). The NASW code of ethics (1996) focuses primarily on the context of clinical practice with individuals, families, and small groups in traditional agency settings. Though the NASW code contains many principles for action that also pertain to the work of the organizer, it does not begin to cover many of the practice situations a typical organizer may encounter outside agency settings. Ethical practice in community organization can be said to differ from that of clinical practice in that:

1. Social transformation is the primary goal of intervention.
2. The social worker must develop a critical consciousness about social and economic conditions that contribute to the marginalization of oppressed groups.
3. Development of critical consciousness among constituency group members is also one of the goals of ethical practice.
4. Clients are primarily constituency group members, residents of target communities, and members of oppressed populations. In many instances, organizers will not have direct contact with all members of the client group.
5. Most interventions take place in alliance with constituency group members. In some situations, the constituency group employs the organizer.
6. Practice is devoted to increasing the power of marginalized groups. Community organization should not be used to sustain oppressive systems.
7. The primary purpose of community organization practice is empowerment. It is recognized that involvement in government and private agency decision making has positive effects on individuals, increasing a sense of mastery over one's environment and improving self-concept (Parsons, Gutierrez, & Cox, 1998).
8. Working with people to gain power requires the use of confrontation tactics, targeting powerful groups in society. Gaining recognition from the public and access to decision making often requires tactics that make the targets uncomfortable (Alinksy, 1971; Reamer, 1999). It also requires risk taking on the part of constituency group members.
9. Ethical conduct is often viewed as situational, requiring that the organizer assess the seriousness of the situation, the accessibility of the decision makers, and the possible risks to targets before deciding on the appropriate use of tactics (Warren, 1971).

Lowenberg and Dolgoff (1996) distinguish between values and ethics: "Values are concerned with what is 'good' and 'desirable,' while ethics deal with what is 'right' and 'correct'" (p. 21). In other words, values are statements of an ideal that we may strive to achieve, whereas ethics offer us a directive for actions that are derived from the desired values. A number of basic values characterize community organization practice. Some of these values are included in the NASW code of ethics; others are not mentioned in the code but are identified throughout the community organization literature (Freire, 1970; Gil, 1998; Gutierrez & Alvarez, 2000; Hardcastle, Wenocur, & Powers, 1997; Kahn, 1991; Rivera & Erlich, 1998; Weil, 1996; Zachary, 2000):

- Diversity and cultural understanding
- Self-determination and empowerment
- Development of a critical consciousness
- Mutual learning
- Commitment to social justice and the equal distribution of resources

Diversity and Cultural Understanding

Standard 1.05 (a) of the NASW code of ethics states: "Social workers should understand culture and its function in human behavior and society, recognizing the strengths that exist in all cultures." Standard 1.05 (b) requires that social workers demonstrate cultural competence in service delivery. Cultural competence requires that the social worker obtain knowledge about a variety of cultural groups, understand the concept of cultural identity, be open to different perspectives, and be able to communicate across these differences (Gutierrez & Alvarez, 2000).

Lum (1996) defines culture as the "lifestyle practices of particular groups of people who are influenced by a learned pattern of values, beliefs, and cultural modalities" (p. 72). Hence, the term "culture" refers not only to ethnic populations, but also to groups that engage in behaviors and practices that make them distinct and separate from the dominant culture. For example, cultural groups can include lesbian, gay, bisexual, and transgendered (LGBT) individuals, people with disabilities, or members of Amish communities. The Council on Social Work Education (CSWE) requires that schools of social work provide a curriculum that focuses on the following diverse groups: women, LGBT individuals, and people of color (CSWE, 1994). In addition, the curriculum must contain content on populations at risk that includes such factors as age, culture, ethnicity, physical or mental disability, religion, and social class.

Community organizers recognize that "oppression originates in and is maintained by the normative group through institutional and economic power and through institutional and individual violence" (Van Voorhis, 1998, p. 122). hooks (1984) defines oppression as the "absence of choices." Opportunities are limited for certain individuals and groups in terms of class, race, age, physical or mental abilities, gender, and gender orientation. Understanding culture requires that a practitioner understand not only the cultural values and meanings associated with certain decisions and actions, but also how oppression is experienced by members of various cultural and demographic groups. For example, Steinberg, Sullivan, and Loew (1998) surveyed deaf consumers and identified a number of cultural and linguistic barriers to mental health access for new immigrants from non–English-speaking cultures. Many of the respondents struggled to find accessible mental health services delivered by therapists fluent in American Sign Language (ASL); English-language mental health terms such as "depression" or "addiction" were unfamiliar to many of the people surveyed (although many were familiar with these terms in ASL). Consequently, mental health services for these consumers were substantially less accessible than similar services for members of the dominant (English-speaking) culture.

Young (1990) uses the following criteria to determine whether individuals are oppressed by the dominant culture:

1. The benefits of their work or energy go to others.
2. They are excluded from participation in many employment opportunities and social activities.
3. Many aspects of their lives are undertaken under the authority of others.
4. They are stereotyped by the dominant culture.
5. Aspects of their lives are often "invisible" to members of other population groups.
6. They seldom are asked for their perspectives or input on social issues or governance.
7. They may experience harassment or violence. (p. 128)

Community organization requires actions to facilitate equal access to resources and participation in policy-related decision making for members of marginalized cultural groups. Standard 6.04 of the NASW code of ethics states that:

Social workers should act to prevent and eliminate domination of, exploitation of, and discrimination against any person, group, or class on the basis of race, ethnicity, national origin, color, sex, sexual orientation, age, marital status, political belief, religion, or mental or physical disability. (NASW code of ethics as cited in Reamer, 1998, p. 284)

Although this statement seems quite explicit, Lum (1996) argues that the Code of Ethics offers insufficient information about how a social worker should interact with cultural groups. He has suggested that the following statements be incorporated into the code:

1. Social work values family unification, parental leadership, respect for the elderly, and collective family decision making.

2. Social work encourages the healthy application of religious and spiritual beliefs and practices, which join the individual and family to collective institutions and cosmic forces in the universe, resulting in harmony, unity, and wholeness.
3. Social work seeks to use family kinship and community networks as supportive means of treatment for persons who are able to benefit from collective help.
4. Social work values the rediscovery of ethnic language and cultural identity, which strengthens a person's relationship to his or her heritage. (p.62)

Self-Determination and Empowerment

The principle of self-determination (Standard 1.02, NASW code) makes it clear that social work clients and constituents should be involved in intervention decisions and should be able to choose how the intervention is applied and the outcome that it produces. Note, however, that the NASW code places limits on self-determination in situations in which a client's actions may cause personal harm or hurt others. In such situations, the social worker can use professional judgment to override what the client wants. Again, this provision of the code is most often viewed as pertinent to clinical situations in which a client is not competent to make sound judgments about his or her actions (Reamer, 1998).

Community organizers often reject the idea that people are not competent to choose appropriate interventions. With empowerment as one of the primary goals of community practice, constituent involvement in decision making is viewed as paramount (Kahn, 1991). Many organizers feel that traditional models of both micro and macro practice place power in the hands of the social worker rather than the client. The social worker's professional degree gives him or her the power to determine who receives benefits and when and whether to intervene (Hardina, 1990). Manning (1997) argues that even advocacy practice threatens the autonomy of the person who receives the help. "It is difficult to speak and act for another person, because practice is often with strangers and the values of clients are not always known" (p. 227).

Rapp, Shera, and Kisthardt (1993) define empowerment as "confidence, control, decision authority, influence, autonomy and self-trust" (p. 733). Constituent involvement in decision making is typically viewed as containing therapeutic elements that can be used to assist members of marginalized groups obtain a sense of self-mastery. Empowerment practice is essential because oppressed people often internalize their treatment by the dominant culture and thus acquire negative self-images (Simon, 1994).

Though the community organization process should lead to empowerment, organizers cannot assume a paternalistic role and "empower" individuals and groups:

> If empowerment in the social services environment is a process that can be initiated and sustained only by those who seek power and self-determination, then it cannot legitimately be conferred by others who can define the parameters of such power. Thus, mere consumer participation allowed in professionally run services must be seen as distinct from true consumer control. (Segal and Silverman, 1993, p. 710)

Empowerment is acquired through the acquisition of leadership and decision-making skills. Organizers provide constituents with opportunities to develop and use these skills. For example, serving as a member on a board or advisory council, forming a constituency group for parents of schoolchildren, knocking on doors to organize a block club for neighborhood residents, giving testimony at a public hearing, and confronting public officials at a community forum are all avenues for attaining empowerment-oriented skills. Transmission of advocacy skills empowers both the users of the information as well as the practitioners who transmit these skills, increasing the effectiveness of social change efforts (Hardina, 1997).

Public and private organizations typically empower citizens by giving them formal roles in decisions that affect their lives (Forester, 1999). For example, organizations can confer power by involving individuals in the creation of community plans or allocating seats on government commissions. However, as Arnstein (1969) has written, sometimes these positions offer no real opportunity for citizens to actually give input or have control (see figure 2.1). Even in situations where power brokers make well-intentioned efforts to include underrepresented groups in the planning process, all potential participants may find that their perspectives on the issue are ignored (Baum, 1998; Tauxe, 1995). Young (1990) argues that special efforts must be made to ensure that oppressed peoples are included in decision making because:

> The privileged are usually not inclined to protect and further the interests of the oppressed, partly because their social position prevents them from understanding those interests, and partly because to some degree their privilege depends on the continued oppression of others. Therefore, a major reason for explicit representation of oppressed groups in discussion and decision making is to undermine oppression. (p. 129)

Consequently, social workers must take a lead role in social service organizations to establish institutional structures that place constituents (i.e., community residents, low-income consumers, members of culturally oppressed groups) in decision-making roles. Seats on boards of directors or advisory panels, or simple partnerships with organizers in planning direct actions are mechanisms typically used to empower low-income consumers.

Figure 2.1. Arnstein's Ladder of Citizen Participation.

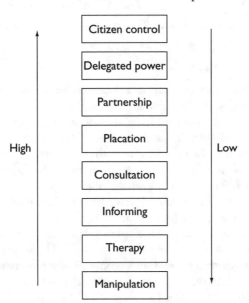

Source: Arnstein, S. (1969). A ladder of citizen participation. *Journal of the American Institute of Planners, 35*(4), 216–24.

Hardina and Malott (1996) note that members of marginalized groups may experience further oppression when given token roles on decision-making boards. Staff and middle- or upper-income board members often have professional degrees that serve to increase their power advantage vis-à-vis representatives of low-income or other marginalized groups. The technical language professional staff use presents a formidable obstacle to the inclusion of nonexperts in the decision-making process (Barr, 1979).

Oppressed groups have few power resources (e.g., money, contacts with politicians, and social status), which further limits their ability to bargain with professional staff and government officials (Winkle, 1991). O'Neill (1992) argues that representatives of low-income and other marginalized groups are more effective on boards when they represent powerful community constituency groups. Such groups obtain power through their membership (strength in numbers), ability to influence the media, and linkages with community institutions. O'Neill identifies four characteristics of successful constituency group leaders:

1. A source of adequate and accurate information
2. Support from other constituency group members

3. The personality to stand up to administrators and other decision makers
4. Established mechanisms for feedback from constituency groups

Development of a Critical Consciousness

To be an effective organizer, one must "realize that prevailing conditions of multidimensional social inequalities were established, and are being reproduced, by overt and covert coercion and socialization rather than by 'acts of gods,' or by voluntary, democratic choices" (Gil, 1998, p. 49). Development of a critical consciousness means that the organizer must not only recognize how society operates to foster oppression, but he or she must also continue to observe and gain knowledge about oppressive social structures and decision-making processes (Freire, 1970). In addition, the organizer must communicate knowledge to others. A central component of the change process is that the organizer must interact with individuals and groups so that they will develop a critical consciousness as well. An understanding of the oppressive nature of social and economic institutions will transform individuals into activists and subsequently help change society. As more people are transformed, social structures will become more humane and more responsive to the needs of individuals. Understanding how society functions to marginalize women, LGBT individuals, people of color, older persons, people with disabilities, the poor, and diverse social groups will help individuals overcome their own prejudices. It will also reduce social stigma and prevent the internalization of oppression (self-blame) by members of marginalized groups (Gutierrez & Alvarez, 2000).

According to Gil (1998), development of a critical consciousness among constituency group members requires both dialogue and education. The transformative process contains the following elements:

- Common perceptions of social reality
- Beliefs and assumptions
- Perceptions of individual and societal needs
- Values and ideologies, which are derived from perceptions of need (p. 49)

These ideologies determine the choices available to individuals and actions that can be taken by change agents. In community organizing, the process of conscientization must take place in the context of mutual learning.

Mutual Learning

The social worker's own "values, beliefs, behaviors and customs may distort communication and promote domination" (Uehara & Sohng, 1996, p. 616).

Consequently, social workers must become active learners, gaining knowledge about the cultural backgrounds of their constituent partners in the organizing process (Gutierrez & Alvarez, 2000; Wint & Sewpaul, 2000). Successful practice, however, requires much more than simply a willingness to learn about the experiences of those who are oppressed. Social workers must be able to "elevate consumers from the role of client to the roles of teacher and partner in a collective learning enterprise" (Rapp et al., 1993, p. 734). According to Van Voorhis (1998), "Mutually empathic, collaborative relationships are fostered by social workers who help clients develop a well-defined sense of self, validate the clients' experiences, build collaborative relationships, and share power" (p. 127).

According to Zachary (2000), group processes that emphasize shared-power rather than authoritarian-style decision making should be used when recruiting community leaders. Zachary's approach to training community leaders includes three primary elements:

- Locates power and meaning in the collective, not the individual leader.
- Considers leadership a largely functional position that does not confer special privileges and status.
- Views mutual dialogue between leaders and members as the dominant method for charting future directions. (p. 75)

In short, organizers must recognize constituents as equal partners in the change process while acknowledging that most constituency groups do not have equal rights in economic, political, and social systems. All constituents in the community-organization process are equal partners in social change: MSWs, lawyers, Ph.D.s, doctors, and elected officials have the same status in the change process as paraprofessionals, high school dropouts, the homeless, and people who receive welfare. All constituents should be treated with dignity and respect and their opinions valued. Consequently, the organizer (especially an organizer with an MSW) must possess *humility* (Burghardt, 1982).

Mutual learning can be defined as a skill that must be developed to maintain equality in relationships among participants in the organizing process. It also requires that the organizer reject, in principle, patterns of domination and authority inherent in hierarchical decision-making structures. As noted in the feminist literature on community organization practice (Gutierrez & Lewis, 1998; Hyde, 1994), equal partnerships characterized by cooperation, power sharing, and consensus building are considered an essential component of practice. However, historical and procedural barriers often block attainment of this in practice. Classism and racism as well as differences in educational achievement and cultural values often create environments in which white professionals dominate the decision-making process. Organizers must make special efforts to foster trust as well as mutual learning across these differences.

Ethical Dilemma #1

You are an organizer for a tenant's-rights organization. Your group has worked with the city government to force a slum landlord to bring his buildings up to code. Repeated court orders and fines have not been effective. Tenants in one of the worst buildings currently have no heat or hot water (it is late fall; winter temperatures in your city often fall below 0 degrees Fahrenheit). The apartments are full of roaches, and a rat has bitten a small child. In consultation with the tenants, you decide that the best way to force the landlord to bring his building up to code is by picketing his home. Two successive days of picketing produce only anger on the part of the landlord and distress in his family members (including several small children). One of the neighbors advises you that the landlord recently brought his wife home from the hospital. She has terminal cancer and has requested that she be allowed to die at home. What do you do?

1. Cancel further plans to picket the landlord's home. Picket the landlord's business instead.
2. Consult with the tenants about whether to proceed with picketing in front of the landlord's home. Advise tenants to discontinue the action.
3. Consult with tenants about whether to proceed with picketing in front of the landlord's home. Advise tenants to continue their efforts.
4. Consult with tenants about whether to proceed with picketing in front of the landlord's home. Make no attempt to influence the decision.
5. Do nothing.

Commitment to Social Justice and the Equal Distribution of Resources

According to Uehara and Sohng (1996), the goal of multicultural social work "is social justice and the transformation of contemporary sociocultural structures and processes that support injustice and inequality" (p. 616). Therefore, community organization practice places social workers "on the side" of groups who have experienced oppression. Although the NASW code of ethics is explicit about the responsibility of social workers to promote social justice (Standards 6.01–6.03), many macro practitioners argue that the profession has largely abandoned its commitment to social change in favor of psychotherapeutic approaches (Abramovitz, 1993; Specht & Courtney, 1994).

Manning (1997) argues that to work for social justice, social workers must become "moral citizens," fighting against organizational and professional practices that are harmful. Social justice can be defined as values that support "justice and fairness to individuals, a sense of collective societal responsibility for the welfare of individuals, and a sense of altruism that accepts personal responsibility for solving problems" (Mondros & Wilson,

1994, p. 15). Social workers generally regard social justice as requiring the equal distribution of resources, opportunities, civil rights, and benefits to all members of society (Reamer, 1998; Robinson & Reeser, 2000).

Much of recent modern thought on social justice is derived from the philosophy of John Rawls (1971). In *A Theory of Justice*, Rawls describes his belief that individuals in the founding stages of a new society, operating under a "veil of ignorance," would choose a set of principles that would ensure the creation of a "just" society, based on the principle of fairness. These principles would likely be chosen because the founders would have no idea about how they would benefit from them. One primary component inherent in these principles is the "maximin rule," the idea that all policies must benefit the least advantaged members of society (Abrams, 1980). Consequently, the purpose of government would be to constantly adjust resources and opportunities for all citizens. Rawls's concept of social justice requires the use of legal mechanisms (such as legislation and courts) to obtain resources for members of oppressed groups. It also requires social workers to engage in a variety of activities (legislative campaigns, grassroots organizing, and participation in social movements) to obtain justice.

An alternative view of justice is offered by Carol Gilligan (1988). Citing studies that have examined moral reasoning among adolescents, Gilligan argues that men and women tend to view morality differently. Men are more likely to use established systems of obligations and rights to examine questions of resource distribution and ethical imperatives. The concept of "fairness" often guides the decision-making process. Women, on the other hand, are more likely to make ethical judgments based on their personal relationships to others and their own perceptions of "the need of people for help and the ability of people to help one another" (p. xxxv). Moral reasoning is developed through personal interaction with others rather than from a set of ethical principles. Gilligan has called this orientation to ethical reasoning the *ethics of care*. However, Flanagan and Jackson (1990) argue that choices involving justice and care perspectives are not necessarily gender exclusive or dichotomous. Instead, these criteria may be viewed as a continuum with individual choices varying by the situation and the type of problem, and the relationship between the decision maker and the people affected by the decision.

The NASW Code of Ethics and the Community Organizer

The NASW code of ethics is primarily oriented toward situations that affect clinicians and their clients (Reamer, 1998, 1999). The code also pertains to relationships between employers and employees as well as relationships among coworkers. Much of the code describes appropriate behavior in agency settings; only clauses prohibiting sexual relations (with clients or relatives of clients) and conflict of interest and those dealing with social justice specifically pertain to social workers' conduct outside the agency or in the community.

The 1976 version of the code of ethics was particularly problematic for community organizers and agency whistleblowers (Bull, 1989). Competing clauses required the social worker to:

1. Remain loyal to his or her employer and implement agency policies
2. Advocate to help clients obtain equal access to resources

The current code, revised in 1996, makes it clear that the social worker's first duty is to clients or program beneficiaries. Social workers are mandated to act when confronted by policies that are harmful to clients. Social workers also have a duty to report unethical agency practices and unethical social workers to the appropriate supervisory staff, licensing boards, or regulatory authorities. However, the code makes no provisions (nor do national or local NASW chapters) to provide legal defense and other support services to social workers who lose jobs or are otherwise penalized for their efforts (Bull, 1989). Also unclear are actions social workers should take when they confront situations in which no effective agency or government policies pertain. For example, what does a social worker do when she finds that a colleague has repeatedly harassed a member of the agency's clerical staff? If the agency has implemented a sexual harassment policy, then the procedure for making reports should be clear. If no policy exists, the social worker would have a duty under the code to advocate for its implementation (Weil, Hughes, & Hooyman, 1994). However, building the intraagency coalition necessary to construct and implement an appropriate policy would be a long-term goal—the social worker may have few intervention options to deal with the immediate problem.

Uncharted Territory: How Should the Organizer Apply Other Aspects of the Code of Ethics to Community Work?

The types of interventions the organizer uses, the client groups involved, the targets of the social change efforts, and the urgency of the issues create a number of situations that are not adequately covered by the NASW code of ethics. One area in which the code is inadequate to address ethical concerns for organizers involves sexual relations with constituents. Additional areas of concern include the choice of tactics the organizer uses, the concept of "informed consent," and sacrificing short-term goals for long-term gain.

Sexual Relations

If the community is an organizer's client, is he or she prohibited from engaging in an intimate relationship with any member of that community?

Obviously, such a prohibition is unfeasible. Yet where should organizers draw appropriate boundaries for friendships and dating situations? The code of ethics makes it very clear that relationships with subordinates and students are prohibited (Kagel & Geibelhausen, 1994; Reamer, 1999). However, organizers should add board members, employers, and targets (individual decision makers and their associates) to this list. Conflicts of interest are involved that interfere with performance evaluations and the success of organizing efforts. Most volunteers and constituents involved in organizing campaigns are also off-limits. Inexperienced organizers may mistake attraction to the organizing effort or the charisma of the facilitator with genuine regard for the organizer as a person.

Robinson and Reeser (2000) describe the practitioner's responsibility to establish clear boundaries with constituents:

> Because they are in positions of power, and presumably have experience about how relationships can go wrong, they have a special obligation to ensure that the relationship goes well, taking special care to encourage the right sorts of responses and to empower clients to act in their own self-interest. (p. 103)

During the antiwar movement of the 1960s, using sex to generate volunteers was known as "horizontal recruitment." Using such tactics in community practice can lead to charges of exploitation or harassment (NASW code, Standards 1.09, 1.10, 1.11, 2.07, and 2.08). This is particularly of concern in situations where the volunteer does not genuinely support the cause, or when organizing activities may place the volunteer at risk (of arrest, losing a job, etc.). Friendships with members of the constituency group often are essential to the organizing effort, especially when the organizer needs to acquire knowledge about the culture and lifestyle of community members (Congress, 1996; Rivera & Erlich, 1998). Attending birthday parties, weddings, school plays, and block parties is an essential part of the organizer's role. Establishing trusting relationships with volunteers is of the utmost importance. The organizer should use a combination of practice experience, guidance from peers and supervisors, and knowledge of the code of ethics to establish appropriate boundaries with constituents.

Congress (1996) developed a list of criteria that social work academics can use to examine the ethical implications of dual relationships with students. The list is adapted here for use by organizers to examine whether relationships with volunteers or members of the organizer's constituency group are unethical.

1. Does the dual relationship with the volunteer or constituent involve the role of sexual partner?
2. Does the relationship exploit or harm the volunteer or constituent?

3. Does the dual relationship take unclear advantage of the organizer's greater power in the relationship?
4. Does the relationship affect other volunteers or constituents?
5. How do the organizer's colleagues view the relationship?

Reamer (1998) argues that dual relationships in macro practice settings are potentially less exploitative than those that take place within the context of clinical practice. He recommends using the following criteria to determine whether a sexual relationship with a constituent is appropriate: whether a significant length of time has passed since the termination of the professional relationship, the length of the professional relationship itself, the emotional stability of the constituent, and the amount of risk to the constituent. Short-term professional relationships that occurred a number of years in the past and did not involve psychotherapy or potential risk are the most likely not to cause harm if a personal relationship is initiated.

Choice of Tactics

Other ethical issues specific to community organization practice involve use of tactical methods. Alinsky (1971) argued that the "ends justify the means." He believed that any tactic is appropriate if it allows organizers to be successful in fighting for a cause. For example, during one organizing effort, Alinsky threatened to have all the toilets at Chicago's O'Hare Airport flushed at one time (allegedly this would have lowered the city's water pressure) (Fisher, 1994). On a number of occasions, Alinksy brought African American volunteers into white communities and institutions in an effort to both confront and frighten members of white elites engaged in harmful or exclusionary tactics. Consequently, tactics such as these can cause humiliation, social ostracism, or loss of employment and income. Participation in such actions can place members of the constituency group at risk. They can face retaliation from people associated with the target group.

Social action often involves the use of confrontational tactics (Hardina, 1997). These tactics are generally used to increase the power of constituency groups that represent marginalized members of society: the poor, people with disabilities, LGBT individuals, and members of other subordinated groups. Though confrontation most often involves picketing, demonstrations, strikes, and boycotts, it may also require the use of Alinsky-style tactics to force targeted decision makers to change their position on the issue at hand. Similar tactics, commonly used in political campaigns, include negative advertising and mudslinging.

Do the ends ever justify the means? Hardina (2000) surveyed community-organization instructors in schools of social work and asked them to identify tactics they felt were unethical. Respondents identified the following unethical tactics: "violence, deceit, and causing personal degradation or harm" (p. 13). A number of respondents gave examples of specific tactics that might cause personal harm, including going to an individual's home to demonstrate, personal attacks, and "outing" gay men or lesbians. Other unethical tactics respondents identified included lying, "deception and fraud on behalf of the client organization," and putting constituents "at risk without their understanding" (p. 14).

The social work ethics literature generally limits discussions of violence to those in which a therapist has reasonable knowledge that a patient intends to commit a violent act (Reamer, 1998). In such situations, it is generally held that the social worker has a duty to report the client to the appropriate authorities. In community organization, unintended violence can occur in relation to specific social change–related actions (for example, strikes, boycotts, and demonstrations). While most social workers would discourage violent action, the professional literature does not mention the organizer's duty to report such activity. Some organizers believe that the seriousness of the issue (risk of death or injury to innocent populations) could require the escalation of confrontation-related tactics or civil disobedience. For example, one respondent in Hardina's (2000) study of tactical decision making found the following tactics unethical, except in one particular situation:

> Violence, terrorism, destruction of property, lying, stealing (although I would have used any and all of these against the Nazis). I would have no problem with militant direct action, which is non-violent, but against the law. (p. 13)

Ethical Dilemma #2

You have a paid position as a field coordinator for a congressional campaign. Recent polls have revealed that your candidate is losing 47 percent to 53 percent. Both candidates have made a pledge to refrain from negative campaign advertising. You receive an anonymous letter in the mail that provides detailed proof that the opposition candidate has recently purchased cocaine from street dealers. What do you do with this information? Do you:

1. Inform your candidate and the campaign manager. Argue that the release of this information to the press would ensure a victory for your candidate.
2. Inform your candidate and the campaign manager. Argue that this information should be turned over to the opposition candidate.
3. Design an ad campaign that uses this information to discredit the opponent. Convince your candidate that such ads are critical to the success of his campaign.
4. Do nothing. Put the documentation through the office shredder.

Chapter 10 of this book explores decision-making rules that organizers can use to examine the appropriate use of strategies and tactics ranging from cooperation and consensus to civil disobedience.

Value Conflict

An issue specific to organizing has to do with whether the organizer engages in social action efforts that are at odds with his or her own values. If the goal is to promote self-determination and empowerment, shouldn't the organizer follow all directives given by constituency group members? Robert Fisher (1996), in *Let the People Decide*, described Alinsky's efforts to organize cross-culturally in the "Back of the Yards" neighborhood of Chicago. Recruitment of traditional community leaders and institutions to head the organizing process resulted in the organization's adoption of conservative politics (and failure to support integration efforts). A similar dilemma might occur for an organizer in situations where residents decide to organize against the location of a group home or halfway house in their neighborhood. Organizers need to weigh specify ethical values (such as self-determination and social justice) and assess personal risks and benefits before taking action to resolve such conflicts. For example, is the loss of one's job the potential price for challenging one's employer? Can or should the organizer live with the ethical dilemma involved in following through with employer or constituent demands for actions that conflict with his or her professional values?

Informed Consent

Two issues tangential to discussions of ethical tactics are informed consent and sacrificing short-term benefits to constituents for long-term societal change. Informed consent in clinical practice often requires that clients sign written statements that list the benefits and risks associated with specific interventions. Though organizers generally dispense with written consent, it is assumed that they will be explicit with constituents about the consequences of participation in organizing efforts. However, without written consent forms, ways to ensure that consent has been obtained are limited (Lowenberg & Dolgoff, 1996). We may assume that lack of a verbal response to a request for action implies consent, when in fact this is not the case. People can decide to withdraw consent in risky situations simply by failing to act or refusing to attend certain events. One procedure organizers use to obtain consent involves a meeting in which all members debate the risks and benefits of the proposed action and attempt to reach a consensus on the tactics to be used (Lee, 1986). This procedure is probably the best method of establishing consent. However, this process is also time-consuming; it may not always be possible to achieve a consensus or to fully consult with all potential participants before the action takes place.

In some instances, organizers may ask constituents to make personal sacrifices so that social justice goals might be achieved. For example, animal rights organizers may encourage members to spray paint on the mink coats of patrons entering or leaving furriers' establishments. The risk of arrest may be viewed as essential in stopping inhumane practices in the fur industry. Constituents should be fully informed about specific consequences of their action, especially in instances where personal sacrifices (e.g., job loss, arrest, social stigma) are great.

Long-Term versus Short-Term Gains

Organizers also confront situations in which short-term help for individuals is sacrificed for long-term goals (Bailey & Brake, 1975). For example, in lieu of helping an individual replace stolen food stamp benefits for the previous month, we may ask her to participate in a class-action suit that challenges the way that food stamps are allocated and delivered to participants. In such cases, the individual's immediate well-being is sacrificed for the greater good. The principle of self-determination identified in the NASW code requires that constituents be fully informed and involved in making such decisions. Organizers can often soften the blow of short-term sacrifices by helping constituents acquire resources (such as emergency food) from other agencies or donors.

Reporting Criminal Activity to Authorities

Many states require that individuals in social work positions report individuals engaged in abusive behavior (primarily toward children or the elderly)

Ethical Dilemma #3

You are recruiting employees of a tomato-processing plant during a union organizing drive. One prospective recruit tells you that she fears she will be fired by her employer or subjected to on-the-job harassment. She asks you to describe the protections the union provides to new members. She also wants you to be candid about the possible risks of taking action. You know that during previous organizing attempts at this plant, union supporters have been fired. The union has been able to provide only $200 and a few bags of food to each terminated employee. What do you tell her?

1. Tell her that the long-term benefits of unionization for her and other employees outweigh the risk.
2. Tell her that there are no risks.
3. Candidly discuss the risks and benefits of joining the union.
4. Tell her nothing and let her make her own decision.

---

to the proper authorities. Though the protection of dependent persons is often viewed as an important principle in social work practice, the obligations of social workers who are not clinicians are ambiguous. Community organizers often encounter situations where constituency group members engage in activities that the dominant culture views as deviant or criminal. Consequently, the organizer's responsibility to report individuals who potentially could harm themselves or others is unclear. Reporting individuals to authorities for minor offenses conflicts with efforts to establish trust with members of marginalized groups. It can also be argued that some behaviors that the dominant culture typically punishes or frowns upon can be an essential component of everyday survival among members of some nondominant groups: selling food stamps, underreporting job-related income to welfare authorities, and some types of criminal acts (such as petty thievery, drug dealing, or prostitution).

Inexperienced organizers may misinterpret statements about these activities or try to prevent their occurrence. Consequently, reporting these events can damage the organizer's reputation and conflict with constituent self-determination. It is critical that constituents be involved in organization decision making in partnership with the organizers, that the use of strategies and tactics be planned in advanced, and that the organizer make every effort to be knowledgeable about the ramification of his or her actions as well as pertinent legal statutes. In addition, the organizer must be knowledgeable about prevailing cultural norms, traditions, and sanctions imposed for extralegal or unsanctioned behavior.

Complicating the issue of the duty to report is the fact that social workers in most states are required by law to report child and elder abuse. Social workers should examine state statutes on mandatory reporting and consult with other professionals to examine their responsibilities under the law. Although community organizers are often not explicitly identified in the statutes as mandatory reporters, such responsibilities can be required for those social workers in integrated (micro and macro) practice or those who work as organizers for public and private child-welfare agencies. In such cases, the organizer may face a number of ethical dilemmas.

Ethical Decision-Making Tools for the Organizer

There are no specific provisions in the NASW code of ethics that help the organizer sort out "means versus ends" dilemmas (Reisch & Lowe, 2000). According to Hardcastle et al. (1997), ethical dilemmas occur when "two ethical dilemmas require equal but opposite behavior and the ethical guidelines do not give clear directions or indicate clearly which ethical imperative to follow" (p. 22). Dilemmas must be linked to specific outcomes that the organizer hopes to achieve (Rothman, 1998).

Often the organizer can use prevailing theories to sort out ethical dilemmas and establish appropriate goals. Theories may be deontological, involving "good" or "right" *motives*, or teleological, involving "good" or "right" *outcomes* achieved by the social change effort in question (Rothman, 1998). Adherents of the deontological perspective (also called ethical absolutism) believe that certain actions must always be taken as a matter of principle (Reamer, 1998). For example, a deontologist would maintain that the principle of self-determination must always be followed, even in situations where time, resources, and limited access to information do not permit full consultation with constituents. Alternatively, a teleological (also called consequentialist or ethical relativism) perspective requires that the action taken must always produce the greatest good for individuals or society as a whole. One teleological approach, utilitarianism, mandates that all ethical decisions produce the greatest good for the greatest number (Lowenberg & Dolgoff, 1996). A teleologist could conceivably argue that mudslinging in a political campaign is appropriate if it results in the election of a public official who supports progressive or social work–related causes.

Using the NASW Code of Ethics

Some ethical dilemmas social workers face in community practice can be addressed using the NASW code of ethics. Lowenberg and Dolgoff (1996) developed an ethical rules screen. They advise the social worker to determine whether principles in the code apply to the ethical dilemma examined. If the situation is not identified in the code or if two or more ethical principles conflict, the ethical rules screen should be applied. The principles in the screen are to be applied in descending order:

Principle #1   Protection of Life
Principle #2   Equality and Inequality
Principle #3   Autonomy and Freedom
Principle #4   Least Harm
Principle #5   Quality of Life
Principle #6   Privacy and Confidentiality
Principle #7   Truthfulness and Full Disclosure (p. 63)

In addition to these principles, Lowenberg and Dolgoff also recommend that the worker examine the impact of the decision on the recipient of the action and assess whether he or she can explain the rationale behind the decision to others. The organizer must determine who exactly is the primary recipient of his or her actions. Is the constituent or client an individual, a group of people, or society in general? Also problematic are situations in which the organizer's actions may benefit members of one marginalized group while putting another marginalized group at risk. For example, locating a homeless shelter in an area with a large transient population may

---

Ethical Dilemma #4

You are an organizer who has just been assigned to work with a group of welfare mothers. You are of a different ethnic background and social class than the members. The mothers tell you about problems with their welfare workers. Since the welfare office is in a "rough" neighborhood, most of the caseworkers assigned to the office are male. All of the mothers receive welfare checks of less than $400 a month. Rents for the slum apartments in this neighborhood often exceed $500. Many of the mothers supplement their welfare checks by engaging in illegal activities such as drug dealing or prostitution. Their caseworkers know that these recipients must have income other than welfare to pay their bills. Consequently, some of the male caseworkers are demanding that the women provide them with sex to avoid having their grants cut due to the unreported funds. The mothers want you to help them deal with this type of sexual harassment. However, one mother suggests that the best solution is to have fathers and boyfriends "beat up" the workers when they leave the office at the end of the day. Do you:

1. Take this threat seriously and report it to your supervisor, the police, the appropriate welfare officials, or a combination of these.
2. Work with the group to identify and implement nonviolent strategies for dealing with this issue.
3. Ignore this suggestion, realizing that group members might be "pulling your leg" due to your inexperience, ethnicity, and social class.
4. On your own, report to appropriate welfare officials what the mothers have told you about sexual harassment in the local welfare office.
5. Do nothing.

---

seem to be a good solution to address a difficult social problem. However, if the site is adjacent to an elementary school (and parents have reason to be concerned about substance abuse and prostitution-related activities near the shelter), the proposed solution may put small children at risk.

Development of One's Own Framework for Ethical Decision Making

Reisch and Lowe (2000) developed a series of steps that will help organizers resolve ethical dilemmas:

- Identify the ethical principles that apply to the situation at hand.
- Collect additional information necessary to examine the ethical dilemma in question.
- Identify the relevant ethical values, or the rules that apply to the ethical problem, or both.
- Identify any potential conflict of interest and the people who are likely to benefit from such conflicts.

- Identify appropriate ethical rules and rank order them in terms of importance.
- Determine the consequences of applying different ethical rules or ranking these rules differently. (p. 26)

Because this decision-making model allows the organizer flexibility in choosing and prioritizing ethical rules, different organizers will achieve different outcomes. Reisch and Lowe also note that some situations that appear to contain ethical dilemmas for the organizer are actually problems that should be addressed by others (for example, constituency group members or targets). Consequently, before confronting the dilemma in question, the organizer must determine whether he or she is actually responsible for handling the problem.

Use of Consultation

An additional option for the organizer facing an ethical dilemma is the use of consultation. Appropriate people to consult in ethical decision making include the following:

1. Constituency group members and beneficiaries of social change processes. This process upholds the basic social work values of self-determination and empowerment.
2. Peers. One's colleagues are often knowledgeable sources of information about ethics and established procedures. They may also have immediate knowledge about the situation at hand; organizational or legal procedures; and organizational, cultural, or community norms and values.
3. Agency supervisory staff. The professional literature contains little information on the use of supervision in community practice. Gamble, Shaffer, and Weil (1994) have argued that knowledge of macro practice among field instructors in schools of social work is limited.
4. Agency directors and board members. In some instances, the organizer can obtain feedback from his or her organization, consulting with both the agency's executive director and, in some cases, members of the organization's board (Tropman, 1997). This is essential in instances when social change activities can jeopardize the organization's nonprofit status or place the organization in legal jeopardy.
5. Mentors. Many practicing organizers find mentors (often staff from other agencies or community activists) who help them obtain the skills necessary to become social change agents (Kaminski, Kaufman, Graubarth, & Robins, 2000). However, little is known about how this process occurs in community practice and whether such mentors are even social workers.

Ethical Dilemma #5

You are a social planner employed by a private redevelopment agency associated with a major university. You have been asked to evaluate two proposals for the use of a vacant lot adjacent to an elementary school. One proposal calls for the lot to be annexed to a nearby park. Another proposal calls for the lot to be used to construct condominiums that will be sold to university professors and other middle-income professionals. Your employer has expressed a preference for the condominium proposal (it will enhance the university's ability to hire nationally prominent faculty). To assess the feasibility of the park expansion approach, you collect data on the number of people who use the Spruce Elementary School Park on a regular basis. You also, for comparison, collect data on Willow Park a few blocks away. Your figures show that both parks attract roughly the same number of people when hours of operation are held constant. Your supervisor advises you, however, to use figures that support the university's argument that the park adjacent to the elementary school is seldom used:

| Number of people using Spruce Park | 9:00 a.m. | Monday | 10 |
| Number of people using Willow Park | 5:00 p.m. | Friday | 50 |

You point out to your supervisor that the comparison is not appropriate. Little League games are held in Willow Park at 5:00 each Friday night. In contrast, few people other than mothers with toddlers use Spruce Elementary School Park early on Monday morning.

Do you:

1. Follow your supervisor's advice.
2. Assume that your employer is your client. Argue for the appropriate use of data but recommend that the vacant lot be used for condominiums.
3. Assume that the community at large is your client. Write a report that supports the use of the vacant lot for additional parkland because it will benefit the public good.
4. Lobby your supervisor and other administrators in support of the parkland proposal.
5. Suggest that the community be involved in choosing between the two proposals. With your employer's consent, organize a community meeting.
6. Quit your job.

6. Professional organizations. Organizers often have a love-hate relationship with NASW. Historically, few organizers joined NASW because of its focus on clinical social work practice. However, this organization may provide some resources and support for organizers involved in organizing for better working conditions or to provide better services for clients or constituents.[1] Other professional organizations include the Association for Community Organization and Social Administration (ACOSA) and the (non–social work–related) National Organizer's Alliance.

Summary

Social work practice requires that the community organizer put values into action: cultural diversity, social justice, equality, critical consciousness, mutual learning, and self-determination. Often these values conflict, creating ethical dilemmas that the organizer must resolve in consultation with constituency group members. The NASW code of ethics provides guidance to the organizer in resolving many dilemmas associated with agency-based practice. However, community organization practice does not always take place in agency settings, nor does it always involve face-to-face interaction with individual clients. Strategies and tactics may harm some groups while providing benefits to others. Consequently, organizers must develop their own set of principles to guide the resolution of ethical problems. Chapters 3, 4, and 5 describe theoretical frameworks that organizers can use to identify community problems and guide practice.

■ QUESTIONS FOR CLASS DISCUSSION

1. What do you think are the most important principles for an organizer to follow?
2. What principles in the NASW code of ethics are most important for community practice?
3. What principles do not seem to be relevant to community practice? Why? How can they be changed to make them relevant?
4. How should the organizer use informed consent?
5. Identify at least three situations in which community practice would put constituents at risk. Are these risks worth taking? What ethical principles should apply to situations that involve risk taking?
6. The NASW code of ethics places restrictions on the use of client self-determination. Are there some situations in community practice in which the client is not always capable of making decisions?
7. What are some of the barriers to mutual learning and equal partnerships between organizers and constituents?
8. What types of dual relationships are likely to be found in community

practice? What techniques can organizers use to establish appropriate professional boundaries?

■ CLASS EXERCISES

1. What are the practice principles inherent in ethical dilemmas 1–5?
2. Rank order each of these principles.
3. Apply the Reisch and Lowe (2000) decision-making model to each case scenario.
4. How should each of these dilemmas be resolved?
5. Do your decisions differ if you utilize the Lowenberg and Dolgoff (1996) ethical decision screen to rank order basic ethical principles? Why?
6. How would the outcomes in each case differ if the decision was made by a deontologist (adheres absolutely to an ethical principle) or a utilitarian (seeks the greatest good for the greatest number)?
7. In ethical dilemma 4, is it the organizer's responsibility to change the behavior of the welfare recipients identified in the scenario?

■ SAMPLE ASSIGNMENTS

1. Find a newspaper or journal article about ethical dilemmas in a social service agency, in social welfare policy, or in an organizing effort. Write a two- to five-page paper about this problem. Identify the ethical issues discussed. Describe actions that are likely to be taken to resolve the identified problem. Are the actions consistent or at odds with the NASW code of ethics? What actions should an organizer with a social work degree take to resolve this problem?
2. Identify an ethical dilemma that affects your job, your field setting, or your educational experience. Write a 5- to 10-page paper on this dilemma. Describe the problem; rank order the ethical principles you feel are important. Use the guidelines developed by Reisch and Lowe (2000) to develop a solution for the problem. Be sure to incorporate your ethical principles in the solution you propose.
3. Review your state's mandatory reporting laws for child and elder abuse. Do you think an organizer is required to comply with these laws? Under what circumstances? Write a two- to five-page paper that describes the scope of these laws, who is covered, and how these statutes could affect what a social worker can do.

Note

1. The president-elect of NASW in 2001 was Terry Mizrahi, a community organizer. Other organizers have taken on leadership roles in the national organization and in state chapters.

References

Abramovitz, A. (1993). Should all social work students be educated for social change? *Journal of Social Work Education, 29* (1), 6–10.

Abrams, R. (1980). *Foundations of political analysis.* New York: Columbia University Press.

Alinsky, S. (1971). *Rules for radicals.* New York: Vintage Books.

Arnstein, S. (1969). A ladder of citizen participation. *Journal of the American Institute of Planners, 35*(4), 216–24.

Bailey, R., and Brake, M. (1975). *Radical social work.* London: Routledge and Kegan Paul.

Barr, D. (1979). The Regents Park community services unit. In B. Wharf (Ed.), *Community work in Canada* (pp. 27–49). Toronto: McClelland & Stewart.

Baum, H. (1998). Ethical behavior is extraordinary behavior; it's the same as all other behavior. *Journal of the American Planning Association, 64*(4), 411–24.

Bull, D. (1989). The social worker's advocacy role: A British quest for a Canadian perspective. *Canadian Social Work Review, 6,* 49–68.

Burghardt, S. (1982). *The other side of organizing.* Cambridge, MA: Schenkman.

Congress, E. (1996). Dual relationships in academia: Dilemmas for social work educators. *Journal of Social Work Education, 32*(3), 329–38.

Council on Social Work Education. (1994). *Curriculum policy statement for master's degree programs in social work education* [On-line]. Available: http://www.cswe.org/mswcps.htm.

Fisher, R. (1994). *Let the people decide* (updated ed.). New York: Twayne.

Flanagan, O., & Jackson, K. (1990). Justice, care, and gender: The Kohlberg-Gilligan debate revisited. In C. Sunstein (Ed.), *Feminism and political theory* (pp. 37–52). Chicago: University of Chicago Press.

Forester, J. (1999). *The deliberative practitioner: Encouraging participatory planning processes.* Cambridge, MA: Massachusetts Institute of Technology.

Freire, P. (1970). *Pedagogy of the oppressed.* New York: Continuum Books.

Gamble, D., Shaffer, G., & Weil, M. (1994). Assessing the integrity of community organization and administration content in field practice. *Journal of Community Practice, 1*(3), 73–92.

Gil, D. (1998). *Confronting injustice and oppression.* New York: Columbia University Press.

Gilligan, C. (1988). Adolescent development reconsidered. In C. Gilligan, J. Ward, & J. Taylor with B. Bardige (Eds.), *Mapping the moral domain: A contribution of women's thinking to psychological theory and education* (pp. vii–xxxix). Cambridge, MA: Harvard University Press.

Gutierrez, L., & Alvarez, A. (2000). Educating students for multicultural community practice. *Journal of Community Practice, 7*(1), 39–56.

Gutierrez, L., & Lewis, E. (1998). A feminist perspective on organizing women of color. In F. Rivera & J. Erlich (Eds.), *Community organizing in a diverse society* (3d ed., pp. 97–116). Boston: Allyn & Bacon.

Hardcastle, D., Wenocur, S., & Powers, P. (1997). *Community practice: Theories and skills for social workers.* New York: Oxford University Press.

Hardina, D. (1990). The effect of funding sources on client access to services. *Administration in Social Work, 14*(3), 33–46.

Hardina, D. (1997). Empowering students for community organization practice: Teaching confrontation tactics. *Journal of Community Practice, 4*(2), 51–63.

Hardina, D. (2000). Models and tactics taught in community organization courses: Findings from a survey of practice instructors. *Journal of Community Practice, 7*(1), 5–18).

Hardina, D., & Malott, O. W. (1996). Strategies for the empowerment of low income consumers on community-based planning boards. *Journal of Progressive Human Services, 7*(2), 43–61.

hooks, b. (1984). *Feminist theory: From margin to center.* Boston: South End Press.

Hyde, C. (1994). Commitment to social change: Voices from the feminist movement. *Journal of Community Practice, 1*(2), 45–63.

Kagel, J., & Geibelhausen, P. (1994). Dual relationships and professional boundaries. *Social Work, 39*(2), 213–21.

Kahn, S. (1991). *Organizing: A guide for grass-roots leaders.* Washington, DC: National Association of Social Workers.

Kaminski, M., Kaufman, J., Graubarth, R., & Robins, T. (2000). How do people become empowered? A case study of union activists. *Human Relations, 53*(10), 1357–80.

Lee, B. (1986). *Pragmatics of community organization.* Mississauga, Ontario: Commonact Press.

Lowenberg, F., & Dolgoff, R. (1996). *Ethical decisions for social work practice* (5th ed.). Itasca, IL: F. E. Peacock.

Lum, D. (1996). *Social work practice and people of color: A process-stage approach* (3d ed.). Pacific Grove, CA: Brooks/Cole.

Manning, S. (1997). The social worker as a moral citizen: Ethics in action. *Social Work, 42*(3), 223–31.

Mondros, J., & Wilson, S. (1994). *Organizing for power and empowerment.* New York: Columbia University Press.

National Association of Social Workers. (1996). *Code of Ethics* [On-line]. Available: http://www.naswdc.org.

O'Neill, M. (1992). Community participation in Quebec's health system. *International Journal of Health Services, 22*(2), 287–301.

Parsons, R., Gutierrez, L., & Cox, E. (1998). A model for empowerment practice. In L. Gutierrez, R. Parsons, and E. Cox (Eds.), *Empowerment in social work practice: A source book.* Pacific Grove, CA: Brooks Cole.

Rapp, C., Shera, W., & Kisthardt, W. (1993). Research strategies for consumer empowerment of people with severe mental illness. *Social Work, 38*(6), 727–36.

Rawls, J. (1971). *A theory of justice.* Cambridge, MA: Harvard University Press.

Reamer, F. (1998). *Ethical standards in social work.* Washington, DC: National Association of Social Workers.

Reamer, F. (1999). *Social work values and ethics.* New York: Columbia University Press.

Reisch, M., & Lowe, J. I., (2000). "Of means and ends" revisited: Teaching ethical community organizing in an unethical society. *Journal of Community Practice, 7*(1), 38.

Rivera, F., & Erlich, J. (1998). *Community organizing in a diverse society* (3d ed.). Boston: Allyn & Bacon.

Robinson, W., & Reeser, L. (2000). *Ethical decision making in social work.* Boston: Allyn & Bacon.

Rothman, J. C. (1998). *From the front lines: Student cases in social work ethics.* Needham Heights, MA: Allyn & Bacon.

Segal, S., & Silverman, C. (1993). Empowerment and self-help agency practice for people with mental disabilities. *Social Work, 38*(6), 705–13.

Simon, B. (1994). *The empowerment tradition in social work.* New York: Columbia University Press.

Specht, H., & Courtney, M. (1994). *Unfaithful angels: How social work has abandoned its mission.* New York: Free Press.

Steinberg, A., Sullivan, J., & Loew, R. (1998). Cultural and linguistic barriers to mental health access: The deaf consumer's perspective. *American Journal of Psychiatry, 155*(7), 982–84.

Tauxe, C. (1995). Marginalizing public participation in local planning: An ethnographic account. *Journal of the American Planning Association, 61*(4), 471–82.

Tropman, J. (1997). *Successful community leadership.* Washington, DC: National Association of Social Workers.

Warren, R. (1971). Types of purposive social change at the community level. In R. Warren (Ed.), *Truth, love, and social change* (pp. 134–49). Chicago: Rand McNally.

Weil, M. (1996). Model development in community practice: An historical perspective. The interweaving of community intervention approaches. *Journal of Community Practice, 3*(3/4), 5–67.

Weil, M., Hughes, M., & Hooyman, N. (1994). *Sexual harassment and schools of social work: Issues, costs, and strategic responses.* Alexandria, VA: Council on Social Work Education.

Wint, E., & Sewpaul, V. (2000). Product and process dialectic: Developing an indigenous approach to community development training. *Journal of Community Practice, 7*(1), 57–70.

Uehara, E., & Sohng, S. (1996). Towards a values-based approach to multicultural social work research. *Social Work, 41*(6), 613–22.

Van Voorhis, R. (1998). Culturally relevant practice: A framework for teaching the psychosocial dynamics of oppression. *Journal of Social Work Education, 34* (1), 121–33.

Winkle, C. (1991). Inequity and power in the nonprofit sector. *Nonprofit and Voluntary Sector Quarterly, 20*, 312–28.

Young, I. (1990). Polity and group difference: A critique of the ideal of universal citizenship. In C. Sunstein (Ed.), *Feminism and political theory* (pp. 117–41). Chicago: University of Chicago Press.

Zachary, E. (2000). Grassroots leadership training: A case study of an effort to integrate theory and method. *Journal of Community Practice, 7*(1), 71–94.

3 Theoretical Frameworks for Practice

■ In this chapter, theoretical assumptions associated with community practice in social work are described. Practice perspectives, which provide guidance about how interventions should be carried out, are also presented. Often our practice literature is derived from psychology, political science, and sociology. However, some have argued that social work is not a profession because it does not possess a unique theory base that defines its primary purpose (Reeser & Epstein, 1990; Wakefield, 1996b).

This chapter discusses two primary practice perspectives, empowerment and strengths approaches. A number of theories used to frame community organization practice are described in detail: systems, ecological, power-dependency, conflict, social movement, and social constructionism. The author argues that these theories in themselves are not sufficient to guide practice. Models of practice that link theories to specific types of intervention approaches are described in chapter 4.

Perspectives, Theories, and Models: What Is the Difference?

Some of the theories that guide social work practice are not empirically testable; specific cause-and-effect relationships cannot be tested using quantitative methods because we cannot identify independent and dependent variables. Therefore, some simply offer perspectives about how practice should proceed. Generally, in community practice we utilize practice models to link theories about how society functions to our intervention plans. Models of community practice are described in detail in chapter 4.

The differences among theories, models, and perspectives can be described in the following manner:

Perspective:	An approach to practice that involves basic value assumptions about best practices. Perspectives offer guidance about the best way to intervene and the role of the social worker in the intervention process. Perspectives do not offer detailed prescriptions about outcomes associated with specific practice activities. Often the ideas or constructs associated with the perspective are not easily measurable. Consequently, little research has been conducted to verify whether the practice approach is effective.
Theories:	Assumptions about cause-and-effect relationships that through empirical testing have been established as valid. In community organization, we use theories to understand how communities function, how residents adapt to change, how to influence government policy decisions, and how people can be organized to take power. The theories that guide our work determine what models of practice we will use to plan social change interventions.
Models:	Constructs used to understand or visualize patterns of relationships among concepts, individuals, groups, and organizations. Theoretical models are used to illustrate cause-and-effect relationships between variables (such as the relationship between a particular social work intervention and its anticipated outcome). Models are typically used to guide decision making or to understand how decisions are made (Flynn, 1992).
Practice models:	Detailed frameworks for understanding social problems and developing responses to those problems. In community practice, our model of choice has a number of components: (1) a theoretical framework for understanding social change, (2) an intervention approach, and (3) probable outcomes associated with using this approach. Models determine the strategies and tactics used to address the problem and the individuals and groups involved in problem solving.

Practice Perspectives: Empowerment and Strengths-Based Approaches

Two of the primary perspectives associated with community practice are the empowerment and strengths perspectives. These approaches provide us with a generic description of how we should interact with constituents, recognizing their strengths and abilities and valuing their right to make decisions that affect their lives. The value assumptions associated with each of these approaches are easily incorporated into theoretical frameworks and practice models associated with community work. Both perspectives focus on the importance of client or constituent self-determination as specified in the National Association of Social Workers (NASW) code of ethics.

The Empowerment Perspective

As noted in chapters 1 and 2, empowerment produces powerful effects. The inclusion of disadvantaged members of society in organization or political decision making can alleviate the harmful psychological effects of social inequality by increasing the power of individuals to change those environmental conditions responsible for their problems. From this perspective, social problems are viewed as originating from the inequitable distribution of resources and decision-making authority (Freire, 1970; Parsons, Gutierrez, & Cox, 1998).

Empowerment also refers to the process through which people maintain control over their own lives and communities (Solomon, 1976; Staples, 1990). Empowerment decreases feelings of alienation from the dominant culture, helps individuals develop the capacity for collective action, and leads to the development of a sense of community or responsibility for and ability to resolve local problems (Simon, 1990). To be empowered, members of oppressed groups must be able to recognize the degree to which social structures limit life opportunities (Freire, 1970).

Empowerment can be defined along three dimensions. An individual is empowered when his or her self-esteem or self-efficacy is increased. At the intrapersonal level, empowerment comes through the construction of knowledge and analysis of social problems acquired through shared experience. At the community level, empowerment occurs through the development of service resources and social change strategies, which in turn help individuals gain mastery over the environment (Labonte, 1990). Involvement in community-based social change efforts is thought to provide opportunities to empower low-income people and members of other oppressed groups along all three of these dimensions.

According to Parsons et al. (1998), empowerment practice originates in the dialogue conducted among service professionals and constituents involved in the organizing effort. It has the following primary components:

1. The validation of the experiences that shape the lives and values of the constituent group
2. An examination of the self-perceptions of constituency group members in terms of their ability to gain mastery over the environment
3. A critical analysis of the impact of the sociopolitical environment on the lives of constituency group members
4. Increased knowledge and skills for critical thinking and action
5. Action taken for political as well as personal change (p. 20)

The implication of this model for community organization practice is that the organizer is to take great pains to establish decision-making processes and structures that support and encourage constituent involvement in problem identification, community assessment, goal setting, implementation of strategies, and evaluation (Zachary, 2000). However, as noted in chapter 2, the decision-making process takes place in a context of equal exchange or dialogue between constituents and the organizer.

The Strengths Perspective

The strengths perspective assumes that residents of low-income and other marginalized groups have skills, resources, and knowledge that they can utilize to transform their lives (Lum, 1996; Saleebey, 1997). The purpose of the strengths perspective is to counteract traditional approaches to social work practice that emphasize personal deficits and consequently result in the victimization of people in need.

Drawing from Freire's work (1970), the strengths perspective assumes that the person who receives the service also is the best "expert" about his or her own life. The strengths perspective emphasizes mutuality in all helping relationships, including one-on-one relationships between clients and social workers. This approach implies that the individual's culture is an asset that should be used in the change process.

This perspective can be incorporated into community practice in several ways. Saleebey (1997) describes community practice from the strengths perspective as oriented toward developing the capacities of individuals to change their own lives as well as the quality of community life. It focuses on "resilience"—the idea that people who have been marginalized and oppressed by society can persevere over hardships. Saleebey argues that the best way to do this is through forming social bonds with other individuals and community associations:

> Community development involves helping unleash the power, vision, capacities, and talents within a (self-defined) community so that the community can strengthen its internal relationships and move closer

toward performing the important functions of solidarity and support, succor and identification and instructing and socializing. (p. 202)

In community organizing, the informal networks found within ethnic communities are central to the completion of successful organizing efforts (Delgado, 2000). Community residents use networks to establish a process of mutual assistance between those in need and other community residents. Such networks can also be used to facilitate community decision making. For example, an organizer interested in enrolling Hmong immigrants in Medicaid may begin the organizing process by asking local clan leaders to put the word out to community residents.

Limitations of Empowerment and Strengths Perspectives

While these perspectives contain important prescriptions for practice, they do not always link specific activities to outcomes. Although empowerment and strengths perspectives are often thought to produce improvements in self-esteem or feelings of control over one's environment, methods for measuring these outcomes are limited (Gutierrez, 1995; Israel, Checkoway, Schulz, & Zimmerman, 1999; Zimmerman, 1990). Consequently, little empirical evidence exists that establishes cause-and-effect relationships between practice activities and specific intervention outcomes. Though some work has been done to establish theoretical frameworks to support this empirical research, most efforts have focused on practice with individuals and small groups (Parsons, et al., 1998). The lack of empirical literature on the effects of empowerment- or strengths-oriented practice in community work may simply be due to the primary role assigned to these values. Many organizers assume that this type of practice is necessary for the success of community projects. However, it is not clear that all organizers actually incorporate such values into their practice. Some traditional models of social action–oriented community organizing involve approaches in which the organizer takes a lead role in guiding or directing intervention processes (Alinsky, 1971).

Theoretical Perspectives on Community Practice

Most of the theories associated with community organization practice help us understand the role of the social change organization within the context of the larger society. These theories also examine the role of social class and competing interests in the political process. Most importantly, these theories help us understand one of the primary concepts inherent in community organization practice: *power*. What is power? How is it obtained? What do social change organizations need to do to maintain their power base?

Systems Theory

In social work, we tend to use systems theory to examine small systems such as families or larger organizational systems. However, systems theory also pertains to the life of the community. We can examine communities in terms of subsystems comprised of individuals and groups. The community is a subsystem of the larger environment, or suprasystem, that includes other communities, the city as a whole, and other political entities (county, state, nation). Community subsystems can include organizations that serve neighborhood residents, businesses, and local institutions (schools, churches, and hospitals). The community is also affected by changes in the political, economic, and social systems (Fellin, 1995). Any action in one component of the system produces changes in all of the subsystems.

Community boundaries may be open or closed to communication and feedback from these larger systems. Communities are dynamic; to survive, organizations must be able to adapt to communication and feedback (Norlin & Chess, 1997). As with any system, the primary purpose of the community is to link individuals with the larger society and to achieve stability or a steady state. Community systems promote pattern maintenance, goal attainment, integration, and adaptation to the demands of the environment (Knuttila, 1992; Norlin & Chess, 1997; Parsons, 1971). Pattern maintenance involves socialization, the transmission of common values and behaviors throughout the community. Integration refers to the process in which people are made to adopt values and behaviors. This process is also referred to as social control. Adaptation focuses on the ability of the community's economic subsystem to acquire the resources it needs to function. Goal attainment refers to the ability to use these resources to accomplish tasks. It can be argued that all community subsystems must function at adequate levels so that community resources can be used to meet goals. While government may be the primary avenue to produce goal attainment (Parsons, 1971), community institutions, businesses, community organizations, and informal groups of residents can organize to produce results. Warren (1978) identifies a number of subsystems, which carry out basic community functions (see table 3.1).

The implications of systems theory for community practice are as follow:

1. A change in the suprasystem will produce a reaction in some aspect of community life. For example, government welfare reform legislation will have an impact on how residents in a low-income community obtain income and find employment.
2. Actions in any community subsystem affect the whole community as well as components of that system.
3. Communities perform all of those functions identified by Warren (1978). Some communities perform these functions less well than others.

4. The purpose of organizing is to restore the community to a steady state where all residents can participate in the life of the community.

Ecological Theory

Ecological theory is also known as population ecology. This approach has its roots in Darwin's biological determinism—"survival of the fittest." Population ecologists believe that social structure develops through the interaction among individuals, groups, and surrounding physical environment (Norlin & Chess, 1997). Changes in the environment occur due to natural forces such as population density or the movement of ethnic subpopulations into or out of the community. These forces will seek equilibrium or to maintain an ecological balance that allows the community to maintain regular patterns of activities.

The community ecosystem includes a variety of components: residents, housing structure, population density, land use, and social structure (Delgado, 2000; Fellin, 1995). The various groups in the community may compete for land, housing, jobs, and other resources. Those who can acquire these resources can dominate others. Those groups who do not successfully compete adapt to existing structures and processes. For example, new immigrants may move into a neighborhood with few services or convenience stores. They adapt to this problem by creating informal structures (street vendors, in-home sales) for the delivery of goods and services (Hardina, Palacio, Lee, & Cabrera, 1999).

Groups may also adapt by finding a specific niche or role in the community that allows them to acquire power or survive. Venkatesh (1997) examined the relationship between physical structures and social organization in a low-income community. He found few informal groups or organizations

Table 3.1 Community Subsystems and Their Functions

Function	Subsystems
Production-distribution-consumption	Economic subsystem, including businesses and employers
Socialization	Family, schools, religious institutions, peer groups
Social control	Government, judicial system, religious institutions
Social participation	Informal groups, formal organizations
Mutual support	Government social welfare programs
	Nonprofit organizations
	Informal helping networks

Source: Warren, R. (1978). The community in America, 3d ed. (Chicago: Rand McNally).

in the community that were effective in performing essential social control functions. However, local street gangs occupied the organizational void. Gang members enforced local norms, provided protection, and punished social deviants. Gangs established rules of inclusion and exclusion—for example, who belongs and who does not belong in the neighborhood. Graffiti and other physical markers (streets or buildings) were used to define the geographic neighborhood. Consequently, access to the neighborhood was controlled or limited by gang members.

Following are the implications of ecological theory for community practice:

1. Groups compete for scarce resources. The strong are able to dominate community life.
2. Other groups must adapt to the surrounding environment.
3. The physical environment has an important role in defining how social structure is created. Low-income communities are often characterized by deteriorating infrastructures and housing stock. Changing the physical environment will produce changes in the community's social life.

Limitations of Systems and Ecological Approaches

Both systems theory and ecological theory have limitations for use in community practice. Both lack specific directives for practice and may represent an inherently conservative approach because of the focus on adaptation (Delgado, 2000). Even proponents of systems and ecological theories have argued that they are not theories in the classic sense; cause-and-effect relationships have not been established through empirical testing (Wakefield, 1996a, 1996b). In addition, both theories fail to recognize the role of power in limiting the life opportunities of low-income people (Cloward and Piven, 1975).

Theories Related to the Acquisition of Power

Power is one of the most important concepts in community organization. Without power, people would have limited ability to acquire goods, resources, and decision-making authority (Alinsky, 1971; Kahn, 1991). Primary theories that link the acquisition of resources to an individual's or organization's ability to acquire power are power dependency, conflict, and resource mobilization theories. Each of these theories has a specific application to community organization practice.

Power Dependency Theory

Blau (1964) argues that power is inherent in all helping relationships between resource-rich donors and poor recipients. Blau's theory can be applied to society in general and has specific applications to understanding the political process. However, it is most often used to examine how organizations acquire and disperse power. Its basic premise is that social service organizations depend on the receipt of funding to survive. Nonprofit organizations target their services to the poor. Although they may sell their services to consumers under a limited number of circumstances, most clients cannot afford to pay for them. Consequently, the organization must rely on grants and contracts from external donors. This is particularly problematic for organizations serving impoverished communities; it is unlikely that funds to ensure the organization's survival can be raised from sources inside the community (Hardina, 1993).

According to Blau (1964), the receipt of this money represents a free good or service and requires that the organization remain obligated to the funder, doing as the donor demands (this usually means complying with government regulations or grant specifications). The only way that the organization can avoid compliance with funder demands is to do one or more of the following:

1. Supply the donor with a good or service of equal value
2. Obtain the service from another source
3. Learn to live without the service
4. Coerce the donor to provide the service

The dependence of the organization on the donor can result in goal displacement, loss of autonomy, or limitations on the organization's ability to lobby for or against government policies. Power dependency theory can also be used to explain the relationship between those people who receive services and the organizations that provide them. People who receive free services from the organization become dependent on and obligated to the organization for the continued delivery of goods and services. Consequently, the organization plays a mediating role in implementing regulations associated with government funding; it must comply with government demands, and it must enforce government policies in its interaction with clients (see figure 3.1).

A number of implications exist for community practice associated with power dependency theory:

1. Demands associated with external funding may limit a community organization's ability to fight for social change.
2. People who receive free social services may be reluctant to advocate for themselves, believing that they may lose services.
3. Social change takes place in an atmosphere that focuses on the exchange of resources. People who receive jobs, political favors, and other resources may be obligated to vote for or support the donor.

Figure 3.1.   Power-Dependency Model

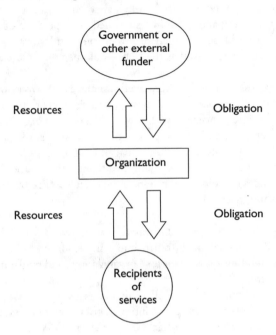

Conflict Theory

Conflict theory focuses on the interaction of groups in society. It is most concerned with groups formed through the process of social stratification—groups that are identified as different on a demographic basis from one another. Marx wrote about the struggle of workers to gain equality with dominant elites. Government, the "State," was viewed as a tool the elite used to oppress the poor to accept "wage slavery" (Knuttila, 1992). These groups form naturally as a function of both social class and ethnicity and consequently have different interests. For example, conflict theorists assume that wealthy individuals have access to most of the goods and services they need. Alternatively, low-income people are assumed to have limited access to resources. These groups are commonly referred to in the conflict theory literature as the "haves" and the "have-nots." It is further assumed that most of the interaction among the various social classes and ethnic groups involves competition for scarce resources. The haves want to hold on to wealth and the power that accrues from wealth. The have-nots want to acquire access to money, jobs, education, decision-making authority, and other power "resources" (Alinsky, 1971).

Two predominant approaches to conflict theory have influenced community organization practice in the United States. One is based on the work of Alinksy (1971, 1974), who believed strongly that all people should have access to goods and services. In Alinsky's view, American society promotes economic well-being and should be sustained. The purpose of community organization should be to organize low-income and working-class communities so that they, as well as the rich, would benefit from capitalism:

> *The Prince* was written by Machiavelli for the Haves on how to hold power. *Rules for Radicals* is written for the have nots on how to take it away . . . we are concerned with how to create mass organizations to seize power and give it to the people to realize the democratic dream of equality, justice, co-operation, equal and full opportunities for education, full and useful employment, health, and the creation of those circumstances in which man can have the chance to live by values that give meaning to life. (Alinsky, 1971, p. 3)

Alinsky's approach to organizing was to use power to force the haves to hand over decision-making authority and other resources. Power was to be acquired by building mass "people's" organizations and confrontation with authority figures.

The second approach to conflict theory is associated with Marxism. Marx, however, offered few prescriptions about how oppression operates and its effect on the various social classes (Marx, 1965). In the twentieth century, neo-Marxist theory evolved to create an explicit theoretical framework for examining how government and the capitalist elite interact to control the economy and subordinate the lower classes (Knuttila, 1992). Neo-Marxist theory has expanded to recognize gender, age, physical ability, and gender orientation as well as race and social class as factors that promote conflict among social groups.

Neo-Marxists have examined the role of social workers and the social welfare system in capitalist societies. The government, or State, primarily serves the haves, or dominant classes; it mediates competition among interest groups within the elite and relations among the social classes (Gough, 1979; Panitch, 1977). The State has two primary functions: capital accumulation; and legitimation, or the promotion of social harmony (Burghardt & Fabricant, 1987). Social welfare institutions are used to maintain social harmony but do not produce profits for private capital. Since capital accumulation is primary, social welfare expenditures are usually quite limited. If the working class is powerful, the State will need to increase expenditures for legitimation. According to Schreader (1990), "State ideological practices produce particular kinds of problem definitions, needs, and methods for dealing with them. These practices are observed to bring into existence certain types of activities and social relations to the exclusion of others" (p. 186).

In their book *Regulating the Poor,* Piven and Cloward (1971) examined social welfare policy in the United States from a neo-Marxist perspective. They argue that historically, social welfare expenditures have been increased during periods of political unrest (the Depression and the 1960s). Social welfare benefits have been reduced during periods when corporations have demanded access to a large pool of low-income labor. People without access to public assistance, who have few skills or job options, will work for very low wages if there are no alternatives.

From the neo-Marxist perspective, the State uses social workers to change the behavior and attitudes of the working class in order to reinforce support for the forces of capital (Burghardt & Fabricant, 1987). Consequently, the capacity of the social work profession to engage in social action is determined by the State. The contradictory nature of the social work profession (workers provide services to meet client needs while acting as agents of social control) can be used to explain why social workers have had some limited ability to control their work (professional autonomy) but little power to change the social welfare system (Burghardt, 1982). Social workers often experience this contradiction as role strain or burnout (Freidson, 1986; Garner & Zald, 1987). One means of coping with this contradiction is participation in social movements that promote increased welfare spending and improved social conditions for oppressed groups.

The primary assumptions of conflict theory as they apply to community practice are as follow:

1. The haves and the have-nots compete for societal resources.
2. The haves hold a resource and power advantage over the have-nots.
3. Much of the oppression that marginalized groups experience has its origins in classism, racism, ableism, ageism, sexism, and heterosexism.
4. The haves control government and other avenues of decision-making authority.
5. The purpose of community organization is to work with members of oppressed groups to acquire power and access to jobs, education, money, and other power resources.
6. Community organizers work to establish other sources of power (strength in numbers, votes, the media) that can be used to increase have-nots access to decision-making authority.

Resource Mobilization Theory

Resource mobilization theory explicitly explores the role and limitations of social movement organizations (Pfeffer & Salsnick, 1978; McCarthy & Zald, 1976). Social movements can be defined as "coalitions of loosely connected groups that attempt to change a social target" (Swank & Clapp, 1999, p. 50). Typical targets are communities, government, industries, or cultural norms and practices. There are two primary types of social movements:

(1) movements oriented toward establishing civil rights for groups that do not have full representation in political, social, or economic systems (for example, the women's movement and the civil rights movement), and (2) movements developed with altruistic motives, helping entities that can't represent themselves to acquire recognition and promote changes in legislation or policies (for example, the animal rights movement and the environmental movement) (Rothman, 1996). Recently there has also been a resurgence of social movements intended to support conservative cultural and religious values associated with the dominant culture (Fisher, 1994; Hyde, 1994).

Resource mobilization theory builds on power dependency and conflict theories to examine whether efforts to develop social movements will be effective. Specific aspects of social movements are examined:

- Where are the resources for the movement?
- How are they organized?
- How does the State facilitate or impede mobilization?
- What are the outcomes? (Muller, 1992, p. 3)

According to resource mobilization theory, organizations must be developed to recruit members, raise funds, and hire qualified staff. These organizations must also find ways to develop legitimacy with the public and with influential decision makers. They must also be able to mobilize their members to take action (writing letters, signing petitions, voting, participating in demonstrations). Member mobilization depends on the organization's ability to communicate its philosophy or ideology to potential members. The organization must be able to rely on current members to recruit others. Such recruitment usually occurs through social networks of friends, relatives, and neighbors.

It is also essential that the social movement organization foster a sense of collective identity among its members. Collective identity refers to the recognition of group members that they belong to and are committed to a social movement distinct from and more important than all others. Recognition of a collective identity promotes solidarity and group cohesion among members (Hyde, 1994). In social movement organizations with high levels of solidarity, members are more likely to participate in organization activities and to make personal sacrifices for the cause.

To successfully recruit members, a social movement organization must also be able to frame its message in ways that prospective members and the public can easily recognize as important and relevant. Jasper and Poulsen (1995) argue that it is important that these recruitment messages be presented in a way that contains cultural meaning and symbolism. For example, the animal rights movement has relied on images of animals being tortured during product or medical testing to recruit members.

Organizations that have large memberships and budgets are generally viewed as more powerful than organizations that do not have these resources. Powerful organizations also must have access to the media to promote their causes. The greater the dependence of the organization on forces outside the organization for these resources, the greater the ability of these outside forces to control what goes on within the organization. To survive, these groups must be able to recruit many dues-paying members or wealthy contributors (Piven & Cloward, 1979). Such donors may not have the same goals or motivation as the founding members of the organization. Consequently, these organizations may become less radical or less representative of their members. Government may also provide funds for the organization. Acceptance of external funds may pose problems for the organization, however:

> State aid to minority and dissident groups plays an important role in legitimation, in sustaining the view that the State is not the agency of a particular social class but rather the benefactor of all. The acceptance of this view necessarily directs political activity toward conventional channels. (Loney, 1977, p. 453)

Following are the basic assumptions of resource mobilization theory, relevant to the community organizer:

1. Social movements emerge in response to the perception that some groups or ideas are not represented in the political process.
2. Social protest is one of the primary methods for social movement organizations to gain public recognition and legitimacy.
3. The effectiveness of the social movement lies in its ability to recruit members, raise funds, and develop an appropriate organizational structure to carry out these tasks.
4. Successful social movements must create an environment that allows members to establish a collective identity, becoming committed to the cause.
5. The salience of the organization's message, increases membership recruitment.
6. The need to fund-raise acts as a double-edged sword. Money is needed to build an organization, recruit members, and influence policy makers. However, low-income people cannot contribute much in the way of resources. Using government funds or contributions from wealthy donors can lead the organization to abandon the struggle for radical reforms.

Limitations of Power-Related Theories

Power dependency, conflict, and social movement theories require that the community organizer accept that the power and influence of the social elite has negative consequences for society. Approaching community organization practice from this theoretical perspective also requires that community organizers recognize that marginalized groups must acquire power in order to meet their needs. Therefore, strategies and tactics are needed that involve conflict with the power structure rather than efforts to establish consensus. Although these theories offer some guidance about how power functions in society and the source of competition among various constituency groups, they do not present the organizer with a full range of strategic options for resolving community problems.

Social Constructionism

Social constructionism is a framework for the development of knowledge that is relevant to the lives of members of marginalized groups. It can be argued that most of the social science theories used in community practice were developed in accordance with Western cultural values and norms (Sohng, 1998). Consequently, this knowledge has relevance to the lives of people who are not members of the dominant culture. Specifically, they may not be relevant to the lives of people who have little or no income, people of color, women, people with disabilities, older people, and LGBT individuals. Constructionism is associated with postmodernism, an approach to knowledge that focuses on overcoming oppression by constructing new knowledge about the lives and experiences of members of traditionally subordinated groups (Chambon, 1999). According to Rodwell (1998), the concept of constructionism implies that change comes about through "linguistic negotiation generated between individuals who judge and correct until agreement is achieved regarding meaning" (p. 254). This approach requires that individuals and groups become engaged in a process of dialogue to identify meanings associated with social institutions, social customs, and everyday activities (Lee & Green, 1999). Some adherents of this approach distinguish between constructionism and constructivism. Constructionism pertains to an overall approach to generate knowledge and facilitate social change; social workers have used the term constructivism to refer to specific applications of constructionism to research and clinical practice (Rodwell, 1998).

Social constructionism also has its roots in "symbolic interactionism," the idea that people construct everyday activities with meanings associated with cultural norms, values, and the use of language (Chambon, 1999; Lee & Green, 1999). One basic assumption of this theoretical perspective is that knowledge is not objective; there is no one overall "truth." Instead, knowledge is constructed through social interaction and dialogue within the context of culture, the political structure, the economy, and historical influences. Consequently, no one version of reality can be said to be better or worse than another (Rossiter, 1996). Lee and Green argue that because knowledge is socially constructed, it can vary historically over time and differ across cultural groups that hold diverse beliefs about human development and nature. Given that values, norms, beliefs, attitudes, traditions, and practices vary from one cultural group to another, so does the social construction of knowledge. (p. 25)

Social constructionists argue that knowledge creation also varies from individual to individual, because each person experiences a different reality and interprets that reality based on his or her own values and personal experiences (Chambon, 1999; Rodwell, 1998). Existing theories are a mechanism the dominant culture uses to maintain institutional structures that oppress individuals and members of marginalized groups. Therefore, they should be discarded and new ways of understanding developed.

In terms of social work practice, this perspective suggests that the work of social workers has been socially constructed as a function of society's need to regulate and control individual behavior (Hardcastle, Wenocur, & Powers, 1997; Moffat, 1999). Therefore, the meaning that client groups assign to the intervention process may be far different from the meaning of this process to the social worker. Members of the client group may internalize the helping process, associating it with society's need to control behavior. People seeking help come from a variety of income and ethnic groups. They often experience social oppression because of gender, sexual orientation, disability, or age. Consequently, the meanings associated with the helping process can be infinite, and the social worker must have appropriate interpersonal and research skills to examine what the helping process means to these individuals and offer assistance in overcoming oppression (Rossiter, 1996).

Epstein (1999) argues that the development of new theories and ways of understanding culture and the everyday lives of people is critical for the development of social work practice. This is necessary because "the standard history [of the profession] fails to analyze the effects of embracing social science in such a way that the dominance of men over the epistemology and purposes was given distorted power, the nature of the work 'masculinized'" (p. 15).

A social constructionism perspective requires that the social worker be able to accomplish the following:

1. Understand how the social, economic, and political structure shapes individual behavior and the meanings attached to cultural values and norms
2. Engage in dialogue with others to determine cultural symbols and meanings that influence practice
3. Conduct collaborative research in marginalized communities to gain insight on how those communities interpret reality and internalize oppression by the dominant culture

4. Develop new knowledge and theories about how social forces and power affect members of marginalized groups

Limitations of a Social Constructionism Perspective

A primary limitation of this method is the view that there is no one correct view of reality. Holding this perspective means that once one acknowledges that knowledge is socially constructed, communication of theories associated with the dominant culture should be rejected as an educational method. Therefore, social constructionism requires that classroom education focus on establishing dialogue among students, exchanging ideas, and looking for meaning behind various situations and behaviors. Students must also attempt to reconcile a variety of different perspectives and examine their own value assumptions (Lee & Green, 1999).

In addition, constructionism requires that the practitioner develop situation-specific theories about appropriate practice interventions. These interventions should be specific to the needs and values of the constituency groups served. Dialogue among group members is necessary to develop a framework that constituents can use for viewing society, the power dynamics associated with social institutions, and the meanings associated with the specific strategies and tactics used in the organizing effort. The need for a situation- or population-specific framework limits the degree to which an organizer can rely on existing theories to guide practice.

Summary

In this chapter, perspectives and theories associated with community organization practice were described. Empowerment and the strengths perspectives were examined in terms of value assumptions about how social workers in community practice should regard the people they serve. Recognition that all people have strengths and skills that they can use to increase their own mastery over the environment is an important value inherent in the helping process.

Three primary theoretical approaches to community practice were also examined: approaches that look at communities as systems, approaches that look at the role of power in society, and social constructionism. This third theoretical perspective offers a criticism of previous theoretical approaches that may not be relevant to the members of groups that are often marginalized by the dominant culture. None of these approaches really provides the community organizer with an explicit guide to practice. In chapter 4, these theories are linked with specific practice models. The prescriptions for action in the models incorporate the basic values and ethics for community practice described in chapter 2. Practice models provide organizers with action protocols and practice principles that can be used in a variety of situations.

■ QUESTIONS FOR CLASS DISCUSSION

1. How do the empowerment and strengths perspectives link community organization to practice with individuals, groups, and families?
2. Are the systems and ecological approaches consistent with the application of these theories to practice with individuals?
3. Is the acquisition of power consistent with basic social work principles? Why?
4. Should government and private donors be able to influence the change strategies that social movement organizations adopt?
5. Do you agree with the social constructionists that knowledge is not objective? Why or why not?

■ SAMPLE ASSIGNMENTS AND EXERCISES

1. Divide the class into two equal groups. Flip a coin to determine which group will assume the role of the haves and which will become the have-nots. The instructor announces that the haves will all receive As in the course. The have-nots will all receive Fs. Each group should identify strategies they will use to either (1) remain the dominant group and receive an A, or (2) acquire power to overturn the instructor's decision.
2. Write a five-page paper that compares a low-income neighborhood to a middle- or upper-income neighborhood. Collect most of your data using observational methods. You may supplement data collection with interviews with residents and information from local newspapers. Compare these two neighborhoods in terms of physical structure (condition of apartments and houses, street maintenance, parks and playgrounds, businesses and community institutions, and garbage collection). What do these physical conditions tell you about the neighborhood residents; the level of interaction among neighbors; and access to jobs, shopping, and services outside the neighborhood? How would you apply ecological theory to what you have observed?
3. Use resource mobilization theory to examine a social movement (for example, civil rights, women's, Christian right, pro-life, or pro-choice movement). Choose a movement for which a great deal of historical information sources or recent newspaper accounts are available. What factors do your sources identify as critical for the success of these movements? Describe, at a minimum, the methods a social movement organization uses to raise funds and recruit members.

References

Alinsky, S. (1971). *Rules for radicals*. New York: Vintage.
Alinsky, S. (1974). *Reveille for radicals*. New York: Vintage.
Blau, P. (1964). *Exchange and power in social life*. New York: Wiley.

Burghardt, S. (1982). *The other side of organizing.* Cambridge, MA: Schenkman.

Burghardt, S., & Fabricant, M. (1987). Radical social work. In A. Minihan (Ed.), *The encyclopedia of social work* (18th ed., Vol. 2, pp. 455–62). Silver Spring, MD: National Association of Social Workers.

Chambon, A. (1999). Foucault's approach: Making the familiar visible. In A. Chambon, A. Irving, & L. Epstein (Eds.), *Reading Foucault for social work* (pp. 51–81). New York: Columbia University Press.

Cloward R., & Piven, F. F. (1975). Notes toward a radical social work. In R. Bailey & M. Brake (Eds.), *Radical social work* (pp. vii–xi). London: Routledge and Kegan Paul.

Delgado, M. (2000). *Community social work practice in an urban context.* New York: Oxford University Press.

Epstein, L. (1999). The culture of social work. In A. Chambon, A. Irving, & L. Epstein (Eds.), *Reading Foucault for social work* (pp. 1–26). New York: Columbia University Press.

Fellin, P. (1995). *The community and the social worker* (2d ed.). Itasca, IL: Peacock.

Fisher, R. (1994). *Let the people decide* (updated ed.). New York: Twayne.

Flynn, J. (1992). *Social agency policy* (2d ed.). Chicago: Nelson-Hall.

Freidson, E. (1986). *Professional powers: A study of the institutionalization of formal knowledge.* Chicago: University of Chicago Press.

Freire, P. (1970). *Pedagogy of the oppressed.* New York: Continuum.

Garner, R. A., & Zald, M. N. (1987). The political economy of social movement sectors. In N. Zald & J. D. McCarthy (Eds.), *Social movements in an organizational society: Collected essays.* New Brunswick, NJ: Transaction Books.

Gough, L. (1979). *The political economy of the welfare state.* London: Macmillan.

Gutierrez, L. (1995). Understanding the empowerment process. Does consciousness make a difference? *Social Work Research, 19*(4), 229–47.

Hardcastle, D., Wenocur, S., & Powers, P. (1997). *Community practice: Theories and skills for social workers.* New York: Oxford University Press.

Hardina, D. (1993). The impact of funding sources and board representation on consumer control of service delivery in organizations serving low-income communities. *Nonprofit Leadership and Management, 4,* 69–84.

Hardina, D., Palacio, R., Lee, S., & Cabrera, H. (1999, March). *Residential segregation and social isolation among residents of a low income neighborhood.* Paper presented at the Annual Program Meeting of the Council on Social Work Education, San Francisco.

Hyde, C. (1994). Commitment to social change: Voices from the feminist movement. *Journal of Community Practice, 1*(2), 45–63.

Israel, B., Checkoway, B., Schulz, A., & Zimmerman, M. (1999). Scale for measuring perceptions of individual, organizational, and community control. In M. Minkler (Ed.), *Community organizing and community building for health* (pp. 278–381). New Brunswick: Rutgers University Press.

Jasper, J., & Poulsen, J. (1995). Recruiting strangers and friends: Moral shocks and social networks in animal rights and anti-nuclear protests. *Social Problems, 42,* 493–513.

Kahn, S. (1991). *Organizing: A guide for grass-roots leaders* (revised ed.). Washington, DC: National Association of Social Workers.

Knuttila, M. (1992). *State theories: From liberalism to the challenge of feminism.* Halifax, Nova Scotia: Fernwood.

Labonte, R. (1990). Empowerment: Notes on professional and community dimensions. *Canadian Review of Social Policy, 26,* 64–75.

Lee, M., & Greene, G. (1999). A social constructivist framework for integrating cross-cultural issues in teaching clinical social work. *Journal of Social Work Education, 35*(1), 21–37.

Loney, M. (1977). The political economy of citizen participation. In L. Panitch (Ed.), *The Canadian state and political power* (pp. 446–72). Toronto: University of Toronto Press.

Lum, D. (1996). *Social work practice and people of color* (3d ed.). Pacific Grove, CA: Brooks/Cole.

Marx, K. (1965). *Capital* (Vol. 1). Moscow: Progress. (Original work published 1867)

McCarthy, J., & Zald, M. (1976). Resource mobilization and social movements: A partial theory. *American Journal of Sociology, 82,* 1212–41.

Moffat, K. (1999). Surveillance and government of the welfare recipient. In A. Chambon, A. Irving, & L. Epstein (Eds.), *Reading Foucault for social work* (pp. 219–45). New York: Columbia University Press.

Muller, C. M. (1992). Building social movement theory. In Morris, A. D., & Mueller, C. M. *Frontiers in social movement theory* (pp. 3–25). New Haven, CT: Yale University Press.

Norlin, J., & Chess, W. (1997). *Human behavior and the social environment: Social systems theory.* Boston: Allyn & Bacon.

Panitch, L. (1977). The role and nature of the Canadian state. In L. Panitch (Ed.), *The Canadian state and political power* (pp. 3–27). Toronto: University of Toronto Press.

Parsons, R., Gutierrez, L., & Cox, E. O. (1998). Introduction. In L. Gutierrez, R. Parsons, & E. O. Cox (Eds.), *Empowerment in social work practice: A source book* (pp. 3–23). Pacific Grove, CA: Brooks/Cole.

Parsons, T. (1971). *The system of modern societies.* Englewood Cliffs, NJ: Prentice-Hall.

Pfeffer, J., & Salanick, G. (1978). *The external control of organizations.* New York: Harper Collins.

Piven, F. F., & Cloward, R. (1971). *Regulating the poor.* New York: Pantheon.

Piven, F. F., & Cloward, R. (1979). *Poor people's movements: Why they succeed, how they fail.* New York: Vintage.

Reeser, L. & Epstein, I. (1990). *Professionalization and activism in social work.* New York: Columbia University Press.

Rivera, F., & Erlich, J. (1998). *Community organizing in a diverse society* (3d ed.). Boston: Allyn & Bacon.

Rodwell, M. (1998). *Social work constructivist research.* New York: Garland.

Rossiter, A. (1996). A perspective on critical social work. *Journal of Progressive Human Services, 7*(2), 23–41.

Rothman, J. (1996). The interweaving of community intervention approaches. *Journal of Community Practice, 3*(3/4), 69–99.

Saleebey, D. (1997). *The strengths perspective in social work practice* (2d ed.). New York: Longman.

Schreader, A. (1990). The state-funded women's movement. In R. Ng, G. Walker, & J. Muller (Eds.), *Community organization and the Canadian state.* Toronto: Garamond.

Simon, B. (1990). Rethinking empowerment. *Journal of Progressive Human Services,* *1*(1), 27–40.

Sohng, S. S. L. (1998). Research as an empowerment strategy. In L. Gutierrez, R. Parsons, & E. O. Cox (Eds.), *Empowerment in social work practice: A source book* (pp. 187–201). Pacific Grove, CA: Brooks/Cole.

Solomon, B. (1976). *Black empowerment: Social work in oppressed communities.* New York: Columbia University Press.

Staples, L. (1990). Powerful ideas about empowerment. *Administration in Social Work,* *14*(2), 29–42.

Swank, E., & Clapp, J. (1999). Some methodological concerns when estimating the size of organizing activities. *Journal of Community Practice, 6*(3), 49–69.

Venkatesh, S. (1997). The social organization of street gang activity in an urban ghetto. *Social Service Review, 103,* 82–111.

Wakefield, J. (1996a). Does social work need the eco-systems perspective? Part 1: Is the perspective clinically useful? *Social Service Review, 70*(1), 2–32.

Wakefield, J. (1996b). Does social work need the eco-system perspective? Part 2: Does the perspective save social work from incoherence? *Social Service Review, 70*(2), 183–213.

Warren, R. (1978). *The community in America* (3d ed.). Chicago: Rand McNally.

Zachary, E. (2000). Grassroots leadership training: A case study of an effort to integrate theory and method. *Journal of Community Practice, 7*(1), 71–94.

Zimmerman, M. (1990). Taking aim on empowerment research: On the distinction between individual and psychological concepts. *American Journal of Community Psychology, 18*(1), 169–77.

4 Practice Models

Linking Theory with Action

■ Though theories give us an idea of how groups in society function and the efficacy of social change efforts, they do not tell us how to organize. In fact, most of the theories described in chapter 3 cannot be used to establish direct relationships between intervention approaches and likely outcomes. In community practice, we rely on models to "provide a level of abstraction and simplification that assists in comparing interventions and selecting appropriate models of action for particular situations" (Weil, 1996, p. 6). Mondros and Wilson (1994) identify several components inherent in practice models:

- A change goal
- Specific roles for staff, leaders, and members
- A process for selecting issues
- An identification of the target of the change effort
- An assessment of how cooperative or adversarial the target will be
- A change strategy
- An understanding of resources needed to produce change
- An understanding of the role of an organization in the change process (p. 240)

Models of practice contain two types of primary goals: process goals and task goals. Process goals pertain to the methods or means used to carry out organizing activities. Task goals focus on the outcomes or the end results of organizing efforts. Some types of community intervention focus almost exclusively on process—the way in which we organize is more important than the outcome of organizing efforts. Other types of organizing focus exclusively on outcomes—what we achieve is of ultimate importance. In the first section of this chapter, models of practice are used to describe three primary intervention models, developed by Rothman (1995). Next, additional models of practice that expand on Rothman's original framework by identifying practice roles and responsibilities are identified in the second section of the chapter. In the third section of this chapter, models that focus on the relationship between organizers and constituents are examined.

Intervention Approaches

Models of community practice vary in terms of the strategies and tactics used to carry out intervention plans, their orientation toward the power structure, and the use of process versus task accomplishment. The three most widely known community practice models are those identified by Rothman (1976, 1995):

- Locality (also called community) development
- Social planning
- Social action

Locality Development

Locality development focuses on correcting problems in geographic communities. It has its intellectual roots in systems or ecological perspectives on community institutions and natural processes that work for or against community stabilization (see table 4.1). All groups in the community are viewed as necessary for developing a positive environment. In addition to residents, representatives of businesses, schools, churches, hospitals, community organizations, social service organizations, and the judicial system are seen as critical to the process of creating positive changes in the community. All these community groups are considered potential partners in the social change process. It is assumed that differences among group members can be resolved through negotiation, consensus building, and collaboration.

The main goal of locality development efforts is to address alienation, the perception by residents that they are excluded from community life and can do little to resolve community problems. Consequently, the focus of community development efforts is on process, relationship building, and problem solving. Creating the atmosphere in which these can happen and bringing groups together are the organizer's primary roles. He or she brings the various community groups together to identify common problems and solutions. How this is accomplished is often more important than accomplishment of a particular goal. It is assumed that simply the act of relationship building will be sufficient to remedy residents' feelings of alienation and powerlessness. Consequently, the strength of this approach is that it can be used to bring diverse individuals and groups to the bargaining table and foster alliances between the haves and the have-nots. Social change is often difficult to achieve unless people with power and influence (those with money, elected officials, businesspeople, media representatives) are involved in the process (Rubin, 1997).

One of the limitations of locality or community development is that it is often difficult and time-consuming to achieve consensus and cooperation among all parties in community change efforts (Warren, 1971). A second problem with this approach is that it assumes that all parties have common interests that transcend boundaries associated with ethnicity, gender, social class, age, physical or mental abilities, gender orientation, and ethnicity (Hyde, 1989; Rivera & Erlich, 1998). A third limitation is that powerful decision makers can refuse to participate or come to the bargaining table. Such individuals can temporarily block or effectively prevent social change. Achieving change often requires strategies that involve confrontation with the power structure (Hardina, 1997; Mondros & Wilson, 1994).

Social Planning

The intellectual roots of social planning probably lie in Weber's (1984) description of organizations as rational entities in which goals are accomplished. The process of planning is often described as having distinct components: problem identification, assessment, goal development, implementation, and evaluation. Social workers will recognize this as the problem-solving model. Most social workers engaged in planning activities are employed by government or private organizations to develop new health- or social service–delivery systems.

The planner's role is to gather data about the scope of an identified problem and to conduct the background research needed to select the best solution for the problem. The planner then makes a recommendation to his or her employer about the best course of action. The planner can also be involved in guiding implementation of the plan and the evaluation of outcomes.

This model requires that the planner be recognized as having "expert" knowledge and is thereby qualified to make such a recommendation. The use of the rational model implies that the planner has the time and resources to collect all necessary information about the problem and choose the best

Table 4.1 Rothman's Models of Community Practice

Practice Model	Change Goal	Staff Role	Constituents	Target of Change	Change Strategies
Locality/ community development	Increasing community capacity and integration	Coordinator Enabler Catalyst	Citizens Participants	Programs or service-delivery systems	Developing a consensus among a variety of community groups
Social action	Change power dynamics and resources	Advocate Negotiator Activist	Victims of oppression Constituents Employers	The power structure	Mobilizing constituents to take action against the power elite
Social planning	Use a problem-solving approach to address social problems	Expert Data analyst Problem solver Employee	Consumers of service	Community systems	Collecting data and choosing the best plan for implementation

Source: Adapted from Rothman, 1995, Approaches to community intervention, in F. Cox, J. Erlich, J. Rothman, and J. Tropman, eds., *Strategies of community organization*, 5th ed., pp. 26–63 (Itasca, IL: F. E. Peacock).

option. It also implies that the recommended option will be logical and decided upon rationally, without the incorporation of bias or political influence.

One of the limitations of this model is that few planners have the luxury of unlimited time and resources. Rarely is the planning process not influenced by political considerations. In many instances, a planner may be called on to work with community groups to obtain a consensus about the best proposed solution for a problem (Forester, 1989). The planner is often required to use conflict-oriented approaches to influence members of the power structure to adopt specific plans (Friedmann, 1987). The planning literature defines several approaches to practice that involve modification of the rational planning model to incorporate aspects of political practice: incremental, advocacy, Marxist, and transactive planning (Hudson, 1983). These approaches will be described in detail in chapter 11.

Social Action

Social action is the most widely known form of community organization practice, but perhaps the least well understood (Hardina, 2000). The theoretical framework that guides this form of practice is associated with conflict, power-dependency, and social movement theories. Its basic premise is that many groups in society experience oppression because of race, gender, social class, ableism, ageism, and heterosexism. To gain access to jobs, education, and the political decision-making structure, these groups must organize. Power comes through strength in numbers or coercion (participation in strikes, boycotts, or other types of protest). Consequently, social action often involves confrontation with members of the power structure. People who make decisions that affect the political, economic, and social systems are viewed as members of the power elite—or enemy targets. The role of the organizer in this process is to advocate on behalf of oppressed populations. He or she may be employed by community organizations to plan interventions on behalf of organization members or constituency groups.

Social action is primarily focused toward task accomplishment. Consequently, process (use of appropriate decision-making structures or relationship building) may be ignored. The term social action is often used generically to describe a wide range of tasks used to influence social policy and legislative changes, including organizing protests, lobbying for legislation, developing mass organizations, and involvement in political campaigns. Many of these activities do not require direct confrontation with the power structure. However, the common bond among these activities is that acquiring goods, resources, and decision-making authority requires power. The act of organizing requires that the organization compete with other groups for access to resources.

One of the limitations of this model is that some practitioners may limit their practice activities to those that require confrontation in all situations. This may result in further polarization of all the parties involved and make it very difficult for the desired outcome to be achieved (Netting, Kettner, & McMurty, 1993). A second limitation is that some organizers and many constituents are not comfortable with strategies that involve confrontation (Burghardt, 1979, 1982). A third limitation associated with this model pertains to some of the ethical issues described in chapter 2. Confrontation can place constituents and organizers at risk or cause humiliation to targets. Some types of confrontation are illegal and should be used only on a very limited basis in dire situations, if at all. All participants should be fully informed of the risks involved.

Supplementing Rothman: Model Subtypes that Specify Organizer Roles and Tasks

A number of theorists have expanded on Rothman's models, focusing on models that explicitly define specific roles that organizers play and the tasks accomplished in achieving intervention goals. Consequently, these models suggest that organizing approaches are situational, dependent on the task at hand. Most of these model subtypes add to our knowledge base about social action and community development–oriented organizing.

Social Action–Related Models

Mondros and Wilson (1994) identify three practice methods that fall within the parameters of the social action model: grassroots practice, lobbying practice, and mobilizing approach. The grassroots practice method focuses on working with constituents in a geographic area to gain power. The targets for the organizing effort are people with the authority to make decisions affecting the community. The organizer works in conjunction with the constituents to identify appropriate strategies. Often these strategies are confrontational. One of the primary outcomes of this practice method is the development of a highly structured organization to carry out future organizing efforts.

Lobbying is the second type of practice method Mondros and Wilson identified. It involves identifying issues of concern to the public and analyzing how current or pending legislation affects these issues. Lobbyists monitor legislative decision making and make direct efforts to influence government decision makers to adopt their organization's position on the issue. Advocacy organizations can assign staff members to conduct one-on-one lobbying with individual legislators and other government officials. However, these organizations also rely on staff to recruit members who can participate in petition drives, letter-writing campaigns, rallies, and meetings with lawmakers.

Mobilizing involves bringing together large groups of people who are traditionally excluded from participation in the political process. The media and mass education are used to create public consciousness of political and economic issues. Participants may use disruptive tactics such as demonstrations, boycotts, and guerrilla theater to confront the power structure. Although this approach requires the formation of a social movement to effect change, Mondros and Wilson (1994) argue that acts of disruption may be more important than developing strong organizations to work for social change.

Fisher (1995) and Haynes and Mickelson (1991) describe a fourth type of social action: political practice. The goal of political practice is to elect public officials who will support policies that uphold social work values. No particular model or prototype specifies how a social worker engaged in politics should conduct interventions. In general, political practice (involving campaign work) contains many similarities to other types of social action organizing. The emphasis is placed on task accomplishment rather than process. Organizers recruit volunteers or constituency group members and raise funds for the cause. The media is used to send messages to the public about the candidate's ideology or position on the issues. However, campaign work takes place in a limited time frame—the focus is on winning, and organizations constructed to carry out the primary tasks are often transitory.

The social work literature on political practice does specify some specific tasks and roles. Political practice can include employment-related activities as well as volunteer work. Political campaigns may employ community organizers to carry out such tasks as recruiting volunteers, organizing precinct workers, planning media campaigns, and conducting research to identify likely voters. Community organizers can also run for political office. Organizers can also volunteer on political campaigns, working as office volunteers or precinct captains, canvassing voters, or raising funds.

Reeser and Epstein (1990) identify a number of political action–related activities that do not involve hands-on participation in a campaign: making a campaign contribution, attending meetings where political speeches are made, becoming a member of a political party, or signing a petition in support of a candidate. Opportunities for political involvement are also offered as part of the field education experience in a number of schools of social work. Students are placed in political campaigns or in constituency offices maintained by legislators (Fisher, 1995). Constituency office tasks tend to focus on activities related to casework, such as helping voters obtain government-funded services (Hoefer, 1999).

Community Development–Oriented Approaches

Kretzman and McKnight (1993) developed a model of practice that focuses on community strengths or assets rather than deficits. They argue that service-based approaches in which organizers identify neighborhood needs often result in the dependence of community residents on outside social service organizations. The Kretzman and McKnight model focuses on helping residents identify personal strengths and skills, create informal networks with strong social bonds, and develop mechanisms for neighbors to exchange skills and resources. This model also calls for strengthening neighborhood associations by increasing resident participation. These associations and neighborhood institutions (e.g., schools, churches, and hospitals) are recruited to donate resources (facilities, staff time, equipment, and money). Consequently, most help is derived from neighborhood-based resources. However, Kretzman and McKnight also recommend finding outside sources to invest funds in the community. Initial steps for using the community assets approach call for the identification or "mapping" of all community resources; building strong relationships among the people, groups, and institutions that possess these assets; and creating a neighborhood organization to develop a plan for community renewal.

Influenced by Kretzman and McKnight, Delgado (2000) developed the capacity enhancement model for community organization. This model focuses on the use of open space in inner-city communities of color. One basic premise of this model (supported by ecological theory) is that the physical environment, often characterized by poor housing and limited institutional resources, is harmful to residents. Consequently, community residents are the focus of the change effort. They are involved in identifying community assets, primarily the use of open space that can be utilized to provide services residents need (such as playgrounds and community gardens) or projects that can be used to create community pride and solidarity (community murals). Projects are carried out through the creation of partnerships between local organizations and residents. Residents take the lead role in identifying community problems, finding solutions, and carrying out the tasks needed to effectively utilize open space. This strategy is intended to enhance residents' skills and knowledge (i.e., strengths) and to bring about substantial changes in the surrounding physical environment.

A third approach that relies on an ecosystems perspective is community economic development (Midgley & Livermore, 1998; Raheim & Alter, 1998; Rubin & Rubin, 1992). Unlike social action, which often identifies corporate interests as the enemy target, economic development focuses on establishing cooperative relationships with area businesses. The purpose of economic development is to improve employment, small business, housing, and investment opportunities in economically depressed communities. This work is accomplished as a variety of constituency groups (lending institutions, employers, educational facilities, churches, and other community leaders) seek government and private investments to improve the community's physical structure and business climate.

Much economic development work in the United States is conducted through community-based development organizations. Some critics of this approach have argued that the focus on business development and investment has led these organizations to neglect service provision and advocacy for the needs of low-income people. However, Rubin (1997) has argued that this approach empowers residents by increasing employment opportunities and economic well-being.

Outside the United States, much of the focus of economic development work has been on creating new industries and self-employment opportunities for people (women, indigenous groups) who have not had previous access to employment opportunities. Consequently, economic development provides an avenue for underrepresented groups to gain economic parity and political recognition (Durst, 1991; Jansen & Pippard, 1998)

Models that Look at Roles and Functions

Weil and Gamble (1995) constructed an eight-model framework for understanding the various approaches to community organization. Their framework builds on the models constructed by Rothman (1995) and differs in a number of ways:

1. It distinguishes between organizing geographic communities and organizing functional communities. According to Lee (1986), functional communities occur naturally or are developed because of a specific common attribute (such as ethnicity or gender) or a common function (for example, owners of "mom-and-pop" grocery stores).
2. It includes three types of social change efforts: political and social action, coalitions, and social movement organizing.
3. It adds a second planning-related activity, program development and liaison, to distinguish the planning model that focuses on the use of "expert" knowledge from one that requires extensive contacts and negotiation with community residents.
4. It recognizes economic development as a distinct organizing model but combines it with an approach called social development. Social development is defined as the "development of people—their capacities and skills—so that they can initiate and maintain grassroots plans and projects, improve their social and economic conditions and support and sustain their home environment and resources" (Weil, 1996, p. 49). For a description of professional roles and tasks associated with these models, see table 4.2.

Limitations of Models that Identify Roles and Tasks

Although these models help us identify the types of activities organizers typically perform, it is unlikely that these categories of practice models are

Table 4.2 Weil and Gamble's Eight-Model Framework: Roles and Tasks for the Organizer

Practice Model	Change Goal	Staff Role	Constituents	Target of Change	Change Strategies/Tasks
Neighborhood and community organizing	Quality of life in the geographic area	Organizer Teacher Facilitator	Residents of neighborhood	Government, developers, community residents	Develop capacity of members to organize
Organizing functional communities	Advocacy for an issue or subpopulation	Organizer Advocate Communicator Facilitator	Like-minded people, not confined to a specific geographic community	Government, the public	Advocate for social justice
Community economic and social development	Income and social support development, improvements in education and leadership skills	Negotiator Promoter Teacher Planner Manager	Oppressed populations within a specific geographic area	Banks, developers, foundations, residents	Initiate development; prepare citizens to make use of social and economic resources

Social planning	Development of programs; creation of service networks for coordination	Researcher Proposal writer Communicator Manager	Elected officials, agency directors, and interagency collaboratives	Perspectives of community leaders and social service administrators	Develop planning proposals to address social problems
Program development and community liaison	Development of services for specific population groups	Spokesperson Planner Manager Proposal writer	Agency boards or administrators; community residents	Funders of agency programs, beneficiaries of services	Improve agency services; create new service-delivery systems
Political and social action	Development of a political power base; changing institutions	Advocate Organizer Researcher Candidate	Citizens within a particular political entity	Voters, elected officials	Influence policy changes
Coalitions	Issue advocacy	Mediator Negotiator Spokesperson	Organization members within the coalition	Elected officials, government	Build a multi-organization power base to influence policy change
Social movements	Social justice	Advocate Facilitator	Leaders and organizations	The public, the political system	Take action to promote social justice

Source: Weil, M., & Gamble, D. (1995), Community practice models, in R. L. Edwards, Ed., *Encyclopedia of social work*, 19th ed., pp. 577–94 (Washington, DC: National Association of Social Workers).

necessarily mutually exclusive or exhaustive. Organizers are most likely to adjust their practice activities in response to situational demands, personal comfort with various strategies, and the preferences of constituents or supervisors. Few organizations that employ organizers are large enough to hire more than a handful of organizers at one time. Consequently, it is difficult for an organizer to specialize exclusively in one area of community practice. Some of the models listed here contain substantial overlap. For example, it may be difficult to determine the difference between a social planner and a program developer (Weil & Gamble, 1995), or community development as opposed to some types of economic development. (For example, community development activities might focus on developing new businesses or increasing employment.) As described later in this chapter, the typical organizer is most likely to use a mixture of approaches for attaining successful outcomes.

Transformative Models: Looking at the Relationship of the Organizer and the Constituency Group

A number of models of practice have been designed specifically for work with oppressed populations. One key component of these models is an understanding of how the dominant culture has used power to limit access to goods, services, and decision-making authority to ethnic and other marginalized groups. One primary component of practice models is the assumption that power derived through the acquisition of authority or resources has harmful effects. Therefore, the organizing process is characterized by the rejection of authority; all participants in the organizing process (organizer and constituents) will function as equals. "Experts," those possessing professional knowledge, have the same status as other group members. These three models are the transformative model, the multicultural practice model, and the feminist model. One of the basic assumptions of these models is that participants focus on personal as well as political change or transformation.

Transformative Model

The transformative model has its roots in both conflict theory and social constructionism, an approach intended to increase our understanding of how social structure constrains the lives of people in the subordinate classes. Freire (1970) developed the transformative model as a mechanism to educate impoverished and oppressed populations in Brazil. People learned to read by discussing their experiences with oppression and putting those experiences into written form. The teacher provided basic instruction in reading and writing. However, students were recognized as the "best experts" about those experiences that had formed their lives. Consequently, teacher and students were peers, equals in the learning processes. The teacher was educated about oppression and the culture-specific experiences of his or her students. In addition to reading and writing, the students gained knowledge about how oppression affected their lives. They were empowered by the literary instruction they received and their ability to apply their skills to developing solutions to common problems. Much of this knowledge was gained through dialogue among group members and instructors. Freire calls this process the development of "critical consciousness"—understanding how individuals, their values, and opportunities are shaped by political and social structures. Carniol (1990) describes why critical consciousness is an essential part of the organizing process:

> It seems clear that basic change for the better becomes a possibility only when many individuals develop a shared consciousness of oppression, for example, of gender, race or class . . .Change, then, is inevitably induced by the system itself, because its exploitative institutions, over time, work to generate negative feelings and a political response from those of us who are subject to their top-down control. The other essential part of change is our own response as individuals—our attitudes and our actions at both personal and political levels. (p. 118)

The development of critical consciousness is an ongoing process; all participants, instructors, and students become "active learners." The purpose of the educational process is to transform the lives of group members. By transformation, Freire hoped that participants obtain some mastery over the environment and become aware of their own strengths and abilities to effect social change. Freire (1970) used the term "praxis" to describe the interplay between reflection (understanding the common origins of individual problems) and taking action to resolve those problems.

Although intended for use in Brazil, various components of the transformative model have been integrated into community organization practice in the United States and Canada. The primary components North American social workers use are as follow:

1. Dialogue to gain insight into cultures and values in instances when group members come from a variety of diverse ethnic groups.
2. The requirement that the professional (teacher or social worker) become an active learner, gaining knowledge about the lives and cultural backgrounds of group participants.
3. An acknowledgment that professionals who lead groups should participate in the groups as equal partners.
4. The purpose of community work with groups should be to create an environment that promotes the development of critical consciousness among group members.

5. The recognition that participation in the process of education for social change leads to personal as well as political transformation.

Multicultural Practice

A number of social workers (Gutierrez & Alvarez, 2000; Lum, 1996; Rivera & Erlich, 1998) have adopted some of Freire's (1970) work and incorporated it into a model of practice designed for working with communities of color. Lum (1996) defines culturally diverse social work practice as intervention that

> recognizes and respects the importance of difference and variety in people and the crucial role of culture in the helping relationship. Its primary group focus is on people of color—particularly African Americans, Latino Americans, Asian Americans, and Native Americans—who have suffered historical oppression and continue to endure subtle forms of racism, prejudice, and discrimination. (p. 12)

Although Lum's work primarily focuses on clinical practice, he has identified a number of components essential for practice with people of color:

- The worker must be able to understand the social, economic, and cultural customs of the community served.
- The worker must be aware of his or her own feelings regarding race and class.
- Research must be conducted on specific behaviors associated with other cultural groups.
- Theoretical constructs designed for and by whites must be replaced by those appropriate for people of color.
- Social work training must communicate a culturally sensitive practice approach.

Efforts to develop a multicultural approach in community practice have used Freire's concepts of dialogue and the development of critical consciousness to educate culturally competent students in community practice (Gutierrez & Alvarez, 2000). Inside the classroom, students have been encouraged to identify their own cultural biases while learning about the cultural backgrounds of other classroom members (Garcia & Van Soest, 1997; Nagda et al., 1999). It is expected that students will continue to use these skills in working with oppressed communities, becoming active learners to identify customs and norms that differ from those of the dominant culture. They would then be able to use what they have learned to develop culturally competent approaches to practice. Consequently, this approach differs in a number of ways from Freire's transformative model:

1. There is an assumption that the organizer (regardless of his or her own cultural reference point or location in the organizing process) will take on the role of the professional or "expert."
2. Most participants in the dialogue (including the organizer) will be able to gain knowledge from their own experiences with oppression.
3. All community organizers will have opportunities to practice cross-culturally.

Feminist Organizing

The basic assumption of feminist theory is that women are oppressed by patriarchy. Compared to men, women have limited access to employment opportunities, political power, and other resources. Another basic assumption of feminist theory is that we actually know very little about how women of various ethnic groups and social classes have experienced oppression in this society. Most theories about the manner in which society operates have been developed by men. The intention of feminist research is to obtain more information about the experiences of women in society. Feminist practice in community organizing is oriented toward the development of theories and skills that are suitable for working with women (Gutierrez & Lewis, 1994).

Feminist theory has been used to examine the role of women in social welfare organizations. Dressel (1992) argues that women are often locked into frontline positions as opposed to management jobs due to stereotypes about appropriate roles for women in society. Tasks involved in the delivery of clinical or casework services are believed to involve nurturing, a trait primarily associated with women. Management tasks, on the other hand, are believed to require an instrumental or task-oriented approach. This approach is believed to be associated with male traits or characteristics. Gender division of labor in most social service organizations is supported by the hierarchical nature of the organization and the power and authority vested in male administrators.

This type of analysis implies that the power inherent in traditional hierarchical organizations is associated with the continued oppression of women. Consequently, feminist organizers have often sought to develop "feminist organizations" to deliver health and domestic violence–related services to women. These organizations have power structures that emphasize the equal distribution of decision-making authority among all members of the organization: board members, administrators, frontline staff, and individuals who receive the service (Hyde, 1994). Consequently, feminist organizations place a heavy emphasis on collaboration and cooperation in decision-making processes. Feminist organizing approaches also use collaboration and cooperative approaches in bringing women together to promote social change. In this regard, feminist organizing can be said to be associated with community development–oriented approaches to community practice (Rothman, 1995).

Gutierrez & Lewis (1994) identify the following characteristics as components of feminist organizing:

1. The assumption that sexism negatively affects the lives of all women.
2. The assumption, as in community development, that the process of practice rather than outcome is most important, with a focus on decision making oriented toward equality and collectivity.
3. The use of consciousness-raising techniques to make the connection between personal experiences and the political environment.
4. The use of a "bottoms-up" or grassroots approach to service delivery that focuses on women's unique needs rather than funding availability or traditional service structure.
5. Promotion of diversity among women through the amelioration of differences in class, ethnicity, sexual orientation, age, and physical ability.
6. The recognition that organizing is holistic and may contain emotional as well as rational elements.

Limitations of Transformative Approaches

Many of the concepts inherent in transformative approaches to practice (critical consciousness, equal status among participants, mutual learning) have been incorporated into community work in North America. However, organizers should be aware that the model developed by Freire (1970) was both culturally specific (Brazil) and intended for use with low-income people by an educator of the same culture. While the organizer was expected to transcend boundaries associated with social class, the focus was on the personal and political development of marginalized groups rather than on the personal development or cultural competency of the organizer. This method was conceived as a multistage process that focused on the education of participants as well as social change. The use of dialogue among participants to achieve goals is time-consuming and may not always serve the needs of constituents and organizers in crisis situations.

Not all of the participants have the same values or goals. As noted in chapter 2, the values of the organizer can be in conflict with those of his or her constituents. Rivera and Erlich (1998) have argued that it is possible for organizers to address such problems. They feel that the best way to do this is for organizers to focus their practice exclusively on members of their own ethnic group. The potential for "mistakes" or domination by the organizer of "other group" members is too great for the organizer to risk working cross-culturally.

Other organizers have argued that oppression is complex, not limited to ethnicity and operating on a number of different levels (Morris, 1993). One individual may experience oppression from a number of different sources. For example, a woman of color with a physical disability could experience racism, sexism, and ableism. According to Moreau (1990):

> Real people are always more than the single categories, by which they are described, defined and kept in their place. Moreover, divisions based on hierarchical gradations of power exist within and between inferiorized groups . . . . All forms of oppression are in reality inter-related, mutually reinforcing, and overlapping. (pp. 63–64)

Consequently, it may be almost impossible for the organizer to experience all the sources of oppression that members of the organizer's constituency group face. Many organizers work with organizations in which many cultural groups are represented (Mizrahi & Rosenthal, 1993). Cultural competency, the ability to be aware of and responsive to cultural differences and the impact of oppression, is therefore an essential component of community practice (Lum, 1996). However, as noted by Hyde (1989, 1994), in many organizations ethnic and class differences (as well as the types of oppression included in the CRAASH typology in chapter 1) make it difficult to achieve consensus. Although some feminist and ethnic organizations foster real collaboration and participation among members, organizations must adopt the values and practices of the dominant culture (for example, hierarchical decision-making structures). Often organizations must meet the requirements of donors (such as the appointment of a central decision maker or director) in order to survive financially.

Choosing an Approach to Practice

In general, the philosophy or mission of the organization that employs the community organizer determines the model of practice used to effect change. Community development organizations use approaches that foster cooperation among various constituency groups. Social planning organizations make recommendations for new services, and social movement organizations organize protests. In addition, the preferences of constituents are also of critical concern. An individual organizer who is asked to recommend a model of practice should consider five primary factors:

1. The constituents' needs and cultural values
2. The organizer's theoretical framework
3. The organizer's own personality
4. The organizing problem or situation
5. The ethical ramifications of organizing strategies

The organizer should use his or her own theoretical perspective to help frame or understand the practice situation and suggest a course of action. Organizers who are most comfortable with systems or ecological theory will probably be oriented toward community development approaches. If the organizer uses conflict theory to understand the interplay between the haves and the have-nots, social action is the model of choice. If the organizer believes that interventions should be constructed by data gathering and choosing among available options, social planning may be the best option. The organizer who believes that these models will not serve the interests of members of historically marginalized groups should choose models influenced by conflict theories (transformative, multicultural, and feminist) (see table 4.3).

Mondros and Wilson (1994) have argued that the organizer's personal preferences as well as his or her own degree of comfort with specific tactics are important factors that determine the selection of an organizing model. Burghardt (1979) argues that an organizer must be comfortable with the practice approach used. The organizer who is most comfortable with a process-oriented approach, inclusive of the preferences of group members, will choose community development or the social planning model. The organizer who is more task-oriented and directive should choose social action. Mondros and Wilson (1994) believe that the organizer's use of a practice framework is determined by his or her perceptions of the legitimacy of the political system and personal feelings of alienation from decision makers. Organizers who believe that social change is easily achievable and that decision makers are reasonable people who will support realistic proposals will choose community development approaches. Those organizers who believe that society is controlled by the elite who will not readily give up power will choose social action.

The only framework social work practitioners have for making decisions about appropriate practice models and the strategies associated with them was developed by Warren (1971). Decisions on strategies and tactics are determined by three primary factors: the degree of consensus among the groups involved in the change effort, the relationship of the action system to the target population, and whether the goal can be achieved within the existing power structure (see chapter10 for further discussion on the choice of tactics).

Rothman (1995) reminds his readers that models of practice are not mutually exclusive. He advocates a "mixing and phasing" approach (see chapter 10). For example, a community group may use community development to bring community groups together, engage in social planning activities to develop a program in response to community needs, and then use social action approaches to lobby government for funds. Bradshaw, Soifer, and Gutierrez (1994) also recommend using different styles of practice in different phases of the organizing process.

Table 4.3 Theories, Models of Practice, and Practice Subtypes

Theory	Systems Theory, Ecological Theory	Conflict Theory, Power Dependency Theory, Social Movement Theory	Rational Theory/ Problem-Solving Model	Constructivist Theory
Model Model Subtype	**Community development** Economic development Capacity enhancement Assets-based model Feminist organizing	**Social action** Lobbying Mobilization Grassroots organizing Political organizing Feminist organizing	**Social planning** Rational Advocacy Incremental Transactive Marxist	**Transformative model** Multicultural model Feminist organizing

Note: Some model subtypes can be linked to more than one theoretical framework.

Toward an Integrated Model of Practice: Identifying Basic Practice Principles

Although a variety of factors contribute to the choice of an appropriate practice model, the following basic principles are offered here as a framework for practice:

1. The basic premise of organizing is to empower individuals and communities.
2. Organizers must recognize the inherent strengths, skills, values, and capacities of the communities they serve.
3. Organizers who work cross-culturally or who work in multicultural settings must be culturally competent; acquiring skills for understanding the values and traditions of the communities they serve. Strategies and tactics used in organizing efforts must be culturally appropriate.
4. Organizers must recognize that their primary practice goal is to help marginalized groups acquire the goods and resources that they deserve.
5. Organizers must recognize that the various types of oppressions are overlapping; no one form of oppression is necessarily better or worse than another.
6. Organizing efforts must contain structures that promote full inclusion of constituents in decision making, including all steps in the problem-solving process (problem identification, assessment, goal setting, implementation, and evaluation).
7. Organizers must work to promote the development of decision-making structures that recognize the equality of professional staff members, paraprofessional workers, and constituents.
8. Organizers must acquire negotiation and bargaining skills to reconcile the needs and preferences of various constituency groups represented by the organizer and his or her employer. These skills are also needed to promote collaborative decision-making structures.
9. Organizers must develop a personal framework for making ethical decisions in choosing appropriate strategies and tactics.
10. Organizers must choose practice approaches that are consistent with the problem at hand, recognizing that no one "right" approach exists. To be effective, the organizer must be prepared to use different approaches during successive stages of the organizing process.

Summary

Community organizers have a wide variety of practice models to choose from when planning interventions. The choice of an appropriate model depends on (1) the preferences of constituency group members, (2) the organizer's personal preferences, (3) the issue or situation at hand, and (4) the ethical implications of using various strategies and tactics. Organizers need to be culturally competent, recognizing the strengths of partners and constituents in the organizing process. Organizers also need to establish dialogue with constituents to develop a critical understanding of the issue and the benefits and weaknesses of proposed solutions. In chapter 5, the term community is defined and theories that describe how communities function are described.

∎ QUESTIONS FOR CLASS DISCUSSION

1. What model of practice do you think you would prefer? Why?
2. Hardina (2000) conducted a survey of community organization instructors. She found that though most instructors in schools of social work preferred social action to other models of community practice, they were most comfortable with strategies and tactics associated with locality or community development: consensus, cooperation, and negotiation. Why do you think social workers would prefer this model?
3. Do you think that social workers should use strategies associated with conflict or those associated with confrontation? Why?
4. Identify two or more oppressed groups. What strategies do you think would be most appropriate for organizing efforts that involve these groups?
5. Why is cultural competency important for the success of organizing efforts? How should one go about becoming culturally competent?
6. Do you agree with Rivera and Erlich (1998) that organizers should work only within their own ethnic group? Why?

∎ SAMPLE ASSIGNMENT: USING MODELS OF PRACTICE

1. Identify a problem in your field setting that could be addressed through community organization practice.
2. Identify constituency groups you would like to involve in the organizing process.
3. Describe your primary goal.
4. Identify available resources (volunteers, staff, members, community institutions, money, media resources, etc.) that could be used to achieve your goal.
5. Describe any diversity issues that could enhance or impede the organizing process.
6. Identify the model or models of practice that would best help you meet your goal.
7. What do you think are the benefits or weaknesses of the models you have chosen?

References

Bradshaw, C., Soifer, S., & Gutierrez, L. (1994). Toward a hybrid model for effective organizing in communities of color. *Journal of Community Practice 1*(1), 25–41.

Burghardt, S. (1979). Tactical use of group structure and process in community organizations. In F. Cox, J. Erlich, J. Rothman, and J. Tropman (Eds.), *Strategies of community organization* (3d ed., pp. 112–37). Itasca, IL: Peacock Press.

Burghardt, S. (1982). *The other side of organizing.* Cambridge, MA: Schenkman.

Carniol, B. (1990). *Case critical.* Toronto: Between the Lines.

Delgado, M. (2000). *Community social work practice in an urban context.* New York: Oxford University Press.

Durst, D. (1991). Unemployment and aboriginal peoples. A new perspective. In G. Riches & G. Ternowetsky (Eds.), *Unemployment and welfare: Social policy and the work of social work* (pp. 195–212). Toronto: Garamond Press.

Dresser, P. (1992). Patriarchy and social welfare work. In Y. Hasenfeld (Ed.), *Human services as complex organizations* (pp. 205–23). Newbury Park, CA: Sage.

Fisher, R. (1995). Political social work. *Journal of Social Work Education, 31*(2), 194–203.

Forester, J. (1989). *Planning in the face of power.* Berkeley: University of California Press.

Freire, P. (1970). *Pedagogy of the oppressed* . New York: Continuum.

Friedmann, J. (1987). *Planning in the public domain: From knowledge to action.* Princeton: Princeton University Press.

Garcia, B., & Van Soest, D. (1997). Changing perceptions of diversity and oppression: MSW students discuss the effects of a required course. *Journal of Social Work Education, 33,* 119–29.

Gutierrez, L., & Alvarez, A. (2000). Educating students for multicultural community practice. *Journal of Community Practice, 7*(1), 39–56.

Gutierrez, L. M., & Lewis, E. (1994). Community organizing with women of color: A feminist approach. *Journal of Community Practice, 1*(2), 23–44.

Hardina, D. (1997). Empowering students for community organization practice: Teaching confrontation tactics. *Journal of Community Practice, 4*(2), 51–63.

Hardina, D. (2000). Models and tactics taught in community organization courses: Findings from a national study. *Journal of Community Practice, 7*(1), 5–18.

Haynes, K., & Mickelson, J. (1991). *Affecting change* (2d ed.). New York: Longman.

Hoefer, R. (1999). The social work and politics initiative: A model for increasing political content in social work education. *Journal of Community Practice, 6*(3), 71–87.

Hudson, B. (1983). Comparison of current planning theories: counterparts and contradictions. In R. Kramer & H. Specht (Eds.), *Readings in community organization practice* (3d ed., pp. 246–62). Englewood Cliffs, NJ: Prentice-Hall.

Hyde, C. (1989). A feminist model for macro-practice: Promises and problems. *Administration in Social Work, 13,* 145–81.

Hyde, C. (1994). Commitment to social change: Voices from the feminist movement. *Journal of Community Practice, 1*(2), 45–63.

Jansen, G., & Pippard, J. (1998). The Grameen bank in Bangladesh: Helping poor women with credit for self-employment. *Journal of Community Practice, 5*(1/2), 103–24.

Kretzman, J., & McKnight, J. (1993). *Building communities from the inside out.* Chicago: ACTA.

Lee, B. (1986). *Pragmatics of community organization*. Mississauga, Ontario: Commonact Press.

Lum, D. (1996). *Social work practice and people of color: A process-stage approach* (3d ed.). Pacific Grove, CA: Brooks/Cole.

Midgley, J., & Livermore, M. (1998). Social capital and local economic development: Implications for community social work practice. *Journal of Community Practice, 5*(1/2), 29–40.

Mizrahi, T., & Rosenthal, B. (1993). Managing dynamic tensions in social change coalitions. In T. Mizrahi & J. Morrison (Eds.), *Community organization and social administration* (pp. 11–40). New York: Haworth.

Mondros, J., & Wilson, S. (1994). *Organizing for power and empowerment*. New York: Columbia University Press.

Moreau, M. (1990). Empowerment through advocacy and consciousness-raising. *Journal of Sociology and Social Welfare, 17* (2), 53–67.

Morris, J. K. (1993). Interacting oppressions: Teaching social work content on women of color. *Journal of Social Work Education, 29*(1), 99–110.

Nagda, B., Spearmon, M., Holley, L., Harding, S., Balassone, L., Moise-Swanson, D., & de Mello, S. (1999). Intergroup dialogues: An innovative approach to teaching about diversity and justice in social work programs. *Journal of Social Work Education, 35*, 433–49.

Netting, E., Kettner, P., & McMurty, S. (1993). *Social work macro practice*. New York: Longman.

Raheim, S., & Alter, C. (1998). Self-employment as a social and economic development intervention for recipients of AFDC. *Journal of Community Practice, 5* (1/2), 41–62.

Reeser, L., & Epstein, I. (1990). *Professionalization and activism in social work*. New York: Columbia University Press.

Rivera, F., & Erlich, J. (1998). *Community organizing in a diverse society* (3d ed.). Boston: Allyn & Bacon.

Rothman, J. (1995). Approaches to community intervention. In F. Cox, J. Erlich, J. Rothman, & J. Tropman (Eds.), *Strategies of community organization* (5th ed., pp. 26–63). Itasca, IL: F. E. Peacock.

Rothman, J. (1996). The interweaving of community intervention approaches. *Journal of Community Practice, 3*(3/4), 69–99.

Rubin, H. (1997). Being a conscience and a carpenter: Interpretations of a community-based development model. *Journal of Community Practice, 4*(1), 57–90.

Rubin, H., & Rubin, I. S. (1992). *Community organizing and development* (2d ed.). Columbus, OH: Macmillan.

Warren, R. (1971). Types of purposive social change at the community level. In R. Warren (Ed.), *Truth, love, and social change* (pp. 134–49). Chicago: Rand McNally.

Weber, M. (1984). Bureaucracy. In F. Fischer & C. Sirianne (Eds.), *Critical studies in organization and bureaucracy*. Philadelphia: Temple University Press.

Weil, M., (1996). Model development in community practice: An historical perspective. The interweaving of community intervention approaches. *Journal of Community Practice, 3*(3/4), 5–67.

Weil, M., & Gamble D. (1995). Community practice models. In R. L. Edwards (Ed.), *Encyclopedia of Social Work* (19th ed., pp. 577–94). Washington, DC: National Association of Social Workers.

5 Defining Community

■ Communities can be thought of in terms of place, interest, and identity. Geographic communities are also called neighborhoods. In most communities, explicit and implicit boundaries delineate community members from nonmembers. This chapter defines the term community and describes factors used to determine who is included in or excluded from the various communities. Three models commonly used for analysis of geographic communities are examined. Links between community interventions and common community problems are also described.

Communities and Neighborhoods

Norlin and Chess (1997) define community as "an inclusive form of social organization that is territorially based and through which most people satisfy their common needs and desires, deal with their common problems, seek means to advance their well-being, and relate to their society" (p. 55). Most community organizers believe this definition, relying solely on a geographic conception of community, is insufficient. Fellin (1995b) defines communities as entities "constituted when a group of people form a social unit based on common location, interest, identification, culture, or common activities" (p. 114).

Communities are most often defined in terms of geographic location, identification, and interest. As described in chapters 3 and 4 geographic communities may be functional, meeting the needs of residents. Communities can also involve patterns of social interaction or networks. They can also be viewed as a process or entity that provides members with a sense of collective identity (Cnaan & Rothman, 1995). Nongeographic communities are "bound together by historical and/or contemporary circumstances; racial, religious, or national origins; and . . . share a common set of values, mutual expectations, and aspirations" (Pantoja & Perry, 1998, p. 225). Consequently, communities can be defined by ethnicity, culture, social class, gender, physical or mental disabilities, gender orientation, age, and common problems (Fellin, 1995b; Kahn, 1991). Individuals can be members of more than one community: neighborhood of residence, demographic characteristics, or identification with a specific population group.

Community organization practice focuses on helping people become attached to and identify with a specific community. Biklen (1983) offers an explanation as to why community membership is valued:

when people find community, they find they have greater power over their lives. They find ways of resolving problems. They find support and a sense of belonging. They find greater meaning in life. By the same token, when people are forcibly isolated, they frequently become victims of exploitation, authoritarianism, and alienation. (p. 5)

Geographic communities contain a variety of features that make each one unique. However, urban communities share a large number of common characteristics (G. Delgado, 1997). Note, however, that community organization can be practiced in localities outside large cities—suburbia as well as rural areas. Travel distances; ethnic, cultural, and social class stratification; and labor market effects often pose special challenges for rural organizers (Cummins, First, & Toomey, 1998; Davis, 1994).

The strength of interpersonal relationships and links between individuals and community institutions are also important for an understanding of community well-being. Toennies (1957) described communities as either gemeinschaft, characterized by strong but informal interrelationships among members, or gesellschaft, characterized by a high degree of alienation from one another and local institutions. In gesellschaft communities, relationships are formal, impersonal, contractual, and used to achieve a goal. Interpersonal relationships may be horizontal. Horizontal relationships take place among residents or among organizations of equal strength and status (Chaskin, 1997). Vertical relationships involve people and organizations of varying power and influence competing for resources; individuals and organizations with greater power or authority are able to control or restrain the activities of others.

Barriers to Participation in Community Life: Understanding the Rules of Inclusion and Exclusion

Communities can be perceived as distinct from one another simply because members and society at large follow implicit and explicit rules that distinguish members from nonmembers. Economic inequality is the most important predictor of social problems that affect geographic communities. Neighborhood poverty is largely "determined by overall economic conditions prevailing in a metropolitan area and level of segregation by race and income" (Jargowsky, 1997, p. 6). Discrimination in employment and housing creates an environment in which people have few options about where they live. Despite federal civil rights laws, segregation still exists. Research suggests that the concentration of low-income people in certain inner-city communities actually increased during the 1980s and 1990s (Chow & Coulton, 1998; Jargowsky, 1997). According to Massey (1990),

> Segregation heightens and reinforces negative racial stereotypes by concentrating people who fit those stereotypes in a small number of highly visible minority neighborhoods—a structural version of "blaming the victim"—thereby hardening prejudice, making discrimination more likely, and maintaining the motivation for segregation. (p. 353)

In isolated communities, people have few options for finding work. Spatial mismatch theory indicates that most employment opportunities can be found in suburban areas whereas the people who need jobs live in inner-city neighborhoods or rural areas (Ong & Blumenberg, 1998). Often public transportation is inadequate to link people with jobs. Consequently, drug dealing, prostitution, and informal, "off-the book" labor may be the only types of employment accessible to people in low-income communities (Anderson, 1990; Wagner, 1994).

Though such theories can be applied to geographic communities, they also pertain to other oppressed groups. According to Brzuzy (1997), "Persons with impairments are perceived and treated differently and are consequently excluded from the mainstream. Impairments become disabilities when societies create structures which limit people's opportunities and access to resources" (p. 81). While these barriers serve to limit participation in economic and social life, they also act to distinguish various communities from one another. Types of community boundaries include physical barriers, common problems, political entities, ethnicity, culture, gender, social class, collective identity, formal networks, and informal relationships. These boundaries can be symbolic, designed to separate people from one another, or based on friendship or functional links among individuals and organizations. Boundaries can also be explicated via written membership bylaws or adherence to implicit rules designed to exclude nonmembers.

Physical Barriers

Physical barriers separate neighborhoods from outside communities. Such barriers may include busy streets or highways, railroad tracks, geographic barriers such as hills or rivers, or implicit boundaries that neighborhood residents will not cross (Kahn, 1991; Lee, 1986), Often residents obtain services from institutions located outside the neighborhood or travel to and from their places of employment. Buildings and streets also play a role in determining who belongs to or who is excluded from the neighborhood (Lee, 1986; Venkatesh, 1997). Sometimes buildings and other physical structures are covered by gang graffiti to further define gang territory and safe or unsafe space.

Physical barriers also limit the participation of persons with disabilities in community life. Curbs and steps restrict the movement of wheelchair users and people who use canes, crutches, or walkers; public transportation is often inaccessible to many persons with disabilities. Visually impaired, deaf, and communications-disordered persons face special problems involving communication and information gathering (Mackelprang & Salsgiver, 1999). Difficulties that persons with disabilities face in obtaining income or insurance coverage also limit mobility. Persons with disabilities often cannot obtain medical equipment, computers (often necessary to facilitate communication), or appropriately equipped vehicles that will permit them to participate in economic and social life.

Political Entities

School districts and other areas constructed for political and decision-making purposes (towns, cities, counties, state assembly and senate districts, congressional districts, states, special assessment or planning zones) also influence the development of common interests (Kahn, 1991; Lee, 1986). Voters may organize within these entities to identify common problems and achieve solutions. Consequently, those planners who set these boundaries have the power to determine who participates in decisions. These decisions are primarily based on a political rationale. Some groups may be deliberately excluded or included within these districts in order that certain types of candidates are elected or the interests of dominant ethnic groups or social classes are represented.

Ethnicity and Culture

Members of ethnic groups who are not part of the dominant culture often face discrimination. They may have difficulty finding job opportunities and housing; they may be paid at lower rates than white Americans and are less likely to have access to college and other educational opportunities. Results from a survey conducted by the Urban Institute indicate that African Americans are twice as likely to live in poverty as non-Hispanic whites, Hispanics, and Native Americans (see figure 5.1). They are three times more likely to be poor than white Americans (Staveteig & Wigton, 2000). Members of nondominant groups are less likely to participate in the political process, vote, and be elected to office (Jackson, Brown, & Wright, 1998; Verba, Scholzman, & Brady, 1997). Consequently, their access to political power, jobs, and wealth is much lower than that of the dominant group.

Anticipated demographic changes during the first half of the twenty-first century are expected to shift the balance of power. The total U.S. population is expected to increase 50 percent (from 255 million to 383 million) between 1990 and 2050. The proportion of whites in the total population is expected to decrease from 75 to 53 percent (G. Delgado, 1997). The proportion of Latinos in the general population is expected to double (9 to 21%) and the proportion of Asians will increase from 3 to 11 percent.

Figure 5.1. People in poverty by ethnicity.

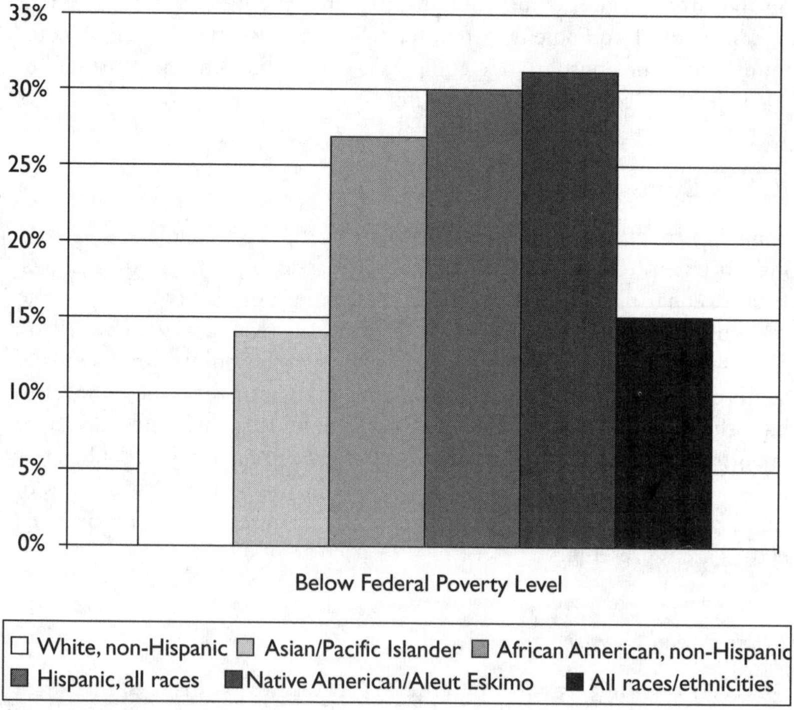

Below Federal Poverty Level

☐ White, non-Hispanic ☐ Asian/Pacific Islander ☐ African American, non-Hispanic
■ Hispanic, all races ■ Native American/Aleut Eskimo ■ All races/ethnicities

Source: Staveteig, S., & Wigton, A. (2000). *Racial and ethnic disparities: Key finds from the national survey of America's families* [on-line]. Available: http://newfederalism.urban.org.html.

Members of nondominant groups also experience discrimination because their cultural norms and values are perceived to differentiate them from the dominant culture.

According to Mackelprang and Salsgiver (1999), "Culture is developed as a social legacy, learned as a result of belonging to a group" (p. 21). Behaviors, attitudes, symbols, music, recreational activities, child-rearing patterns, "slang" vocabulary, folk stories, and decision-making processes are all components of culture. Cultural patterns that are inconsistent from the mainstream may be viewed as inappropriate and labeled "deviant" by social institutions, public officials, and uninformed citizens. Mackelprang and Salsgiver (1999) describe the development of "deaf culture":

> Within programs devoted exclusively to deaf people, a culture of deafness has developed over the years. This culture has been built upon language, shared experiences, and a sense of identity. As deaf children have grown up, they have established lifelong friendships and a world of Deaf culture. Deaf clubs have provided opportunities for further Deaf culture, and national associations for Deaf people have given them political voice. Relationships that preserve and enhance Deaf people as a diverse group have flourished. (p. 112)

Citizenship Status

Federal and state legislation adopted in the 1990s limited the right to receive public benefits for some categories of immigrants (Voelker, 1995). Fear of deportation also discourages people who have immigrated illegally from applying for public benefits. This has resulted in differences in legal status and entitlements among citizens, legal residents, and undocumented people (Fix & Passel, 1999; Halfon, Wood, Valdez, Pereyra, & Duan, 1997). In addition, language and discrimination limit employment opportunities for new immigrants. Immigrants (regardless of educational status) may be relegated to temporary and low-wage employment (Tienda & Singer, 1995). According to Portes and Zhou (1993), the children of immigrants encounter different paths to economic security: some assimilate into the larger society while others remain isolated in ethnic communities and remain in poverty. Other second-generation immigrants are able to preserve family traditions and culture while experiencing economic gains. Isolation from the dominant culture often requires that new immigrants look for support from ethnic group members and create social networks and institutions to respond to their needs (Sherraden & Barrera, 1997).

Social Class

Fellin (1995b) defines social class as "a community of identification, based on subjective measures such as class consciousness, class awareness, class identity, and cognitive maps—all images individuals have about their location in the class structure" (p. 118). Class can also be defined in terms of the income or lifestyle (values, employment, leisure activities, interpersonal relationships, and memberships in associations) (Fellin, 1995a).

Neighborhoods and ethnic groups may be stratified by class; members will encounter different experiences and opportunities based on their parents' position in the class structure. In geographic communities, people may prefer to live among people with similar economic status, employment, or education (Fellin, 1995a). Alternatively, many people are limited by residential segregation and market prices in choosing a home (Jargowsky, 1997). Institutional arrangements affecting employment and education may limit the entry of low-income people into the ranks of the middle- and upper-income classes.

Although class differences in the United States may not seem as obvious as those in other countries, wealth (the accumulation of assets) and income from work or investments determine one's life chances. People with greater wealth have more choices in terms of education and employment opportunities. They do not have to rely on nonprofit social service organizations or public assistance benefits for goods and services; they can purchase the things they need. However, many community organizers argue that agricultural subsidies, corporate tax breaks, and tax shelters are government assistance for the rich (Biklen, 1983; Kahn, 1991).

An analysis of wealth and income completed by the Center for Budget and Policy Priorities illustrates that wealth is concentrated in the hands of only a few Americans. These data show that the top 1 percent of all Americans (in terms of wealth) possess 39 percent of the wealth and 13 percent of all after-tax income. The bottom 80 percent of Americans possesses 50 percent of the income and only 16 percent of the wealth (see figure 5.2). Recent changes in income and wealth indicate that the overall concentration of wealth is greater than at any time since the Depression (Shapiro & Greenstein, 1999).

Common Interests

One of the basic premises inherent in community organization practice is that problems are not unique to individuals but that in any group of people, many individuals will experience problems that have common origins. These common problems require common solutions often involving joint action by group members. Solving the problem for one individual is insufficient to keep the problem from recurring and affecting others (Epstein, 1981; Hardina, 1995).

Conflict theory (see chapter 2) describes society as a competitive field in which some groups are more successful than others in competing for resources, social status and political power. Social structure (the economic and

Figure 5.2. Share of after-tax income and share of wealth: Comparing the top 1 percent of households to all others.

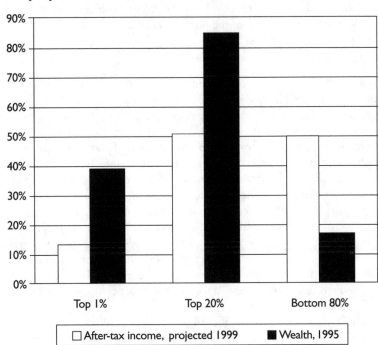

Source: Shapiro, I. and Greenstein, R., (1999). *The widening income gulf* [on-line]. Available: http://cbpp.org/99tax-rep.htm.

social status of the various subpopulation groups) and institutional arrangements that serve to maintain elite dominance and keep others "in their place" is viewed as the origin of a variety of social problems: poverty, crime, substance abuse, teen pregnancy, and a variety of health care problems (Kahn, 1991; Moore, Vandivere, & Ehrle, 2000). In U.S. society, white males possess most of the wealth and decision-making authority. Consequently, members of oppressed groups (persons of color, LGBT individuals, women, older people, and persons with disabilities) are more likely to experience social problems than others. These population groups also have difficulty finding public benefits and social services to meet their needs (Baker, 1997; Chow, 1999; Halfon et al., 1997; Pampel, 1994; Sherman, Amey, Duffield, Ebb, & Weinstein; 1998; Torrez, 1998; Weisner & Schmidt, 1992). They are more likely to interact with the justice, public welfare, and child welfare systems. For example, people of color are more likely to be imprisoned than whites; children of color are more likely to enter into foster care (Courtney et al., 1996; Kilty & Joseph, 1999; Ross & Hawkins, 1995).

Members of dominant groups also experience common problems that limit the quality of life and access to goods and services (for example, substance abuse or health care problems). However, some problems will not be as prevalent among members of the dominant class.

Collective Identity

Common problems often foster a sense of community or collective identity among the affected individuals. Collective identity can be defined as a state of recognition among community members that they belong to the specific community in question (Lee, 1986). The development of a sense of collective identity is essential for recruiting members, motivating volunteers, and creating social movements to foster long-term change (see chapter 2). In organizing work, it is often sufficient to define members as in a "potential" state of consciousness about their inclusion in the community (Lee, 1986). Consequently, the organizer's focus involves helping community members attain a collective identity about their inclusion in the community.

People often develop a collective community identity when they organize to defend or preserve their community against outside interests or danger (Cnaan & Rothman, 1995). For example, the disability rights movement has also fostered the development of a collective identity among persons with disabilities (Mackelprang & Salsgiver, 1999).

Gary Delgado (1997) describes the development of community organizations that have moved away from examining common interests based on geographic location to examine common identity based on gender, physical or mental disabilities, ethnicity, and gender orientation:

> Solidarity based on identity has been particularly important for disposed constituencies. Women, people of color, disabled people, and gays and lesbians have formed organizations and taken leadership very often denied them in neighborhood groups, on issues and concerns that would not have been raised in traditional community organizations. (p. 56)

Informal Networks

Informal networks are made up of members of one's primary group: relatives, friends, and neighbors. Members of such a group can provide friendship; mutual support; nurturance; health care for a sick relative or friend; child care; child-rearing tips; or help with financial support, housing, or food. Informal networks can also help individual members find work, transition off welfare, provide information about public programs and services, or help mitigate the effects of substance abuse (El-Bassel, Chen, & Cooper, 1998; Hemmens, Hoch, Hardina, Madsen, & Wiewel, 1986; Jackson, 1998; Oliker, 1995; Popkin, 1990; Stack, 1974).

Many programs that community-based nonprofit organizations and public agencies offer have relied on informal networks to get the word out about their services or have linked up with existing networks to provide services. In some cases, local organizations hire "natural helpers" or community leaders to provide health care information and other services to friends and neighbors (Lowe, Barg, & Stephens, 1998; Muquiz, 1992). Community organizations use informal networks to recruit volunteers and organize social action campaigns. Community-development efforts often focus on creating strong informal networks as a means of reducing feelings of alienation among community residents and increasing neighborhood ability to address problems such as drug dealing and gang violence.

Conquergood (1992) provides an example of the impact of strong interpersonal ties among neighborhood residents. He conducted an ethnographic study of low-income tenants in an apartment building in Chicago. The tenants were members of a variety of ethnic groups; many of them were new immigrants. Some of these immigrants were Hmong; others were from Mexico or Central America. Conquergood found a complex set of interactions among building residents based on exchanges of goods and services and family relationships. Many of these interactions were oriented toward increasing the odds of economic survival among all the building's tenants. Interaction patterns were similar across and among ethnic groups. These tenants successfully united across ethnic boundaries to fight eviction by a slum landlord.

Formal Organizations and Networks

Neighborhoods can be distinguished from one another by their links with local institutions such as churches, schools, and hospitals (Fellin, 1995a). Backman and Smith (2000) argue that nonprofit organizations are essential components of community networks because they are able to link together members of the community through volunteer activities and programs. These organizations can also link residents with institutions such as city governments, the health care system, schools and universities, employers, and lending institutions. However, Backman and Smith warn that such links may result in a decrease in social action–oriented activities.

Members of ethnic groups may find traditional social service organizations inaccessible to them due to language and cultural barriers, social stigma, or lack of information about service availability (Chow, 1999; Iglehardt & Becerra, 1995). Many ethnic communities respond to systemic discrimination by creating their own organizations and service networks to meet their needs. Ethnic organizations are established, in part, to help preserve unique aspects of the group's culture. This phenomenon is not limited to ethnic communities, however. According to Milofsky (1988), many community-based organizations are developed in response to national recognition of common social problems or discriminatory practices. For example, organizations that serve the gay and lesbian community were developed during the 1980s and 1990s in response to the AIDS epidemic, teen suicides, assaults on gay men and women, and discrimination (Ault, 1997; Winkle, 1991).

Informal networks and formal organizations play a vital role in the delivery of services to low-income people and members of oppressed groups. These organizations also help people come together and form mutual aid associations and organize politically. Consequently, they help people acquire power (Kahn, 1991). In some instances, for-profit businesses such as grocery stores and beauty shops can be part of the helping network. In many ethnic communities, small businesses provide free services such as counseling, credit, and emergency food in ethnic communities (M. Delgado, 1996, 1999).

Models of Community Life in Neighborhoods

Researchers have identified a variety of cause-and-effect models that can be used to differentiate between well-functioning geographic communities and those communities that are inadequate to meet the needs of residents. The recent theoretical literature identifies three models that can be used to examine how well basic community functions are carried out: social isolation (Wilson, 1987, 1996), social disorganization (Figueira-McDonough, 1991), and residential segregation (Jargowsky, 1997). These theories examine levels of informal and formal networks, residents' ties to external institutions, population mobility, and the overall degree of poverty within neighborhoods. Some of these concepts can be applied to the formation and maintenance of nongeographic communities.

Social Isolation Theory

Wilson (1987, 1996) uses social isolation theory to describe the effects of concentrated neighborhoods in contributing to a number of social problems. Such neighborhoods are characterized by a sense of hopelessness and powerlessness. Residents of concentrated-poverty neighborhoods are segregated from the larger society. They tend to have difficulty gaining access to jobs that are located outside the community; employment opportunities in the community itself are few. Well-paying industrial jobs that require few skills or little education have declined in number and are no longer available to members of minority groups. Upwardly mobile members of minority groups leave inner-city areas; consequently, young people have few mentors or role models. Crime and other social problems (welfare dependency; teen pregnancy) flourish in neighborhoods that are socially isolated from other communities. In addition, many youth lack education and skills, and as the number of unskilled and semiskilled jobs has decreased relative to highly skilled jobs, young minorities are entering the job market in low-level jobs that have fewer prospects for advancement. Consequently, residents of these neighborhoods adopt culture values and beliefs that sustain a culture of poverty.

Wilson (1996) also links unemployment to the neighborhood's ability to prevent crime, gang violence, drug dealing, and family breakups as well as other types of family problems. He believes that neighborhoods that experience high rates of poverty also have low rates of social organization. Further, social organization permits adults to exercise control and limit negative behavior among neighborhood youths. Social organization can be defined in terms of the prevalence and strength of social networks and friendship ties, rate of resident participation in voluntary and formal organizations, and the density and stability of formal organizations.

Wilson (1996) also identifies four ways in which social isolation becomes a factor in the behavior of inner-city residents:

1. Parents isolate and attempt to protect their children from crime by prohibiting contact with other neighborhood residents.
2. Residents (both adults and children) have limited contact with individuals and institutions outside the neighborhood.
3. Decreases in the proportion of working-class and middle-income people who live in the neighborhood make it less likely that unemployed residents will interact with people who work. Consequently, access to the informal networks that can generate job contacts is limited.
4. Children in the neighborhood have few adult role models who work. (pp. 20–21)

Wilson's theories have been highly influential in guiding federal policies on neighborhoods and crime prevention (Rosenthal, 1999; Walker, 1998). However, some critics argue that Wilson's theories are inaccurate or incomplete. Massey (1990) believes that residential segregation rather than the flight of middle-income African Americans from inner-city communities is responsible for the prevalence of economic deprivation in these neighborhoods. Lee, Campbell, and Miller (1991) conducted research that suggests that informal networks and associations are actually more prevalent in African American communities than in white communities. Note that Wilson applies his theories exclusively to urban and predominantly African American communities. They may not be relevant to poverty neighborhoods that are multicultural; rural or exclusively Latino, Asian, or white.

Social Disorganization Theory

Figueira-McDonough (1991) also believes that informal networks and links with formal organizations are central to understanding communities. However, she argues that poverty and mobility are the most valid predictors of social disorganization. Neighborhoods with few ties among residents, limited opportunities for people to participate in formal organizations, and few external ties to other communities will have the highest rates of youth crime and violence. She describes the disorganized community as having

> population characteristics (transiency and lack of resources) that make it difficult to develop both formal and informal networks. Lacking both sources of internal control, this community is usually controlled from the outside by such agencies as the police and the welfare system. While transiency could facilitate external links, lack of resources hampers their maintenance . . . . Strong ties among neighborhood residents may serve to mitigate the effects of poverty and population mobility. (p. 79)

Figueira-McDonough (1991) believes that all communities can be categorized in terms of the overall level of social organization or disorganization. The two dimensions in her typology are the overall level of population mobility in the community and the degree of poverty. Established communities have low poverty rates and a low level of population mobility. Therefore, they can be expected to maintain a high degree of activity in informal and formal networks. Links to institutions and organizations outside the community of origin are likely to be few; longtime residents will simply have no need to go outside their community of origin for goods and services. In contrast, highly disorganized communities are those in which poverty rates are high and the population is highly transient. These communities are characterized by few informal and formal networks and few ties to institutions in surrounding neighborhoods (see table 5.1). Figueira-

Table 5.1 Typology: Community Types by Degree of Mobility and Poverty

	Mobile	*Stable*
Nonpoor	Stepping-stone community	Established community
	Low primary networks	High primary networks
	High secondary networks	High secondary networks
	High external links	Low external links
Poor	Disorganized community	Parochial community
	Low primary networks	High primary networks
	Low secondary networks	Low external networks
	Low external links	Low external links

Source: Figueira-McDonough, J. (1991), Community structure and delinquency: A typology. *Social Service Review, 65,* 68–91.

McDonough suggests that policy makers should focus on increasing community control through formal organizations as a mechanism for decreasing gang violence and other social problems in disorganized communities.

Residential Segregation

Jargowsky (1997) argues that only the concentration of poverty, not the level of social organization, predicts the deterioration of communities. He also believes that some obvious reasons exist for population mobility in high-poverty neighborhoods. Neighborhoods with high poverty rates (poverty rates over 40%) have physical characteristics that distinguish them from neighborhoods where residents have higher incomes. These characteristics include vacant units, older buildings in need of repair, and a low proportion of homeowners. High numbers of rental units make it easier for residents to leave (homeowners are less likely to move than renters). In addition, owners of rental units often abandon their buildings when the cost of maintenance outweighs income from rental units.

Jargowsky found empirical evidence (concentration of poverty within census tracts) that verifies that only 12 percent of all U.S. residents live in high-poverty neighborhoods. However, residency in low-income communities is highest for African Americans and Puerto Ricans and lowest for Caucasians and Cuban Americans (Jargowsky did not examine rates for Asian Americans). Consequently, Jargowsky rejects Wilson's idea that economic conditions, social class, and isolation create unique cultural values and beliefs that make it difficult for people to leave poverty. Instead, poverty is associated with residential segregation and conditions that create limited job opportunities. He suggests that residents in these neighborhoods are not likely to remain in poverty once economic conditions improve. He believes the contribution of culture to such social problems as substance abuse and teen pregnancies is limited; such effects are identified in the literature simply because most of the research is conducted in high-poverty communities. He argues that poverty can be alleviated by relocating inner-city residents to areas where they have access to good jobs and a better education system.

Community-Building

Contrary to Jargowksy's (1997) assumptions about the limited importance of neighborhood in sustaining poverty, much of the recent poverty research has focused on the role of geographic communities in exacerbating or alleviating social problems. For example, high rates of teen pregnancy, Aid to Families with Dependent Children (AFDC) receipt, family dysfunction, gang membership, and violent crime have been associated with high rates of neighborhood poverty and population mobility (Anderson, 1990; Brooks-

Gunn, Duncan, Klebanov, & Sealand, 1993; Jencks & Mayer, 1990; Mercy, Rosenberg, Powell, Broome, & Roper, 1993; Reiss & Roth, 1993; Vartanian, 1997, 1999). According to Stern and Smith (1995):

> Neighborhoods and communities affect the consequences of poverty for families by further reducing the availability of social and other resources that support parenting. Both economic hardship and neighborhood disadvantage are associated with extreme forms of parenting dysfunction, including child maltreatment. (p. 706)

Given Wilson's (1987, 1996) theories and much of the recent research literature, government policy makers and several large foundations have funded a number of community interventions (such as community-building efforts and "weed and seed" programs; see next paragraph) to improve the life chances of low-income people.

During the Clinton administration, the federal government released funds and encouraged local governments to adopt community policing programs. In these programs, police walk a beat and get to know community residents. They work with neighborhood residents and local institutions (schools, businesses, community organizations, and landlord associations) to improve neighborhood quality and reduce crime. The basic assumption behind such programs is that criminal activity will decline if criminals and drug dealers are removed or "weeded" from the neighborhood—hence the term "weed and seed." Walker (1998) describes the assumptions behind weed and seed programs in this way:

> The growth in the nonwhite share of the population is distressingly bound up with the persistence of and even increases in certain familiar pathologies of disenfranchisement—substance abuse, teenage pregnancy, family disintegration . . . . Within this matrix, there is another subset of problems that might be characterized as new "social diseases." By social disease, we mean a mixed bag of pathologies—some physical, some psychological, some both. They range from homelessness among veterans and others to child abuse, with its long-term neuropsychological impacts from substance dependency to obesity. (p.12)

In the "seed" phase of such programs, the police engage local groups in community-building and neighborhood-revitalization efforts. Police learn to problem solve in order to "stabilize and control" situations (Community Policing Pages, 1998, p. 1). In theory, residents are empowered by engaging in decision-making processes with police officers and representatives of the private sector to identify and propose solutions for crime-related problems in their neighborhoods (U.S. Department of Justice, 1998). One criticism of these programs is that neighborhood residents often have limited input into the decision-making process (Community Policing Pages, 1998). Consequently, the police or other groups from outside the neighborhood may impose solutions for the crime problem. In such situations, weed and seed programs run counter to traditional organizing approaches that emphasize the role of community residents in defining community problems and generating solutions (Freire, 1970; Rivera & Erlich, 1998).

Many organizations use an intervention called community building as an alternative to the deficit model of community inherent in the weed and seed approach. Community building focuses on involving community residents in the decisions that affect their lives:

> Community building addresses the developmental needs of individuals, families, and organizations within the neighborhood. It changes the nature of the relationship between the neighborhood and the systems outside its boundaries. A community's own strengths—whether they are found in churches, block clubs, local leadership, or its problem-solving abilities—are seen as central. (Schorr, 1997, p. 361–62)

One of the models of community practice described in chapter 4, community development, specifically focuses on improving bonds among community residents and between residents and local institutions. It is also intended to help residents develop a sense of community or collective identity and ameliorate feelings of hopelessness and alienation. However, as previously noted, the strategies and tactics associated with this model are not always sufficient to address community problems. Social action, social planning, and transformative approaches are also needed to change communities, depending on situational factors, intended outcomes, and the preferences of community residents.

Summary

Community organization practice requires interventions that focus on community of place (neighborhoods) as well as communities of interest and identity. However, it is essential that members identify with or participate in that community. In most communities, clear boundaries define who is a member of the community and who will be excluded. Some communities are defined in terms of the socioeconomic characteristics of their members. These definitions are determined by community members or by the dominant society and its institutions. Communities can also be examined in terms of informal networks; links with formal institutions; and the degree of isolation from other groups, organizations, or neighborhoods. Community organization as a practice method requires that the organizer work to develop relationships and links among residents and between residents and institutions. In chapter 6, methods used for the assessment of community problems are described in detail.

■ QUESTIONS FOR CLASS DISCUSSION

1. Identify the communities in which you have membership.
2. Have students in your social work program formed a community? Why or why not?
3. Identify at least one community (geographic, functional, interest) of which you have knowledge. What are the rules of inclusion or exclusion for this community?

■ SAMPLE ASSIGNMENTS AND EXERCISES

1. Find a case study of a community or a community organization effort in a professional journal such as the *Journal of Community Practice*. Write a three- to five-page paper describing how the author defined community, explicit rules of inclusion and exclusion, and the method used to bring the community together to accomplish goals.
2. Choose a geographic community in your area. Write a five-page paper applying one of the three models of community life described in this chapter to your target community. How does your target community conform to or differ from the model you've chosen in terms of at least five of the following factors?

> Concentration of poverty
> Segregation from surrounding communities
> Availability of work
> Ethnic composition
> Informal networks
> Prevalence of formal organizations
> Links between residents and organizations outside the target
>   community

> Sources of information can include interviews with neighborhood residents or organization leaders, census records, newspaper articles, and funding proposals written by neighborhood organizations or government agencies.

References

Anderson, E. (1990). *Streetwise: Race, class, and change in an urban community*. Chicago: University of Chicago Press.

Ault, A. (1997). When it happens to men it's "hate" and a "crime": Hate crime policies in the context of gay politics, movement organizations, and feminist concerns. *Journal of Poverty, 1*(1), 49–64.

Backman, E., & Smith, S. R. (2000). Healthy organization, unhealthy communities. *Nonprofit Management and Leadership, 10*(4), 355–73.

Baker, M. (1997). Service needs, usage, and delivery: A look at the imbalance for African American elderly. *Journal of Poverty, 1*(1), 93–108.

Biklen, D. (1983). *Community organizing: Theory and practice.* Englewood Cliffs, NJ: Prentice-Hall.

Brooks-Gunn, K., Duncan, G., Klebanov, P., & Sealand, N. (1993). Do neighborhoods influence child and adolescent development? *Social Service Review, 99* (2), 353–95.

Brzuzy, S. (1997). Deconstructing disability: The impact of definition. *Journal of Poverty, 1*(1), 81–91.

Chaskin, R. (1997). Perspectives on neighborhood and community: A review of the literature. *Social Service Review, 71*(4), 521–47.

Chow, J. (1999). Multiservice centers in Chinese American immigrant communities: Practice principles and challenges. *Social Work, 44*(1), 70–87.

Chow, J., & Coulton, C. (1998). Was there a social transformation of urban neighbourhoods in the 1980's?: A decade of worsening social conditions in Cleveland Ohio, USA. *Urban Studies, 35*(8), 1359–75.

Cnaan, R., & Rothman, J. (1995). Locality development and the building of community. In J. Rothman, J. Erlich, & J. Tropman (Eds.), *Strategies of community organization* (pp. 241–56). Itasca, IL: Peacock.

Community Policing Pages (1998). Horror stories [On-line]. Available: http:// www.concentric. net/.

Conquergood, D. (1992). Life in Big Red: Struggles and accommodation in a Chicago polyethnic tenement. In L. Lamphere (Ed.), *Structuring diversity: Ethnographic perspectives on the new immigra*tion (pp. 95–144). Chicago: University of Chicago Press.

Courtney, M., Barth, R., Berrick, J., Brooks, D., Needell, B., & Park, L. (1996). Race and child welfare services: Past research and future directions. *Child Welfare, 75*(2), 99–137.

Cummins, L., First, R., & Toomey, B. (1998). Comparisons of rural and urban homeless women. *Affilia, 13*, 435–54.

Davis, C. (1994). Domestic food programs, hunger and undernutrition in rural America. *Review of Black Political Economy,* 179–83.

Delgado, G. (1997). *Beyond the politics of place: New directions in community organizing.* Berkeley, CA: Chardon.

Delgado, M. (1996). Puerto Rican food establishments as social service organizations: Results of an asset assessment. *Journal of Community Practice, 3*(2), 57–78.

Delgado, M. (1999). *Community social work practice in an urban community.* New York: Oxford University Press.

El-Bassel, N., Chen, D., & Cooper, D. (1998). Social support and network profiles among women on methadone. *Social Service Review, 72*(3), 379–401.

Epstein, I. (1981). Advocates on advocacy: An exploratory study. *Social Work Research and Abstracts, 17*, 5–12.

Fellin, P. (1995a). *The community and the social worker* (2d ed.). Itasca, IL: Peacock.

Fellin, P. (1995b). Understanding American communities. In J. Rothman, J. Erlich, & J. Tropman (Eds.), *Strategies of community organization* (5th ed., pp. 114–28). Itasca, IL: Peacock.

Figueira-McDonough, J. (1991). Community structure and delinquency: A typology. *Social Service Review, 65,* 68–91.

Fix, M., & Passel, J. (1999). *Trends in noncitizens' and citizens' use of public benefits following welfare reform, 1994–1997* [On-line]. Available: http://www.urban.org/immig/trends.html.

Freire, P. (1970). *Pedagogy of the oppressed.* New York: Continuum.

Halfon, N., Wood, D., Valdez, R., Pereyra, M., & Duan, N. (1997). Medicaid enrollment and health service access by Latino children in inner-city Los Angeles. *Journal of the American Medical Association, 274*(8), 636–42.

Hardina, D. (1995). Do Canadian social workers practice advocacy? *Journal of Community Practice, 2(3),* 97–121.

Hemmens, G., Hoch, C., Hardina, D., Madsen, R., & Wiewel, W. (1986). *Changing needs and social services in three Chicago communities.* Chicago: School of Urban Planning and Policy, University of Illinois at Chicago.

Iglehart, A., & Becerra, R. (1995). *Social services and the ethnic community.* Boston: Allyn & Bacon.

Jackson, A. (1998). The role of social support in parenting for low-income single, black mothers. *Social Service Review, 72* (3), 365–78.

Jackson, R. A., Brown, R. D., & Wright, G. C. (1998). Registration, turnout, and the electoral representativeness of U.S. state electorates. *American Politics Quarterly, 26*(3), 259–72.

Jargowsky, P. (1997). *Poverty and place: Ghettos, barrios, and the American city.* New York: Russell Sage Foundation.

Jencks, C., & Mayer, S. (1990). The social consequences of growing up in a poor neighborhood. In L. Lynn & M. McGeary (Eds.), *Inner-city poverty in the United States* (pp. 111–86). Washington, DC: National Academy Press.

Kahn, S. (1991). *Organizing: A guide for grassroots leaders.* Washington, DC: National Association of Social Workers.

Kilty, K., & Joseph, A. (1999). Institutional racism and sentencing disparities for cocaine possession. *Journal of Poverty, 3*(4), 1–17.

Lee, B. (1986). *Pragmatics of community organization.* Mississauga, Ontario: Commonact Press.

Lee, B., Campbell, K., & Miller, O. (1991). Racial differences in urban neighboring. *Sociological Forum, 6*(3), 525–50.

Lowe, J., Barg, F., & Stephens, K. (1998). Community residents as lay health educators in a cancer prevention program. *Journal of Community Practice, 5*(4), 39–52.

Mackelprang, R., & Salsgiver, R. (1999). *Disability: A diversity model approach in human service practice.* Pacific Grove, CA: Brooks/Cole.

Massey, D. (1990). American apartheid: Segregation and the making of the underclass. *Social Service Review, 96,* 329–57.

Mercy, J., Rosenberg, M., Powell, K., Broome, C., & Roper, W. (1993). Public health policy for preventing violence. *Health Affairs, 12,* 7–29.

Milofsky, C. (1988). *Community organizations: Studies in resource mobilization and exchange.* New York: Oxford University Press.

Moore, K., Vandivere, S., & Ehrle, J. (2000). Sociodemographic risk and child well-being [On-line]. Available: http://newfederalism.urban.org/html/series.

Muquiz, G. (1992, September/October). Oregon programs reach farmworker families and elderly farmworkers through two new outreach models. *Migrant Health Clinical Supplement,* 1–2.

Norlin, J., & Chess, W. (1997). *Human behavior and the social environment: social systems theory.* Boston: Allyn & Bacon.

Oliker, S. (1995). The proximate contexts of workfare and work. *Sociological Quarterly, 36,* 251–72.

Ong, P., & Blumenberg, E. (1998). Job access, commute, and travel burden among welfare recipients. *Urban Studies, 35*(1), 77–93.

Pampel, F. (1994). Population aging, class context, and age inequality in public spending. *American Journal of Sociology, 100* (1), 153–95.

Pantoja, A., & Perry, W. (1998). Community development and restoration: A perspective and case study. In F. Rivera & J. Erlich (Eds.), *Community organizing in a diverse society* (3d ed., pp. 220–42). Boston: Allyn & Bacon.

Popkin, S. (1990). Welfare: Views from the bottom. *Social Problem, 37,* 65–79.

Portes, A., & Zhou, M. (1993). The new second generation: Segmented assimilation and its variants. *Annals of the American Academy of Social Sciences, 530,* 74–97.

Reiss, A., & Roth, J. (1993). *Understanding and preventing violence.* Washington, DC: National Academy Press.

Rivera, F., & Erlich, J. (1998). *Community organizing in a diverse society* (3d ed.). Boston: Allyn & Bacon.

Rosenthal, S. (1999). How liberal ideology assists the growth of fascism: A critique of the sociology of William Julius Wilson. *Journal of Poverty, 3*(2), pp. 67–87.

Ross, L., & Hawkins, D. (1995). Legal and historical views on racial biases in prisons. *Corrections Today, 57*(2), 192–96.

Schorr, L. (1997). *Strengthening families and neighborhoods to rebuild America.* New York: Anchor.

Shapiro, I., & Greenstein, R. (1999). *The widening income gulf* [On-line]. Available: http://cbpp.org/99tx-rep.htm.

Sherman, S., Amey, C. Duffield, B., Ebb, N., & Weinstein, D. (1998). *Welfare to what?: Early findings on family hardship and well-being* [On-line]. Available: http://www.childrensdefense.org.

Sherraden, M., & Barrera, R. (1997). Family support and birth outcomes among second generation Mexican immigrants. *Social Service Review, 71*(4), 607–33.

Stack, C. (1974). *All our kin.* New York: Harper & Row.

Staveteig, S., & Wigton, A. (2000). *Racial and ethnic disparities: Key finds from the national survey of America's Families* [On-line]. Available: http://newfederalism.urban.org/html/series_b/b5.html.

Stern, S., & Smith, C. (1995). Family processes and delinquency in an ecological context. *Social Service Review, 69,* 703–31.

Tienda, M., & Singer, A. (1995). Wage mobility of undocumented workers in the United States. *International Migration Review, 29,* 112–39.

Toennies, F. (1957). *Community and society.* Lansing: Michigan State University Press.

Torrez, D. (1998). Health and social service utilization patterns of Mexican American older adults. *Journal of Aging Studies, 12*(1), 83–100.

U.S. Department of Justice. (1998). *National weed and seed program* [On-line]. Available: http://www.ojp.usdoj.gov/eows/.

Vartanian, T. P. (1997). Neighborhood effects on AFDC exits: Examining the social isolation, relative deprivation, and epidemic theories. *Social Service Review, 71,*548–73.

Vartanian, T. P. (1999). Adolescent neighborhood effects on labor market and economic outcomes. *Social Service Review, 73,* 142–67.

Venkatesh, S. (1997). The social organization of street gang activity in an urban ghetto. *Social Service Review, 103*, 82–111.

Verba, S., Schlozman, K. L., & Brady, H. E. (1997, May/June). The big tilt: Participatory inequality in America. *American Prospect*, (32), 74–80.

Voelker, R. (1995). Impact of proposition 187 is difficult to gauge. *Journal of the American Medical Association, 273*, 1641–46.

Wagner, D. (1994). Beyond the pathologizing of nonwork. Alternative activities in a street community. *Social Work, 39*, 718–28.

Walker, B. (1998). *What can the federal government do to decrease crime and revitalize communities: The context* [On-line]. Panel paper, Research forum. U.S. Department of Justice, Office of Justice Programs, National Institute of Justice, Executive Office of Weed and Seed. Available: http://ncjrs.org/txtfiles/172210.txt.

Weisner, C., & Schmidt, L. (1992). Gender disparities in treatment for alcohol problems. *Journal of the American Medical Association, 268*(14), 1872–77.

Wilson, W. (1987). *The truly disadvantaged.* Chicago: University of Chicago Press.

Wilson, W. (1996). *When work disappears.* New York: Vintage.

Winkle, C. (1991). Inequity and power in the nonprofit sector. *Nonprofit and Voluntary Sector Quarterly, 20*, 312–28.

PART TWO

Problem Identification and Assessment

6 Needs Assessment

■ Community organizers must work with community residents to identify local problems and assess the root causes of those problems. Problem identification and assessment are the first two components of the problem-solving model. In clinical practice, a social worker may work alone or engage in dialogue to identify client problems and needs. In community practice, needs assessment is much more complex. Social workers use a variety of interpersonal and research techniques to engage residents, constituency groups, and community leaders in the needs-assessment process. This chapter describes both qualitative and quantitative approaches to problem identification and needs assessment. Social workers use qualitative approaches to engage with a broad range of individuals and groups to understand their problem, perspectives, or culture. Previous chapters examined the importance of qualitative approaches in developing knowledge about cultural norms and practices for the culturally competent practitioner. In this chapter, the actual application of these methods to needs assessment is described.

Chapter 6 also includes a description of methods used to identify common problems and solutions using a community forums approach. A third approach to needs assessment involves using quantitative methods to collect information in a structured, standardized way. Standardized approaches can include structured surveys, program monitoring techniques, social indicator analysis, population forecasting, or time series analysis. Also included in this chapter are methods used to examine physical and spatial attributes of the community: community mapping and geographic information systems. The chapter concludes with a section on social network analysis, a method that allows the researcher to examine links among individuals and organizations.

Assessment of Need in Community Practice: Using Multiple Methods

Community organizers conduct assessments to determine what services or interventions community residents want, need, or will utilize. Generally, needs assessments are conducted to determine what services community residents need. Services that community assessments can identify may include garbage pickup, street cleaning, parks, recreational services for youths, day care, jobs, or traditional types of social and health services. Residents may also be concerned about the quality of community life: crime, street gangs, shopping facilities, parking, or getting to know one's neighbors. Consequently, in community practice, assessments typically cover a variety of issues and can be conducted using a number of different data-collection methods. Assessments can target specific constituency groups or are inclusive, reaching a wide spectrum of community residents, service professionals, businesspeople, and church leaders.

A typical needs assessment focuses on the perceptions of community residents, service professionals, leaders, and other key informants (Burch, 1996). It identifies social problems that affect the community. Respondents may be asked to identify those services that could address the perceived needs. Needs assessments can also focus on service availability, coordination of service systems, service gaps, and whether services are accessible (Burch, 1996; Royse & Thyer, 1996). An analysis of service gaps requires that the researcher explore whether services target all population groups who need them (see figure 6.1). Accessibility assessments examine whether it is easy for people to find and obtain services. Factors that can limit accessibility include location, availability of public transportation, parking facilities, hours of operation, cost of the service, waiting time for services, and length or complexity of applications (Hardina, 1993; Iglehart & Becerra, 1995; Lipsky, 1980).

Needs assessments may be limited to impressionistic approaches, techniques used simply to gain insight into constituent perspectives on the problem, or may involve a more formal, systematic approach to data collection and analysis. A formal needs assessment usually combines interviews or surveys with key informants and analysis of existing data, available from the U.S. Census or agency databases. Questions included in a needs assessment focus on two main categories: resident needs and services offered (see table

Figure 6.1. Looking for Service Gaps in the Fairtown Community: Who Is Not Served?

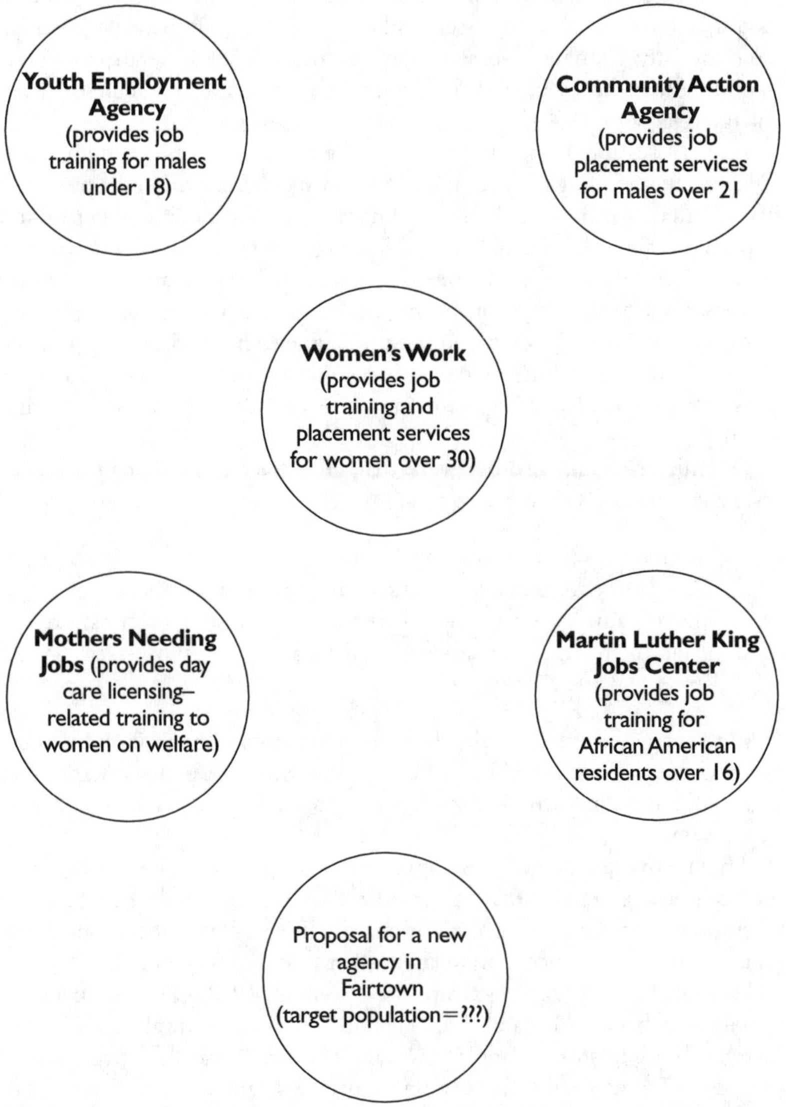

6.1). However, as Kretzmann and McKnight (1993) point out, assessments that focus exclusively on community deficits mandate a service-based approach to needs identification rather than an approach oriented toward identification of community assets and the strengths of individual residents. Consequently, a strengths-based approach to needs assessment can involve a community audit, used to identify assets that can be used to facilitate social change (Delgado, 1996).

Needs assessment often requires that the organizer employ a number of different methodologies to examine the problem from different perspectives. Different groups in the community may have very different attitudes or opinions about local problems. Collecting data from a variety of sources improves the reliability of the needs assessment. If data from a number of sources point to the same conclusion, the researcher can be confident that he or she has correctly identified the problem (see figure 6.2). The process of using a number of different data sources and research methods to conduct an assessment is called triangulation or convergent analysis (Royse & Thyer, 1996).

Organizers should also be aware that the choice of methods for needs assessment depends on three factors:

1. The time allotted to conduct the study
2. The resources necessary to actually implement the study
3. The organizer's orientation toward the inclusion of constituency group members in the study (Marti-Costa & Serrano-Garcia, 1995; Royse & Thyer, 1996).

Organizers may use pre-existing problem indicators when time and money are of concern. The availability of resources often determines whether the views of more than one constituency group are included in the needs assessment.

The use of the empowerment approach or strengths perspective in community practice requires that the organizer take steps to make sure that the views of many community groups, especially those of low-income and marginalized people, are incorporated in the research study (Durst, MacDonald, & Parsons, 1999; Reisch & Rivera, 1999; Sohng, 1998). This is especially important when the organizer is engaging in cross-cultural practice. An understanding of cultural norms and values is essential to the correct interpretation of study results. In addition to surveying members of less powerful groups, it is also possible, and in many situations essential, to involve community residents in research design, data collection, and data analysis phases of the study (Johnson, 1994). According to Marti-Costa and Serrano-Garcia (1995):

> Needs-assessment methodology, if it is to respond to a commitment to the powerless and to the fostering of social change, must (a)

emphasize techniques that singly or in combination facilitate grouping and mobilizing people; (b) foster collective activities; (c) facilitate leadership development; and (d) involve residents in the entire research process. (p. 260)

While many of the techniques described in this chapter are intended to foster the involvement and empowerment of community residents, other techniques involve complex technical skills. Often such analysis is best done by individuals or small groups. Although community residents may not be directly involved in all aspects of the needs assessment, they can serve to guide the project. Many experts on needs assessment suggest that a steering committee, made up of residents or other constituency groups, be established and function as the governing body for the project. The steering committee approach helps ensure that the findings are reliable and that they accurately reflect the community's needs. Steering committees also help establish the legitimacy of research efforts and ensure that the data will actually be used to facilitate social change (Warheit, Bell, & Schwab, 1984).

Using Qualitative Approaches to Gather Information from Individuals

Qualitative approaches to needs assessment focus on gathering information to form impressions about community problems and needs. The purpose of such approaches in community practice is to establish a direction for further research and to identify a problem that can be used to initiate organizing efforts. To ensure that organizing efforts are salient to community residents and that issues truly of concern to the community are raised, the organizer must use techniques that allow for the examination of needs from community residents' perspectives. It is also important that the organizer understand cultural values and norms that often determine how ethnic groups and other subpopulations outside the dominant culture view their lives and the troubles they encounter. Three of the primary qualitative approaches for collecting data from individuals are informal conversational interviews; formal interviews; and the ethnographic research approach.

Informal Conversational Interviews

Most community-organizing efforts require that the organizer develop an impression of the community and its people. The first step in this process is for the organizer to engage in informal interviews with community residents (Meenaghan, Washington, & Ryan, 1982). Rubin and Babbie (1997) define an informal conversational interview as an "unplanned and unanticipated interaction between an interviewer and a respondent that occurs naturally during the course of fieldwork observation" (p. 388). Conversational

Table 6.1 Questions Addressed through Needs Assessment

Resident Perspectives on the Community	What social problems do individuals and groups in the community experience?
	How should these problems be addressed?
	What actions can residents take to address these problems?
	What actions should government agencies take to address these problems?
	What actions should local institutions and businesses take to address these problems?
Resident Perspectives on Service Needs	Are services offered in the community to address these problems?
	Do residents feel that they need services to address the problems identified?
	Do community residents use available services to address these problems?
	Are these services accessible to community residents?
	Are there some community residents who do not receive these services?
	What additional services should be provided?
Service Provider/ Key Informant Perspectives on Community Needs	What types of services do community residents need?
	What services are currently provided by local organizations?
	Are comparable services offered by more than one organization?
	Are specialized or unique services offered by some of these organizations?
	Are these services adequate to meet the needs of community residents?
	Are these services accessible to community residents?
	Are there some community residents who do not receive services?
	What additional services should be provided?
	How are services coordinated among organizations (shared resources, referrals, case management, co-location)?
	When we look at the service system as a whole, what services are not provided?

Table 6.1 *(continued)*

Community Assets	What are the skills and resources of individuals in the community?
	What organizations and institutions are located in the community? What assets are associated with these organizations?
	What are the links among local organizations? How can they best be used in the organizing process?
	What are the physical attributes of the communities? Can buildings and open space be used to enhance the organizing process?
	What resources from outside the community can be used to enhance the organizing process?

Adapted from Kretzmann & McKnight, 1993.

Figure 6.2.   Information Sources for a Needs Assessment of Domestic Violence in a Native Community

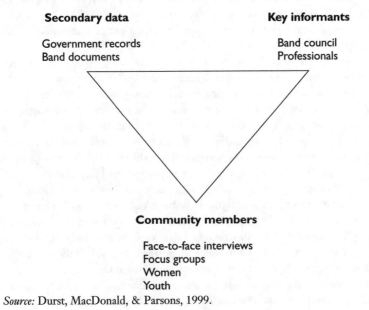

Secondary data

Government records
Band documents

Key informants

Band council
Professionals

Community members

Face-to-face interviews
Focus groups
Women
Youth

Source: Durst, MacDonald, & Parsons, 1999.

interviews differ from other, more formal types of interviews or surveys in that the questions the interviewer asks often occur spontaneously in response to a specific situation or issue. Though the organizer may have a topic that he or she wishes to examine, no questions are prepared. Each question asked flows naturally from the informant's previous responses and the interviewer's informational needs. The respondent may not even recognize that an interview is taking place; he or she is simply participating in a conversation with the organizer.

The conversational interview is used in community practice as both an information-gathering tool and a means to start organizing around a specific issue or problem of concern to community residents. When the organizer recognizes a common theme or pattern in the responses, he or she can focus on one issue. Once the issue has been identified, the organizer takes the opportunity to link people together, identifying common themes and problems. Participants are asked to recruit additional members and organizations to address this problem (Meenaghan et al., 1982).

Formal Interviews

The researcher can schedule formal meetings with people believed to be key informants, those who possess "expert" knowledge about specific social problems or community conditions. Key informants can represent a variety of constituency and interest groups including residents, businesspeople, elected officials, social service or public health professionals, and other community leaders (Chambers, Wedel, & Rodwell, 1992). These interviews can be conducted over the phone or in person.

Most often, the interview format involves open-ended questions that allow respondents the opportunity to give detailed, complex answers. The researcher can conduct the interview using an interview guide that contains a general outline of questions to address during the interview. No constraints are put on the interviewer about question order or wording. Alternatively, the interviewer may use a standardized interview instrument. In this case, the user is required to ask each question in the same order using the same wording. This approach is believed to ensure reliability or consistency in the data collection process (Rubin & Babbie, 1997). The researcher may (with the respondent's permission) tape-record the interview. However, it is also important to take detailed notes during or just subsequent to the interview (tape recorders, and tapes, have been known to break!). Data analysis for information collected through interviews requires that the research identify common themes and patterns that respondents raise (Strauss & Corbin, 1990). A number of computer software packages, including Nud*ist and Ethnograph, allow users to analyze interview data.

Selection of respondents usually relies on informal or nonprobability sampling techniques: the availability of potential subjects, existing groups of people, and all members of small subpopulation groups (for example, all agency directors in the target community or all residents of a four-block area). The organizer will want to select people who represent a variety of community constituency groups as well as differ in age, gender, and ethnicity. Alternatively, the organizer may choose to interview only those people viewed as having special insight into specific problems. For example, an organizer conducting an assessment of the needs of youth in the community might interview only young people under 18. More formal nonprobability sampling techniques such as quota or snowball sampling can also be used to select respondents (Rubin & Babbie, 1997). An organizer who decides that ethnicity is an important factor that could determine responses may opt to use quota sampling. After obtaining a list of potential interviewees and determining the proportion of people within that community by ethnicity, the organizer makes sure that the chosen sample includes the same proportion of people within each ethnic group category (see table 6.2). In snowball sampling, the organizer starts with a small group of people who may have special knowledge about a problem or who fit a particular demographic profile. Each person interviewed is then asked to recommend friends, colleagues, and neighbors who may be willing to talk to the researcher about the same subject.

Ethnographic Approaches

Ethnography is an approach to research that requires that the practitioner examine cultural norms and practices associated with marginalized populations. Though ethnography is most often associated with research involving specific ethnic or cultural groups, it can also be used to examine the lives of people outside the dominant culture. To become culturally competent, community organizers must use research methods associated with

Table 6.2 Quota Sampling: Choosing Respondents in the Mid-Fairtown Neighborhood

Ethnic Group	Proportion of Population in 2000 Census	Number of People in Each Subpopulation to be Surveyed (N = 200)
African American	20%	40
American Indian	5%	10
Asian/Pacific Islander	15%	30
Latino/Hispanic	30%	60
White	28%	56
Other	2%	4

ethnography to gain insight into how community residents perceive community problems and appropriate solutions for those problems. Ethnographic research is often referred to as a field study. Many of the techniques used are associated with the type of anthropological research conducted by Margaret Mead (Hardcastle, Wenocur, & Powers, 1997).

Ethnography is "a process that attempts to describe and interpret social expressions between people groups" (Berg, 1998, p. 121). This method usually combines in-depth interviews with the researcher's observations. The interviewee's surroundings and appearance are as relevant to the research process as the words used to respond to the interview. Researchers also study the interactions that take place among individuals within naturally occurring groups (extended families or social networks) and between groups. The meaning behind certain activities and the social context in which these activities occur are also examined (Berg, 1998; Kirby and McKenna, 1989; Sohng, 1999). The purpose of ethnography is to gain understanding of the lives and beliefs of the group under study. Ethnographic approaches have been used successfully to examine gang membership, social interactions, and economic survival patterns in low-income communities (Anderson, 1990; Decker & Van Winkle, 1996; Menjivar, 1995; Wagner, 1994).

Ethnographic research requires that the organizer or researcher gain entry to the community of interest. This involves establishing trust and legitimacy with residents (Berg, 1998). Low-income or otherwise marginalized people may not wish to be scrutinized by outside researchers and other professionals from outside the community. Researchers may be viewed as agents of the government who will inform on community members or put people at risk of losing welfare or other benefits (Guerra, 1999; Reisch & Rivera, 1999).

Kirby and McKenna (1989) recommend that researchers gain access by invitation from potential subjects, working in collaboration with one or more members of the target population, or using social networks to establish appropriate contacts. The researcher can conduct informal or formal interviews with members of the population group, attend cultural events or community meetings, and in some instances move into the community to gain insight into the personal everyday experiences of community members.

Berg (1998) notes that ethnography can also document day-to-day activities in institutions such as mental hospitals or prisons. To protect the privacy of subjects, the researcher must obtain permission to conduct formal studies in these settings. An additional issue of concern is whether the research will be conducted overtly, with subjects aware of the research, or covertly. Covert researchers become members of the community, participating in many of the activities of the community under study. Both approaches can involve risks; subjects may change their behavior because of the researcher's actions, regardless of whether they know the purpose for the researcher's participation. A covert researcher, if exposed, may be seen as having betrayed community members' trust.[1]

Data analysis for ethnography requires that the researcher keep detailed notes of his or her observations and interviews. The researcher then writes a narrative description of his or her findings. This may be limited to an identification of common themes, patterns of behavior, or cultural norms. However, ethnographers can also choose to write a thick description, creating a picture of the "observed events, the actors involved, the rules associated with certain activities, and the social contexts in which these elements arise" (Berg, 1998, p. 152).

One of the ways in which ethnography varies from other objective forms of research is that the researcher's feelings and perspectives are considered relevant data (Kirby & McKenna, 1989). For example, the researcher may keep a diary to record his or her reactions to various situations or respondents. Consequently, the researcher's values and beliefs (as well as those of the research subject) are incorporated into the descriptive narrative. Reimer (1997) used the thick description approach to analyze data from an ethnographic study of a program that helped welfare recipients obtain jobs as nursing assistants:

> Funneled into low-wage, high-turnover, gendered jobs, the women's experiences at work were not so much a manifestation of their former welfare status as they were the result of the blending of race, socioeconomic status, and gender in the workplace. No different from their nurse assistant colleagues at Church Hall, the women found themselves in jobs that minimized their knowledge and experience, squashed their enthusiasm and motivation, and provided wages insufficient to create safe and stable lives for themselves and their children. (p. 232)

Using Qualitative Approaches to Gather and Synthesize Information

Organizers must determine what community problems should be addressed. The best way to do this is to ask those individuals and groups affected by the problem. However, numerous people will have a variety of different perspectives about these problems. Consequently, the organizer uses a variety of informal techniques designed to forge a common perspective about important problems that can become the focus of any organizing effort. Many of these techniques employ qualitative research methods and include the community forum approach, the use of dialogue between organizers and constituents, nominal group technique, focus groups, and the Delphi technique. With the exception of the Delphi technique, all of these methods can be used during a community event or forum.

Using Community Forums to Collect Information

Often community organizers use needs-assessment techniques not only to collect data on community issues but also to foster a shared perception among community residents of problems and possible solutions. The primary method they use to do this is conducting community forums, which are very easy to set up and use. Residents are invited to give their input into community problems at a meeting set for a specific time and date. Chambers et al. (1992) distinguish between public hearings, used to solicit comments on government programs or plans, and the forum approach. In public hearings, citizens are given the opportunity to make comments about specific proposals or the scope of specific social problems. A needs assessment can be written based on an analysis of all written and verbal comments participants make. The government agency responsible for conducting the hearing can publish and disseminate a summary of these comments. A disadvantage of this approach is that it is often unstructured (participants may simply be invited to step up to the microphone) and difficult to control. A small number of individuals or groups may dominate the hearing, refuse to yield the microphone, or simply attempt to disrupt the meeting (Burch, 1996; Chambers et al., 1992). It may also be difficult to determine whether participants and their views are actually representative of the community (Royse & Thyer, 1996).

Organizations conduct community forums to document residents' perceptions of community problems and needs. The forum may be open to the public or by invitation only to people the sponsoring organization believes are representative of the community. Participants may be given a thumbnail sketch of the scope of a specific problem and be asked to provide comments and feedback. Alternatively, participants may be asked to identify important community problems and to propose solutions to these problems. As with public hearings, it may be difficult to maintain control (Hardcastle et al., 1997). However, many community forums employ structured approaches for soliciting information from participants. Methods can include structured dialogue, nominal group technique, and focus groups. All of these methods are used to bring participants to a common or shared perception of the problem at hand. A fourth qualitative research method, the Delphi technique, is also used to foster shared perceptions of problems. However, this approach is not used in conjunction with community forums.

Using Dialogue to Identify Common Problems

The purpose of dialogue is to enable a group of people to develop a shared understanding of community problems and agree on a joint action to address them. In community practice, it is generally accepted that the organizer will take the role of the facilitator or planner, bringing participants together. The organizer engages in dialogue with group members. Common sources of oppression or community problems that affect more than one resident are identified. Common origins of these problems are also examined. The dialogue process is also used to identify possible solutions to the problems and resources needed to effectively address them. Outcome goals are established and action plans developed. Consequently, what actually occurs during the dialogue is that the facilitator guides the group through the problem-solving process: problem identification, assessment, goal setting, implementation planning, and identification of evaluation criteria.

Meenaghan et al. (1982) identify two primary approaches to conducting dialogues: the collective capacity model (associated with community development approaches) and the partisan model (associated with social action). Using the collective capacity model, the organizer's main purpose is to establish linkages among community residents and maintain involvement in a plan or project. Creating a cooperative working environment is more important than successful accomplishment of the project.

Meetings focus on identifying common perceptions about the origins of community problems and appropriate actions to resolve those problems. Differences that emerge between individuals and groups are talked through; conflicts are minimized. If the power structure is believed to contribute to community problems, these powerful individuals and organizations are recruited to take part in the intervention process. The organizer helps the group weigh the costs and benefits of various options for action. Decisions are made through consensus, and a temporary structure is set up to carry out the action plan.

Meenaghan et al. (1982) identify a number of limitations associated with this model. There may be insufficient time to develop consensus among members, and it may be difficult to get people involved if the focus is on talking rather than action. Task-oriented organizers may have difficulty waiting patiently for the group to "gel" and focus on the issues.

The partisan model involves some very different assumptions about the role of the organizer and that of participants (Meenaghan et al., 1982). It is assumed that people and groups have different interests and power to influence change, depending on their location in the social structure. The organizer's role is to help participants understand what they have and do not have in common with one another. Groups with varying interests may interact with one another. Consequently, this interaction may be adversarial. For the process to be effective, the organizer must work with the group to analyze community power relationships, raise issues that may be of concern to participants, and provide training in organizing strategies and tactics.

Meenaghan et al. (1982) identify a number of problems with this model. The organizer can take on a directive role, performing some of the key tasks. Consequently, group maintenance and involvement can be difficult. In addition, the group may not define an issue or may fall apart when the primary problem is addressed. Reliance on conflict-oriented tactics as well as the emphasis on distinguishing between the haves and the have-nots could foster conflicts within the group that cannot be resolved.

Nominal Group Technique

Nominal group technique is another method of fostering a shared understanding of problems affecting the community. In many instances, it also is used to identify a goal and develop an action plan. With this method, the facilitator asks individuals to write down a list of problems or issues affecting the community. Each individual then reads his or her list out loud. The facilitator or a designated recorder writes down the identified problems on a blackboard, flip board, or butcher paper taped to a wall. Many of the meeting participants will list the same issues. However, each issue is listed only once. The facilitator may choose to comment on common themes or to articulate that the issues raised are similar in nature (Chambers et al., 1992). Once the list has been constructed, group participants are given time for discussion. The discussion period deepens participant understanding of the issues identified.

At the conclusion of the discussion period, members are asked to rank order the top three to five issues—to assign a 1 to the issue he or she feels is most important, a 2 to the second-most-important issue, and so on. The facilitator reads each issue off the list, then calls on each participant to give it a ranking. The rank that each individual assigns the issue is posted on the board. Most often, this process clearly identifies the issues of greatest importance to group members. In the event of ties among issues, the facilitator can calculate rankings by averaging the scores for each issue (see table 6.3). If there seems to be much disagreement among group members and no consensus about the most important issue has been reached, the facilitator can call for another round of rankings. In this case the facilitator identifies three to five issues ranked highest by the participants. Each participant then

Table 6.3 Rankings Using Nominal Group Technique

Issue	Ranking, Person 1	Ranking, Person 2	Ranking, Person 3	Ranking, Person 4	Ranking, Person 5	Mean Score	Final Rank[a]
City services	4	1	3	5	3	3.2	3
Crime	1	3	2	2	1	1.8	1
Drug abuse	3	2	1	4	5	3.0	2
Homelessness	2	4	5	3	4	3.6	5
Unemployment	5	5	4	1	2	3.4	4

[a] 1 = the most important problem, 5 = the least important. Mean scores were calculated by adding all rankings for each issue and dividing by the number of participants who provided rankings.

assigns a ranking to each of these issues. The facilitator should continue with this process until a clear consensus about the issue emerges from meeting participants.

Focus Groups

Focus groups are an additional technique that organizers can use to identify common perspectives about a community problem of concern. Focus groups can take place within the context of a community forum, in lieu of structured dialogue or nominal group technique. They can also be used as a stand-alone technique for gathering data about community problems or to supplement other methods of data collection (Chambers et al., 1992).

Using this technique, researchers choose six to eight participants who they feel best represent the interests of various community groups (Royse & Thyer, 1996). In some cases, a number of focus group interviews may be set up for representatives of specific interest groups. The rationale for doing this involves confidentiality or creating an atmosphere in which participants are comfortable with one another. Because the result of using a focus group to collect data is to identify common perspectives about the problem in question, the researcher will want to minimize conflict among members but must also incorporate a number of diverse views on the issue.[2]

A moderator administers to the participants an interview guide with six to eight open-ended questions. The moderator allows each participant some time to answer each question. Responses are usually tape-recorded with the permission of group members. Although each participant may provide detailed information about his or her own perspective, the group process encourages full discussion about the issue. According to Berg (1998), focus groups permit "interactions among and between group members which stimulate discussions in which one group member reacts to comments made by another" (p. 95).

Focus groups work best when participants are asked to describe how or why something happens rather than simply to identify community problems. For example, the moderator may ask participants to describe their experiences with the welfare system and why problems with application processing occur. In community practice, we might ask neighbors to describe recruitment methods a community organization could use to reach new members. Responses to how and why questions often produce a group perspective about the issue under discussion. In instances where opinions diverge among group members, the researcher will analyze individual responses to identify common themes and ideas. Majority and minority viewpoints among group members are described in the analysis.

Delphi Technique

The Delphi technique is used outside the context of a community forum. It may be conducted through the mail or using E-mail technology and relies on the perceptions of "expert" key informants. Key informants may include academics, social service professionals, businesspeople, community leaders, and health care workers—anyone who is expected to have insight into a predetermined community problem. For example, if high infant mortality rates within the African American community have been identified as the primary issue of concern, Delphi panel members might include pregnant women, doctors, public health nurses, church leaders, social workers, and representatives of local community organizations. Members of the panel are sent a survey consisting of several open-ended questions. They are asked to give in-depth responses that represent their views on the issue. Once the surveys are returned, the researcher synthesizes the information received. He or she summarizes, in a few short paragraphs, participant perceptions of the issue, then sends the summary to panel members for revisions. Using these revisions, the researcher revises the summary and again returns it to panel members. This process may require several more rounds until the responses of the panel members move to the center, or form a consensus. Extreme responses on either side of the issue are eliminated. The result is that the research obtains an assessment of the issue that represents a common perception among panel members (Chambers et al., 1992).

Using Quantitative Methods to Identify Needs

Researchers use a number of approaches to gather standardized information about the community that can be used to describe the depth and scope of community problems. They can also use standardized information to make comparisons among community or demographic population groups, to examine trends over time, and to make forecasts about how the problem is likely to affect the community in the future. This section examines a number of quantitative approaches to needs assessment, including structured surveys, program monitoring, social indicator analysis, population forecasting, and time series analysis.

Structured Surveys

Researchers may conduct survey research using structured or semistructured questionnaires. Surveys can be conducted through the mail, over the phone, or using one-on-one or group interviews (Burch, 1996). The difference between the formal interviews described previously and surveys is that on a questionnaire, the respondent is asked to choose among the response categories listed. The advantage of using a survey to document community needs is that responses will be standardized. The researcher does not need to identify common themes or ideas subsequent to data collection. In addition, participant responses are not likely to vary greatly if there are only a few predesignated response categories to choose from (Rubin & Babbie,

1997). Structured questionnaires also allow the comparison of responses made by members of different demographic groups (for example, differentiated by age, gender, and ethnicity). This approach also allows for comparison of responses made by various constituency groups in the community. For example, responses made by landlords can be compared to those made by tenants of rental units (see table 6.4).

One of the major disadvantages of this approach is that the researcher must determine likely response categories in advance. However, the researcher can structure questions to allow respondents to write in other responses or can allow room on written surveys for additional comments (Chambers et al., 1992). Another disadvantage of this approach is that members of different constituency groups, social classes, and ethnic groups can describe community problems differently and may prefer different solutions to the problem. The language used in the questionnaire will determine whether constituency group members perceive the questions as relevant to their lives. Consequently, the use of language (both the manner in which the question is written and translation into languages other than English) determines whether individuals will complete and return the survey.

The use of technical language to describe needs, services, and social problems may discourage responses from low-income or marginalized groups (Hardina & Malott, 1996). Translation into other languages, using inappropriate words or in some instances formal rather than informal language (or vice versa), can also discourage respondents. As in any study with predetermined questions, researchers should conduct a pretest to determine whether questions are worded in an appropriate, nonoffensive manner. A pretest consists of asking a small number of people who fit the demographic profile of intended respondents to complete the survey; this helps to establish the "face validity" of the research instrument (Rubin & Babbie, 1997).

Table 6.4 Comparing Needs Assessment Data Collected from Tenants and Landlords: What Is the Most Urgent Housing Problem in the Fairtown Community?

Housing Problems	Landlords	Tenants
Nonpayment of rent	32%	2%
Poor condition of rental units	6%	38%
Noisy or disruptive tenants	22%	15%
High rents	0%	27%
Broken light fixtures in hallways	0%	10%
Inadequate parking	2%	7%
Rents are inadequate to reimburse landlords for maintenance costs	38%	1%
Total	100.0%	100.0%

Using Technical Language in Generating Responses across Constituency Groups

The Children's Network, a coalition of neighborhood agencies, conducted a needs assessment to determine how best to expand services for children. Structured questionnaires were distributed to three constituency groups: agency directors, frontline staff, and the parents of children these agencies served. The questionnaire developed for this project contained a list of 40 types of services that could be used by children with physical, developmental, and mental disabilities. Participants were asked to rank order the five most important services they would like to have for their children (with 1 as the most important, 2 the second most important, and so on). The language that described these services was quite technical. The categories were generated by the staff of the Children's Network upon consultation with the agency directors who attended coalition steering committee meetings.

The response rates varied for the different target groups surveyed. One hundred percent of the agency directors returned the survey. The response rate for frontline staff was 68 percent. Only 40 percent of the parents who received the survey returned it. However, when the responses were analyzed, all three groups assigned the highest ranking to the same response: a centralized community assessment center. The Children's Network had difficulty formulating a plan for such a center. No one on the Network's board or staff was sure what services should be provided. Was it to be a place that used a battery of assessment tools to determine the best package of services (from a variety of agencies) for each child? Would it allow a family in need to do "one-stop shopping," finding information about appropriate neighborhood services for each child? Could a standardized assessment tool be used to determine eligibility for services from all the child-focused agencies in the neighborhood?

The Children's Network's steering committee suggested that additional research be conducted to

1. determine what services an assessment center provides,
2. assess how this service should be operated (hours of operation, staffing, location, funding, feasibility), and
3. more fully explore parental perceptions of the services needed.

The researcher can choose a number of methods to select a sample. As with formal interviews, nonprobability sampling can be appropriate for conducting needs-assessment research. In many cases, the population of possible respondents will be so small that more sophisticated sampling techniques are unnecessary. However, government agencies and foundations that fund needs-assessment research may want some verification that the sample is representative of the community. The researcher who has both time and money can use probability sampling methods: random samples (choosing at random a small number of people from the population), systematic samples (choosing every nth person from a list), and cluster sampling. Cluster sampling involves selecting pre-existing groups (for example, census tracts areas or blocks), using random sampling methods to select among these groups, and then randomly selecting individuals from within these groups to participate in the study.

Data analysis for standardized questionnaires can be analyzed simply by calculating the frequency of responses and making comparisons among the different demographic groups represented in the study. Percentages and means are typically used to make comparisons.

Program Monitoring for Service Utilization

Often agency records give much information about community needs and the effectiveness of health and social service agencies in meeting those needs. An analysis of data already collected by one or a number of agencies can be a quick and simple method for assessing need. Because this approach involves looking at data about those people who are served by the agency in question, it is sometimes called the rates under treatment approach (Chambers et al., 1992). Questions typically asked include the following:

1. Are people using all the program's services?
2. Is the program serving everyone who requests service or is eligible for the service?
3. Does the demand for service exceed the supply?
4. Are community residents requesting services not currently supplied by the agency?

Researchers typically look at agency records to determine whether members of the target population actually obtain services. This is referred to as program coverage. Program bias is the term used to describe whether specific population groups have access to services in direct proportion to their membership in the target population (Rossi & Freeman, 1982).

One indicator of service need often used in needs assessment is demand (Burch, 1996). Demand for service is a measure of the number of people who have actually requested the service. This figure may be very different from the number of people who have received the service. Applicants can be deemed not eligible, referred elsewhere, or refused the service if it is in short supply. Often the need for emergency food, shelter, or jobs programs is expressed in terms of demand. For example, the U.S. Conference of Mayors has conducted a study of demand for emergency food every year beginning in 1983. In 1997, demand for emergency food from city governments increased by 16 percent from the previous year (Food Research Action Center, 1999).

Another indicator of program effectiveness in reaching people in need is the percentage of people served who drop out of the program before completion (Chambers et al., 1992). If a high percentage of enrollees drop out, this indicates that:

1. The program has not been effective in meeting the needs of participants.
2. There exist unanticipated barriers to participation (such as transportation, day care, and hours of operation).
3. The program is not responsive to culture values and norms among the population groups served (Rossi & Freeman, 1982).

Social Indicator Analysis

Social indicator analysis requires that the researcher rely on data that has already been collected by government agencies as well as private health and social service organizations (Royse & Thyer, 1996). The most commonly used data is that collected by the U.S. Census Bureau. Every U.S. household is asked to participate in a survey conducted at 10-year intervals. The most recent census was conducted in 2000. Data the census collects includes the age, gender, and ethnicity of each resident; quality and type of housing; occupation of each adult resident; and income (see table 6.5). Consequently, this data can be used to identify needs, particularly needs associated with poverty and population density. Data are reported for the nation as a whole as well as by state, county, Standard Metropolitan Statistical Area, (SMSA), census tract, and some ethnic population groups (Chambers et al., 1992). Census tracts are geographic areas containing approximately 5,000 people. Sometimes census tracts coincide with community boundaries. In many instances, however, census tracts may include several different communities that vary in terms of demographic composition and income levels (Burch, 1996).

Federal and state governments also compile data on unemployment, health, safety, and crime rates. All of these data are available to the public by individual request, in published reports, in CD-ROMs that can be purchased, or through the Internet. The Census Bureau has made its data very accessible to the public. In addition to its Web site, it also maintains partnerships with data banks maintained by state agencies and universities. Census data are available to the public at these sites. Much of the census data can easily be used for community analysis. However, using census records presents a number of limitations:

1. A complete census that includes most U.S. households is completed only once every 10 years. Data collected for 2000 may be substantially out

Table 6.5 Questions in Census Forms

Social Characteristics	Economic Characteristics	Physical Characteristics of Housing	Financial Characteristics of Housing
Marital status	Current labor force status	Units in structure	Value of home
Place of birth/citizenship	Place of work	Number in rooms	Monthly rent
Year of entry	Journey to work	Number of bedrooms	Shelter costs
Education	Work status last year	Plumbing and kitchens	
School enrollment	Industry/occupation	Year structure built	
Educational attainment	Income (previous year)	Year moved into unit	
Ancestry/Race/Ethnicity		Housing heating fuel	
Residence 5 years ago		Telephone	
Language spoken at home		Vehicles available	
Veteran status		Farm residence	
Disability			
Grandparents as caregivers			

Source: U.S. Census, 2000.

of date by 2008. The usefulness of these data may depend on whether the analysis can use trends explicit during previous time periods to make population forecasts for the years in question. Many state and local agencies use statistical procedures to make forecasts. The Census Bureau also makes its own forecasts using indicators such as poverty and income. Data are also available from a smaller survey conducted monthly, the Current Population Survey and the Survey of Income and Program Participants.[3]

2. Census records can be inadequate in documenting the lives of low-income people. The census habitually undercounts the homeless, undocumented immigrants, and other people in poverty. The U.S. Census Bureau proposed to use a sampling procedure to control for the effects of undercount in the 2000 census. This procedure would have assigned a statistical weight to those low-income or homeless households actually counted in the census. The weighting procedure was thought most likely to produce an accurate estimate of traditionally undercounted groups. However, in a lawsuit filed by the Republican Party, the Supreme Court has ruled that the Census Bureau may not use this procedure for determining population counts that would affect congressional district reapportionment. Consequently, the Census Bureau linked up with a variety of nonprofit groups to conduct outreach to low-income communities for the 2000 census.[4] The Census Bureau also made efforts to count the homeless by surveying people residing in shelters or who received service from emergency food providers (U.S. Census Bureau, 1999a).[5]

3. Previous census data have come under criticism for the categories respondents are required to use to indicate ethnicity. Sometimes these terms are ambiguous or are considered stereotypical or demeaning (for example, there is controversy surrounding the terms Indian, Native American, and American Indian). It can be difficult for individuals of mixed race to complete the form. In 2000, the U.S. Commerce Department allowed respondents to check off multiple categories to reflect their racial ancestry (U.S. Census Bureau, 1999a). All respondents were also asked to indicate whether they are Hispanic, recognizing that Latinos/Hispanic peoples can be members of a number of racial groups.

Another area of controversy involves the construction of social indicators by government agencies. The government develops measures for such concepts as poverty and unemployment. To be unemployed, a person must be actively searching for work. People who have stopped job hunting or who are employed part-time but want full-time work are not counted in government employment surveys (Burch, 1999; Chambers1993).

The poverty indicator is especially problematic. This measure was initially constructed using data from a consumer survey during the 1950s that determined that households typically spend 30 percent of their income on food. Consequently, the poverty measure is constructed using U.S. Department of Agriculture figures on the approximate cost of a minimally adequate diet for households of various sizes. The poverty rate by household size is then calculated by multiplying this figure by three (Eisinger, 1996). The market value of this prototypical basket of food is updated each year using the Consumer Price Index. Both the U.S. poverty rate and food stamp allotments are determined based on this assumption.

Recently, the Census Bureau devised a number of alternative models to determine the best way to revise the poverty indicator to reflect current household needs (Short, Iceland, & Garner, 1999). The U.S. Department of Agriculture added several questions on hunger and hunger risk to the Current Population Survey administered by the Census Bureau each year. Findings from this study were used to estimate that 10 million U.S. households (9.7 percent) are "food-insecure" (Nord, Jemison, & Bickel, 1999). Food insecurity was defined as "not always having access to enough food to meet basic needs" (p. 1). (see figure 6.3). A number of Federal agencies and private advocacy organizations have also developed hunger indicators (Eisinger, 1996; FRAC, 1999).

Population Projections and Forecasting

Data from population surveys and government databases are used to provide information about the scope and depth of problems (Burch, 1996; Rossi & Freeman, 1982). For example, we can determine problem incidence and prevalence. Incidence refers to the number of new cases of an identified problem within a specified geographic area or time. Prevalence refers to the number of existing cases in a particular area or among a particular population group during a specific time. Incidence and prevalence allow researchers to communicate about patterns of occurrence. Knowing where and when a problem originates allows intervention efforts to be focused in the most efficient manner. For example, public health planners have responded to information about the incidence of the AIDS virus among low-income communities of color by developing AIDS education and prevention programs for these communities.

Researchers also identify population groups at risk and populations in need. Population at risk refers to the segment of the community that is likely to develop a specific problem. Often we hear about population groups at risk of hunger or homelessness. People at risk of hunger are assumed to be those with incomes below the poverty line. People at risk of homelessness are often considered those who are living "doubled up" with other family members (Choi & Synder, 1999; Wright, Caspi, Moffitt, & Silva, 1998). Populations in need are those people who currently have a problem. For example, the Food Research Action Council(FRAC) (2000) estimates that 4 million children under 12 go hungry and that another 9.6 million are at

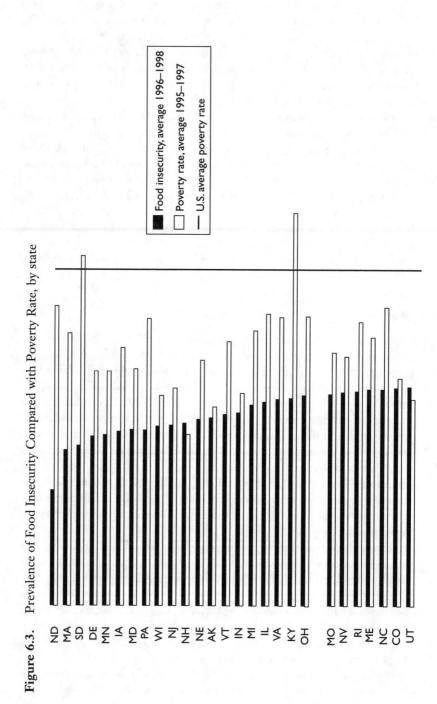

Figure 6.3. Prevalence of Food Insecurity Compared with Poverty Rate, by state

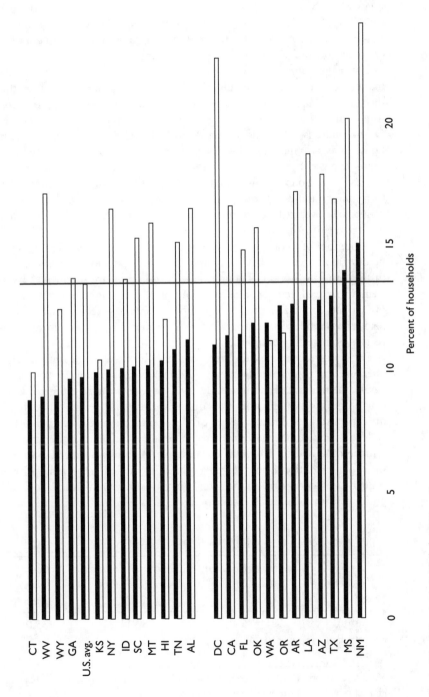

Percent of households

Source: Nord, Jemison, & Bickel, 1999, p. 9.

hunger risk. We most often talk about risk and need in terms of the percentage of the population who experience or may experience the problem. For example, FRAC's figures indicate that approximately 29 percent of all children under 12 are either hungry or at hunger risk.[6]

Rates are a third method used to communicate about need. A rate is the number of people in the population who have that problem. If we say that the unemployment rate is 10 percent, we mean that 10 out of 100 people who want jobs are actually looking for work.[7] If the poverty rate for children 18 and under is 30, we mean that for every 100 children, at least 30 live in households with income below the poverty line. It is often necessary to use percentages and rates to indicate the scope of the problem if we want to make comparisons among population segments or among communities. Community and population segment size vary substantially. Raw number counts will overestimate or underestimate the prevalence of the problem (see table 6.6).

A number of mathematical techniques allow us to use available data to predict future trends. These techniques include population estimation, forecasting, and projection. Though these three terms are often used interchangeably, each technique differs in terms of data sources and the degree of certainty in which a prediction can be made. These techniques are tools planners use to facilitate programmatic decisions made by organization directors or government officials.

Estimates require that indirect measures be used to measure a social phenomenon that cannot be measured directly (Klosterman, 1990). For example, the number of children under five in a county can be estimated using data on the total number of births during the past five years. Although this may seem to be a direct measure of the phenomenon studied (number of children), any number of factors may determine the actual rather than the estimated number of children. For example, high infant mortality (death) rates, out-migration from the geographic area studied, or an influx of new residents can contribute to the actual number of children under age five. A projection involves the creation of a scenario for the future based on a

Table 6.6 Comparing Child Poverty in Three Counties

County	Population of Children Under 18 2000	Number of Children Under 18 in Poverty 2000	Percentage of Children in Poverty
County A	25,496	8,911	35.0%
County B	14,537	2,572	17.7%
County C	39,218	9,699	24.7%

Note: The county with the largest number of children in poverty does not have the highest poverty rate among the three counties.

number of if-then assumptions (Klosterman, 1990). Predictions are made based on whether a particular phenomenon occurs. Generally, planners create a number of scenarios using different assumptions about what will happen in the future. The development of these different alternatives allows decision makers to plan for a variety of contingencies. For example, demand for day care slots for children under five could vary considerably if the yearly growth rate for this subpopulation was 2, 5, or 10 percent (see table 6.7).

A population forecast is a judgment about what will happen (Klosterman, 1990). The planner makes a determination about what will most likely occur in the future. Alternative scenarios are not prepared to guide planning decisions; the expert judgment of the planner preparing the forecast is believed to be adequate to predict future trends. Forecasts differ from projections in that projections are only conditional statements based on a well-articulated set of assumptions. An analyst making a forecast does not offer different scenarios but implies that his or her prediction will hold true regardless of situational variations. For example, a planner might forecast that unemployment rates will continue to be under 5 percent in all regions of the United States between 2000 and 2005.

The data planners use to make projections and forecasts involve trend analysis. Because of unanticipated events, it is highly unlikely that social problems or population will remain at current levels in future years. To predict what will happen in the future, planners use social indicators or population measures from previous years to find patterns that may carry over into the next year and over the next 5, 10, or 20 years. They can calculate trends mathematically by determining rates of changes in indicators between time periods. The average rate of change is used to calculate the predicted rate of change for the next time interval. The formula for calculating rates of change is

$$\sum_{t}^{m} \frac{Y_t + 1 - Y_1}{m}$$

Table 6.7 Mid-state County: Projections for Growth in Demand for Child Care Slots

Number of children in child care slots	16,685
Number of children on waiting lists	5,809
Total demand for child care slots	22,494
5% increase in demand	23,619
10% increase in demand for slots	24,743
20% increase in demand for slots	26,993

Where t is the total number of time periods, m is the total number of intervals between time periods, Y_1 is the population in the first time period in the sequence, and Y_{t+1} is population in the next time period. Σ indicates that the differences in population between time periods should be added. The sum of the differences is then divided by m. The formula can be applied to the population figures in table 6.8.

To calculate expected population change for the time periods in table 6.7,

$$\frac{(30{,}052 - 20{,}500) + (44{,}598 - 30{,}052) + (40{,}943 - 44{,}598) + (51{,}799 - 40{,}943)}{4}$$

$$= \frac{9{,}552 + 14{,}546 + -3655 + 10{,}856}{4} = 7{,}825$$

To calculate population growth for 2010, simply add
7,825 to 51,799 = **59,624**
To calculate population growth for 2030, multiply 7,825 by 3 and add
the total to 51,799 = **75,274**

Planners should be cautious about using these numbers to forecast population growth. Unforeseen events can alter expected growth. For example, economic downturns may stall growth, or the location of new industries in a community can stimulate growth well beyond expectations. The wise planner could, as described earlier, estimate population growth using a number of different scenarios. For example, the average rate of population change in the preceding example is 28 percent. Population growth projections using rates of change of 25, 30, and 35 percent could be provided to decision makers as well to allow for fluctuations or unanticipated events. (see table 6.8). The formula for calculating the yearly rate of change is

$$\text{Rate} = \frac{Y_{t+1} - Y_1}{Y_1}$$

where Y_1 is the first time period and Y_{t+1} is the subsequent time period (Klosterman, 1990). Simply calculate the average rate of change during the entire time span to determine an appropriate rate of change for your projection. Calculate the percentage of change for each time interval and then calculate the average percent of change (see table 6.9).

Table 6.8 Population growth in Fairtown, 1960–2000

	1960	1970	1980	1990	2000
Population of Fairtown	20,500	30,052	44,598	40,943	51,799

Table 6.9 Calculating Rate of Population Change

Time Period	$Y_{t+1} - Y_1$		Rate of Change
Period 2 − Period 1	= (30,052 − 20,500)/ 20500	= 9,552/ 20,500	47%
Period 3 − Period 2	= 44,598 − 30,052/ 44,598	= 14,546/ 30,052	48%
Period 4 − Period 3	= 40,943 − 44,598/ 40,943	= −3,655/ 44,598	−9%
Period 5 − Period 4	= (51,799 − 40,943)/ 51,799	= 10,856/ 40,943	27%
Average rate of change			28%

Using the preceding example, with a 25 percent growth rate, the population of Fairtown would be 64,749 (51,799 + 12,950) in 2010. With a 30% rate of change, the population would be 67,399 (51,799 + 15,540) in 2010.[8]

Time Series Analysis

Time series analysis is another method used to examine future trends. The researcher plots census data or social indicators on a graph to examine changes in population, program participation, or problem scope. Time series can also be used to examine whether social programs or changes in social policy have made any impact on the problem. This method requires that data points collected at yearly or monthly intervals be plotted on a graph. Information about the population or the number of people experiencing the problem is plotted at the y or left axis. Time periods are plotted along the x or bottom axis.

The primary method of analysis simply requires that the researcher look for obvious patterns that indicate whether the problem has increased or decreased. However, time series does not establish causation; it offers no evidence about what originally caused the problem or if program changes have actually alleviated the problem. Unanticipated events could explain time series patterns (Rubin & Babbie, 1997). For example, analysts offered a number of explanations for a drop in homicide rates during the late 1990s (Associated Press, 1999). Some of the explanations offered included a decline in the use of crack cocaine and the aging of the baby boomer population (older people are less likely to engage in crime).

Researchers conducting time series analysis must offer explanations about the way patterns have changed. In the absence of concrete proof, many of these explanations are purely speculative. Because time series analysis involves data that pertain to the entire population, people cannot be assigned to experimental and control groups to examine policy impacts. Consequently, behaviors associated with these social problems cannot be controlled. Unanticipated events might determine some of the patterns observed in time series data. Anticipated or general patterns of behavior can also determine patterns in the time series. For example, employment is generally affected by seasonal patterns in hiring. Some industries may be more likely to hire employees at certain times during the year. Monthly variations or patterns in time series data that occur almost without variation from year to year create an effect called seasonality (see figure 6.4).

In addition to seasonality, time series data has three components: trend, cycle, and stochastic fluctuations (Dattalo, 1998). Trend is a long-term increase or decrease in a time series. A cycle is a pattern that repeats itself during periods of three or more years. This differs from seasonality in that seasonal patterns take place during shorter periods and often occur annually. Stochastic fluctuations are changes in data values that take place with no apparent pattern. This effect is also called random error. Fluctuations include any changes that are evident after trends, seasonality, and cycles are removed.

Figure 6.5 contains data on Medicaid enrollment. These data were obtained from one county's Medicaid record-keeping system to aid in determining whether outreach efforts by local nonprofit organizations were effective in increasing program enrollment. Outreach efforts started in April and were completed in November. The chart shows an obvious upward trend, although enrollment drops occurred in June and February. The impact of seasonal variations cannot be measured, however, unless we were to

Figure 6.4. County Unemployment Rates Over a Three-Year Time Span

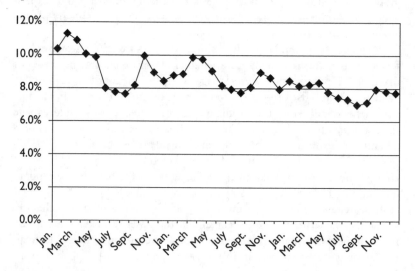

Figure 6.5. Medicaid Enrollment During Outreach Campaign (Number of Approved Cases)

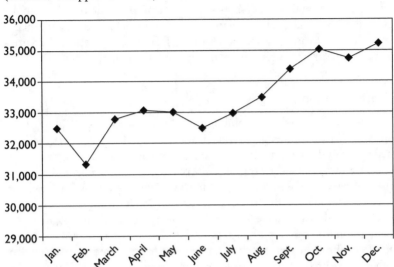

compare enrollments (and patterns of increases and decreases) from previous years. We would also need to adjust the figures to control for stochastic fluctuations. To assess program effectiveness, we might also want to compare the time series data to information collected from other counties, enrollment data for similar programs (for example, whether enrollments increased for food stamp or Temporary Assistance for Needy Families [TANF] programs), or other indicators that might be associated with Medicaid enrollment (for example, county unemployment rates).[9]

Most analysis of time series data focuses on isolating trends and seasonal variations. Although it is possible to control for random error and seasonality using sophisticated statistical software packages, Dattalo (1998) recommends using a simple statistical procedure that requires only a calculator or spreadsheet. Moving averages are calculated for the numbers in the time series, using data from the time series in figure 6.5.

1. Enrollment figures for January, February, and March are added and divided by 3.
2. Enrollment figures for February, March, and April are added and divided by 3 (January figures are dropped from the calculation).
3. Enrollment figures for March, April, and May are added and divided by 3 (February figures are dropped from the calculation).
4. These calculations are repeated until moving averages for each data point (month) are calculated.

The data points obtained through the calculation of the moving averages are then plotted on a graph (see figure 6.6). The trend line has been smoothed out, and the increases in enrollment are made obvious. Similar procedures can be used to isolate seasonality in time series data available for successive years. One method for minimizing seasonal effects is to present the data for three-month (quarterly) periods rather than monthly.

Spatial Analysis

As described in chapter 4, a community's physical attributes (buildings, open space, streets, and other geographic features) often determine both the characteristics of the community and resources available to community residents for organizing to address problems. We need to know how buildings are used, if parks are used for recreation, if any unclaimed space is available, and whether geographic barriers limit access to and from the community. We also need to identify less-tangible barriers that may limit movement and land use in the community, such as graffiti that marks gang territory or the location of nearby drug markets. How these features interact with one another to create or prevent problems is also important. Two techniques that help us examine the spatial attributes of a community are community mapping and geographic information system (GIS) analysis.

Figure 6.6. Isolating Trends in Time Series Data by Calculating Moving Averages: Medi-Cal Outreach Data (Approved Cases).

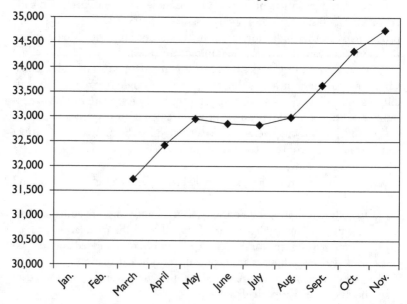

Community Mapping

Community mapping refers to the use of neighborhood street or area maps to chart the location of buildings, parks, and other neighborhood institutions. Mapping is an important means to identify problems related to access. It can also be used to pinpoint the location of trouble spots in the community. Color-coded pushpins can be used to identify locations of specific community features (Delgado, 2000). For example, community mapping can be used to identify rental properties that have not been kept up to code. Such properties may be colocated in specific pockets of the community or may be owned by one or two landlords (it may take additional research on property titles and holding companies to verify this, however). Community residents can and should be involved in creating community maps and examining ways that existing facilities and open space can be used to promote economic development and neighborhood well-being. Delgado (1996, 2000) recommends using mapping to find alternate uses for open space, such as the creation of parks or murals that can unite community residents behind a goal. He also recommends maps as a tool for conducting an asset assessment, examining how existing facilities are and can potentially be used to deliver needed services to the community. For example, Delgado (1996) has written about how Puerto Rican–owned grocery stores are used to deliver, on an informal basis, social services and consumer credit.

The mapping process can also be used to examine access issues. Do residents have access to institutions or services within or outside the community? Is shopping available within the community? (Many low-income communities do not include full-service grocery facilities.) How easy is it for residents to travel to the nearest clinic or hospital? Is public transit available? Are public institutions close to bus lines, or will residents need to walk blocks or miles to obtain services? Where are neighborhood schools located? Are they near busy streets? Can children reach them safely? Residents can be involved in creating the map and identifying problem areas or barriers that affect their lives. Often their perceptions are essential for preparing maps that accurately reflect how land in the community is actually used.

Note, however, that community mapping to examine physical structures and the use of space is used in a different context in the community maps proposed by Kretzmann & McKnight (1993). They suggest that organizers create lists of skills, facilities, institutions, relationships among residents and between residents and institutions, and potential external investors. Spatial analysis is not conducted using this model, however. Community mapping offers an easy method to examine community problems and involve residents in the research process. For example, the community map displayed in figure 6.7 indicates the location of rental apartments and fraternity houses in a small neighborhood near a university. The map also shows the location of a church and a recreational facility. Also apparent from viewing this map is that the neighborhood contains a cul-de-sac with a dead-end

Figure 6.7. Community Map

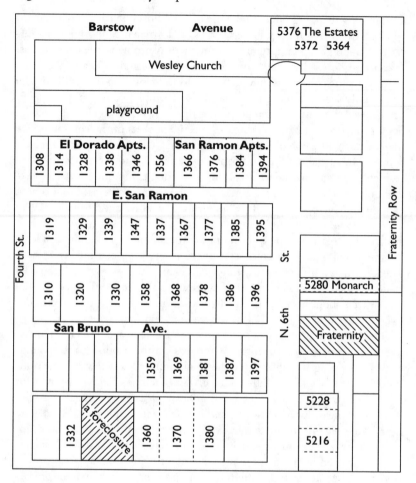

street (limiting resident access into and out of the neighborhood). There are no businesses located inside this neighborhood.

Geographic Information Systems

Geographic information systems are also a tool for mapping community problems. However, they require access to computers, printers, scanners, software, and other types of specialized equipment (Hoefer, Hoefer, & Tobias, 1994). In addition to computers and software, GIS analysis requires maps and databases. Computers serve to link the data with the map (Clarke, 1999). GIS systems are often established in conjunction with management information systems maintained by public agencies. Consequently, community problems and service utilization can often easily be mapped using GIS.[10] For example, the San Francisco Department of Health (2000) has published GIS data that indicate that most San Francisco residents with AIDS live in one of two communities: either the Castro (residents are primarily middle-income white males) or the Tenderloin neighborhood (residents are primarily low-income; this community also contains a great number of injection-drug users). Due to the prevalence of AIDS there, most of the AIDS caregiver organizations in San Francisco are located in these two communities (see figure 6.8).

GIS systems allow the researcher to input data on street addresses or other types of location information on a street or area map. The advantage of this method is that it allows the researcher to plot this information on the map in several layers or overlays so that multiple features of a specific geographic area can be viewed. Street map layers include street grids, cities or towns, and zip code boundaries (Weir & Robertson, 1998). Three additional types of data can be mapped: points (building, park, or problem incident locations; addresses of service consumers), lines (streets, railroad

Figure 6.8. Geographic Information System Map: People Living with AIDS and Locations of AIDS Care Providers in San Francisco

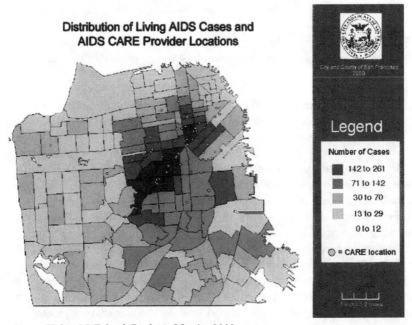

Source: Kohn, McFaland, Bock, & Martin, 2000.

lines, bus routes), and areas (service regions). All information entered into the system must have a geographic identifier (census block or tract number, zip code, city or state code) that creates a link to a specific spatial area (Hoefer et al., 1994). Using the computer to map community areas allows the researcher to change the overlays to explore different questions about community problems (Weir & Robertson, 1998). According to Clarke (1998), GIS serves as a tool to measure human behaviors:

> Human activities create geographical patterns and distributions. They lead to the population map, census map, distribution of disease incidence, location of infrastructure, and so on, all related to how people live their daily lives. The "event" part of GIS implies that geographic data fall not only into space but also into time. (p. 4)

Relationship Analysis: Mapping Social Networks

Another community attribute of interest to organizers are social networks: patterns of relationships that link residents to one another or that link residents to organizations and community institutions. Murty (1998) defines a network as "a set of actors linked by a specific set of relations" (p. 22). Social network analysis is conducted using individuals or organizations as units of analysis. Researchers examine three different types of relationships:

- Relationships between individuals, households, families, peer groups or other small units
- Relationships between organizations
- Relationships between organizations and individuals or other small units

Social network analysis assumes that these relationships are used to provide social support, goods, services, and other intangible resources that increase individual well-being or help organizations survive.

Social network analysis requires that researchers survey individuals or organization administrators about their linkages with others. Respondents can be asked to describe relevant people or organizations in their networks and the resources that these individuals or entities provide. Alternatively, respondents can be given a list of people or organizations in their community who provide these services. They are asked to simply check whether they have received specific resources from these sources (Murty, 1998). This technique requires, however, that the community in question be narrowly defined with a small population. Using either technique, respondents are also asked to assess the strength of their relationships with others.

The second stage of social network analysis requires that the researcher create a mechanism to illustrate information obtained about the networks.

A matrix can be constructed to indicate a set of interrelated relationships among members of the network. In addition, the researcher can map or graph the relationships among individuals or organizations in the network. Either technique can be used to answer questions about the strength of relationships among network members, the resources given or exchanged, and the density of networks. Density refers to the number of interrelationships that can be found among network members. Other attributes of relationships that can be measured are frequency, duration, intensity, and importance as well as negative and positive aspects of the relationship (Murty, 1998).

Using a matrix, the researcher can look at the relationships among network members (Murty, 1998; Scott, 1991). Dichotomous data can be used to indicate that a relationship exists among network members (1 = yes, 0 = no). The research can also substitute measures of other characteristics associated with the network (for example, frequency) that can be represented using ratio level variables (beginning with a 0 to indicate that the characteristic is not present or certain activities did not occur). For example, if we wanted to indicate the frequency of visits between neighbors per week, our rating scale could be 0, 1, 2, 3, etc. (see table 6.10). Matrices have their limitations, however. They cannot be used to indicate multiple attributes of relationships among members. In addition, there must be agreement between the two parties in the relationship about the attribute measured. If not, information from one individual or party can be included in the matrix but should be interpreted cautiously (Murty, 1998).

Relationships can also be illustrated using graphs. The smallest unit represented is the dyad, or relationship between two actors (Murty, 1998). Graphs illustrate the complexity of relationships among network members. One component of the graph may be the primary egonet, or the group of actors that interact with a focal individual or organization (see figure 6.9). Secondary egonetworks can also be used to examine relationships associated with a single individual, a small group, or an organization. However, these

Table 6.10 Sample of a Social Network Matrix

Ego	1	2	3	4	5
1	–	0	0	1	1
2	1	–	1	0	1
3	0	1	–	1	0
4	1	0	0	–	1
5	1	1	1	1	–

Note: 1 = Relationship
   0 = No relationship
   – = No data collected

Figure 6.9.   Social Network Map for a Primary Egonet

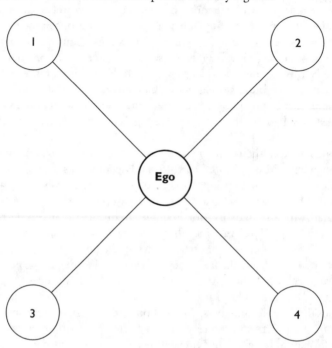

relationship maps focus on linkages among all the actors in the network (Wasserman & Faust, 1994). These maps can provide information about the density of the network or the number of actual links among members. They can also include information about the strength of the relationship between two actors (dark lines indicate a strong relationship; weak relationships are indicated by lighter lines) and the degree of reciprocity in the relationship. Arrows are used to indicate if the relationship is one-way (only one of the actors receives support, goods, or services) or if the actors participate in activities that suggest mutual exchange (see figure 6.10).

Organizers can use social network analysis to examine the strength and density of relationships in one neighborhood. Because community development approaches require that organizers strengthen ties among residents to reduce alienation (Rothman, 1995), social network analysis can be used to assess the degree of community linkages. This approach also allows the organizer to examine how communication, resources, and services flow through the community. Network analysis can be used to examine interconnections among elite members of the community, interlocking boards of corporations, and various interest groups in a variety of community issues (Scott, 1991; Wasserman & Faust, 1994). Note, however, that most organizers do not have the resources to examine entire communities. Therefore,

Figure 6.10. Secondary Egonetworks

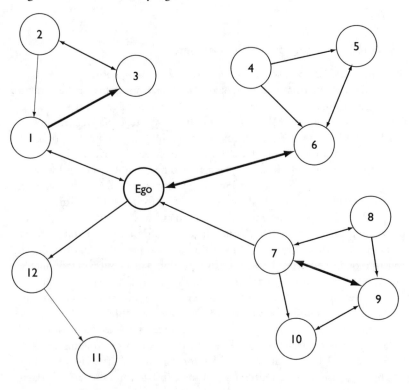

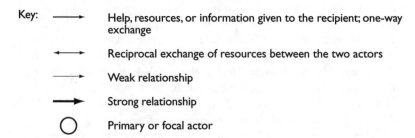

Key: ——→ Help, resources, or information given to the recipient; one-way exchange

←——→ Reciprocal exchange of resources between the two actors

——→ Weak relationship

——→ Strong relationship

○ Primary or focal actor

it is important to limit the analysis to a community segment or target group (Murty, 1998).

Social network analysis is often used to examine relationships among community-based organizations, both membership groups and social service agencies. Typical research questions deal with the exchange of information, referrals, and clients among members of organization networks. Do all the organizations provide equal amounts of resources to one another?

Are relationships reciprocal or are there identifiable givers and receivers (Wasserman & Faust, 1994)?

Using the Internet for Needs Assessment

The Internet is a good source of data for needs assessment. Thousands of sites offer information about the scope of social problems in the United States and Canada: homelessness, mental illness, hunger, child abuse, etc. (see, for example, the Web site maintained by the U.S. Department of Health and Human Services, http://www.os.dhhs.gov). State and local advocacy organizations also include statistical data on Web sites.

Data for social indicator analysis can also be obtained via the Internet. Many states post welfare utilization, social service, and health statistics on their own sites. You can obtain much of this information by visiting your state's Web site and using the search command to locate various state departments. Departmental Web sites often include a link to statistical or demographic data. The U.S. Census Bureau also provides data from each census (conducted every 10 years), Current Population Surveys (conducted monthly), and the Survey of Income and Program Participants (conducted every several years). Data from the American Community Survey, an ongoing survey of some geographic areas, are also available.

The Census Bureau also provides several other services that make social indicator research user-friendly. The bureau's home page contains a link to "Quick Facts." Users can easily find information from the last census by city block, census tract, county, congressional district, and state. A new data-retrieval system, American FactFinder, permits individual users to access data on specific geographic areas directly from the census database (U.S. Census, 1999c). This innovation should result in a great increase in public access to information. The Census Bureau also makes detailed street-level maps available to the public on the Web. These maps may be downloaded free of charge directly from the Census Bureau Web site. Maps generated through the TIGER mapping service can be used with GIS technology (U.S. Census Bureau, 1999c).

A number of additional federal government sites, including the Center for Disease Control, the Department of Health and Human Services (HHS), and the Justice Department, also contain statistical indicators. A number of private databases constructed by advocacy organizations also compile statistical indicators that are available to the public. A number of national advocacy organizations, including Children Now, the Children's Defense Fund, and the Center for Budget and Policy Priorities, also analyze trends in government indicators. The National Neighborhood Indicators Partnership (http://www.urban.org/nnip/tool.html) provides a wealth of information on constructing neighborhood indicator systems and includes guides and catalogues of information sources.

Indicators for participation in state-operated programs are also available, in many cases, on Web pages maintained by various state health and welfare departments. Be aware, however, that politically sensitive or difficult-to-compile data may not be available to the public. Many states make such data available only by personal request. In some cases, indicators are available but few details are given in terms of how the data were collected and basic assumptions made to construct the indicator. The researcher may need to calculate his or her own estimates to make comparisons of these indicators by geographic area and year.

Summary

A wide variety of methods are available to the organizer for identifying needs in the community. Many of these methods (conversational interviews, formal interviews with individuals, and ethnography) focus on the perceptions of individuals and subgroups. Other techniques (community forums, dialogue, nominal group technique, and the Delphi approach) help the organizer develop a shared or common perspective of community problems among the parties involved in organizing efforts. Quantitative approaches (structured surveys, social indicator analysis, program monitoring, population forecasting, and time series analysis) help the organizer communicate about the scope and breadth of problems affecting the community.

These approaches also allow for comparison of needs across subpopulations and different communities. Techniques such as community mapping, geographic information systems, and social network analysis help the planner examine how physical space and relationships among individuals influence community problems. Organizers should keep in mind that all of these approaches should empower community residents and incorporate their views about community problems into any plan of action. The next chapter describes techniques for analyzing community power dynamics.

■ QUESTIONS FOR CLASS DISCUSSION

1. What are the obvious gaps in service in figure 6.1?
2. How do you feel about involving constituents in planning and conducting needs assessments? What are the advantages and limitations of doing this?
3. In what ways could community forums be disrupted? What procedures could be used to control public input while maximizing participation?
4. What are the advantages of using a number of different research methodologies for gathering data from a number of different groups in conducting the needs assessment?
5. How could population projections and forecasts be used to plan programs? Would you feel confident about predictions made using these types of approaches?

6. Identify a number of different unforeseen events that could affect population growth within specific geographic areas.

7. What unanticipated events could explain patterns in Medicaid enrollment presented in figure 6.5? Can we be confident that outreach efforts alone explain the increase in enrollment? Why or why not?

8. How could you apply geographic information systems to problems in your community? What physical aspects of the community are important in determining service needs? How does the location of people in need impact the ability of public and private organizations to provide services?

9. Identify community assets included in the map in figure 6.7. How could these assets be used to improve neighborhood quality?

10. How can social network analysis be used to help organizers plan community interventions?

■ CLASS ASSIGNMENTS AND EXERCISES

1. Examine the Children's Network scenario in "Using Technical Language in Generating Responses across Constituency Gaps." What additional needs-assessment methods could the Children's Network use to determine the services that the assessment center will provide? Who should be surveyed in this supplemental research study? How could the steering committee better involve target groups in planning the needs assessment and the data analysis?

2. Conduct an Internet search to find either county or statewide monthly unemployment data for the past year. Once you find these data, plot them on a chart. Place the number of unemployed on the y- (left) axis and the months on the x- (bottom) axis of the chart. Identify any seasonal patterns in the data. What explanation can you offer for these variations? Are some industries in your state and county more likely to hire or lay off employees during specific times of the year? (For example, employment in agriculture is most likely to be higher in the summer months; temporary employment in retail sales is most likely to be high in November and December.) Why?

3. Calculate the average rate of population change for people in poverty in Fairtown using the numbers in table 6.11. Make a projection (using at

Table 6.11 Number in Poverty

	1960	1970	1980	1990	2000
Number of People in Fairtown with Incomes Below the Poverty Line	3,333	5,554	12,278	21,633	28,758

least two different scenarios) about the expected number of people in poverty in 2010.

4. Use social network analysis techniques to map your own social network. How would you assess the strength of your personal network?

5. Find a map of your community: a simple street map or a map downloaded from TIGER at the Census Bureau Web site or through your university library. Identify important physical barriers (busy streets, railroad tracks, barrier walls, cul-de-sacs, or speed bumps) that limit or enhance access to residents and members of subpopulation groups. Indicate the location of these barriers on the map. Also, pinpoint the location of community institutions, parks, businesses, and open space. Analyze the spatial aspects of the community. How does the community's infrastructure enhance or impede resident access to services, institutions, and recreational facilities? If there appears to be a problem with access, make recommendations for change.

Notes

1. Researchers conducting formal ethnographic studies will want to protect participants from harm and preserve their privacy by insisting on human subject reviews conducted by the researcher's employing institution or any agency in which such research will be conducted.

2. Separate focus groups for different constituency groups are often established to minimize problems associated with social distances among participants. For instance, in most focus groups oriented toward needs assessments, sessions will provide separate groups for clients and agency staff.

3. The Current Population Survey is conducted each month by the Bureau of Labor Statistics. It involves a survey of 50,000 households. Data from the survey are used to develop estimates for the nation as well as states, counties, and smaller geographic areas. Survey questions include age, sex, race, school enrollment, education, occupation, and industry of workers (U.S. Census, 1999a). The Survey of Income and Program Participation is conducted every several years and is intended to provide a comprehensive database on income and household participation in government programs.

4. Census data is used to determine congressional district boundaries. The more people found in urban areas, the more likely it is that congressional districts will include cities and low-income people. Low-income residents are believed to be more likely to vote Democratic. Consequently, Republicans were opposed to sampling techniques that would eliminate undercounts in urban areas (Sample, 1999; U.S. Census Bureau, 1999a).

5. In 2001, the U.S. Census Bureau decided not to use sampling techniques to adjust any of the data collected in the 2000 census. The Supreme Court ruling had pertained only to data used for redistricting purposes.

6. FRAC's estimate of child hunger was calculated using a survey of more than 5,000 families nationwide with incomes below 185 percent of the poverty line.

7. Some rate indicators are used to indicate the prevalence of the problem for every 1,000 people (for example, infant mortality and low birth rates).

8. To calculate growth rates for more than one time interval, simply add an exponent equivalent to the number of time periods to the formula. This allows a geometric measure to be constructed that assumes that the rate of growth from time period to time period will stay constant.

$$\text{Rate} = \frac{Y_{t+1} - Y_1}{Y_1}$$

For example,

If a population of 100 grows at 6 percent in year 1, there will be $100 * (1.06)^1 = 106$ in year 1.

If the population in year 2 (106), grows by another 6 percent in year 2, the population will be $100 * (1.06)^2 = 112$.

If the population in year 3 (112) grows by another 6 percent in year 3, the population will be $100 * (1.06)^3 = 119$.

(See Klosterman, 1990)

9. Greater numbers can be expected to apply for Medicaid during economic downturns.

10. This requires that such databases contain files that are complete, with very limited amounts of missing or incorrect data.

References

Anderson, E. (1990). *Streetwise: Race, class, and change in an urban community*. Chicago: University of Chicago Press.

Associated Press. (1999, December 31). Homicide rates fell this year in many U.S. cities. *San Francisco Chronicle*, p. A3.

Berg, B. (1998). *Qualitative methods for the social sciences* (3d ed.). Boston: Allyn & Bacon.

Burch, H. (1996). *Basic social policy and planning*. New York: Haworth.

Burch, H. (1999). *Social welfare policy analysis and choices*. New York: Haworth.

Chambers, D. (1993). *Social policy and social programs: A method for the practical public policy analyst*. Boston: Allyn & Bacon.

Chambers, D., Wedel, K., & Rodwell, M. (1992). *Evaluating social programs*. Boston: Allyn & Bacon.

Choi, N., & Snyder, L. (1999). Homeless families with children: Barriers to finding decent housing. *Journal of Poverty, 3*, 43–66.

Clarke, K. (1999). *Getting started with geographic information systems* (2d ed.). Upper Saddle River, NJ: Prentice-Hall.

Dattalo, D. (1998). Time series analysis: Concepts and techniques for community practitioners. *Journal of Community Practice, 5*(4), 68–85.

Decker, S., & Van Winkle, B. (1996). *Life in the gang*. New York: Cambridge University Press.

Delgado, M. (1996). Puerto Rican food establishments as social service organizations: Results of an asset assessment. *Journal of Community Practice, 3*(2), 57–78.

Delgado, M. (2000). *Community social work practice in an urban context*. New York: Oxford University Press.

Durst, D., MacDonald, J., & Parsons, D. (1999). Finding our way: A community needs assessment on violence in native families in Canada. *Journal of Community Practice, 6*(1), 45–59.

Eisinger, P. (1996). Toward a national hunger count. *Social Service Review, 70*(2), 214–34.

Food Research Action Center. (2000). Hunger in the U.S. [On-line]. Available: http://www.frac/org/html/hunger_in_the_us/hunger_index.html.

Guerra, L. (1999). *Technical assistance and progressive organizations for social change in communities of color: A report to the Saguaro grantmaking board of the funding exchange* [On-line]. Available: http://comm-org.utoledo.edu/papers.htm.

Hardcastle, D., Wenocur, S., & Powers, P. (1997). *Community practice: Theories and skills for social workers.* New York: Oxford University Press.

Hardina, D. (1993). The impact of funding sources and board representation on consumer control of service delivery in organizations serving low-income communities. *Nonprofit Leadership and Management, 4,* 69–84.

Hardina, D., & Malott, O. W. (1996). Strategies for the empowerment of low income consumers on community-based planning boards. *Journal of Progressive Human Services, 7*(2), 43–61.

Hoefer, R. A., Hoefer, R. M., & Tobias, R. A. (1994). Geographic information systems and community practice. *Journal of Community Practice, 1*(3), 113–27.

Iglehart, A., & Becerra, R. (1995). *Social services and the ethnic community.* Boston: Allyn & Bacon.

Johnson, A. (1994). Linking professionalism and community organization: A scholar/advocate approach. *Journal of Community Practice, 1*(2), 65–86.

Kirby, S., & McKenna, K. (1989). *Methods from the margins.* Toronto: Garamond Press.

Klosterman, R. (1990). *Community analysis and planning techniques.* Savage, MD: Rowman & Littlefield.

Kohn, R., McFarland, W., Kellogg, T., Bock, K., & Martin, R. (2000, Nov. 14). *Use of geographic information system technology for HIV prevention planning, evaluation, and surveillance.* San Francisco: Department of Health.

Kretzmann, J., & McKnight, J. (1993). *Building communities from the inside out.* Chicago: ACTA.

Lipsky, M. (1980). *Street-level bureaucracy.* New York: Sage Foundation.

Marti-Costa, S., & Serrano-Garcia, I. (1995). Needs assessment and community development: An ideological perspective. In J. Rothman, J. Erlich, & J. Tropman (Eds.), *Strategies of community intervention* (5th ed., pp. 257–67). Itasca, IL: Peacock.

Meenaghan, T., Washington, R., & Ryan, R. (1982). *Macro practice in the human service.* New York: Free Press.

Menjivar, C. (1995). Kinship networks among immigrants: Lessons from a qualitative comparative approach. *International Journal of Comparative Sociology, 36* (3–4), 219–33.

Murty, S. (1998). *Network analysis as a research methodology.* In R. MacNair (Ed.), Research methods for community practice (pp. 21–46). New York: Haworth.

Nord, M., Jemison, K., & Bickel, G. (1999). *Prevalence of food insecurity and hunger, by state, 1996–1998.* Washington, DC: U.S. Department of Agriculture, Food and Rural Economics Division, Economic Research Service.

Reimer, F. (1997). Quick attachments to the workforce: An ethnographic analysis of a transition from welfare to low-wage jobs. *Social Work Research, 21*(4), 225–32.

Reisch, M., & Rivera, F. (1999). Ethical and racial conflicts in urban-based action research. *Journal of Community Practice, 6*(2), 49–77.

Richards, L., & Richards, T. (2000). Non-numerical unstructured data indexing search and theorizing (Nud*ist) data analysis (Version 5). Melbourne, Australia: Qualitative Solutions and Research.

Rossi, P., & Freeman, H. (1982). *Evaluation: A systematic approach* (2d ed.). Beverly Hills, CA: Sage.

Rothman, J. (1995). Approaches to community intervention. In F. Cox, J. Erlich, J. Rothman, & J. Tropman (Eds.), *Strategies of community organization.* Itasca, IL: Peacock.

Royse, D., & Thyer, B. (1996). *Program evaluation: An introduction* (2d ed.). Chicago: Nelson-Hall.

Rubin, A., & Babbie, E. (1997). *Research methods for social work.* Pacific Grove, CA: Brooks/Cole.

Sample, H. (1999, September 5). State battles echo in Congress: Impending redistricting means victors get considerable spoils. *Fresno Bee,* p. A8.

Scott, J. (1991). *Social network analysis: A handbook.* Thousand Oaks, CA: Sage.

Seidel, J. (1998). Ethnograph (Version 5.04). Salt Lake City: Qualis Research Associates.

Short, K., Iceland, J., & Garner, T. (1999). Experimental poverty measures: 1998 [On-line]. Available: http://www.census.gov/hhes/poverty/povmeas/exppov.html.

Sohng, S. S. L. (1998). Research as an empowerment strategy. In L. Gutierrez, R. Parsons, & E. O. Cox (Eds.), *Empowerment in social work practice: A source book* (pp. 187–201). Pacific Grove, CA: Brooks/Cole.

Strauss, A., & Corbin, J. (1990). *Basics of qualitative research.* Newbury Park, CA: Sage.

U.S. Census Bureau. (1999a). Census 2000, Frequently asked questions [On-line]. Available: http://www.census.gov/dmd/www.genfaq.htm.

U.S. Census Bureau. (1999b). Small area income and poverty estimates: A basic explanation of confidence interviews [On-line]. Available: http://www.census.gov/hhes/www.saipe/stcty/ci.html.

U.S. Census Bureau. (1999c). *TIGER mapping service: The "coast to coast" digital map database* [On-line]. Available: http//tiger.census.gov/general.html.

Wagner, D. (1994). Beyond the pathologizing of nonwork: Alternative activities in a street community. *Social Work, 39,* 718–28.

Warheit, G., Bell, R., & Schwab, J. (1984). Selecting the needs assessment approach. In J. Rothman, J. Erlich, & J. Tropman (Eds.), *Tactics and techniques of community intervention* (2d ed., pp. 41–59). Itasca, IL: Peacock.

Wasserman, S., & Faust, F. (1994). *Social network analysis: Methods and applications.* New York: Cambridge University Press.

Weir, K., & Robertson, J. (1998). Teaching geographic information systems for social work applications. *Journal of Social Work Education, 34* (1), 81–97.

Wright, B., Caspi, A., Moffitt, T., & Silva, P. (1998). Factors associated with doubled-up housing—a common precursor to homelessness. *Social Service Review, 72* (1), 92–111.

Web Resources

Needs Assessment

Children's Defense Fund (contains a state-by-state database on the status of children)—http://www.childrensdefense.org/

Children Now—http://www.childrennow.org/

National Center on Child Abuse and Neglect—http://www.calib.com/nccanch/

The National Neighborhood Indicators Partnership—http://www.urban.org/nnip/tools/html

U.S. Administration for Children and Families—http://www.acf.dhhs.gov/

U.S. Census Bureau—http://www.census.gov/

U.S. Census Bureau, TIGER Mapping Service—http://tiger.census.gov/

U.S. Centers for Disease Control—http://www.cdc.gov/

U.S. Department of Agriculture (contains information on food programs)—http://www.ers.usda.gov/

U.S. Department of Housing and Urban Development—http://www.hud.gov/

U.S. Health Care Financing Administration (contains information on health care funding and hospital utilization)—http://www.hcfa.gov/

Youth Indicators—http://www.ed/gov/pubs/YouthIndicators

7 Power Analysis

■ Power is an important component of the political process. It is one of the few ways, other than persuasion, that we have to influence others to change their decisions or behaviors. Groups with limited amounts of financial or political power can be excluded from the decision-making process. Power can be actual, used to influence social change, or potential, not used but available to those who possess power. It can also be positive, used to persuade a decision maker to take action, or negative, used to prevent someone from taking action. (Meenaghan, Washington, & Ryan, 1982).

This chapter describes power resources and the role of power in the community decision-making process. Organizational structures used to bring people together to increase their power—interest groups, coalitions, and social movements—are examined. This chapter also identifies models that can describe how group interaction influences community and government decision making and describes analytical techniques that can identify power inherent in community decision-making structures.

Power Resources

Power resources may include (but are not limited to) goods, services, money, votes, public support, authority, professional status, knowledge, information, ability to influence the media, and links to other powerful people (Haynes & Mickelson, 1991; Jansson, 1999). The power associated with authority comes by virtue of the ability to make or influence a decision. For example, people can acquire power if they hold one of the following positions: elected official, executive director of an organization, a university president, religious leader, or expert in a particular field. Social workers acquire a number of power resources by virtue of having a bachelor's or master's degree in social work. Sources of social worker power include professional status; knowledge; and information about policy impacts, service-delivery systems, and client need. Social workers also derive power through their role as gatekeepers—deciding who should receive goods, services, and referrals. They also have the power to deny or reduce government-funded benefits to low-income people (Hardina, 1993; Lipsky, 1980).

Power can be derived from authority, the ability to make decisions that affect the lives of others. In social service organizations, administrators and supervisors have the authority to hire and fire staff and to decide how organizational policies will be administered. Elected officials, government agency administrators, and frontline government employees (welfare workers, police officers, employees of the Department of Motor Vehicles) have power derived from holding these positions as well as from their ability to make certain types of decisions.

Power is also derived through election to office. Consequently, votes and the money to run campaigns to get these votes are important power resources.

French and Craven (1968) identified five types of power:

1. Coercive power—the ability to sanction an individual or a group for noncompliant behavior
2. Reward power—the ability to provide a benefit for appropriate behavior
3. Legitimate power—the ability, derived from a position of authority, professional status, or public recognition, to reward and sanction behaviors or make certain decisions
4. Expert power—derived from recognition that the power holder has the experience or education to make certain decisions
5. Referent power—derived from a subordinate's desire to identify with the power holder, due to personal admiration.

Power is also derived from the personal attributes associated with the power holder. For example, an individual can attain power due to personal attractiveness, charisma, or celebrity. People often follow charismatic leaders, believing they have legitimacy and the expertise to make certain types of decisions (Jansson, 1999; Mondros & Wilson, 1994). Often, politicians gain public support and recognition because of their ability to influence people and their vision of a just society. Recent examples of charismatic leaders include presidents Bill Clinton and Ronald Reagan as well as British prime minister Tony Blair. Individuals can also have the power to influence political decisions due to their successes and public recognition in other fields such as acting, music, sports, or the military. For example, Bill Bradley (a former professional basketball player) was a candidate in the Democratic presidential primary in 2000; actors Warren Beatty and Cybill Shepard also considered announcing their candidacy for the presidency in 2000.

Power can also be derived from one's position in the social structure. Positional power in society is generally thought to accrue from gender, race, education, and wealth (Kahn, 1991). Educated, heterosexual white males with access to money or influential connections are generally believed to have more power than others in society: women, gay men and lesbians, people of color, and those with limited income. If oppressions can be overlapping (see chapters 2 and 4), so is power. A man of color, for example, may be powerful in terms of gender relationships but is less powerful than white males of comparable income and education.

Community organization can be considered the practice of increasing the power of individuals and groups with little status, money, and decision-making power in society. One method for increasing the power of marginalized groups involves bringing together large numbers of people to meet with, call, or write to public officials (Haynes & Mickelson, 1991). Organizing protests, particularly the type of protest activities that draw media attention, additional participants, and sympathy for the cause, is a typical method for developing power among groups that have limited money or political and media connections (Mondros & Wilson, 1994; Swank & Clapp, 1999).

Individuals working alone seldom have sufficient power to influence political decision making (Kahn, 1991). Consequently, individuals join interest groups to influence political decision making. Interest groups generally consist of formal organizations such as business, professional, or trade associations; unions; and advocacy or social movement organizations. For example, the National Association of Social Workers is a professional organization that lobbies for legislation that will improve pay and workplace conditions for social workers while expanding services to people who need assistance. Interest groups try to influence the development of legislation that will be beneficial to them (or, alternatively, that will do them minimal harm) by using a variety of power resources such as money, media, and promises to organize voters on behalf of a candidate who supports their positions. These groups lobby in support of their vested interest. A vested interest usually involves personal motivation or a rationale for participating in a group or supporting a cause.

Interest groups use a variety of strategies and tactics to increase their power to influence social change. Strategies, as described in chapter 4, are long-term action plans used to achieve a specific goal. Warren (1971) identified three primary strategies or orientations to change: collaboration, campaign, and contest. Collaborative strategies are used when groups can agree on joint actions. Campaign strategies are used to persuade opponents to come to the bargaining table. Contest or conflict is used to pressure decision makers to adopt policies or take action supported by opposition groups. Tactics are short-term activities undertaken as part of a change-oriented strategy. Tactics can include cooperation, negotiation, public education, persuasion, media influence, lobbying, public appeals, demonstrations, boycotts, strikes, and civil disobedience (Warren, 1971).

Community Power Structures

Meenaghan et al. (1982) identified two primary types of power structures in communities: elitist communities and pluralist communities. The term power structure refers to how community decisions are made and who makes them. These decisions can be governmental, involving the adoption or implementation of new laws. They can also be made by the private sector, such as the development of new businesses, recognition of individual achievements or awards, fund-raising, or providing emergency assistance or local responses to natural disasters.

Elitist Decision Making

In elitist communities, decision making is confined to specific social classes or groups (most often wealthy individuals or people with professional status). Often, only a few key people are involved in all important decisions. Few mechanisms exist for linking people across income levels or ethnic groups. Groups maintain separate public or private organizations and do not form coalitions to accomplish tasks. Members of the community elite are isolated from other groups and often fail to recognize community needs. People and groups that could potentially influence social change because of their own power resources (professionals and members of formal organizations) are reluctant to challenge the power structure. They perceive themselves as having limited ability to change the status quo and may perceive that negative consequences (for example, possible loss of income or status) are associated with standing up to the elite. Most citizens are reluctant to become politically involved and have problems communicating with the elite or find it difficult to obtain information about current social problems or policies. Consequently, the public perception is that change is not possible.

Pluralist Decision Making

In pluralist communities, there are numerous issues for members of the community to address. Key decision makers vary depending on the issue of concern. People with power are associated with three different community sectors: business, government, and the professions (e.g., doctors, lawyers, social workers, etc.). None of these sectors is assumed to dominate the others. Involvement in decision making often depends on the decision maker's occupation. organizational affiliations, or election to public office. Interest groups form around specific issues. These groups often form coalitions to apply pressure on decision makers. The alliances that coalition members form often shift response to the issue at hand, with opponents becoming allies and allies becoming opponents as the group members' vested interests change over time.

Meenaghan et al. (1982) identified a number of questions that can be used to conduct a basic power analysis:

1. What is the nature of business in the community?
2. What is the pattern of business in the community (how many businesses exist; are there more than one or two primary industries)?
3. What is the political character and tradition of the community? Do influential individuals or groups represent one or more specific political viewpoints?
4. What is the demographic composition of the community? Do obvious class differences exist? Is there a variety of ethnic or cultural groups?
5. How much conflict is there among the various groups in the community? Are there powerful economic or political groups in the community?
6. What sources of power are associated with the various groups identified? (pp. 122–24)

These questions help distinguish heterogeneous communities from those that are homogenous. In communities where individuals come from the same ethnic group and there are few distinctions made by social class, less conflict exists. Residents of such a community often have similar interests and values. Alternatively, ethnic or class divisions in a community can promote conflict. These questions also help to distinguish communities controlled by a small elite from those in which a number of interest groups actively compete for resources. Communities dominated by a handful of industries are less diverse and more likely to limit decision making to a few insiders with ties to the business elite.

This information can be used to create maps of social networks and relationships among organizations adopting techniques associated with social network analysis (see chapter 6). The researcher can simply create a map illustrating the relationships among members of one interest group or create maps of several groups and compare both membership and the strength of relationships among members (see figure 7.1). A map of a pluralist community can be expected to illustrate shifts in organization mem-

Figure 7.1. Map of social networks and relationships among interest groups.

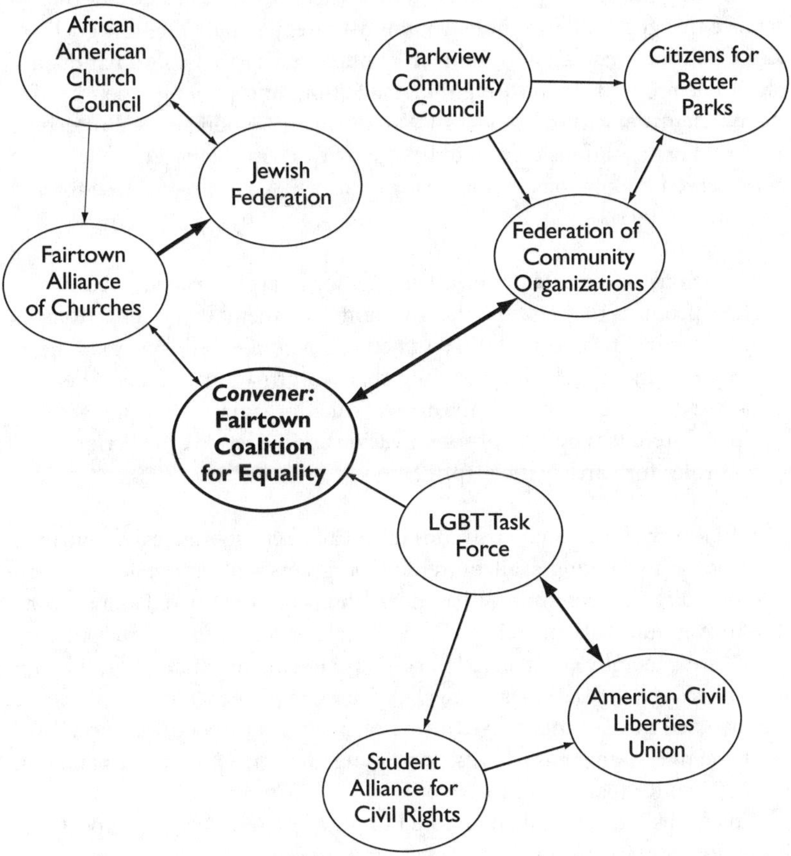

bership among interest groups. In an elitist community, the same organizations will be members of each interest group. Mapping techniques can also illustrate the relationships among individuals who are in positions of decision-making authority or who take an active role in community issues.

Coalitions and Social Movements

Interest groups may form alliances or coalitions with other organizations to educate the public about certain issues and influence public policies and legislation. Formation of coalitions increases member organizations' ability to derive "strength from numbers" and provides members with greater access to goods and services through resource sharing (Weingarten & Nemon,

1999; Yamatani, Soska, & Baltimore, 1999). Roberts-DeGennaro (1997) defines coalition as an "interacting group of organizational actors who a) agree to pursue a common goal, b) coordinate their resources in attempting to achieve this goal, and c) adopt a common strategy in pursuing this goal" (p. 92). Coalitions may serve a number of purposes: service coordination and planning, program monitoring and evaluation, and pooling resources for the efficient delivery of services (Wandersman, Goodman, & Butterfoss, 1999). Many coalitions combine these activities with advocacy on behalf of underserved populations or support for a cause. According to Mizrahi and Rosenthal (1993):

> Coalitions are often a preferred vehicle for intergroup action because they promise to preserve the autonomy of member organizations while providing the necessary structure for unified effort. Enabling people to link special interests and share information and diverse expertise, coalitions are also means by which organizations can clarify their differences and incorporate various skills, levels of experience, and roles for participation. (p. 12)

Often service-oriented coalitions (also called collaboratives) are formed in response to funding availability; federal grants and private foundations often require that community-based coalitions be constructed as a precondition of funding (Yamatani et al., 1999). However, advocacy-related coalitions are generally constructed in response to situational needs. Lobbying for policies and legislation is more effective when greater numbers of people are involved in the process. Member organizations can pool resources, recruit members, and raise funds, increasing the impact of the organizing effort (Wandersman et al., 1999).

Coalitions are generally composed of a variety of interest groups. Coalitions of interest groups concerned about obtaining rights for disadvantaged groups come together to form social movements (Mizrahi & Rosenthal, 1993). Social movements may form when coalition groups gain national recognition or initiate organized campaigns to improve the status of disadvantaged groups in society or change laws and policies (Jasper & Poulsen, 1995; Rothman, 1995).

Social movements often form in response to public recognition that the political process has not been effective in helping groups obtain social change (Piven & Cloward, 1979). Social movements may initially use protest-related strategies (strikes, demonstrations, boycotts) to put forward their agendas. A social movement involves a handful of core organizations with large numbers of members or supporters. However, as noted in chapter 3, to mobilize members for social action, social movements must develop a formal organizational structure and raise funds to maintain the organization. Consequently, social movements evolve from informal organizations that sporadically stage protests into formal organizations that represent the vested interests of specific groups. These organizations may have the structure, funds, and influence to engage in legislative politics (Hrebenar, 1997; Piven & Cloward, 1979).

Interest Groups and Elites in the Political Process

We must also examine interest group interaction to understand the role of power in legislative decision making. Interest groups come together because they recognize common needs or goals. As described previously, the motivation to participate in an interest group is often described as vested interest. For example, the CEO of a corporation that manufactures cigarettes may have a vested interest in efforts to prevent the government from labeling tobacco as an addictive substance. Hrebenar (1997) identifies six factors that contribute to the power of interest groups to influence legislators.

1. The size, wealth, information, services, and degree of group cohesion the group can provide to the legislator
2. The importance and reliability of the group
3. The type of interest the group represents (businesses are likely to be more highly regarded than groups who represent consumers)
4. Whether the group wants to prevent or support a piece of legislation (prevention may be easier)
5. Whether, and in what degree, the legislator's political party supports or opposes the issue
6. The degree of competition among interest groups on the issue in question. (p. 290)

Interest groups can be understood as mechanisms through which organized groups pool their power resources. Political scientists have developed four primary models of interest group participation: elitist, pluralist, public choice, and neo-elitist (Dye, 1998; Heffernan, 1979). The models used here provide theoretical frameworks that describe interest group interaction rather than prescriptions for action. Dye (1998) defines the decision-making model used for this type of analysis as an "abstraction or representation of political life" used to simplify reality, provide meaningful communication about what is happening, and offer explanations about cause-and-effect relationships that are empirically testable (p. 38).

Elitist Model

C. W. Mills (1956) developed the term elitist model to examine decision-making processes in which only a small number of people or the elite make decisions. He described the elite as "the members of a top social stratum, as a set of groups whose members know one another, see one another socially and at business and so, in making decisions, take one another into account" (p. 11). Members of the elite often attend the same university, serve on boards of directors, or intermarry. As a result, they have similar views on political issues.

The basic assumption inherent in the elitist model is that members of the elite control all decision making (Dye, 1998; Heffernan, 1979). This group has no communication with the great majority of people in society (the masses). The elite therefore make decisions to benefit their own interests. They communicate with the masses through a group of intermediaries (called minions), usually employees of government bureaucracies or members of the professional classes (see figure 7.2). As noted in chapter 3, some proponents of this model believe social workers to be intermediaries that help the elite implement laws and policies needed to control the masses (Burghardt & Fabricant, 1987). The welfare system is viewed as a process established by the elite to control political dissent and regulate the work behavior of low-income people (Piven & Cloward, 1971).

Pluralist Model

A pluralist policy model assumes that the policy process is characterized by conflicts among interest groups (Heffernan, 1979). These groups act to in-

Figure 7.2. Elitist decision-making model.

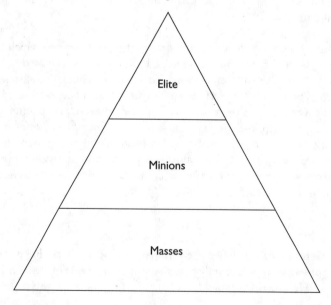

crease the likelihood that their preferred policy options will be selected in the political process. Each of these groups has varying interests, values, and goals. They may form coalitions with other interest groups in order to increase their power resources. However, these coalitions are often temporary. Once a goal has been abandoned or achieved, the interest group is likely to pursue a different goal that will benefit the interest of its members. This may require that the interest group join an entirely different set of allies. For example, the Children's Defense Fund allied itself with the Clinton administration in 1992 to support an expansion of programs that would benefit children. However, in 1996 the Children's Defense Fund aggressively lobbied against the welfare reform bill signed by President Clinton, arguing that the bill would force more than a million children into poverty (Children's Defense Fund, 1996).

The pluralist model assumes that policies are generated through the competition among these various interest groups. Government facilitates compromise between the groups. Compromise results in policy decisions that are incremental in nature and that represent small changes in previous policies. This is known as incremental decision making (Lindblom, 1959). Incremental decision making occurs because it is almost impossible for a large number of interest groups to agree on large-scale changes (for example, the Clinton administration's attempt at health care reform). Interest groups will attempt to attain a certain level of satisfaction with a particular policy. Lindblom has called this process "satisficing." One interest group may be satisfied with one aspect of a piece of legislation and dissatisfied with other aspects. Other groups may find satisfaction with different components of the legislation (see figure 7.3).

This model also assumes that some groups possess more resources and have more power to influence decisions than others. Interest groups gain political power by trading votes and campaign donations with elected officials in return for their support on specific issues. It is also assumed, due to government's role as a mediator in this process, that pluralism results in government policies that benefit the national interest (Lindblom, 1959).

Public Choice Model

The public choice model combines aspects of both elitist and pluralist models of policy making (Brooks, 1989). It assumes that individuals and groups do use monetary resources, media influence, and votes to purchase favorable political decisions. Another basic assumption is that this is an appropriate and efficient mechanism for the allocation of resources in society. Politicians who must acquire votes and campaign contributions function as gatekeepers, allowing access to government decision-making processes to people and groups with money and power (see figure 7.4).

Adherents of this model are influenced by classical economic theory, the

Figure 7.3. Pluralist decision-making model.

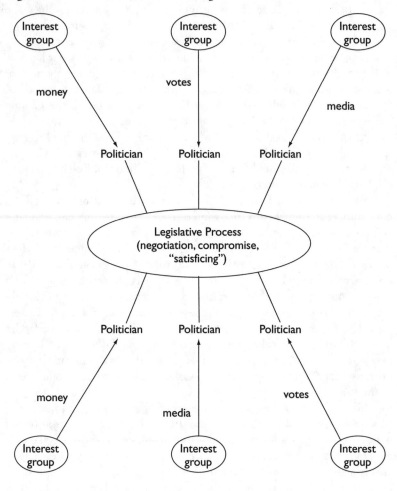

idea that in capitalist societies the most appropriate distribution of goods and services is through the "free hand of the market," or nonregulation of economic activity. The basic assumption of the public choice model is that those with the most resources and willingness to invest in favorable political decisions should be free to influence political decision making. As with classical economics, however, the public choice model of policy development does not describe the actions or behaviors of those people (such as the poor) who are excluded from participation in the market.

This model also assumes that all political actors react in ways that maximize their own self-interest (Dye, 1998). Politicians are primarily interested in maximizing votes and campaign contributors. Individual campaign do-

Figure 7.4. Public choice decision-making model.

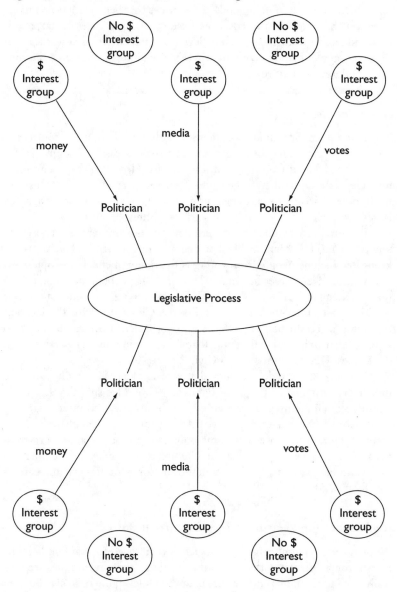

nors try to obtain special benefits and privileges. Interest groups also maximize their power to obtain goods and services that benefit their members. Government disperses the costs of these special privileges to taxpayers. Some adherents of this approach believe that interest group power leads to the creation of a market economy where special interests benefit from subsidies and government regulation.

Neo-Elitist Model

The neo-elitist policy model assumes that although all interest groups have access to government, not all groups have equal access. Some groups are effectively excluded from the political process. However, this exclusion is not due to some deliberate conspiracy on the part of the elite. Instead, institutional barriers to participation have been created. In addition, some issues are excluded from policy discussion simply because they have not traditionally been handled by government, or government has chosen to ignore them (Heffernan, 1979). For example, one institutional barrier that keeps low-income people from voting is the requirement that people need to reregister every time they move. Low-income people tend to be transitory. Consequently, it is more difficult for them to register and vote than it is middle- and upper-income groups (Piven & Cloward, 1988). The location of polling places in buildings that are not wheelchair accessible may also represent an unintentional action that limits voting among persons with disabilities (U.S. Commission on Civil Rights, 2001).

The neo-elitist model assumes that social change is possible with the monetary assistance of the elite (Panitch, 1977). This support is possible because not all members of the elite have the same vested interests; coalitions between the more progressive members of the elite and social movement organizations representing the poor can shift and change in relation to the issues. As described in chapter 3, monetary resources and membership mobilization are essential elements in the development of social movements (see figure 7.5).

Techniques for Measuring Interest Group Power

To plan social action campaigns, social workers need to examine how interest groups interact with one another. Though these techniques are typically used to examine power at the community level, they can also be used to examine government decision making. Meenaghan et al. (1982) describe two approaches to identifying power resources and the interrelationships among interest groups: issues analysis and the positional approach. Issues analysis requires that the researcher identify four or five issues of concern to the public or members of specific interest groups. Sources of information could include interviews with residents, information provided at public

Figure 7.5. Neo-elitist decision-making model.

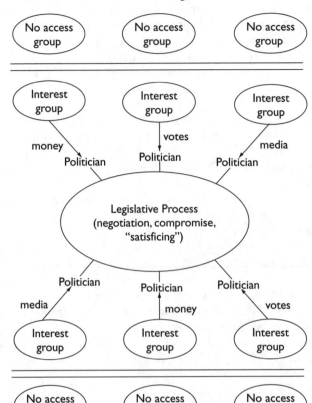

meetings, and media reports. Once the issues are identified, the researcher should identify a number of key decision makers associated with each issue. If the names on the list vary by issue, the decision-making structure probably can be characterized as pluralist. If the same names are associated with most of the issues, then the community or government body has an elitist decision-making structure.

The positional approach requires that the researcher list all major organizations involved in the decision-making process. Leaders of these organizations (administrators as well as board members) are then identified. Expect overlap in many of these organizations (Meenaghan et al., 1982). For example, a business leader would be likely to sit on the boards of several major community institutions (schools, hospitals, social service organizations) or a number of corporate boards. Decision-making structures are likely to be elitist when there are a great number of links among organizations but only a handful of powerful individuals who make decisions for these organizations. On the other hand, the decision-making structure is most likely to be pluralist in nature if there are a large number of individuals involved in decision making. Diversity by gender and ethnicity also is an indicator of pluralism (Hardina & Malott, 1996).

Interest group interaction may be examined using the following guidelines:

- Look at those organizations the interest group typically works with on a variety of issues. Also, examine the groups that it typically opposes on an issue.
- Does membership in alliances shift or remain constant as the issues change?
- Examine the demographic profile of interest group members. Look at gender, ethnicity, professional affiliations, social class, religion, and political party affiliations.
- Are participants members of disadvantaged groups or members of the political, economic, or social elite?
- Are decisions made by a small number of individuals and groups or by a variety of organizations that represent diverse interests?
- Was the final decision made because of conflict? Are there clear winners and losers on the issue in question?
- Are decisions made through negotiation and bargaining? Are the preferences of different groups expressed in the decision? (Meenaghan et al., 1982)

Sources of information for this type of interest group analysis can include newspaper and magazine articles, personal interviews with decision makers, annual reports issued by interest group organizations, lists of board members (available on organization letterheads), and Web sites maintained by interest groups. Federal, state, and local governments also require that political campaigns file reports that list donors, the amounts of donations, and the donors' industry affiliations. The Federal Elections Commission and a variety of private organizations make this information available to the public on the Internet. Chapters 8 and 9 contain detailed information about using data on campaign donations to examine the power of interest groups to influence political decision making.

Summary

To facilitate social change, community organizers must use power resources such as professional status, knowledge, and information to influence decision makers. Strength in numbers is also a key to influencing political change. Community organizers may join or form interest groups in order to support or oppose public policies and legislation. Coalitions and social movements are also formed to influence social change. Organizers should conduct power analyses to assess whether interest groups will be successful in influencing policies and legislation. To examine how the preferences of influential groups are incorporated into laws and policies, organizers must understand how interest groups interact with one another. Information on interest group power is also critical for understanding how individual legislators can be influenced in the political process. Chapters 8 and 9 contain information about conducting research on power and its effect on legislative and political processes. Chapter 10 describes the use of strategies and tactics to increase the power of interest groups and organizations to influence social change.

■ QUESTIONS FOR CLASS DISCUSSION

1. How much power do you think social workers have to influence social change? Why?
2. What source(s) of power do you have as a student or practicing social worker? What types of things can you do to influence change?
3. Why would social workers involve themselves in coalitions and social movements?
4. In what current movements do social workers participate?
5. What activities have state and National Association of Social Workers organizations pursued to facilitate social change?
6. Are these activities consistent with social work values as expressed in the code of ethics? Why?

■ ASSIGNMENT: ANALYZING DECISION-MAKING PROCESSES

Analyze a current social, economic, or political issue (policy or legislation). Describe the issue and the positions of proponents and opponents.

- Describe the issue (policy, plan, or legislation) under discussion.
- Identify the decision makers and interest groups that will influence the decision.
- For each decision maker or interest group you identify, assess the person's or group's
  a. position on the issue.
  b. source of decision-making power.
  c. vested interest or motivation.
- Identify environmental influences (economic, political, cultural, or media).
- Identify alliances or coalitions among the decision makers and interest groups.

- Describe strategies used by at least one interest group to influence decision makers or the public.
- Examine how the decision was made (through cooperation or conflict, negotiation among interest groups or by political elites, radical change from previous policy or incremental changes made).

Use newspapers, magazines, televised city council or legislative hearings, interviews with key informants, and reports prepared by interest groups or government agencies.

References

Brooks, S. (1989). *Public policy in Canada.* Toronto: McClelland & Stewart.

Burghardt, S. & Fabricant, M. (1987). *Radical social work* (18th ed., Vol. 2, pp. 455–62). Silver Springs, MD: National Association of Social Workers.

Children's Defense Fund (1996). CDF summarizes conference bill [On-line]. Available: http://www.handsnet.org/handsnet2.

Dye, T. (1998). *Understanding public policy* (9th ed.). Saddle River, NJ: Prentice-Hall.

French, J., & Craven, B. (1968). The bases of social power. In D. Cartwright & A. Zander (Eds.), *Group dynamics: Research and theory* (pp. 259–69). New York: Harper & Row.

Hardina, D. (1993). The impact of funding sources and board representation on consumer control of service delivery in organizations serving low-income communities. *Nonprofit Leadership and Management, 4,* 69–84.

Hardina, D., & Malott, O. (1996). Strategies for the empowerment of low-income consumers on community-based planning boards. *Journal of Progressive Human Services, 7*(2), 43–61.

Haynes, K., & Mickelson, J. (1991). *Affecting change: Social workers in the political arena.* New York: Longman.

Heffernan, J. (1979). *Introduction to social welfare policy.* Itasca, IL: Peacock.

Hrebenar, R. J. (1997). *Interest group politics in America* (3d ed.). Armonk, NY: M. E. Sharpe.

Jansson, B. (1999). *Becoming an effective policy advocate.* Pacific Grove, CA: Brooks/Cole.

Jasper, J., & Poulsen, J. (1995). Recruiting strangers and friends: Moral shocks and social networks in animal rights and anti-nuclear protests. *Social Problems, 42,* 493–513.

Kahn, S. (1991). *Organizing.* Silver Springs, MD: National Association of Social Workers.

Kahn, S. (1997). Leadership: Realizing concepts through creative process. *Journal of Community Practice, 4*(1), 109–36.

Lindblom, C. (1959). The science of muddling through. *Public Administration Review, 19,* 79–88.

Lipsky, M. (1980). *Street-level bureaucracy.* New York: Russell Sage Foundation.

Meenaghan, T., Washington, R., & Ryan, R. (1982). Inferring community power. *Macro practice in the human services* (pp. 116–36). New York: Free Press.

Mills, C. W. (1956). *The power elite.* New York: Oxford University Press.

Mizrahi, T., & Rosenthal, B. (1993). Managing dynamic tensions in social change coalitions. In T. Mizrahi & J. Morrison (Eds.), *Community organization and social administration* (pp. 11–40). New York: Haworth.

Mondros, J., & Wilson, S. (1994). *Organizing for power and empowerment.* New York: Columbia University Press.

Panitch, L. (1977). *The Canadian state and political power.* Toronto: University of Toronto Press.

Piven, F. F., & Cloward, R. (1971). *Regulating the poor.* New York: Pantheon.

Piven, F. F., & Cloward, R. (1977). *Why Americans don't vote.* New York: Pantheon.

Piven, F. F., & Cloward, R. (1979). *Poor people's movements: Why they succeed, how they fail.* New York: Vintage.

Roberts-DeGennaro, M. (1997). Conceptual frameworks of coalitions in an organizational context. *Journal of Community Practice, 4*(1), 91–107.

Rothman, J. (1995). Approaches to community intervention. In F. Cox, J. Erlich, J. Rothman, & J. Tropman (Eds.), *Strategies of community organization* (5th ed., pp. 26–63). Itasca, IL: F. E. Peacock.

Swank, E., & Clapp, J. (1999). Some methodological concerns when estimating the size of organizing activities. *Journal of Community Practice, 6*(3), 49–69.

U.S. Commission on Civil Rights. (2001). Status report on probe of election practices in Florida during the 2000 Presidential Campaign [On-line]. Available: http://www.usccr.gov/Vote2000/flstrpt1.

Wandersman, A., Goodman, R., & Butterfoss, F. (1999). Understanding coalitions and how they operate. In M. Minkler (Ed.), *Community organizing and community building for health.* New Brunswick, NJ: Rutgers University Press.

Warren, R. (1971). Types of purposive social change at the community level. In R. Warren (Ed.), *Truth, love, and social change* (pp. 134–49). Chicago: Rand McNally.

Weingarten, H., & Nemon, H. (1999, March). *A practitioner's guide for working with community collaboratives: From collaboration to conflict to collaboration.* Paper presented at the Annual Program Meeting of the Council on Social Work Education, San Francisco.

Yamatani, H., Soska, T., & Baltimore, T. (1999, March). *A study of community collaboratives: Effective, efficient, and holistic service systems.* Paper presented at the Annual Program Meeting of the Council on Social Work Education, San Francisco.

8 Legislative Analysis

■ In chapter 4, we identified lobbying as a component of social action–oriented practice. Assessment is a critical component of the lobbying process. To influence the development of legislation, we must know the content of the legislation, specific procedures established for legislative decision making, and the status of the bill. We must also identify the power resources and vested interests of individual legislators and interest groups that will try to influence the content of the legislation. This chapter describes the role of the community organizer as lobbyist and examines procedures used for legislative analysis. Internet applications for tracking the progress of pending legislation and looking at the content and potential impacts of legislation are described. This chapter also includes a discussion of the use of E-mail and other Internet applications for contacting legislators and organizing lobbying campaigns.

Community Organizers as Lobbyists

Lobbying is the process through which individuals and interest groups attempt to persuade elected officials and other policy makers to adopt the group's or individual's position on the issues. Community organizers may lobby as part of their duties as frontline or supervisory personnel in agencies, as executive directors or other management staff, as staff members in advocacy organizations or interest groups, or as volunteers in social movement organizations (Ezell, 1991; Haynes & Mickelson, 1991; Pawlak & Flynn, 1990).

Lobbying Activities

Community organizers often contact legislators or legislative staff to oppose or support specific pieces of legislation. They can also contact legislators to maintain or increase fiscal resources for specific programs that can benefit client groups or the agency that employs them. Methods for influencing legislators on issues include letters, phone calls, and personal visits to the legislator's office. Lobbyists also use fax machines and E-mail to contact legislators. Interest groups can ask members to fax their legislators, make phone calls, or send E-mail on specific days so that legislative staff will record or otherwise take note of the high volume of messages on the specific issue of concern.

Many groups ask members to fill in personal information on preprinted postcards or letters. Individuals, social workers, and interest groups may also set up meetings with legislators at local constituency offices or in state capitols. Lobbyists also meet with governors, members of Congress, state and federal cabinet secretaries, and, in some instances, the president. In most cases, meetings with legislators must be set up in advance. Unless the lobbyist has established a good working relationship with a legislator, the meeting may be brief due to constraints on the legislator's time (Children's Defense Fund, 1991).

Restrictions on Lobbying

Currently, nonprofit organizations are subject to some restrictions on the funds they spend for lobbying activities. Currently, any organization that has received 501(c)(3) status from the U.S. Internal Revenue Service is restricted to spending up to 20 percent of any funds raised on lobbying activities (Chisholm, 1987). An additional 25 percent of the permitted lobbying amount may be spent on grassroots lobbying (communications oriented toward voter education that make recommendations among candidates). During the early 1980s, President Reagan issued an executive order, still in effect, that prevents nonprofits that receive federal funds from lobbying the federal government with those funds (Independent Sector, 1984).

Some organizations are incorporated explicitly for lobbying purposes under section 501(c)(4) of the tax code. Although these organizations cannot, in most situations, provide money to political candidates, they often form political action committees (PACs). Under federal law, PACs are permitted to contribute money to individual candidates and political parties. Often we

Analyzing Legislative Content and Processes

Lee Vang has been hired to work for a newly incorporated advocacy organization, Humans Against Handguns (HAH). State assemblywoman Muriel Jackson has called the organization to request its support for legislation requiring mandatory safety locks on all privately owned handguns. The executive director of HAH has asked Lee to research the following issues:

1. Is the content of the legislation in keeping with HAH's views on handguns?
2. Have other states passed similar laws?
3. How do experts on gun safety perceive this law?
4. Is there research evidence that suggests this law will be effective?
5. Is this legislation likely to receive support in the state senate and state assembly?
6. Which legislators have supported similar legislation? Who has opposed it?
7. Is the governor likely to sign this legislation or veto it?
8. At what point in the legislative process should HAH be prepared to contact legislators or provide testimony at legislative hearings?
9. How can HAH best use its resources to lobby for this legislation?

can trace lobbying activities by examining donations made by interest group–affiliated PACs to individual candidates (Gross, 1999). Donations made by people who are members of specific groups also allow us to link the vested interests of professional associations and industry-affiliated PACs to money contributions to candidates. We can also link contributions to the votes of those politicians who have received money from these donors.

Analyzing Legislation

All bills move through a set of predetermined legislative procedures. Because there are numerous stages in the process, many opportunities exist for advocates to lobby for legislation. In some instances, interest groups may have a role in actually drafting the legislation. In other situations, advocates who have not been successful in blocking legislative approval may lobby to keep the chief executive (president or governor) from signing the bill into law.

If the lobbyist knows where a bill stands in the legislative process, he or she can decide which decision makers to pressure for changes in the content of the bill. If, for example, a legislator is thinking about introducing legislation that will affect welfare recipients, the lobbyist can schedule a meeting with that legislator and offer to help draft the bill. If a state assembly committee is reviewing the bill, the lobbyist can try to be placed on the committee's agenda to provide public testimony on that legislation. To determine how best to influence decision making related to specific pieces of legislation, it is important for lobbyists to be familiar with the following information:

- The legislative procedures that guide the decision-making process
- The stage of the legislative process that the bill has reached
- The sponsor of the bill
- The cosponsors and other legislative supporters
- The legislative committees that will discuss the bill; the chairpersons of these committees
- The legislators opposed to the legislation
- How legislators have voted in the past on similar issues
- Interest groups that support the bill as well as interest groups opposed to the bill
- The vested interests of those interest groups that are likely to influence the legislative process
- Alliances between legislators and members of the interest groups.
- The vested interests of individual legislators, especially those who are in a position to control whether legislation is scheduled for a vote or a committee hearing.
- Legislative staff members who can serve as links between a lobbyist and the legislator.

Most of this information is available from legislative sources or from interest groups. Key decision makers may be available for discussions about the legislation and its implications. Vested interests of those groups involved in lobbying for the issue are usually explicit. Many of these groups publish their own analyses of the legislation. Information about the vested interests of individual politicians may be more difficult to find. It can often be inferred, however, through available information about the content of the legislation, by analyzing the campaign donations made to the legislator, or by examining public information about the politician (family connections, friends, social networks, past employment, and political allies). Most politicians are motivated by the need to acquire votes and campaign donations for reelection (Jansson, 1999; Richan, 1996). Good publicity or media attention can also motivate legislators to take action.

Conducting Formal Assessments of Legislative Content and Processes

In addition to acquiring basic information needed for effective lobbying, a legislative analyst may also wish to conduct formal assessments in relation to pending legislation. Such assessments are used to inform the public or to gain insight into how legislation is formulated (Dye, 1998; Gil, 1998).

There are two primary types of legislative analysis:

1. Content analysis: The analyst must assess the content of a piece of legislation. Is it consistent with the goals of the lobbyist or the lobbyist's employer?
2. Process analysis: The analyst must examine the legislative process. How is a legislator likely to vote? Is the legislation likely to be approved? Who is likely to support or oppose it?

Content Analysis

Analysts conduct content analysis before government policies and legislation are actually implemented. While most government policies are derived

---

Lobbying with Sister Julia

The Support our Families Coalition was concerned about reports that Temporary Assistance to Needy Families (TANF) benefits were to be cut. The governor had asked the state legislature to approve a 5 percent cutback for all welfare families. The state assembly was about to vote on this budget recommendation. The staff organizer for the coalition, Michelle Moseley, was able to schedule a meeting with the Speaker of the General Assembly, Jeff Jones, just prior to the vote. This meeting was important. The Speaker could influence the votes of other assembly members, especially his fellow party members.

Most of the coalition board members, including social service agency directors and a number of welfare recipients, were scheduled to attend. One of the board members, Sister Julia, had had a previous relationship with Speaker Jones. She was one of his teachers in elementary school and had remained in contact with him. A number of newspaper reporters and television stations planned to cover the meeting.

The coalition had collected over 10,000 signatures on a petition in opposition to the cuts and planned to present the petition to the Speaker. The Speaker had been lobbied heavily by the governor to support the cuts. The public also seemed to support them. Editorials in major newspapers across the state were also in support of the governor's budget recommendations. However, newspaper, TV, and radio coverage portrayed the cuts as harmful to poor families, especially as Christmas approached.

What were the coalition's power resources?

What were the Speaker's power resources?

How could the coalition maximize its power resources? Is it likely that it was able to influence the Speaker's vote?

---

from legislation, some policies are set by the executive branch (president, governor, or mayor), are regulations implemented by government bureaucracies, or are simply proposals for new legislation made by interest groups. Content analysis can be used to prepare testimony for legislative hearings or position papers on the issue in question. The goals of a particular piece of legislation and the impact it may have on beneficiaries or other groups affected by those policies are examined. Ideally, policy or legislative analysis is conducted based on the assumption that policies are made rationally, using the problem-solving model. Legislative analysts identify the problem, conduct an assessment, identify policy goals, select the most appropriate goals, implement an intervention, and then evaluate the effectiveness of the intervention (Haynes & Mickelson, 1991). Recommendations among various policy or legislative options are, ideally, to be made objectively and without bias, based on the information available (DiNitto, 1991). Few policies, however, are actually based on rational choices. It is more likely that policies are made through the political process. Seldom is there sufficient time or resources to review all options. Decision makers are influenced by their values and vested interest in the issue.

Legislative options differ substantially by political ideology (Gil, 1998; Dunn, 1981). Liberals typically use such values as adequacy and equality to evaluate policies, tending to favor programs that focus on the adequacy of benefits or the distribution of resources to low- or moderate-income voters (Gilbert & Terrell, 1998). Conservatives tend to favor values such as efficiency and personal responsibility. Because most policies typically result from compromises among a number of interest groups in society, any one piece of legislation or policy may express conflicting values (Lipsky, 1980).

Analysts typically construct models to examine the content of policies. The development of the model requires the analyst to select four or five attributes or values and then to examine the legislation in terms of whether it upholds these values. Social workers typically use policy values expressed in the National Association of Social Workers (NASW) code of ethics to evaluate policies: client self-determination, individualization, identity, confidentiality, and social justice (Flynn, 1992).

Social justice is a value of special concern to community organizers. It is related to the distributional effects of a policy (Gil, 1998). As specified in the NASW code of ethics, social workers have a responsibility to make sure that all people, especially members of the oppressed groups, have access to resources (see chapter 2). We determine if a policy supports social justice by looking at which societal groups will benefit as a consequence of the policy and which groups will lose resources or status (Gilbert & Terrell, 1998). Few policies provide new benefits, money, tax relief, or increased social status to one social group without taking these resources from other groups (Pampel, 1994). These groups typically include service beneficiaries, the government, and taxpayers.

Even if a policy creates no real winners or losers, it can have differing effects on different segments of the population (children, the elderly, people with disabilities) or ethnic groups. For example, we know that African American children remain in foster care for longer periods than children from other ethnic groups (Courtney et al., 1996). Characteristics of the population therefore interact with the policy in a manner that creates unique effects.

To examine the content of policies, the analyst must choose a policy model—one developed by another policy analyst, or one constructed using values that are important to the analyst or the organization that employs him or her. The next step in a content analysis is applying the model to the legislation of interest. The analyst also uses these value criteria to assess alternatives to the legislation and to choose the most appropriate policy option based on the criteria in the model (DiNitto, 1991).

Analyzing Legislative Processes

There are three primary approaches to analyzing legislative processes:

1. A historical study (who did what and how the decision was influenced)
2. A present-day study of interaction among interest groups
3. A study of institutional processes that affect the decision making

When we examine groups involved in the decision-making process, we are primarily concerned with how they use their power and influence to gain the policy changes they want (Flynn, 1992; Heffernan, 1979). Both historical and interest group analysis focuses mainly on the interest groups involved in the decision-making process, the role of political leaders and their positions on the issues, and the use of strategies and tactics to influence outcomes (see chapter 10). Important for this type of analysis is identification of power resources associated with proponents and opponents of the change (Jansson, 1999). Analysis can also focus on the process of agenda setting—the activities that were necessary to make decision makers and the public aware of the issue (Kingdon, 1984). Historical, cultural, social, and economic trends also contribute to whether the issue comes to the public's attention and is successfully addressed through the legislative process (Gil, 1998).

When we examine institutional structures, we are primarily concerned with the "rules of the game," or government-established procedures that interest groups can use to bargain, negotiate, or contest changes in policy (Warren, 1971). Such rules include those established for political campaigns or the introduction, amendment, and approval of bills as they move through the legislature (Haynes & Mickelson, 1991). Many studies of policy processes include an assessment of both institutional procedures and interest group influence.

We also need to know how the public currently views the problem or policy and the values and preferences that will guide the final policy decision (Gil, 1998). Is the public concerned about adopting policies that will reinforce personal responsibility for dealing with problems, or do they prefer policies intended to protect vulnerable members of society? For example, they could support federal regulations to prevent children from smoking. Alternatively, public sentiment could indicate a preference for a reduction in government regulation of smoking. Also important are the potential fiscal implications of a policy as well as the public's perception of fiscal impact. For example, are taxpayers more concerned about reducing the federal budget deficit, or would they pay more taxes to reduce class sizes in elementary schools?

Techniques used for conducting a process analysis of legislative decision making may include interviews with participants in the process as well as secondary accounts or descriptions of the process written by reporters or political analysts. Other sources of information can include primary documents such as newspaper descriptions of legislative processes, videotapes of TV news programs or legislative hearings, legislative hearing or debate transcripts, legislative documentation of legislative votes (roll call), and personal notes or diaries about the proceedings written by the participants.

A thorough process analysis will address most, if not all, of the following factors:

1. How does the public become aware of the problem or issue the legislation addresses?
2. What institutional processes or rules are used to facilitate the legislative process?
3. Who sponsored a particular piece of legislation or proposed a policy?
4. Who are the individuals, interest groups, and legislators who support this legislation? Who are their allies and what power do these groups have to influence the legislation?
5. Who opposes the legislation? What power do they have to prevent adoption of the legislation? (Include both interest groups and legislators in your analysis.)
6. Who provides funds to the individuals, groups, and legislators who support or oppose the legislation?
7. What are the values and ideologies of the interest groups and legislators involved in the legislative process?
8. How do these values influence the groups' or legislators' positions on the issue and their ability to negotiate or bargain with opposing individuals or groups?
9. What strategies or tactics do the various groups and legislators use to influence the decision-making process?
10. What environmental factors (historical, economic, social, and cultural influences) have influenced the decision making?

11. Who makes the final decision? Is it made by a small group with decision-making authority or through bargaining and negotiation among a variety of individuals and interest groups?
12. Was the decision made cooperatively or achieved through conflict?
13. Who are the winners and losers in the policy process? Who benefits most from the new policy? Who stands to lose status or resources because of the new policy?

Using the Internet to Find Information about Legislative Content

The Internet provides a huge variety of information about legislation. You can obtain information directly from the legislator's own Web site, from official legislative sites maintained by state governments, and from interest groups. Often interest groups conduct their own analyses of the impact of proposed legislation and post them on the Web.

Sources Maintained by Individual Legislators

Some legislators have their own Web sites that offer information about that legislator and specific pieces of legislation he or she supports. Legislators often use their Web pages to identify their position on the issues. Such descriptions on the Web use value-laden terms to describe why that legislator has taken such a position. For example, the Web sites of Democratic congresswoman Carolyn McCarthy and Republican congressman Bob Barr during the summer of 1999 contained very different proposals for dealing with handgun violence. Sometimes legislators use these sites explicitly to garner public support for a specific piece of pending legislation or to "sell" legislators facing reelection to likely voters (see figures 8.1 and 8.2).[1]

Official Government Sources

Legislation that has been passed by Congress and signed by the president can be found in the U.S. legal code. Access to the U.S. code is available on the Web through a number of sources. Legislation that is moving through Congress is also available on the World Wide Web. Web search procedures allow you to hunt for a piece of legislation using the bill number, the session of Congress in which the bill was introduced, the bill sponsor, or the topic area. Implementation of legislation that is broad and ambiguous requires that federal departments, such as the departments of Health and Human Services (HHS) or Housing and Human Development, develop regulations that specify how the legislation is to be implemented. For example, HHS determines food stamp eligibility requirements and benefit levels that "fit" the intent of legislation approved by Congress. These regulations are published in the *Federal Register* (http://www.access.gpo.gov). Federal law re-

Figure 8.1.   Legislative Web page: Republican Congressman.

Congressman Bob Barr

Text
Only
Version

Seventh District of Georgia
Securing America's Future

Youth Violence Legislation - Both the House and Senate have recently passed youth violence legislation; which is now in conference to reconcile differences between the two bills. I have been selected to serve on that conference and will work to ensure the final bill does not infringe on the rights of law abiding citizens, and focuses instead on the real issues, such as enforcement of existing laws, and strengthening America's ability to restore its moral foundation.

On June 30, 1999 I was named to Speaker Hastert's Special Youth Violence Panel. The panel has been charged with developing recommendations on initiatives to curb youth violence. I am hopeful this panel will develop longer-term solutions to curb youth violence. I believe we ought to look at: violence in the media and in the movies, the prevalence of mood altering drugs by students, federal laws that may tie the hands of school administrators to properly discipline students and enforce codes of conduct, the lack of counselors and school psychologists, parents not stopping kids from behavior that clearly indicates a predisposition to violence, laws not being enforced or enforced inconsistently and the message that sends to our kids, and other aspects of this terrible problem afflicting our society.

Only by addressing this problem comprehensively and responsibly will we do justice to our overall goal of providing security for our children, while respecting the civil rights of all our citizens, and within the bounds of our federalist form of government, in which primary power to address problems resides with the state not the federal government.

back to top

Lawsuits Against Gun Manufacturers - In the wake of the massive tobacco lawsuits, about 40 law firms around the country are teaming up with big city mayors to sue gun manufacturers for the "costs" of responding to shootings and treating gunshot victims. They are not arguing that firearms are manufactured improperly, but that gun companies should be held liable when their fully legal and non-defective product is used by a criminal. This is like holding car manufacturers responsible for homicides committed by drunken drivers, or suing the makers of Swiss Army Knives on behalf of stabbing victims. Such lawsuits spell disaster for product manufacturers in our country. If these suits are allowed to become legal precedent, the cost of products would rise, whole sectors of our economy may be crippled, and numerous Americans could find themselves jobless.

On March 9, 1999, I introduced the **Firearms Heritage Protection Act, H.R.1032**. This legislation, which has the support already of several dozen co-sponsors from both parties, will stop such abusive, frivolous lawsuits against gun manufacturers in both federal and state courts by barring claims for damages from the criminal misuse of such products. It does not in any way affect lawsuits against manufacturers for *defective* firearms or ammunition, or for transferring a firearm to a person who they know will use it in the commission of a crime.

On October 7, 1999, Ohio State Judge Robert Ruehlman dismissed a lawsuit brought by the City of Cincinnati against gun manufacturers, finding the lawsuit vague and unsupported by any legal precedent. His decision marks the first dismissal of the lawsuits filed by cities, states, and trial lawyers against gun manufacturers. None of the other lawsuits have been decided. This decision vindicates the foundational legal principle that only legislatures, not the courts, can pass laws regulating the distribution and sale of consumer products.

back to top

Main Page II Biography II Seventh District Issues II Constituent ServicesII Legislation
IITown Hall Schedule II District InformationII Media Information II National Issues
Interesting Web Sites II Contact Congressman Barr II Search this Site II Send a Letter to the Editor

quires that proposed regulations be published in the *Federal Register* for public comment (written comments must be received within specific periods after publication). Final regulations are also published in the *Federal Register.* The *Congressional Record* (http://thomas.loc.gov/) is a written recording, organized by bill number and topic area, of all floor debates that take place on legislative issues. The *Congressional Quarterly* (http://www.cq.com/) publishes analyses of issues under debate in Congress.

Most states post information on pending legislation on their Web sites.

Figure 8.2.　Congressional Web page: Democratic Congresswoman.

Congresswoman
Carolyn McCarthy
━━━━━ 4th District of New York ━━━

Home Page
Biography
Statements
Press Releases
Photo Gallery
Articles

Write Rep.
McCarthy

Order Flags
Tour Tickets
Order a Bill

Children's Gun Violence Prevention Act of 1999
Bill Description

The Children's Gun Violence Prevention Act, sponsored by Representative Carolyn McCarthy (NY-04), Representative Marge Roukema (NJ-05), Representative John Porter (IL-10) and Senator Edward Kennedy (MA), is designed to prevent children from gaining access to guns, thereby preventing shootings in America's schools. Keeping guns out of the hands of children requires an increased commitment to responsibility, education and safety.

RESPONSIBILITY: The guns children use to shoot other children all start out in the hands of adults. The bipartisan Children Gun Violence Prevention Act of 1998 shuts down the sources of guns for kids by placing increased responsibility on parents and gun dealers. Parents whose children gain access to improperly stored guns in the home will risk facing criminal penalties. Gun dealers will also have to take greater responsibility for keeping weapons out of the hands of children or risk losing their federal firearms license.

EDUCATION: The best way to keep our schools safe is to utilize the hands-on experience of teachers, parents and law enforcement. The McCarthy/Roukema/Porter/ Kennedy bill provides funding for grants to assist successful anti-gun violence programs designed by schools working with local law enforcement, parent-teacher organizations, and community based organizations.

SAFETY: When it comes to children, the safest gun is one that a kid cannot use. The McCarthy/Roukema/Porter/Kennedy bill will require gun manufacturers to produce guns with improved safety features, such as increase trigger resistance standards, child safety locks, manual safeties, and magazine disconnect safeties. The Children's Gun Violence Prevention Act will also authorize the Consumer Product Safety Commission to study the latest and most effective technological advances for making firearms childproof.

BUILDING ON WHAT WORKS AND PROVIDING DATA FOR LAW ENFORCEMENT

The McCarthy/Roukema/Porter/Kennedy bill expands the Youth Crime Gun Interdiction Initiative (YCGII). This cooperative local/state/federal gun tracing program has already helped identify and eliminate illegal sources of guns used in juvenile crime in 27 communities across the country. The Children's Gun Violence Act provides funding for the gun tracing efforts of local law enforcement and will allow more communities to participate in the YCGII.

Finally, the bipartisan Children's Gun Violence Prevention Act will provide policy makers and law enforcement critical children's gun injury data. The bill establishes a youth firearms injury surveillance program at the Centers for Disease Control. The injury surveillance program will provide Congress and the American people fair and accurate information on the costs of gun injuries and deaths. The injury surveillance program will also provide law enforcement with strategic information on the type of weapons used to shoot children and the relationship of the victim and perpetrator.

Full Text of the Bill
Fact Sheet

This information includes the name of the bill sponsor and the last place in the legislative process that action was taken on the bill—whether it was amended, passed, approved by the governor, or filed by the secretary of state. Bills passed by the state assembly and the state senate and signed by the governor are entered into the state legal code.

Analyses by Interest Groups

Many interest groups, such as the Children's Defense Fund, NASW, and the Center for Budget and Policy Priorities, publish regular updates about the status of pending legislation and the effects of the various provisions of specific pieces of legislation. Two Web sites, the Electronic Policy Network (EPN) (http://epn.org) and HandsNet (http://www.handsnet.org), provide links to a number of policy institutes and advocacy organizations that publish regular analyses of federal legislation. EPN contains links to a number of research and policy institutes, including the Center for Budget and Policy Priorities and the Center for Law and Social Policy. HandsNet was founded by the Apple Computer Corporation to assist antihunger organizations with networking, resource sharing, and lobbying activities. HandsNet includes links to a number of welfare and child advocacy groups, including the Child Welfare League of American and the Children's Defense Fund. The NASW Web site also features legislative bulletins on issues of concern to social workers.

Interest groups such as state chapters of NASW and the League of Women Voters also try to influence policies and issue regular reports about the status of legislation. State chapters of other national advocacy organizations also disseminate legislative updates.

Using the Internet to Find Information about Legislative Processes

Newspaper accounts are a great source of information about day-to-day events that influence the legislative process. A variety of national news organizations (all major TV networks, the *New York Times*, the *Washington Post*, the *Chicago Tribune*, and the *Los Angeles Times*) maintain Web sites with information about national politics. Local newspapers also provide extensive coverage of state and local politics. These sites are updated daily.

Interest groups such as the Children's Defense Fund and the Center on Budget and Policy Priorities often post on their Web sites analyses of various pieces of legislation or specific provisions of legislation. Some of these postings coincide with debates in Congress or negotiations between legislators in the House and Senate or between Congress and the White House as they attempt to find a compromise on the wording in the final bill. Often interest group Web sites give specific instructions for individuals wishing to lobby for or against the legislation as it is developed (e.g., E-mail the president, write your local congressional representative, fax the House Majority leader). State chapters of national interest groups, such as NASW, also post information about legislation on the Web. Some of these organizations also post messages urging members to take action in support of or in opposition to specific pieces of legislation.

It is also possible to conduct research on the voting patterns of legislators. *Roll Call* (http://www.rollcall.com/)magazine publishes information about how federal legislators vote on specific bills. Some interest groups also compile legislative "scorecards" that list key votes that uphold the organization's values and mission. These groups post the scorecards on their Web sites; part of the purpose is to inform the public about the voting records of candidates for reelection. Project Vote Smart, the Center for Responsive Politics, and Common Cause maintain databases that contain the scorecards published by a variety of organizations. Organizers can use this information to assess how individual members of Congress and the Senate are likely to vote on similar issues. State advocacy organizations also publish similar scorecards for state legislators on their Web sites.

The Internet can also help you find out whether interest groups have used their political action committees to donate money to candidates for federal, state, and local offices. Donations to candidates may also be made by individuals who are members of interest groups. PACs are required to file regular reports to the Federal Election Commission (FEC). All candidates for federal office file reports on campaign donations (names and business affiliations of donors) with the FEC (see chapter 9 for conducting research on campaign donations).

Candidates for state and local office are also required to file reports on donations with state and local agencies. Many states now require that this information be made easily available to citizens. Consequently, much of it is available on state Web sites. States that put legislative propositions to electoral votes also generally allow interest groups to pay for media and get-out-the-vote campaigns operated in support of or opposition to these referenda (Hrebenar, 1997).[2] Generally, these donations must also be reported to state agencies and may be available on the state's Web site.

Using the Internet to Lobby Decision Makers

The Internet has also proved to be a useful tool for contacting legislators. However, though it increases accessibility for those individuals and organizations lucky enough to have computers with Internet connections, this approach may not be as effective as personal contact or handwritten letters. Addresses, phone numbers, and E-mail addresses for many state and federal legislators are published on federal and state Web sites. Many public officials have procedures in place to respond to E-mail correspondence and count total responses on behalf of and against legislative proposals. As noted earlier, many advocacy organizations post lobbying information and sample letters on their own Web sites. As legislation moves through Congress or state assemblies, the public can check the status of a particular bill and lobby at significant points in the legislative process.

Many organizations also use LISTSERVs, devices that permit E-mail messages to be sent simultaneously to all people on a mailing list. Some organizations will send out weekly E-mails to all members, urging them to lobby on behalf of pending issues. Some organizations send out LISTSERV messages periodically when an issue of concern to the organization requires urgent attention. The process makes it easy for individuals to monitor the legislative process and respond by letter to their elected representatives. However, it is especially convenient for staff lobbyists employed in advocacy organizations across the country. Simply logging onto E-mail each morning can generate legislative updates from a variety of Washington, D.C.–based organizations that regularly monitor the status of new and pending legislation. In addition, the use of LISTSERVs allows the organization to reach an unlimited number of people in a short period at almost no expense.[3]

Some lobbying groups have used E-mail technology to recruit members, fund-raise, and develop powerful organizations. One recent example involves the organization MoveOn. MoveOn was organized by a number of people who were opposed to the impeachment of President Bill Clinton. Initially, MoveOn focused on recruiting people to sign and return an E-mail petition calling for the termination of impeachment proceedings. Organizers used a snowball process for reaching individuals. Those people originally contacted were urged to E-mail a copy of the message to friends and coworkers. MoveOn was successful in generating over one million signatures. Once impeachment proceedings were stopped, MoveOn organizers decided to use their membership base to lobby for gun control and nuclear disarmament (see figure 8.3).

E-mail and the Web have also been used to form virtual organizations (McNutt, 2000). These organizations are often started by individuals who construct Web sites. The existence of the Web site may be sufficient to convince lawmakers and the public that a legally incorporated lobbying organization does exist. Lawmakers may receive messages featuring the organization's logo and Web site address. However, virtual organizations may not have members or funds with which to lobby.

Summary

Legislative analysis is a critical component of community organization practice. It allows the organizer to determine what legislation may be critical for the well-being of his or her constituency group and to determine which legislators should be lobbied. It helps the organizer figure out the final content of a bill. Innovations in technology, such as E-mail and the World Wide Web, allow the organizer to disseminate information about the content of legislation, mobilize constituency group members, and contact legislators. The next chapter will look at additional techniques for examining how politicians are influenced by campaign donations.

■ QUESTIONS FOR CLASS DISCUSSION

1. Identify at least three interpersonal skills associated with clinical practice that could be used to lobby legislators.

Figure 8.3. Legislative alert received by E-mail: MOVEON.

Dear MoveOn Petitioner,

The Senate is poised to reject the Comprehensive Test Ban Treaty, supported by 158 nations and more than 80% of Americans. This would deal a frightening setback to our nation's efforts to prevent nuclear proliferation.

Although supported by a majority of Senators, the treaty needs a 2/3 vote for ratification. Senate leadership has politicized this treaty and seems determined to use it to embarrass the Clinton administration, forcing the treaty to a vote without a proper hearing process.

Key votes to postpone consideration could happen any time in the next few hours. It will be close. Your call could make a difference:

* Contact Majority Leader Trent Lott. In his key leadership position, he needs to hear from the entire country. His contact information is:

The Honorable Trent Lott
D.C Office 202-224-3135
Fax 202-224-2262
State Office 601-965-4644

* Call your Senators directly at
The Honorable Dianne Feinstein
D.C. Office 202-224-3841
State Office 619-231-9712

The Honorable Barbara Boxer
D.C. Office 202-224-3553
State Office 415-403-0100

Once you reach each Senator's office, let the staff member know that you are a constituent (by giving your name and city), and that you support the Comprehensive Test Ban Treaty. If you reach the office after hours, leave a voice-mail message.

low

Express your own personal concerns and ask for a response from your Senator.

FYI, additional information on the Comprehensive Test Ban Treaty is appended below
-Wes Boyd
MoveOn.org

2. Identify at least five elected officials. What values and ideologies are associated with each of these lawmakers? Are their positions on the issues consistent with social work values?

3. Name one lawmaker who has been in the news. What issues has he or she been associated with recently? What could conceivably change this lawmaker's position on these issues?

4. What methods do you think you could use to determine a legislator's vested interest in an issue?

5. How could a social service organization be affected by federal regulations on lobbying?

■ SAMPLE ASSIGNMENTS

1. Draft a letter to the president, a congressional representative, a U.S. senator, a governor, or a state assemblyperson or senator. Send the letter via E-mail.

2. Participate in a campaign to influence a legislator's vote on a piece of legislation of interest to you. Write a two- to five-page paper describing the lobbying campaign, the power resources involved with the individuals and groups associated with the campaign, and the tactics used to influence the legislation. Identify the legislator's personal interest in the issue. Do you think this campaign will be effective? Why or why not?

■ SAMPLE ASSIGNMENT: PROCESS ANALYSIS

Find a piece of pending legislation, either state or federal, on the World Wide Web. Identify the bill's sponsor, the bill number, and any background material (floor debates, government reports, committee reports, or analysis by advocacy groups) on this legislation.

1. Identify interest groups that have an interest in this issue and their power resources.

2. Identify any attempts by interest groups to influence the legislation and the specific tactics used by each group.

3. Identify any proposed amendments to the existing legislation.

4. Give your assessment as to whether the bill will be passed, amended, or tabled.

■ SAMPLE ASSIGNMENT: CONTENT ANALYSIS

Use the following outline to analyze the content of a federal, state, county, or organizational policy.

1. Identify the social problem the legislation addresses.

2. Describe the historical background and environmental factors (economic, political, social, and cultural) that have contributed to the problem the legislation addresses.

3. How have different social, cultural, or economic groups been affected by this problem? Are there identifiable winners and losers?

4. Identify previous legislation used to address this problem. Were these policies successful? Include legislation used in other jurisdictions (cities, counties, states, countries).

5. Describe the goals and objectives of the proposed legislation.

6. Does the proposed legislation represent an incremental or radical change from previous polices?

7. Construct a policy model to evaluate the proposed legislation. Choose four or five values that should be incorporated into the legislation. These values could be a reflection of your own personal values, the NASW code of ethics, or those values included in your organization's mission statement.

8. Describe how the proposed legislation addresses these values.

9. Describe how the legislation contributes to social justice. Are there identifiable winners and losers?

10. Are there feasible alternatives to proposed legislation? If so, describe how these alternatives fit your value criteria. Do they contribute to social justice?

11. What in your opinion is the best legislative option?

12. How politically feasible is the option you've recommended? Is it likely to receive public or legislative support? Why?

Notes

1. Congresswoman McCarthy's vested interest in gun control legislation has been made quite explicit. Her husband was killed and her son seriously wounded by a gunman who shot passengers on a suburban New York commuter train.

2. States that have recently conducted referendums include: Arizona, California, Colorado, North Dakota, Oregon, and Washington.

3. Some organizers will remember the "good old days" when organizations used mass mailings to reach members and raise funds. Printing letters, stuffing and addressing envelopes, and bundling letters by ZIP code for mailing consumed a great deal of staff time. It was also expensive, despite reduced government rates for bulk mailings by nonprofit organizations.

References

Children's Defense Fund (1999). *Congressional workbook: Basic process and issue primer.* Washington, DC: Children's Defense Fund.

Chisholm, L. B. (1987). Exempt organization advocacy. *Indiana Law Journal, 63,* 201–99.

Courtney, M., Barth, R., Berrick, J. D., Brooks, D., Needell, B., & Park, L. (1996). Race and child welfare services: Past research and future directions. *Child Welfare*, 75, 99–133.

DiNitto, D. (1991). *Social welfare politics and public policy* (3d ed.). Englewood Cliffs, NJ: Prentice-Hall.

Dunn, W. (1981). *Policy analysis: An introduction.* Englewood Cliffs, NJ: Prentice-Hall.

Dye, T. (1998). *Understanding public policy* (9th ed.). Saddle River, NJ: Prentice-Hall.

Ezell, M. (1991). Administrators as advocates. *Administration in Social Work*, 15 (3), 1–18.

Flynn, J. (1992). *Social agency policy* (2d ed.). Chicago: Nelson-Hall.

Gil, D. (1998). *Confronting injustice and oppression.* New York: Columbia University Press.

Gilbert, N., & Terrell, P. (1998). *Dimensions of social welfare policy* (4th ed.). Boston: Allyn & Bacon.

Gross, K. (1999). *Lobbying and the law* [On-line]. Available: http://www.opensecret.org/regulation/kgross.htm.

Haynes, K., & Mickelson, J. (1991). *Affecting change: social workers in the political arena.* New York: Longman.

Heffernan, J. (1979). *Introduction to social welfare policy.* Itasca, IL: Peacock.

Hrebenar, R. J. (1997). *Interest group politics in America* (3d ed.). Armonk, NY: M. E. Sharpe.

Independent Sector (1984). *Advocacy is sometimes an agency's best service.* Washington, DC: Independent Sector.

Jansson, B. (1999). *Becoming an effective policy advocate.* Pacific Grove, CA: Brooks/Cole.

Kingdon, J. (1984). Agendas, alternatives, and public policies. Boston: Little Brown.

Lipsky, M. (1980). *Street-level bureaucracy.* New York: Russell Sage Foundation.

McNutt, J. (2000). Organizing cyberspace: Strategies for teaching about community practice and technology. *Journal of Community Practice*, 7(1), 95–109.

Pampel, F. (1994). Population aging, class context, and age inequality in public spending. *American Journal of Sociology*, 100, 153–95.

Pawlak, E., & Flynn, J. (1990). Executive directors' political activities. *Social Work*, 35, 307–12.

Richan, W. (1996). *Lobbying for social change.* New York: Haworth.

Warren, R. (1971). Types of purposive social change at the community level. In R. Warren (Ed.), *Truth, love, and social change* (pp. 134–49). Chicago: Rand McNally.

Web Resources

Code of Federal Regulations—http://www.access.gpo.gov/nara/cfr/
Congressional Quarterly—http://www.cq.com/
Congressional Budget Office—http://www.cbo.gov/
Federal Agencies—http://www.lib.lsu.edu/gov/fedgov.html
Federal Register—http://www.access.gpo.gov/
General Accounting Office—http://www.gao.gov/
Library of Congress—http://lcWeb.loc.gov/

Office of Management and Budget—http://www.whitehouse.gov/OMB

Roll Call magazine—http://www.rollcall.com/

Thomas, Legislative Information—http://thomas.loc.gov/ (includes links to the *Congressional Record*, bill status and summaries, roll call votes, public laws, and the status of appropriation bills)

Contacting Elected Officials

U.S. House of Representatives—http://www.house.gov/

U.S. Senate—http://www.senate.gov/

White House—http://www.whitehouse.gov/

Federal Agencies

Census Bureau—http://www.census.gov

Department of Education—http://www.ed.gov

Department of Health and Human Services—http://www.os.dhhs.gov

Department of Housing and Urban Development—http://www.hud.gov/

Federal Statistics—http://www.fedstats.gov

Food, Nutrition, & Consumer Services (USDA)—http://www.fns.usda.gov/

State and Local Government

National Governors Association—http://www.nga.org
(includes links to state Web pages)

State and Local Government on the Net—http://www.statelocal.gov/

U.S. Conference of Mayors—http://www.usmayors.org/uscm/home.asp

Legislative Information: Interest Groups

American Public Health Association—http://www.apha.org

American Association for Retired Persons—http://www.aarp.org

Children's Defense Fund—http://www.childrensdefense.org

Children NOW—http://www.childrennow.org

Child Welfare League of America—http://www.cwla.org

Electronic Policy Network—http://epn.org/ (includes links to a number of policy research organizations including the Center for Budget and Policy Priorities, the Center for Law and Social Policy, Families USA, OMB Watch, and numerous other private policy institutes, university policy research centers, and private foundations.

Food Research Action Center—http://www.frac.org/

Gray Panthers—http://www.graypanthers.org

Greenpeace—http://www.greenpeace.org

HandsNet—http://www.handsnet.org/

League of Women Voters—http://www.lwv.org

National Alliance for the Mentally Ill—http://www.nami.org

National Coalition for the Homeless—http://www.nationalhomless.org

National Gay and Lesbian Task Force—http://www.nglt.org/

National Organization of Women—http://www.feminist.org

Planned Parenthood—http://www.plannedparenthood.org

Social Work Advocacy and Policy Issues

Influencing Social Policy—http://www.statepolicy.org

National Association of Social Workers—http://naswdc.org/

Note: This is not a comprehensive list. For membership organizations such as NASW and the League of Women Voters, also see Web sites maintained by state chapters.

9 Politics

Analyzing Processes and Outcomes

■ Participation in electoral politics is a type of social work intervention associated with the social action model of community practice (Fisher, 1995; Haynes & Mickelson, 1991; Mahaffey & Hanks, 1982; Rose, 1999). Electoral work requires analytical skills to identify the power resources needed to elect candidates to office. Such analysis helps us plan election campaigns and predict likely outcomes. In this chapter we describe the roles and responsibilities of social workers who work in political campaigns and discuss the importance of community organization practice in linking voters to the electoral process. This chapter also provides a detailed description of the research skills needed to analyze political processes and predict the likely outcome of local, state, and national elections. Internet resources that can be used to examine the way campaigns are conducted and financed are identified.

When Are Social Workers Likely to Engage in Politics?

A number of studies (Ezell, 1991; Hardina, 1995; Mary, Ellano, & Newell, 1993; Pawlak & Flynn, 1990; Reeser & Epstein, 1990) have found that macro practitioners (administrators and community organizers) are much more likely to be involved in election campaigns than micro practitioners (social workers who provide clinical services to individuals, groups, and families). Organizers and administrators are likely to engage in politics in order to influence legislative decision making. Administrators must lobby for funds for their organizations; community organizers often seek to obtain legislative approval or block legislation to facilitate social change efforts.

Reeser and Epstein (1990) surveyed a random sample of National Association of Social Workers (NASW) members in 1984. They asked these

---

Political Analysis and the Community Organizer

Josefina Martinez works for the Immigration Reform Now Coalition, incorporated as a 501(c)(4) social welfare lobbying organization. The coalition has organized opposition to new legislation that allows farmers to bring in "guest workers" from Mexico for farm labor. These workers would be allowed to work for only one employer; most of the wages earned would be "banked" for the worker and released only when the worker returns to Mexico. The incumbent congressman, Joe Stanton, has announced he will support this legislation. The coalition opposes the guest worker bill, believing that it will lead to the exploitation of farmworkers.

Josefina's boss has asked her to determine the likelihood that Representative Stanton, a Republican, will be reelected to Congress in a district that traditionally votes Democratic. In 1996, the voters elected Representative Stanton by a 60 percent to 40 percent margin. District voters also preferred Republican Bob Dole to President Clinton by a 52 percent to 48 percent margin. In the next election, voting preferences in the congressional district are expected to benefit Democratic candidates. Latino voter registration in the district has increased by almost 20 percent during the last five years.

Josefina's boss wants to know if his organization should continue to lobby Congressman Stanton for changes in the immigration legislation. If Congressman Stanton's chances for reelection are good, this may be the coalition's best option for influencing the legislation. The coalition may be able to persuade the congressman that he will obtain the voter support he needs to win the election if he votes against the legislation. Alternatively, if Congressman Stanton's chances for reelection are not good, the coalition may wait until after the election to lobby the winner. The coalition may also choose to engage in voter education activities, releasing information to voters about the position of both candidates on immigration issues. Although the coalition, as a 501(c)(4) organization, is prohibited by federal law from making campaign contributions, individual members of the coalition may wish to support a pro-immigrant candidate or encourage someone with those views to run for the office.

How can Josefina find information about the likely outcome of the election? What data should she obtain?

social workers whether they had engaged in the following political activities during the past year: contributed money to a political campaign, signed letters or petitions supporting a candidate, or attended public rallies or meetings. Eighty-four percent of their respondents reported involvement in two or more of these activities. Domanski (1998) surveyed members of the Society of Social Work Administrators and Health Care of the American Hospital Association. She found that although over 95 percent of respondents voted, only 43 percent were involved in campaign activities (worked for a candidate, had membership in a political party, or attended meetings with members of Congress). Hardina (1995) found a slightly higher level of political involvement (68 percent) among Canadian social workers.

These studies make a strong argument that social workers are more likely to vote than the public at large. Typical voter participation rates for the population at large range from 30 to 60 percent. In the 1998 congressional races, only 36 percent of registered voters participated (Neal & Morin, 1998). Verba, Schlozman, and Brady (1997) estimate that less than 25 percent of all Americans participate (as either volunteers or donors) in political campaigns. Consequently, political participation among social workers also exceeds that of the general population.

It is important for social workers to do more than vote, however. Involvement in election campaigns is an important way to ensure that elected officials support legislation that upholds social work values. A social worker can donate money to a candidate or political party, help register new voters, attend candidate forums, or become active in a political party.

Social workers interested in politics can also join a nonpartisan organization such as the League of Women Voters that provides the public with educational information on the candidates and issues. Other types of election-related work include working as a campaign volunteer or an election judge. Social workers can also accept paid campaign positions or run for office (Haynes & Mickelson, 1991; Reeser & Epstein, 1990). A number of social workers hold federal office (NASW, 2001). Social workers serving in the U.S. Senate in 2001 included Barbara Mikulski (D-Maryland) and Debbie Stabenow (D-Michigan). In addition, four social workers were members of Congress: Susan Davis (D-California), Barbara Lee (D-California), Ciro D. Rodriguez (D-Texas), and Edolplus Towns (D-New York).

Many of the activities involved in running a political campaign are similar to those required in social action–oriented community organizing. To run an effective campaign, you need to acquire money, volunteers, office supplies, lists of likely supporters, media attention, and paid staff. You also need to recruit voters. As discussed in chapter 4, the focus of such efforts is highly task oriented and must often be completed within a short time frame. Disorganization among campaign staff, poor media coverage, lack of contact with likely voters, funding shortfalls, and a host of other factors can have dire effects on the outcome of the campaign.

Political Activities for Social Workers

Entry-Level Campaign Positions

- Helping a candidate get on the ballot by circulating nominating petitions
- Registering new voters
- Volunteering to work in the campaign office (typing, stuffing envelopes, answering phones)
- Canvassing your neighborhood to find out if your neighbors support the candidate
- Calling voters for contributions, for votes, and to recruit new volunteers
- Poll watching for your candidate on election day
- Holding a social event so that your neighbors have a chance to meet the candidate
- Designing or distributing campaign literature

Positions for Middle-Management Volunteers or Paid Staff

- Recruiting campaign volunteers
- Managing the campaign's phone bank
- Organizing fund-raising benefits
- Contacting the media regarding your candidate; sending out press releases
- Scheduling campaign appearances for the candidate
- Planning campaign strategy as a member of the candidate's steering committee
- Recording and analyzing election results
- Organizing the election night party for campaign volunteers

Management Positions

- Working as a paid office coordinator or other frontline staff person
- Working as an analyst to identify issues of concern to voters or individuals who are likely to vote
- Serving as campaign manager
- Running for office as the candidate

Voter Registration: Linking People with the Electoral Process

One of the critical campaign activities is voter registration. Currently, only two-thirds of all adults are registered to vote (Alliance for Better Campaigns, 1998). With turnouts in recent campaigns at about 40 to 50 percent, this means that less than 30 percent of all U.S. adults actually vote. Voters are more likely to be white, age 50 or over, and college graduates and to have higher incomes than nonvoters (Jackson, Brown, & Wright, 1998; Piven & Cloward, 1988; Verba et al., 1997). One of the reasons for limited participation is that laws in many states make voter registration difficult. Potential voters must show identification and travel to designated spots to register. The registration period may end 30 days before the election. New registrations are needed when the individual changes residence or last name due to marriage or divorce. Poor people typically have difficulty with registration requirements; they may be transient, changing residence on a regular basis.

Beginning in the early 1980s, efforts have been made on a state-by-state basis to reform the voter registration laws. The organization behind this effort, Human SERVE, was founded by Richard Cloward, professor of social work at Columbia University, with political scientist Frances Fox Piven. Human Service Employees Registration and Voter Education (Human SERVE) worked to change state laws to permit community groups to register people to vote. In addition, Human SERVE advocated for the National Voter Registration Act (NVRA), passed by Congress in 1993.[1] The NVRA requires that states implement "motor voter" procedures for voter registration. People are encouraged to register when they apply for driver's licenses. In addition, this legislation also requires that people be allowed to register at public assistance offices, at military recruitment offices, and in agencies that serve people with disabilities. People are permitted to update names, addresses, and party affiliation at these sites. The legislation also requires that all states permit mail-in voter registration (Human SERVE, 1999).[2]

Human SERVE believed that these changes in registration would increase voter participation among people in poverty. They also assumed that increases in voter registration among the poor would increase support for the Democratic Party (Knack & White, 1998). Early assessments of the impact of motor voter law suggest that it has had mixed success. Though there was an increase of 11 million registrations in the 1998 Congressional elections, voter turnout (at 49 percent of all registered voters) was significantly lower than previous levels (Alliance for Better Campaigns, 1998). Turnout dropped most dramatically among young, low-income, and transient voters, those people that motor voter laws were intended to reach (Knack, 1999). Registration increased most among those people registered as independents. However, those people who registered at welfare or disability agency sites (rather than driver's license facilities) were more likely to indicate a preference for the Democratic Party.

Are Registration Activities Sufficient to Increase Voter Turnout?

Walzer (1997) argues that motor voter legislation was based on some erroneous assumptions about the likely behavior of new registrants:

> The truth is that a lot of the Americans who don't vote would support conservatives or right-leaning populists . . . . The problem is that many of the non-voters—perhaps especially the long-term non-voters—are not only disengaged but also unaffiliated and unorganized. They have not been educated by a political party or movement; they have little or no experience of the discipline of collective action. (p. 1)

The second problem inherent in the focus on registration is that some people who do register simply don't vote.[3] Though this may be a matter of preference or convenience for some individuals, others, especially those who are low-income, disabled, or persons of color, often face barriers to voter participation (Keyssar, 2000). The U.S. Commission on Civil Rights (2001) identified the following voting problems, attributed to state and county election policies, in Florida during the 2000 presidential election:

- Failure to process motor voter applications in a timely manner
- Polling places that were inaccessible to persons with disabilities
- Failure to provide voting assistance to disabled, elderly, and non-English-speaking voters
- Confusing ballots
- An inaccurate database of individuals with past felony convictions to be purged from the voter registration list[4]

This analysis gives strong support for the role of community organizers in the electoral process. Organizers can lobby for changes in registration laws to increase voter registration among low-income people or other groups historically excluded from participation in voting. Organizers can work through community-based organizations to register people to vote. They can monitor state government to make sure motor voter laws are implemented properly. They can lobby state government for election-day registration or other laws that increase access to the electoral process. According to Keyssar, this work is critical because

> in socially diverse nations, ethnic, racial, and religious antagonisms often have sparked the impulse to suppress or restrict the rights of minorities. Even individual issues have sometimes loomed so important that factions have sought to deny political voice to their adver-

Increasing Access to Participation: Voter Registration Drive

CongressDaily/A.M., July 19, 1999

In N.J., Effort Launched to Register Disabled Voters (New Jersey)

Full Text: COPYRIGHT 1999 National Journal Inc.

WASHINGTON—July 19—(*CongressDaily*) The New Jersey Developmental Disabilities Council and its grassroots affiliate, the Monday Morning Project, a voter registration campaign, are launching a drive to have 10,000 additional disabled state residents registered to vote in time for 2000, the *Trenton Times* reported.

Ethan Ellis, the council's executive director, said the council has registered 3,000 to 4,000 disabled citizens over the last four years through its voter education challenge and grassroots efforts.

Ellis said most counties report to the state that their polling places are 90 percent to 98 percent accessible, but he noted "accessible" could mean a place has ballots available in Braille, but may not be fully wheelchair accessible.

The council and Rutgers University last week released a survey which found people with disabilities are 20 percent less likely to vote than those without disabilities.

Source: *http://Web5searchbank.com/itwsession/151/506/3789847w3/12!xrn_5_0A55194849*

Techniques for Increasing Voter Turnout

- Driving voters to the polls on election day
- Canvassing to find likely voters, then knocking on doors or making phone calls to ensure that people who are likely to vote for your candidate will actually vote
- Releasing poll results just before election day that indicate your candidate will lose by a few votes (making it more likely that your supporters will vote)
- Releasing poll results just before election day that indicate that your candidate cannot be defeated (making it less likely that people will come out to support your opponent)
- Using TV or radio advertising to motivate undecided swing voters
- Targeting get-out-the-vote campaigns to specific ethnic or interest groups likely to support your candidate

saries. On the other hand, there always have been individuals and groups pressing in the opposite direction, for greater democratization and equality. As a result, the very structures and rules of electoral politics periodically become touchstones and lightning rods of conflict. (p. 323)

In addition, community organizers working in election campaigns can develop effective methods getting registered voters to the polls on election day. The establishment of an electorate that is representative of all citizens, including the poor, is imperative for the promotion of social change because

the higher the participation of the lower class, the more generous are state welfare policy efforts . . . . local leaders tend to be more responsive to the citizenry in communities with high participation rates and . . . community leaders are more likely to concur with the policy priorities of active participants. Furthermore, in a situation of low and biased turnout, certain types of citizens (the inactives) may be at a severe disadvantage in agenda setting; the agenda from which elites select policy alternatives may be less likely to reflect the needs and interests of those who are less active. (Jackson et al., 1998, p. 2)

Federal Regulation of Political Activities

Social workers who are interested in electoral activism should be aware, however, that federal and state governments place some restrictions on political activity. The Hatch Act prohibits federal and state government employees from engaging in electioneering when on the job. The act was passed in the late nineteenth century to keep elected officials from pressuring government civil service workers for help with election campaigns. This legislation has been interpreted as prohibiting such on-the-job activities as wearing campaign buttons, canvassing voters, selling tickets to campaign fund-raisers, and running for office. A government employee generally is required to quit or take a leave of absence from his or her job when running for office (Pawlak & Flynn, 1990).

Federal law also prohibits donations to political campaigns by nonprofit organizations. Most nonprofit social service organizations are incorporated under section 501(c)(3) of the federal tax code. Most interest groups are incorporated under Section 504(c)(4) of the tax code. Though lobbying activities by 504(c)(4) organizations are not restricted, these organizations cannot donate to political campaigns. They may make some very limited types of expenditures on behalf of federal candidates, but cannot make direct donations to campaigns, however (Gross, 1999).

Despite these restrictions, interest groups do get involved in election campaigns. Federal law allows the formation of political action committees

(PACs) by interest groups (Haynes & Mickelson, 1991). Originally intended to help small donors pool monetary donations for individual candidates, some PACs have been formed by large organizations and wealthy donors. Democratic Party officials often make an issue of the use of PACs by wealthy businesspeople; Republicans feel that the use of PACs by members of large unions gives labor an unfair advantage in the political process. All PACs are required to report contributions to the Federal Election Commission (FEC). Information on individual donors (usually name, date, and amount) to the PAC is available for public inspection. However, these records do not indicate how much in total dollars has been contributed from each PAC (*Frontline*, 1996). Information on contributions is available from the FEC as well as from a number of private organizations that analyze campaign contributions (Project Vote Smart, 1996).

PACs are operated as either nonconnected committees or separated segregated funds (SSFs). Under FEC regulations, SSFs may be established only by corporations or labor organizations. These PACs may raise funds only from a specific group of individuals and cannot accept donations or reimbursement for most expenditures from the sponsoring organization. In contrast, a nonconnected PAC can be established by any organization and can solicit funds from anyone. The sponsor of a nonconnected PAC may help pay for expenses (Colby & Buffum, 1998).

The NASW has a nonconnected fund PAC, Political Action for Candidate Election (PACE). The PACE board of trustees is appointed by members of the national NASW board. State NASW chapters also maintain PACE committees.

During 1992, the national NASW PACE fund raised $1.4 million, making it the eleventh-ranked nonconnected PAC. Emily's Fund, the top-ranked nonconnected PAC, raised funds exclusively for female candidates. It donated a total of $4,139,346 in 1992. In comparison, the top-ranked SSF PACs in 1992 were the Democratic-Republican Voter Education Committee and the National Rifle Association. These groups donated $9,393,542 and $5,971,253 respectively to candidates in the 1992 campaign (Colby & Buffum, 1998).

Although federal law prohibits donations by individuals and corporations of more than $1,000 to one candidate for president or Congress, there are no restrictions on donations made to political parties. This practice is often referred to as soft money (*Frontline*, 1996). Consequently, this allows corporations, unions, and interest groups that establish PACs to make almost unlimited indirect contributions to election campaigns (Isikoff & Alter, 1996). NASW's PACE made a $5,000 soft money contribution to the Democratic National Committee during the 1997–1998 election cycle.[5] PACE donated no money to the Republican National Committee.

Federal law also allows interest groups to purchase media advertising on behalf of candidates in instances where there are no direct links between the candidate and the interest group. There are currently no restrictions on the dollar amount of issue advertising purchased by these organizations (Magleby & Holt, 1999). Campaign reform legislation was introduced in Congress several times during the 1990s but was repeatedly defeated (Espo, 1999).[6] Reform law opponents have argued that the $1,000 cap on individual donations is too low; restrictions put on donations of any kind are viewed as a violation of free speech rights (Will, 1999).

Assessment of Campaign Outcomes

One of the basic roles for a community organizer in any social change effort is to examine whether elected officials can be persuaded to support or oppose specific pieces of legislation. Two of the primary methods of influencing politicians are through money (campaign contributions) and through votes. Therefore, it is critical for the organizer to determine the reelection prospects of officeholders. Factors usually identified in assessments of campaign outcomes include the following:

- Saliency of the issues raised
- Effectiveness of campaign advertising
- Appeal to traditional voters
- Appeal to new or emerging blocks of voters
- Money raised from interest groups
- Amount of money raised by the candidate
- Power resources associated with the candidate other than money
- Situational factors that can influence election results
- Likely turnout on election day (see table 9.1)

Saliency of the Issues

Saliency of the issues refers to the degree to which the public recognizes the importance of the issues the candidates raise. Candidates often look for issues that are of symbolic importance to the public. For example, in 1999, Republican members of Congress informed the public that they would protect the Social Security surplus (Hager, 1999). Previous administrations added the balance in the Social Security fund to the dollar amount of the federal budget. This accounting device minimized the public's perception of the size of the yearly budget deficit. However, no money was actually borrowed from the Social Security Trust. Announcements that the budget for the fiscal year beginning in October 1999 would not "borrow" from the trust fund were intended to address public fears that the Social Security Trust would not be able to pay out benefits to future retirees.

Campaign Advertising

Campaigns also run print, radio, and television advertising to present their issues to the public. Some of this advertising has been controversial, focus-

Table 9.1 Assessment Tool for Predicting the Outcome of Political Campaigns

Background Information

Candidate name:	Political party:
Major campaign issues:	Party of current office holder:
Major issues identified:	
Situational factors likely to influence campaign:	

Outcome Assessment

Is the candidate an incumbent (currently holds the office in contention)?	1=Yes 2=No
What is the response of the public to the issues raised by the candidate?	1=Positive response 2=Neutral 3=Negative response
How effective is campaign advertising?	1=Very effective 2=Somewhat effective 3=Not very effective
What is the political party affiliation of the majority of voters in this electoral district?	1=Same as the candidate's 2=Majority are Independent 3=Different from the candidate's
Does the candidate's message appeal to traditional voters (white, suburban, upper or middle class)?	1=Yes 2=No
Does the candidate's message appeal to new or emerging blocks of voters (African American, Asian, Latino, LGBT, or female)?	1=Yes 2=No
How much influence are interest groups who support the candidate likely to have on the election?	1=A large amount 2=A moderate amount 3=A small amount 4=None
How does the public perceive the candidate's ethics (for example, honesty or personal conduct)?	1=Better than other candidate(s) 2=About the same 3=Worse than other candidate(s)
Approximately how much of the money donated to the candidate came from identifiable interest groups?	1=A large amount 2=A moderate amount 3=A small amount 4=None
How much money has the candidate raised? (The amount will vary by the type of election. Multiply the base amounts by 10 for U.S. Senate and governor's races. Multiply by 100 for presidential elections.)	1=A large amount (over $200,000) 2=A moderate amount ($50,000 to $199,999) 3=A small amount (under $50,000)
Has the candidate raised more money than his or her opponents?	1=Yes 2=About the same amount 3=No
To what degree are the candidate's power resources (gender, ethnicity, family connections, wealth, professional status, celebrity, etc.) likely to influence voters?	1=High 2=Medium 3=Low

Table 9.1 *(Continued)*

What is the likely rate of turnout on election day for all voters?	1=High 2=Medium 3=Low
What is the likely rate of turnout among traditional voters (white, middle, or upper income) likely to support your candidate?	1=High 2=Medium 3=Low
What is the likely rate of turnout among new or emerging blocks of voters likely to support your candidate?	1=High 2=Medium 3=Low
How do independent analysts assess the outcome of the election for your candidate?	1=Win 2=Too Close to Call 3=Lose
Total Score	

Key:

Likely to LOSE	36 points or more
Race too CLOSE TO CALL	26 to 35 points
Likely to WIN!!!	25 points or less

Note: This scale has not been empirically tested for reliability or validity. It is intended only as a tool that can help the beginning organizer examine critical aspects of an election.

ing on negative aspects of the opposition candidate's personal life (Pinkleton, Weintraub, & Fortman, 1998). Other advertising may focus on the candidate's positive attributes (family man, crime fighter, mother, educator) or identify the candidate's position on issues of concern to the public. The amount and type of advertising used may be influential in bringing likely voters to the polls on election day (Benson, 1999).

Targeting Subpopulations

Candidates often focus their advertising or identify issues of concern to specific population groups. Some candidates embrace issues of concern to traditional types of likely voters. The population groups most likely to vote are older, have more income, and are better educated than those who do not vote (Jackson et al., 1998). Campaign wisdom suggests that these voters are most likely to vote Republican. Many campaigns focus on population groups that have only recently begun to vote in great numbers or make monetary contributions to candidates. Two emerging powerful voting blocks are Latinos and members of the gay and lesbian community. Candidates who are interested in obtaining votes from these population groups often raise issues that appeal to them (Neal & Morin, 1998). For example, in the 2000 presidential primary campaign, former senator Bill Bradley announced his support for full civil rights for gay men and lesbians ("Reaching out to gay voters," 1999). Both Democratic and Republican presidential candidates targeted Latino voters. The Census Bureau estimates that Latinos will emerge as the largest minority group in the United States by the year 2004 (Connolly, 1999a).

New and emerging voter groups are usually viewed as potentially Democratic, especially when these groups are members of subpopulations traditionally excluded from participation in the dominant society. In 1998, Democratic victories in five congressional races and governorships in Alabama and South Carolina were attributed by analysts to get-out-the-vote efforts in the African American community ("Can the black vote hold up," 1999). Candidates also target disaffected white voters. In 1999, Reform Party presidential candidate Pat Buchanan announced plans to target blue-collar conservatives—white, working-class Democrats—during his campaign.

Interest Group Donations to Campaigns

Candidates may also receive support from influential interest groups. These groups rally their members to make campaign contributions. Often the most powerful interest groups represent industries and corporate entities. For example, executives in the tobacco industry may contribute to candidates who do not support additional restrictions on tobacco sales. NASW asks its members to support candidates who favor third-party reimbursements for social work services, health care reform, and funding increases for social services. The power of these groups to influence campaign outcomes is most easily measured by looking at the amount of money they contribute to election campaigns.

The amount of money each candidate raises is usually considered a decisive factor in campaigns. Money is used to develop and staff campaign organizations, recruit volunteers, and pay for pre-election advertising. The ability to raise a large amount of money may help a candidate limit the prospects of potential opponents. For example, George W. Bush's ability to raise $50 million before the Republican primaries in 2000 forced a number of other candidates to drop out of the race (Connolly, 1999b).

Essential to an analysis of individual campaign donations, however, is determining the donor's vested interest (Jansson, 1999). What does the donor reasonably want to achieve by making the donation? In some cases, the donor's vested interest may be obvious. In other situations, the analyst may need to do some supplemental data gathering, using information available from the media, advocacy organizations, and personal interviews with candidates or donors. For example, teachers' unions are likely to give donations to candidates who are supportive of increases in funding for education; tobacco company executives are likely to favor candidates who oppose taxes on tobacco products.

Green et al. (1998) surveyed 200 major congressional campaign contributors in 1997. These contributors donated $200 or more to campaigns. Ninety percent were white; 80 percent were male. Most were age forty-five or older, had college degrees, and were members of high-status professions (doctors, lawyers, or MBAs). Over 50 percent were Republicans, and a third identified themselves as Democrats. Reasons given for supporting individual candidates were ideology (19 percent), issues (16 percent), previous personal relationships with the candidate (16 percent), support for local candidates who can bring back benefits for the community (20 percent), benefiting one's own business (15 percent), and backing likely winners who can provide the donor with access to decision makers after the election (14 percent).

Power Resources and Situational Factors that Influence Outcomes

Money is not the only power resource that wins elections. Incumbents (elected officials running for office) are also more likely to win elections than their opponents. They have greater ability to raise money, can use their decision-making authority to influence supporters, and have greater name recognition. Other power resources that can influence results are professional status (minister, doctor, retired military officer), celebrity, or family connections. For example, a number of candidates for federal office in 2000—Hillary Rodham Clinton, Al Gore, and George W. Bush—were relatives of previous officeholders (Roddy, 1999). Name recognition, political connections, and ability to raise funds provided a huge power advantage for these candidates.

Situational factors can also influence election outcomes. Political scandals, especially those that surface in the media just before the election, can determine results. Public opinion polls predicted that 2000 presidential candidate Al Gore would have trouble defeating George W. Bush because of his association with President Clinton and the Monica Lewinsky scandal (Pew Research Center, 1999). The public's perception of current economic conditions is also a factor in federal election campaigns. A good economy is believed to favor incumbent presidents. A poorly performing economy makes it unlikely that the incumbent will be reelected (MacKuen, Erikson, & Stimson, 1992).

Voter Turnout

Although money is a key factor in determining who will win an election, voter turnout is also very important. Members of historically disadvantaged groups, such as people in poverty, African Americans, and Latinos may not vote because they believe their interests will not be represented ("Can the black vote hold up," 1999; Walzer, 1997). One of a political analyst's key analytical tools is determining what demographic groups are likely to vote and the degree of voter turnout. Polls, conducted by the candidates and by independent polling corporations before the election, generally examine how people will vote and who is likely to vote. In addition, these polls examine whether members of specific subpopulations (usually by income and ethnicity) are likely to vote on election day. One important limitation of these polls is that they are usually conducted by phone. A process called random-digit dialing allows pollsters to reach most households with phones. Households without phones are likely to be excluded. Most often, households without phones are likely to contain families with low incomes (Rubin & Babbie, 1997; Taylor & Terhanian, 1999). Consequently, poll results may not be representative of the general population.[7]

Campaigns often try to fit their messages to target subpopulations of people who are likely to vote. In 1996 presidential, congressional, and local races, campaign resources were targeted to fit a demographic profile of suburban female voters ages twenty-five to fifty-five. The term used to describe these voters was soccer moms (Crone, 1997). Campaigns also target swing voters who are unlikely to come out to vote unless they are motivated by the candidate's message, issues voiced in the campaign, or negative advertising that targets the candidate's opponent (Benson, 1999). Campaign analysts can determine which candidates have support from voters in that district and the probable characteristics of the voters who have selected that candidate (Haynes & Mickelson, 1991).

Though we do not know the names or backgrounds of everyone who voted, we have two key sources of information about voting patterns: exit

---

Social Work Roles and Responsibilities for Increasing Voter Access

V **Volunteer** on a political campaign, register prospective voters, or work as an election judge or poll watcher.

O Conduct **outreach** activities in communities in which residents historically don't vote.

T Provide **training** to election judges, poll watchers, and prospective voters about the Federal Voting Rights Act.

E **Educate** the public about barriers that could prevent individuals from casting their votes. For example, many states have laws that prohibit voting by people who have committed minor felonies in the past. Disproportionate numbers of these individuals are people of color.

R Conduct **research** to identify structural barriers to voting. Any analysis of voting should also include a demographic analysis of likely voters and identification of communities where participation has been low. Such research will help social workers understand the root causes and effects of oppression and how it is expressed in terms of the political power of various subpopulations and marginalized groups.

interviews and demographic analysis by region. Many media sources and research institutes conduct exit interviews with voters as they leave polling places on election day. Questions typically asked in exit interviews deal with the candidates the voter selected, reasons for selection, and the voter's personal characteristics. For example, an analysis of California voters conducted by the Voter News Service in November 1996 found that almost 60 percent of white women going to the polls voted for Proposition 209, a ballot measure that ended affirmative action in state hiring, state contracts, and university admissions (Associated Press, 1996).

Using the Internet to Conduct Research on Candidates and Campaign Issues

Campaign analysis involves three primary types of research. The Internet can be used to obtain most of the necessary information to do the following:

- Conduct research on the campaign platforms and ideologies of individual candidates and political parties as expressed in advertising, debates, and other vehicles that identify campaign issues
- Conduct research on campaign donations and lobbying expenditures
- Identify likely voters and analyze how demographic characteristics of voters will affect election results

Gathering such information allows the analyst to project the likely outcome of the election based on factors such as the saliency of issues raised in the campaign, the power resources possessed by each candidate, and the likely voter turnout on election day.

Issues Analysis

Any number of newspapers, magazines, and television programs present in-depth coverage of candidates and campaign issues several months before an election. Some of this analysis is nonpartisan, but most analysis incorporates some value biases in terms of the issues that the candidates support. Some of the analysis (newspaper columns, television commentaries) is intentionally biased; the commentator will outline his or her value assumptions and describe how the candidate supports or opposes the value assumptions inherent in a discussion of the issue. You may want to do your own in-depth analysis, looking at a variety of media resources.

Newspapers, especially those serving large metropolitan areas, generally provide in-depth coverage during and just subsequent to campaigns. Some journals that offer in-depth coverage of issues (*CQ Voter, Roll Call* magazine, *Atlantic Monthly*, and *Newsweek*) also have Web sites that provide campaign coverage. Major national news outlets (ABC, CBS, CNN, NBC, the *New*

York Times, and the *Washington Post*) have sites that carry breaking news stories about campaign issues and archives that contain new stories about previous elections.

Information on Candidates

Sites maintained by political parties and individual candidates or office-holders provide a good source of primary data on candidates. Candidate sites are intended to promote the individual candidates and are often quite explicit in identifying the candidate's position on the issues. Good sources of campaign information are the Web sites maintained by candidates for reelection. These sites are often promotional in nature and contain information about the individual candidate, the status of current legislation of interest to the candidate (as well as to likely voters), and his or her political ideology (Jalonick, 1999).

Some on-line journals offer in-depth coverage of congressional debates and strategies political parties use to block or gain passage for specific pieces of legislation. The *Congressional Quarterly* and *Roll Call* magazine are two traditional sources of information about the federal legislative process. Both of these journals have Web sites that provide information about the electoral prospects of members of Congress. A number of Web sites for campaign analysis—including Project Vote Smart, Center for Responsive Politics, and Common Cause—contain information about the voting patterns of incumbent officeholders.

Research on Campaign Donations

Another important area of research in campaigns involves analysis of the individuals and interest groups that have donated money to the campaign. Federal law (in effect since the 1970s) prohibited donations of more than $1,000 by individuals or corporations. Many corporations have their top executives make individual donations. In some cases, the spouses of these executives donate to the same candidates in order to double the family's contribution (Marminucci, 1999). Interest groups and corporations can make soft money donations directly to candidates.

Knowing the dollar amount of the total funds contributed by donors to a candidate can help the political analyst predict the outcome of that campaign. Big donations associated with specific industries can also be used to predict how the successful candidate will vote in the future on issues that can be expected to benefit the interest group. For example, members of the entertainment industry might be expected to oppose efforts to censor violence in TV programs, movies, and video games (McNamara, 1999). Candidates who receive a large amount of funding from members of this industry might be expected to oppose efforts to censor entertainment programs.

A number of Web sites contain links to resources for campaign analysis. Many states require that candidates for office file campaign report forms using software technology that allows this data to be posted directly on the Web. Candidates for Congress and the presidency are required to report contributions to the FEC. A number of organizations obtain information on campaign financing from the FEC and post it on their Web sites. Good sites for analyzing campaign donations include the Center for Responsive Politics, Project Vote Smart, Mother Jones' Coin-Operated Congress, Common Cause, and Congress.org. Some of these sites contain databases developed from campaign donation information compiled by the FEC. Some of these sites contain explicit information about the donors' vested interests.

Most of these sites contain information from recent congressional races and information from the campaign fund reports filed by candidates in the 2000 presidential race. Some of these sites also contain information about campaign donations and soft money donations made by individuals and corporations to political parties. A few sites (by Project Vote Smart and the FEC) provide detailed information about campaign finance reporting procedures and regulations.

An analysis of top campaign donors can tell you which interest groups or industries are trying to influence or did influence the outcome of the election. For example, an examination of the top 400 donors to 1996 congressional races by *Mother Jones* magazine (1996) shows that top California donors to Democratic candidates were members of the entertainment industry (including Barbra Streisand and Steven Spielberg) and executives from a number of computer software manufacturing companies.[8] A similar analysis using the Project Vote Smart database on soft money contributions made in 1995 also provides interesting results. These data indicate that most of these donations were made by members of a small number of industries: publishing, gas and oil producers, tobacco manufacturers, utility providers, alcohol manufacturers, and the entertainment industry (see table 9.2).

State governments also require that candidates for state office file campaign finance reports. Some of these states have begun to post this information on the Web. Some of the sites for analysis of federal campaign finances also contain links to state databases. You can also find these sites by looking for links on your state government's Web page.

Information about Voters

The identification of areas with likely voters helps election campaigns target their resources; areas with high concentrations of likely voters will receive a great deal of attention from the candidate, whereas areas with low concentrations of likely voters will receive little attention. Political campaigns generally examine voting within certain areas (precincts or city, state assem-

Table 9.2 Project Vote Smart — 1995 Soft Money Contributions

Contributor	Democrats	Republicans	Interests
Phillip Morris	$199,000	$992,149	Tobacco/food products/ beer
RJR Nabisco	$126,250	$696,450	Tobacco/food products
AT&T	$313,684	$370,000	Long distance phone service
Atlantic Richfield	$185,500	$322,175	Oil & gas/chemicals
Joseph E. Seagrams & Sons	$285,000	$175,000	Beer, wine, and liquor
American Financial Corp.	$100,000	$330,000	Insurance/financial services
MCI Telecommuni- cations Corp.	$279,750	$107,500	Long distance phone services
Dirk Ziff	$380,000	$0	Publishing
Time Warner	$101,000	$250,000	Communications
Archer-Daniels- Midland	$60,000	$255,000	Agriculture services and products
NYNEX	$77,500	$206,405	Local phone utility
Anheuser-Busch	$215,250	$66,000	Beer, wine, and liquor
Lazard Freres & Co.	$235,000	$45,000	Securities and investment
Miramax Films Corp.	$276,000	$0	Movie production
Textron Inc.	$48,150	$218,700	Defense
News America Publishing	$0	$265,000	Publishing
Brown & Williamson Tobacco Corp.	$0	$265,000	Tobacco
Loral Corp.	$240,500	$15,500	Defense
Chevron Corp.	$83,000	$154,400	Oil and gas
Dream Works	$255,000	$0	Movie production

Source: Project Vote Smart, 2000.

bly, state senate, or congressional districts) to determine how much voting strength a candidate has had in that district. Data on the demographic characteristics by congressional district or state are available from the Census Bureau.[9] Private polling firms (such as Gallup and Harris) or public policy research institutes (such as the Roper Center and the Pew Research Center) publish summaries of polling results in presidential and congressional races (see table 9.3). All of the major television networks (ABC, CBS, CNN, and NBC) regularly publish poll results on their Web sites. Major newspapers also publish poll results on the Web. Good sources of poll information for presidential and congressional races include the *New York Times*, the *Los Angeles Times*, and the *Washington Post*. Information on local races can often be found on Web sites associated with local TV stations and newspapers. Most states also post final vote counts from previous elections on the Web. These results can help determine which candidates and political parties are likely to have widespread support from voters in the next election.

Polling firms are also beginning to experiment with on-line polling methods, distributing surveys to known computer users. Names of respondents may be obtained from previous phone surveys, responses to advertisements, and samples drawn from people who subscribe to some Internet services (Taylor & Terhanian, 1999). One important limitation of on-line polling is that only 45 percent of all U.S. adults use the Internet. In addition, Internet users are not representative of the general population or the population of likely voters. They are more likely to be white, and younger than the average voter.

Summary

Electing people to office who support social work values contributes to the development of policies that help social workers and members of disadvantaged groups. However, other groups may be more successful in electing candidates to represent their interests. Community organizers must develop analytical skills that allow them to identify those factors (especially money) that influence election outcomes. Social workers can undertake a number of campaign activities, including voting, volunteering to help a candidate, staffing a campaign, planning electoral strategies, analyzing campaign out-

Table 9.3 1999 Pew Research Center Poll on Likely Presidential Candidates (October, 1999)

	Reason for	
	Supporting Gore	*Supporting Bush*
Ties to administration	30%	49%
Personality/leadership	60%	38%
Other/neither	7%	8%
Don't know	3%	5%
Total	100%	100%

Source: Pew Research Center for the People and the Press, 1999.

comes, and actually running for office. The Internet provides a convenient, cheap, and easy vehicle for social work students to "follow the money" and determine the vested interests of campaign donors and candidates. Knowledge of monetary resources, vested interests, and alliances among decision makers is an important aspect of planning successful community organization strategies and tactics. Chapter 10 describes methods used to develop intervention plans and acquire power.

■ QUESTIONS FOR CLASS DISCUSSION

1. Do you think social workers should work in political campaigns or run for office? Why or why not?
2. Are the values of politicians consistent with those of social workers? Why or why not?
3. How would you expect political campaigns to differ from day-to-day activities encountered in community organization practice?
4. What issues do you think social workers in public office should address?
5. Visit the national NASW Web page (http://www.nasw.org) or the Web page maintained by your state's NASW chapter. What advocacy or legislative issues are identified? What candidates are likely to support these issues?
6. Are you surprised that PACE donated funds to the Democratic National Committee in 1997–1998? Why or why not?

■ SAMPLE ASSIGNMENTS

Write a brief paper (one to five pages) on one of the following topics.

1. Interview a candidate for public office. Ask the candidate to describe his or her position on issues of concern to social workers and members of disadvantaged groups. Describe how well you think this candidate will represent social work values once he or she is elected to office.
2. Visit a campaign office as either a volunteer or an observer. Write a brief paper describing your observations. How does the interaction among staff and volunteers differ from the interaction you typically see in a social service setting?
3. Spend at least four hours registering voters or going door-to-door to canvass prospective voters before an election. What attitudes do people express toward voting? Do you think that these people will actually vote? Why or why not?
4. Use the campaign-assessment tool in table 9.1 to compare the campaigns for at least two candidates for the same office. Use primary and secondary sources to make your assessment. Based on your analysis, who do you think is likely to win this race? Give a written rationale, based on available information, for your response.

■ SAMPLE ASSIGNMENT ON CAMPAIGN CONTRIBUTIONS

Using information published by *Mother Jones* magazine on the top 400 campaign contributors to the 1998 congressional campaigns (http://www.mojones.com/coinop_congress/), answer the following questions about campaign contributors:

1. What industries (industries in which contributors work) support each of the two major political parties?
2. What industries tend to provide campaign funds? Why would members of these industries be interested in influencing federal policies?
3. What issue appears to be of primary importance to Republican women donors?
4. Examine "Snapshots/biographies" for five of the donors. How does *Mother Jones* analyze the vested interest of these donors?

Notes

1. Human SERVE discontinued operations in 1999. For a history of the organization see Piven & Cloward, 2000.
2. Human SERVE reported that there were *70 million* unregistered adults in 1994. Of the 70 million, it is estimated that 16 million could not vote because of felony convictions, residency in mental hospitals, or because they were not citizens.
3. Piven and Cloward (2000) cite research conducted by Human SERVE in the mid-1980s that suggests that at least 70 percent of those who were registered at public welfare and other social service agencies did indeed vote.
4. Laws in some states prohibit voting by people who committed minor felonies in the past. Many of these individuals are disproportionately African American ("Can the black vote hold up?" 1999).
5. This information was obtained from the soft money database maintained by Common Cause [On-line]. Available: http://commoncause.org/campaign2000/body.htm.
6. The McCain-Feingold-Cochran bill on campaign finance reform passed in the U.S. Senate in spring 2001. Prospects for passage in the House of Representatives were believed to be low (Common Cause, 2001). As passed by the Senate, this legislation would ban soft money but raise the cap on individual contributions.
7. Pollsters often use a statistical process called weighting to adjust results so they reflect the preferences of the population of voters.
8. This information is available from Mother Jones' Coin-Operated Congress [On-line]. Available: http://www.mojones.com/.
9. Demographic data by congressional district is available from the Census Bureau Web site (http://www.census.gov/).

References

Alliance for Better Campaigns. (1998). Voter turnout [On-line]. Available: http://www.bettercampaigns.org/documents/turnout.htm.

Associated Press. (1996, November 12). Women helped push through 209. *Fresno Bee*, p. A3.

Benson, M. (1999, October 24). Politicians find U.S. public easy to manipulate. *San Francisco Examiner*, p. A12.

Can the black vote hold up? (1999). *Economist, 351*(i8113), 23.

Colby, I., & Buffum, W. E. (1998). Social workers and PACs: An examination of National Association of Social Workers P.A.C.E. Committees. *Journal of Community Practice, 5*(4), 87–93.

Common Cause. (2001, April 4). McCain-Feingold-Cochran Bill passed in Senate on April 2, 59–41 [On-line]. Available: http://www.common.cause.org/issue_agenda/issues.htm

Connolly, C. (1999a, September 25). Politicians court Hispanic vote. *Washington Post* [On-line]. Available: http://www.washingtonpost.com/wp-srv/politics/campaigns/wh2000/stories/money092599.htm.

Connolly, C. (1999b, September 16). Deep-pocketed Bush could hit Democrats early [On-line]. Available: http://www.washingtonpost.com/wp-srv/politics/campaigns/Keyraces20/hispanics091699.ht.

Crone, B. (1997). Finding priority voters with database overlays. *Campaigns and Elections, 18*(10), 49–52.

Domanski, M. (1998). Prototypes of social work political participation: An empirical model. *Social Work, 46*, 156–67.

Espo, D. (1999, October). Campaign finance reform bill killed by GOP filibuster. *San Francisco Chronicle*, p. A3.

Ezell, M. (1991). Administrators as advocates. *Administration in Social Work, 15*(3), 1–18.

Fisher, R. (1995). Political social work. *Journal of Social Work Education, 3*, 194–204.

Fournier, R. (1999, March). Pat Buchanan making third try for White House. Fosters On-line [On-line]. Available: http://www.fosters.com/news99a/march/02/xx0302f.htm.

Frontline/WGBH Educational Foundation (1996). So you want to buy a president [On-line]. Available: http://www2.pbs.org/wgbh/pages/frontline/president.

Green, J., Hernson, P., Powell, L., & Wilcox, C. (1998, June 9). Wealthy, conservative, and reform-minded [On-line]. Available: http://opensecrets.org/pubs/donors/donors.htm.

Gross, K. (1999). Lobbying and the law [On-line]. Available: http://www.opensecrets.org/regulation/kgross.htm.

Hager, G. (1999, October 11). Logic of "saving" Social Security surplus is pooh-poohed. *San Francisco Chronicle*, pp. A3, A5.

Hardina, D. (1995). Do Canadian social workers practice advocacy? *Journal of Community Practice, 2*(3), 97–121.

Haynes, K., & Mickelson, J. (1991). *Affecting change: Social workers in the political arena*. New York: Longman.

Human SERVE (1999). Summary of the national voter registration act of 1993 [On-line]. Available: http://www.igc.org/humanserve/home.html.

Isikoff, M., & Alter, J. (1996, October 28). The real scandal is what's legal. *Newsweek*, 30–32.

Jackson, R. A., Brown, R. D., & Wright, G. C. (1998). Registration, turnout, and the electoral representativeness of U.S. state electorates. *American Politics Quarterly, 26*(3), 259–72.

Jalonick, C. (1999). Rating presidential campaign Web sites. *Campaigns and Elections, 20*(i6), 36.

Jansson, B. (1999). *Becoming an effective policy advocate.* Pacific Grove, CA: Brooks/Cole.

Keyssar, A. (2000). *The right to vote.* New York: Basic Books.

Knack, S. (1999). Drivers wanted: Motor voter and the election of 1996. *Political Science and Politics, 32*(2) 237–44.

Knack, S., & White, J. (1998). Did state's motor voter programs help the Democrats? *American Politics Quarterly, 26*(3), 344–66.

MacKuen, M. B., Erikson, R. S., & Stimson, J. A. (1992). Peasants or bankers? The American electorate and the U.S. economy. *American Political Science Review, 86*(3), 597–611.

Magleby, D., & Holt, M. (1999). The long shadow of soft money and issue advocacy ads. *Campaigns and Elections, 20*(i4), 22–28.

Mahaffey, M., & Hanks, J. (1982). *Practical politics.* Washington, DC: National Association of Social Workers.

Marminucci, C. (1999, September 16). Patterns emerge on Bush's donor list. *San Francisco Chronicle,* p. A5.

Mary, N., Ellano, C. W., & Newell, J. (1993). Political activism in social work: A study of social work educators. In T. Mizrahi & J. Morrison (Eds.), *Community organization and social administration* (pp. 203–23). New York: Haworth.

McNamara, Eileen. (1999, June 18). Movie choices: Dumb and dumber. *San Francisco Chronicle,* p. A27.

Mother Jones Magazine. List of top 400 contributors to 1996 congressional campaigns [On-line]. Available: http://www.mojones.com/coinop_congress/.

National Association of Social Workers (2001). Social workers in Congress [On-line]. Available: http://www.naswdc/advocacy.congress.htm.

Neal, T. M., & Morin, R. (1998, November 5). For voters, it's back toward the middle. *Washington Post* [On-line]. Available: http://www.washingtonpost.com/wp-srv/politics/campaign/keyraces98/stories/poll110598.htm.

Pawlak, E., & Flynn, J. (1990). Executive directors' political activities. *Social Work, 35,* 307–12.

Pew Research Center for the People and the Press. (1999, October). Candidate qualities may trump issues in 2000 [On-line]. Available: http://www.people-press.org/oct99rpt.htm.

Pinkleton, B., Weintraub, E., & Fortman, K. (1998). Relationship of media use and political disaffection to political efficacy and voting behavior. *Journal of Broadcasting and Electronic Media, 42*(1), 34–50.

Piven, F., & Cloward, R. (1988). *Why Americans don't vote.* New York: Pantheon.

Piven, F., & Cloward, R. (2000). *Why Americans still don't vote.* Boston: Beacon Press.

Project Vote Smart. (2000). 1995 soft money contributions [On-line]. Available: http://www.vote-smart.org

Reaching out to gay voters, Bradley calls for equal rights (October 3, 1999). *New York Times,* p. N28.

Reeser, L.C., & Epstein, I. (1990). *Professionalization and activism in social work.* New York: Columbia University Press.

Roddy, D. (1999, July 17). Gore, Bush: Smoke vs. mirrors [On-line]. *Post-Gazette.* Available: http://www.postgazette.com/columnists/19990717roddy.asp.

Rose, S. (1999). Social workers as municipal legislators: Potholes, garbage and social activism. *Journal of Community Practice, 6*(4), 1–15.

Rubin, A., & Babbie, E. (1997). *Research methods for social work* (3d ed.). Pacific Grove, CA: Brooks/Cole.

Taylor, H., & Terhanian, G. (1999, June/July). Heady days are here again: Online polling is rapidly coming of age. *Public Perspective*, 20–23.

U.S. Commission on Civil Rights. (2001). Status report on probe of election practices in Florida during the 2000 presidential campaign [On-line]. Available: http://www.usccr.gov/Vote2000/flstrpt.htm.

Verba, S., Schlozman, K. L., & Brady, H. E. (1997, May/June). The big tilt: Participatory inequality in America. *American Prospect*, 74–80.

Walzer, M. (1997). The disenfranchised. *New Republic, 216*(1–2), 23.

Will, G. (1999, October 11). Political class is to blame for money games. *San Francisco Chronicle*, p. A23.

Web Resources

Information on Voter Registration

Project Vote—http://www.projectvote.org/
League of Women Voters—http://www.lwv.org/
NAACP Voter Empowerment Project—http://www.naacp.org/workvoter/voter_empowerment.shtml
Rock the Vote—http://www.rockthevote.org/
Southwest Voter Registration Project—http://www.svrep.org/

Campaign Contributions

Center for Responsive Politics—http://www.opensecrets.org/
Common Cause—http://www.commoncause.org/
Congressional Quarterly—http://www.cq.com/
Congress.org—http://www.congress.org/
The Coin-Operated Congress and the *Mother Jones* Magazine MOJO 400 (donors in congressional races)—http://www.mojones.com/
The Federal Elections Commission—http://www.fec.gov/
Project Vote Smart—http://www.vote-smart.org/

Demographic Analysis of Voters and Opinion Polling

U.S. Census Bureau—http://www.census.gov/
Gallup Organization—http://www.gallup.com/
Pew Center—http://www.people-press.org/
Roper Center—http://www.ropercenter.uconn.edu/

News Sources

ABC—http://abcnews.go.com
CBS—http://www.cbsnews.com
CNN—http://cnn.com/
NBC—http://www.msnbc.com/
Los Angeles Times—http://www.latimes.com
New York Times—http://www.nytimes.com (subscription fee required)

Salon.Com—http://www.salon.com (on-line magazine)
Washington Post—http://www.washingtonpost.com

Issue Analysis

American Civil Liberties Union—http://www.aclu.org
American Friends Service Committee—http://www.afsc.org
American Indian Movement—http://www.aimovement.org
Amnesty International—http://www.amnesty.org
Disability Rights Activist—http://www.disrights.org/
Human Rights Campaign (LGBT issues)—http://www.hrc.org
Mexican American Legal Defense and Education Fund—http://www.maldef.org/
National Association for the Advancement of Colored People (NAACP)—http://
    www.naacp.org/
National Association of Social Workers—http://www.naswdc.org
National Council of La Raza—http://www.nclr.org/
Puerto Rican Legal Defense Fund—http://www.igc.org/IPR
Note: Also see the list of interest group Web sites in chapter 8.

PART THREE

Goal Setting and Implementation

10 Intervention Planning

Using Strategies and Tactics

■ The implementation of strategies and tactics takes place in the context of interpersonal interaction among individuals and groups. It is critical that the organizer be able to use practice models, analytical frameworks, and research data to choose situation-specific strategies and tactics that will facilitate social change. Consequently, in this chapter the primary components of intervention plans—strategies and tactics are defined and the role of the action and target systems in community practice is examined. Methods for linking strategies and tactics to models of practice are described, as well as ethical aspects of using strategies and tactics and the importance of participant participation in intervention planning and goal setting. The importance of mixing and phasing the use of practice methods is described. This chapter also addresses evaluation as a component of intervention planning. The chapter concludes with a description of computer resources that can help the practitioner choose and implement interventions.

Defining Strategies and Tactics

Community organization practice requires that social workers use strategies and tactics associated with each model to influence social change. A strategy is a long-term plan of action to address a specific social problem. Mondros and Wilson (1994) define strategy as "a 'game plan.' It is offensive in its attempt to achieve a goal and defensive in that it is influenced by the perceptions of allies and adversaries" (p. 131). Warren (1971) identified three primary strategies or orientations to change: collaboration, campaign, and contest. Collaborative strategies are used when groups can agree on joint actions. Campaign strategies are used to persuade opponents to come to the bargaining table. Contest involves confrontation tactics to pressure decision makers to adopt policies or take actions supported by opposition groups. Collaboration strategies are most often associated with community development; contest-related strategies with the social action model. Campaign-oriented strategies may be used as appropriate with all three models of practice (Warren, 1971).

Tactics are short-term activities undertaken as part of a change-oriented strategy. Tactics can include cooperation, negotiation, public education, persuasion, media influence, lobbying, public appeals, demonstrations, boycotts, strikes, and civil disobedience (Warren, 1971). Collaborative tactics are used to minimize differences between individuals and groups through the identification of common interests, the sharing of resources, the creation of joint plans, and cooperative efforts to address the problem at hand. Collaborative tactics can include consensus, cooperation, problem solving, public education, and persuasion (Brager, Specht, & Torczyner, 1987; Netting, Kettner, & McMurty, 1993; Warren, 1971).

Campaign tactics are used to minimize differences between groups and to develop agreements between opponents (Brager et al. 1987; Rothman, 1995; Warren, 1971). Campaign tactics are often used to determine the rules of engagement, or the manner in which the opposing groups will negotiate with one another (Kahn, 1991). In campaigns, each side makes clear statements about their differences. Common points of interest are also identified. The primary goal of a campaign is (1) forcing one's opponent to engage in dialogue about a problem or issue, (2) creating a situation in which both parties can come to an agreement, or (3) engaging both parties or the public in a decision-making process that will produce a definite outcome.

For example, political campaigns produce clear winners and losers. The process for determining the winner is governed by explicit rules, monitored by public officials and the media, and the outcome is given legitimacy by the public. In addition to political campaigns, organizers engage in media campaigns; public education campaigns; union-organizing drives; and lobbying campaigns to change policies, programs, votes, or opinions. Advocacy organizations can also use campaigns to recruit members and raise funds. Campaign tactics include political maneuvering, bargaining, negotiation, and mild coercion. Sometimes campaigns are conducted to meet multiple organizational goals. For example, an organization interested in protecting the rights of immigrants could seek to inform the public about the impact of anti-immigrant legislation, recruit new members to the organization, and influence legislators to change harmful laws and policies.

Contest or confrontation tactics are most often associated with social action. Confrontation tactics can include such activities as face-to-face meetings with opponents, cutting off or limiting debate, portrayal of opponents in a negative light (mudslinging), and excluding opponents from participation in certain decisions (Hardina, 1997, 2000). Demonstrations, strikes, boycotts, civil disobedience, and picketing also require the ability to confront one's opponents (Bobo, Kendall, & Max, 1991). According to Kahn (1991),

> confrontations work well because they give people a chance to vent their anger. As they confront the individual or individuals who have been responsible for so many of their problems, they recognize their own ability to stand up and fight back. (p. 174)

Confrontation tactics may be problematic for some organizations. For a tactic to be effective, constituents must feel comfortable with the action taken (Bobo et al., 1991). The tactic used must fall within the participant's range of experience and values. Participants who value working within the system may not wish to become involved in confrontation until they face a situation in which less aggressive tactics, such as letter writing or meetings with public officials, fail (Kahn, 1991).

The transformative model of practice and its subtypes, feminist and multicultural practice, are associated with other types of strategic processes and outcomes. Processes include participatory education, constructing knowledge and learning from experience, dialogue between students and educators, and analysis of the impact of oppression institutions (Castelloe and Watson, 1999). Outcomes include leadership development, empowerment of participants, critical consciousness, and collective social action. As participants share experiences and develop knowledge and awareness of the root causes of oppression, they begin to develop action plans to change social institutions and consequently transform their own lives (Freire, 1970). Such action plans employ a variety of collaborative-, campaign-, and confrontation-oriented strategies and tactics (see table 10.1).

Action and Target Systems

Action and target systems are terms organizers use to describe participants in the community change process. The action system refers to members of the group who are seeking social change. Organizers, constituents, coalition members, community-organization staff, concerned citizens, and other prospective beneficiaries are members of the action system. The target system usually consists of individuals whose decisions affect policies: elected offi-

Table 10.1 Models of Intervention, Strategies, and Tactics

Model	Community Development	Social Action	Social Planning	Transformative Model
Primary Strategy	**Collaboration**	**Contest/Campaign**	**Problem solving**	**Popular education**
Tactics	Capacity building Consensus building Education Joint plans/actions Letter writing Persuasion Petitions Problem solving Self-empowerment	Bargaining Boycotts Civil disobedience Confrontation Demonstrations Direct action Hunger strike Influence media Letter writing Lobbying Mild coercion Mobilizing Negotiations Petitions Picketing Political campaigns Public education Sit-ins Strikes Union organizing	Data analysis Fact gathering Lobbying Negotiation Promotes citizen participation and inclusion in planning process Collaboration, campaign, or contest as appropriate to support adoption of plans	Understanding own values and experiences Understanding role of institutional structures Understanding how structures contribute to personal and societal oppression Transforming oneself Taking action (collaborative approaches to working with colleagues who have equal power; contest-oriented tactics for confronting the power structure)

Action System	Community residents; representatives of key community institutions	Constituents; members of oppressed groups	Constituents; beneficiaries; planning agencies; collaborative partners	People who are members of oppressed groups and who have achieved a sense of collective identity
Target System	Partners, collaborators, same as target system	Representatives of oppressive institutions; government decision makers; corporate leaders; members of the political, economic, or social elite	Dysfunctional community, social, or economic systems; decision makers who must be influenced to change the system	Oppressive economic, social, and political systems Harmful values and beliefs perpetuated by oppressive systems

cials, government bureaucrats, and representatives of local institutions (Mondros & Wilson, 1994). Social action–oriented organizers sometimes speak of the target as the enemy. In campaigns, the target can include key decision makers and the general public. Changing public opinion by staging demonstrations, using media campaigns, or educating people about specific issues is often essential in influencing decisions made by public officials. Collaborative strategies require that members of the target system be integrated into the action system. All concerned parties will then cooperate to produce change.

One primary consideration in choosing strategies and tactics is the relationship between the action system and the target system (see figure 10.1). If the action and target systems are the same, use collaborative strategies. If some overlap exists between the action and target systems, use campaign strategies. (Overlap exists when the opposing sides have some members in common or can agree on some common issues.) When the action and target systems are distinct from each other, there is little communication between the two systems, and the power differential between the two groups is large, contest strategies are appropriate (Brager et al., 1987; Kahn, 1991; Warren, 1971).

Figure 10.1. Relationship of action and target systems to strategies.

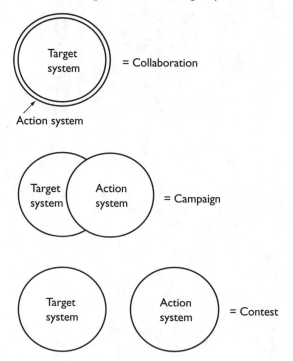

Linking Strategies and Tactics to Intervention Plans

Strategies and tactics are specific steps required to meet a goal (Netting et al., 1993). The effective use of strategies and tactics requires that the organizer create an intervention plan that links models of practice, strategies, tactics, and goals. The organizer's choice of practice model (see chapter 4) should ideally depend on the particular situation, the target of the action, the resources available, the seriousness of the issue at hand, and time constraints (Hardina, 2000; Mondros & Wilson, 1994; Rothman, 1995). Strategies and tactics used to implement the plan should be explicitly linked to the model of practice appropriate for the situation at hand.

Goals may be either long-term or short-term. Long-term goals are focused on the alleviation of social problems or achievement of an ideal state. Short-term goals are objectives or steps toward achieving long-term goals. Goals and objectives used in planning programs or projects should also be an inherent part of any intervention plan (Mondros & Wilson, 1994).

Intervention-related objectives can be task oriented, producing certain specified outcomes, or process oriented. Process-oriented objectives focus on the means, or activities that need to take place so that tasks can be accomplished. For example, a task or outcome objective might be to recruit fifty new organization members. A process objective specifies how this will be done. Here is an example:

The Fairtown Community Organization will conduct ten house meetings to recruit new members.

According to Mondros and Wilson (1994), process objectives in community practice typically pertain to four types of activities: increasing membership, training leaders, strengthening the organization, and public awareness of issues. Process and outcome objectives should be time limited and measurable.

Strategies should be planned well in advance of implementation; be grounded in the culture and experiences of participants; and provide opportunities for people to learn about issues, the power structure, and methods for obtaining power (Mondros & Wilson, 1994). Strategies should also be flexible, changing in response to situational demands or opportunities for action (Kahn, 1991). Plans should also include specific timelines for task accomplishment (Mondros & Wilson, 1994).

Intervention plans should anticipate strategies and tactics opponents will use (Mondros & Wilson, 1994). Organizers should conduct background research to determine how opponents will react to the action system's strategies and tactics (Bobo et al., 1991). Research is also necessary to determine opponents' power resources, their primary interests, and their associations with other power brokers (see chapter 7). It is essential that organizers conduct such research before implementing any intervention plan. Kahn (1991) argues that although in most situations we want to keep our strategies secret from opponents, successful campaign strategies require that organizers let opponents know what their strategy will be. This helps stimulate efforts toward negotiation. The target group can choose between finding common ground and responding to the next steps the action system says it will take.

Mondros and Wilson (1994) characterize good tactics as those that are winnable, unite people, are simple, and help build the organization. Good tactics are also fun—they are enjoyable, provide a chance to socialize with other constituents, and put people at ease. A good or effective tactic is often one that falls outside the opponents' past experience; the targets may not know how to respond to the tactic or may react in a way that the public and the media view as inappropriate or an overreaction (Bobo et al., 1991).

Congruence among Models of Practice, Strategies, and Tactics

Some organizers have difficulty linking models of community practice with strategies and tactics. In her survey of community organization instructors in schools of social work, Hardina (2000) found that respondents preferred social action to other models of practice. However, these respondents identified collaboration as the strategy they most preferred to use. Burghardt (1979) offers one reason that practitioners may be reluctant to use social action: "The relative rarity of social action is also due to the organizational difficulty of maintaining such a conflictual stance over a long period of time" (p. 126).

Mondros and Wilson (1994) argue that organizers seldom use conceptual frameworks to decide when to use strategies and tactics. Instead, their own values and personal comfort level determine practice methods. Consequently, some organizers use the same strategies and tactics over and over. The methods they use do not necessarily vary with the situation or the resources available to them. It is sometimes difficult for social workers to confront members of the power structure (Hardina, 1997). Sometimes the difficulty comes from simply feeling that confrontation is inappropriate or contrary to the principles in the code of ethics. In other instances, it may be difficult for social workers to be assertive enough to engage in direct confrontation. Although workers in some male-dominated professionals (such as business or law) may consider confrontation politics routine, social workers may not have experience in directly challenging decision makers. Consequently, social workers who engage in community organizing may need assertiveness training (Hardcastle, Wenocur, & Powers, 1997).

Reisch and Wenocur (1986) and Specht and Courtney (1994) have suggested that the process of professionalization, or achieving public recognition for the profession, has turned social workers away from social action. Reeser and Epstein (1990), in their study of social action among social workers, found high levels of social work involvement in political action, lobbying for legislation that helps the social work profession, and agency-approved activities. However, they also found that few social workers participated in demonstrations, picketing, or other types of direct social action. It is conceivable that as the profession has given approval to some types of social action (especially activities designed to promote the profession), other types of more militant social action (demonstrations, for example) have lost legitimacy (Wagner, 1990). The rejection of social action–oriented strategies suggests a rejection of social class–based analysis of social problems (Burghardt, 1987; Rivera, 1990).

Choosing Appropriate Tactics

As discussed in chapter 2, many social workers disagree about whether some tactics fall within ethical guidelines established by the National Association of Social Workers (NASW) (Hardina, 2000). Some social worker educators feel that organizers should emphasize collaboration or campaign tactics and use confrontation only as a last resort (Netting et al., 1993). Others feel that social workers have an ethical mandate to produce social change. This ethical commitment includes participation in social movements and the use of a wide variety of tactics (Burghardt & Fabricant, 1987).

The only framework social work practitioners have for making decisions about appropriate tactical methods was developed by Warren (1971). Brager et al. (1987) developed this framework further. Decisions about tactics are determined by three primary factors:

- The degree of consensus among the groups involved about the ultimate goal of the social change effort
- The relationship of the change system to the target system
- Whether the goal can be achieved within the existing power structure

When all parties agree on the desired outcome of the intervention and all groups involved are members of the same system, collaboration can be used. When groups differ on their perceptions of the problem and when there is little communication among groups, contest strategies are used. Campaign strategies are used in situations when overlap exists between the target and action systems and it is possible to establish communication between the two groups.

Brager et al. (1987) have added additional criteria for choosing tactics:

- The seriousness of the issue (will people be harmed if it is not resolved?)
- The public's perception of the legitimacy of the decision-maker.
- The resources available to the change agent.

Community organizations with few funds are more likely to use dramatic or confrontational methods that can be used to get their point across to decision-makers, the media, and the public. Affluent, established organizations often rely on flyers, press conferences, or meetings with newspaper editorial boards to make a point.

The choice of tactics also has to do with the degree of legitimacy the public affords the organization and its members (Brager et al., 1987). Some types of tactics, especially those that involve confrontation, may in the short term anger the public while doing little to persuade people to adopt the group's perspective on the cause. For example, Hardina (1997) describes opposition to Proposition 187 in California. Proposition 187 was intended to cut off access to education, social services, and health care for illegal immigrants. Students who opposed Proposition 187 carried Mexican flags in demonstrations. Such actions (viewed as "anti-American") may have been instrumental in actually generating public support for the proposition, which was approved by California voters.[1] In one instance, college students burned an American flag to protest the vote. This action generated controversy on campus and resulted in a death threat against one of the participants. Consequently, the organization should carefully deliberate the use of confrontation tactics and thoroughly discuss the possible benefits and risks.

An additional concern for organizers is the amount of time available to address the issue. Confrontation tactics may be used in situations in which the organizer has little time to get a point across and when the problem addressed has caused personal harm to individuals. For example, members of the antinuclear and peace movements have often blocked the movement of trains and other vehicles that carried nuclear weapons (Jasper & Poulsen, 1995).

Pilisuk, McAllister, and Rothman (1999) raise the issue of winners and losers in the organizing process. It may be possible for a project to benefit one oppressed group while posing a risk to another. To resolve such ethical dilemmas, organizers must define whether they are working for specific groups, society as a whole, or all disadvantaged people. They must also examine benefits, risks, and long-term consequences of each organizing effort.

Civil Disobedience and Disruption

Not all types of tactics are legal. Organizers and constituents may, depending on the seriousness of the issue and the urgency of working toward a solution, break the law. Cesar Chavez, Gandhi, and Martin Luther King Jr. all engaged in peaceful civil disobedience to gain recognition for causes. Civil disobedience can include sit-ins in restricted areas, marches that have not been sanctioned by public authorities, attempts to block the entry of others into public or private property, nonpayment of taxes, or noncooperation with police or other officials. For example, one of the most famous acts of civil disobedience at the beginning of the civil rights movement was the Rosa Parks's refusal to move to the back of the bus (legally required of African Americans) in Montgomery, Alabama, during the 1950s (Biklen, 1983).

Appropriate use of civil disobedience as a tactic requires that participants be fully committed to the cause; aware of the impact of their actions on themselves and others; and ready to accept any negative consequences of their actions, including jail time, employment loss, and public stigma. Participants in the anti-Vietnam War, civil rights, farmworker, and American Indian movements often risked beatings by the police, were jailed, and in some extreme instances faced death (Carley, 1997). Bobo et al. (1991) argue that civil disobedience is effective when participants are comfortable with the tactic, leadership roles are available for those who do not wish to participate in direct action, and the tactic illustrates to the target that the action system has power. However, they also caution that this tactic can backfire if it limits the organization's ability to recruit new members. Intensive training in the appropriate use of these tactics is mandatory (Lee, 1986).

In some cases, social action organizations deliberately engage in disruptive activities, including direct confrontations with police, rock throwing, and destruction of private property, to convey opposition to government and corporate practices. Disruptive tactics, intended to focus media attention on environmental problems and globalization, were used during the 2000 Republican and Democratic national conventions (Chonin & Wildermuth, 2000). Some of the difficulties inherent in such activities include assignment of responsibility for violence to coalition partners who have not engaged in these activities and the inability of coalition members to control the actions of disruptive organizations or the reactions of the police, the press, and the public (Brager et al., 1987; Lee, 1986). Disruptive events involving physical confrontation or the destruction of property can result in great bodily harm to demonstrators, police, and innocent bystanders and are not recommended.

Brager et al. (1987) offer guidelines for participation in various types of protests (see table 10.2). If the goal of the organizing effort is for both the action system and the target system to make mutually agreed upon adjustments in policies or the manner in which resources are distributed, then the parties can engage in collaboration. If the purpose is to actually transfer resources from one party to another, then campaign is required. If, however, the purpose of the action is to change the status of disadvantaged groups in society (enable them to acquire voting rights, jobs, improvements in education or economic status), then contest or disruption is required. In extreme cases, where the entire system must be restructured, insurrection (which may involve violence or mass civil disobedience) is required. A recent example of effective organizing to restructure the system was the termination of apartheid in South Africa. Tactics used included an international boycott of corporations doing business in South Africa, the campaign to

Table 10.2 Confrontation and the Escalation of Tactics

Goal	Response	Mode of Intervention
Mutual adjustments or rearrangement of resources	Consensus	Collaboration
Redistribution of resources	Difference	Campaigns
Change in social, cultural, economic, or political status and power	Dissensus	Contest or disruption; civil disobedience
Reconstruction of the entire system	Insurrection	Nonviolent, civil disobedience; violence

Source: Adapted from Brager et al., 1987.

free Nelson Mandela from prison, expansion of voting rights to members of oppressed groups, civil disobedience, and use of some violent tactics (African National Congress, 2001). Mass civil disobedience and disruption were also extremely effective in bringing about changes in the former Soviet Union and Eastern Europe without violent resurrection.

Participation in the Decision-Making Process

Constituents and beneficiaries should always be involved in planning interventions (Nettinget al., 1993). As described in chapters 2 and 4, this is particularly critical in situations where the intervention may have harmful consequences, such as jail time, potential loss of employment, or social stigma, for participants. Mondros and Wilson (1994) believe that discussing strategies and tactics with constituency group members is critical to the success of any intervention plan because the organizer, left to his or her own devices, may prefer to use those tactical methods consistent with his or her own values rather than those that are situation specific. In addition, through discussions about tactics, "Members have the opportunity to discuss their fears and reservations about a particular activity" (p. 157). Kahn argues that when participants are involved in the planning process, "They will have much more of a sense of participation and ownership" (p. 178).

It may be difficult to include everyone in decision making. In many organizations, historic patterns of institutional relations exclude women, people of color, persons with disabilities, or LGBT individuals from decision making. Pilisuk et al. (1999) describe dilemmas organizers face as they attempt to include participants in decision-making processes:

> Men may try to speak for women or to withdraw from action led by women. Long-term residents may resent immigrants, who are seen as competition for jobs and services. Most American working people

have never experienced a multiethnic framework of political solidarity, and workers have traditionally belonged to unions and political machines based upon ethnic solidarity and exclusion. (p. 114)

True participation requires preparation and resources (Hardina & Malott, 1996). It also requires that organizers maintain a multicultural perspective. They should also adhere to the social work value of empowerment, promoting inclusion (Gutierrez & Alvarez, 2000). Beresford and Croft (1993) identify the following attributes of an inclusive decision-making process:

- Resources (places to meet, clerical support, publicity, and travel expense coverage)
- Information about the scope of the problem at hand, resources available for remediation, and possible solutions
- Training in participatory processes
- Equal access to services and opportunities to participate
- Appropriate forums and structures that enhance involvement
- Use of language and terminology that is accessible to all participants, including appropriate translation services
- An evaluation mechanism that includes opportunities for constituency group members to participate in research design, data collection, and analysis

Fostering participation in intervention planning also requires that the organizer develop appropriate interpersonal and group work skills. Such skills include leadership development; group facilitation; development of group cohesion; task assignment; volunteer motivation; and ability to work with constituents to identify, attain, and evaluate group outcomes (Burghardt, 1979; Zachary, 2000). Group work styles will vary depending on the strategies used to attain outcomes; community development efforts will employ collaborative approaches that focus on consensus building, group cohesion, and process. Social action–oriented groups are more likely to focus on outcomes as well as specific task accomplishment by members.

Multicultural Organizing and the Choice of Tactics

The choice of tactical methods should include consensus-oriented approaches to organization that are appropriate for working with women or members of Asian, African American, Latino, American Indian, and other ethnic communities. Methods that incorporate traditional cultural values are viewed as more effective than confrontation-oriented tactics used within hierarchical decision-making structures characteristic of white, male-dominated institutions (Rivera & Erlich, 1998; Weil, 1986). Organizers must be prepared to organize within specific ethnic communities as well as across ethnic boundaries.

Ndubisi (1991) describes conflicts that occurred between government planners in Ontario, Canada, and the Grassy Narrow Ojibway community in the development of a community master plan. The plan focused on improvements in the physical environment and social service delivery. The planning agency's institutional structure and hierarchical decision-making approach conflicted with traditional methods of consensus-oriented decision making used by the tribal government. Ndubisi identifies a number of value conflicts that made decision making difficult, including time orientation (past, present, future), conceptualization of space (economic versus spiritual), relationship to the environment (harmony with nature versus control over nature), and self-expression in activities (being versus doing). He argues that much of the conflict could have been avoided if participants had adopted the transformative model of practice and engaged in dialogue to exchange cultural and technical knowledge.

O'Donnell and Karanja (2000) see culturally specific, transformative approaches as essential for the development of effective community-development activities. They define transformative approaches as a process of changing the following:

1. How individual people in the community see themselves, developing deeper understanding of who they are and what they can accomplish
2. How they see themselves in relationship with others in the community, building a collective identity and a sense of common purpose and efficacy
3. How people outside the community view the community and its people. (pp. 75–76)

To recruit and motivate organization members it is essential that organizers be able to articulate issues and use symbols that are culturally appropriate to the target audience. Symbols can include verbal, written, visual, and musical images that communicate a variety of meanings or themes. The use of community leaders, religious figures, or celebrities to publicize a cause also conveys a message about the symbolic importance of an issue. For example, 2000 presidential candidate Al Gore chose a religious Jew, Senator Joseph Lieberman, as his running mate due to public recognition and respect for Lieberman's religious values and his condemnation of President Clinton during the Lewinsky affair. Symbolically, Senator Lieberman indicated that the ticket was dedicated to good moral values.

Symbols and the meaning associated with them are essential components of the organizing process. According to Jasper and Poulsen (1995), "A powerful symbol lends credibility to an explicit argument by connoting the implicit assumptions embedded in worldviews and common sense"(p. 498). Symbols have relevance not only to specific cultural groups, but also to people of specific genders or gender orientations and different physical or mental abilities and social classes. Swerdlow (1993) describes the Women's Strike for Peace in 1961 as successful, in part due to its use of the concept of motherhood to generate support for the cause:

> On 22 September a call was issued from Washington to women across the nation, urging them to suspend their regular routine of home, family, and jobs for one day, in order to "Appeal to All Governments to End the Arms Race—Not the Human Race." The organizational call declared: "We strike against death, desolation, destruction on behalf of life and liberty . . . . Husbands or babysitters take over the home front. Bosses or substitutes take over our job!" (p. 18)

In part, this organizing effort was successful due to its saliency to white, middle-income women. The symbols used in the organizing effort must have saliency (in terms of both personal recognition and emotional response) for members of the constituency group as well as the intended targets. Other examples of effective cultural symbols include the United Farm Workers' eagle (with origins in the mythology associated with indigenous culture), pictures of cute animals subjected to scientific testing, or use of the song "We Shall Overcome" to build support for the civil rights movement during the 1960s. Note, however, that each of these symbols conveys a variety of meanings to different social, cultural, and economic groups.

Reisch and Jarman-Rohde (1999) argue that cultural activities are often one of the only tools that can be used to strengthen group identity and integrate people into community life. In addition, cultural activities play a role in making community-organizing efforts accessible to community residents. They also help constituents examine broader issues by inspiring people to share their own worldview within the creative process. And cultural activities help bring people to the organizing effort simply because they are fun!

Cultural activities are not in themselves sufficient to bring people together across ethnic boundaries, however. Kahn (1991) believes that multicultural organizing cannot succeed without the development of organizational structures that foster equity in resource sharing, administration, and leadership. Such organizations should recruit people from differing ethnic backgrounds and provide ongoing education about race and cultural issues. Cultural and social activities designed to maintain the organization and sustain participation should be culturally appropriate and inclusive. Efforts should also be made to identify common issues that are of sufficient saliency that they can unite members in collective action.

Mixing and Phasing Intervention Approaches

Bradshaw, Soifer, and Gutierrez (1994) recommend an approach to practice that draws on both Alinsky-style (conflict-oriented) social action and feminist practice models for work in ethnic communities. The model is intended to be flexible, with strategies and tactics chosen that fit the situation at hand. When bringing individuals within ethnic communities together, the organizer should utilize collaborative methods to facilitate change. Initial approaches to members of the power structure should also be collaborative in nature. However, it is recommended that the organizer, with the approval of constituents, shift to Alinksy-style methods in situations where the power differential between the decision makers and the community is large.

According to Rothman (1995, 1996), models of practice can also be mixed to create new hybrid forms of practice. Distinct models of practice can also be used during different phases of the organizing process. Rothman identifies three hybrid models of practice:

- Action/planning. The prototypes for this model are consumer advocacy and environmental groups that agitate to inform the public about the seriousness of various issues but also conduct empirical research on the problem and issue detailed plans that can be used to address it. The more powerful the action/planning organization, the more likely it is to see its plans adopted. Some environmental groups have become so powerful that they have been given seats on corporate boards.
- Development/action. Rothman (1996) argues that both feminist and transformative practice fit the development/action model. Work is conducted within specific population groups or geographic communities to bring members together. When members work to identify common problems, they will also be motivated to take action against oppressive institutions in which these problems originate.
- Planning/development. The United Way and local citizen planning councils can be characterized as groups that involve local residents in developing comprehensive plans for health, social services, and economic development. Recruiting individuals to participate in the creation of plans is one of the primary functions of these groups. In addition, these organizations must provide detailed information about the problem and train members to interpret technical reports and propose solutions.

Many social problems are so complex that a variety of strategies must be used to resolve the problem. Consequently, Rothman (1995, 1996) argues that different strategies and tactics (with origins in different practice models) must be used to resolve specific social problems. For example, when crime reduction is a goal, a community organization might undertake the following steps:

1. Use community development and strategies associated with collaboration to bring together community residents and key local institutions including the police, local businesses, and churches.

2. Use social planning–related strategies to conduct research into community problems and create a detailed plan to address the problem. For example, if the problem identified is the length of police response time when crime reports are made, ask constituency group members to come together to create a detailed plan to address this problem.

3. Use social action–oriented strategies involving campaign or contest to acquire resources needed to implement the plan and to persuade politicians to support the plan. For example, the police union may need persuasion to support the plan. The community group may need to persuade local government to provide the additional funds for implementation (see table 10.3).

Some organizers believe that strategies and tactics should be used in phases based on the degree of intensity (Netting et al., 1993). For example, collaboration is usually perceived to require low-intensity actions: a low degree of persuasion or manipulation is required for people to act. If collaborative tactics fail, the organizer can move on to campaign strategies that require a mild degree of coercion. If campaign tactics fail, the organizer and the constituency group can safely adopt contest-related strategies (see figure 10.2). As noted in chapter 4, some organizers reject collaborative strategies, arguing that the acquisition of coercive power is necessary to persuade members of the political or economic elite to accept social change (Bobo et al., 1991; Rivera, 1990).

Evaluation of Intervention Processes and Outcomes

The success of the intervention in community practice is typically measured in relation to whether strategies and tactics were sufficient to achieve long-term outcome goals. Kahn (1991) argues that the achievement of outcomes should be only one measure of successful outcomes. We also need to know how participants felt about the action. How would they assess the quality of the experience, their own reactions, and the reaction of targets?

A series of failures involving the implementation of tactics often requires that the action system revise the intervention plan. It is also important that in response to critical incidents that occur and must be re-

Figure 10.2.   Continuum: Escalation of strategies.

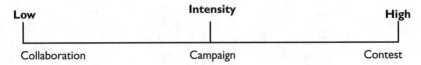

Table 10.3 Creating an Intervention Plan

Long-Term Goal	Intermediate and Short-Term Objectives	Resource Needs	Action System	Target System	Model of Practice	Strategy	Tactics	Evaluation Criteria
Reduce crime in Fairtown			Fairtown Community Organization; local churches, businesses, police, residents		Community development	Collaboration, campaign	Cooperation, negotiation	Reduction in crime reports
	Increase citizen involvement by organizing a neighborhood watch	Outreach workers, funds, publicity		Community residents	Community development		Problem solving, cooperation	Number of block club members recruited

Close at least 2 crack houses per month	Media, police, citizens	Drug dealers	Social action	Contest	Confrontation, neighborhood pressure	Number of houses closed
Decrease police response time to crime reports by 10 minutes	Police, media	Police practices	Community development, social planning	Collaboration, campaign	Problem solving, media advocacy	Length of response time (pre- and posttest)
Improve relations with police through regular meetings	Meeting space, publicity, relationships with public officials	Police practices, community residents, public officials	Community development	Collaboration, campaign	Lobby officials, cooperation, negotiation	Community forums to assess improvements

Source: Adapted from Bobo et al., 1991.

sponded to, intervention plans be amended to prevent harm to individuals or because they provide a window of opportunity to address a social problem (Jenness, 1995). Consequently, most evaluations of intervention plans should develop and change in response to the situation at hand. However, it is critical that an overall outcome evaluation be conducted to assess the plan's effectiveness, with the proviso that in some instances the intended outcome may be modified or changed before the completion of the intervention.

Successful implementation calls for a celebration of the achievement (Kahn, 1991). Parties and other types of celebrations help motivate volunteers and consequently enhance the likelihood of future success as the organization moves forward with the intervention. Mondros and Wilson (1994) believe that it is not sufficient simply to measure success in terms of outcome (see figure 10.3). Process is also important. Has the intervention strengthened the organization, increased members, stimulated leadership development, or increased public awareness of the organization and the issues it supports?

Linking goals and objectives to specific strategies and tactics allows the evaluators to directly assess whether specific actions produced the intended

Figure 10.3. Steps in the intervention plan development process.

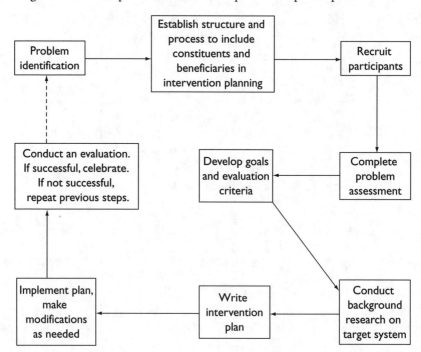

outcomes (see table 10.2). Organizers should identify evaluation criteria before implementing the intervention plan. Quantification of objectives and specific time lines allows the participants to measure success. However, additional measures such as consumer satisfaction surveys, community forums, social indicator analysis, and pre and post tests can be used to provide additional information for any evaluation. Given that constituents should be included in planning and conducting the evaluation, any data collected should be analyzed and reported in a way that makes it easily accessible and understandable to constituents (see chapters 11and 14 for more information on program planning and evaluation).

Computer Resources for Intervention Planning

A large number of Web sites contain information and support services for community organizers. One of these sites is operated by the Association for Community Organization and Social Administration (http://www.acosa .org). Though ACOSA has an interdisciplinary focus, most of its members are social workers. A group called COMM-ORG also maintains a Web page (http://comm-org.utoledo.edu). This site includes working papers, which describe research on community organizing efforts, and helpful information about strategies. Organizers find information about strategies and tactics using the Community Toolbox (http://ctb.lsi.ukans.edu). A number of these sites also provide training and support for organizers interested in using the Internet to facilitate social change (see, for example, HandsNet at http:// www.handsnet-training.org).

Organizers can also use Internet technologies to link with organizations and constituents (McNutt, 2000). They can use E-mail to recruit members and lobby government decision makers and LISTSERVs, bulletin boards, and chat rooms to set up on-line communities in which constituents can discuss common problems and plan for collective action (McNutt, 2000). Organizers can also construct Web pages that provide information on social problems, propose solutions, and describe actions that can address these problems. For a good example of a social action organization's Web page, see the United Farm Workers' site at http://www.ufw.org. It contains information on current issues, upcoming events, pending legislation, and products that members can purchase to help the organization reach its fund-raising goals.

Organizers can also educate the community about using Internet resources so that constituents can make direct use of technology to contact decision makers, inform the public about local problems, gain access to information, and lobby decision makers (Blundo, Mele, Hairston, & Watson, 1999; Schon, Sanyal, & Mitchell, 1999). Later chapters of this book will describe in greater detail how to use the computer for research, data analysis, fund-raising, lobbying, and tracking campaign donations.

Summary

To choose effective strategies and tactics, organizers must be able to analyze the situation at hand, determine the model of practice appropriate to the situation, identify the target and action systems, and determine the amount of power that can be acquired by both systems. In addition, they must identify the resources available to the target system and the amount of time that can be allocated to carry out the action. The organizer and the constituent group must also determine how the intervention will be evaluated. They must use strategies and tactics that fit the experience of the participants and that are culturally appropriate.

Strategies and tactics must be consistent with the model(s) of practice used to implement the intervention and should also be linked to specific goals and objectives as well as to evaluation criteria. The choice of strategies and tactics is also determined by the degree of relationship between the action system and the target system, the degree of public legitimacy associated with the action system, the primary purpose of the organizing effort, and the degree to which the public recognizes the seriousness of the issue to be addressed. Chapter 11 describes techniques that organizers can use to plan programs and choose among goals and objectives.

■ QUESTIONS FOR CLASS DISCUSSION

1. What verbal, pictorial, video, or musical symbols or which celebrities do you associate with social movements and causes (for example, women's rights, gay and lesbian rights, disability rights, pro-choice and/or pro-life, and civil rights)?
2. Identify disruptive tactics. Do you think these tactics are consistent with social work practice? Are there instances in which they should be used? What are some of the consequences of using them?
3. Should social workers engage in civil disobedience? Why or why not? What types of social problems are serious enough to outweigh breaking the law? What are some of the possible consequences of civil disobedience for the social worker? Would you be willing to accept such a penalty?
4. Identify at least three current campaigns (nonpolitical) described in the media. What strategies and tactics were used in these campaigns? How was the public informed about the issues involved in the campaigns? How effective were they? Were the rules of engagement made explicit to nonparticipants?
5. Do you think that it is ethical to use certain types of contest strategies (destruction of property or break-ins) to protest cruelty to animals? Why or why not?

■ ANALYSIS OF CULTURAL SYMBOLS, STRATEGIES AND TACTICS IN SOCIAL MOVEMENTS

Identify a current or past social movement that interests you. Use media accounts, biographies, books (both fiction and nonfiction), personal interviews and narratives, and other archival data to analyze the cultural symbols associated with the movement. For example, an analysis of the antiwar movement in the 1960s might focus on the strategic use of rock music to rally people to the cause. An examination of the United Farm Workers might focus on the use of music, religion, and other cultural symbols.

In your analysis, focus on the following questions:

1. What strategies and tactics did the social movement use to recruit members?
2. What symbols were used to inspire members and what do they mean?
3. What tactics did the primary social action organizations associated with the movement use to recruit organizers and constituents?
4. What strategies and tactics did they employ to garner public support?
5. What resources were used to build the social movement?
6. How were volunteers who were not from the target community utilized?
7. Who were the political allies of the primary social action organizations involved?

   a. Did the primary social action organization share a common cultural orientation and value system with some of its political allies?
   b. What were the potential costs and benefits of the alliance for participant organizations?

8. What was the most powerful interest group that opposed the primary social action organizations involved? What were the group's or institution's power resources?
9. What power resources did the social action organization use to fight this group?
10. How would you assess the effectiveness of the tactics the primary social action organization employed?
11. How did opponents respond to those tactics?
12. What environmental influences (social, cultural, media, political, or economic) were essential to the development of the social movement in question?

■ INTERVENTION PLAN

Develop an intervention plan to address a community problem. Your plan should include the following:

- Identification of the community organization model used to develop the plan (social action, community development, social planning, feminist organizing, transformatives, multicultural, or other models identified in this chapter)
- Identification of the strategies to be used
- Identification of tactics consistent with the model of practice identified
- Identification of both the target system and the action system
- Identification of the power resources associated with both the target system and the action system
- Specification of a timeline for each action to be taken
- Identification of the resources needed to carry out the plan (money, facilities, members, technical expertise, media, influential decision makers, etc.)
- Identification of potential barriers to successful completion of the change effort (opponents, resource limitations, current legislation or policies, etc)
- Your assessment as to whether the change effort is likely to succeed
- Criteria for evaluating action outcomes

In addition, you should create a chart that links goals and objectives to specific strategies and tactics (see table 10.2). At least one of the objectives should be process oriented and at least one should be task oriented.

Note

1. Proposition 187 was contested in the courts by pro-immigrant and civil rights groups and was never implemented.

References

African National Congress (2001). Profile of Nelson Rolihaha Mandela [On-line]. Available: http://www.anc.org.za/people/mandela.html.

Beresford, P., & Croft, S. (1993). *Citizen involvement: A practical guide for change.* London: Macmillan.

Biklen, D. (1983). *Community organizing: Theory and practice.* Englewood Cliffs, NJ: Prentice-Hall.

Blundo, R., Mele, C., Hairston, R., & Watson, J. (1999). The Internet and demystifying power differentials: A few women on-line and the housing authority. *Journal of Community Practice, 6*(2), 11–26.

Bobo, K., Kendall, J., & Max, S. (1991). *Organizing for social change: A manual for activists in the 1990s.* Santa Ana, CA: Seven Locks.

Bradshaw, C., Soifer, S., & Gutierrez, L. (1994). Toward a hybrid model for effective organizing in communities of color. *Journal of Community Practice, 1*, 25–41.

Brager, G., Specht, H., & Torczyner, J. (1987). *Community organizing* (2d ed.). New York: Columbia University Press.

Burghardt, S. (1979). Tactical use of group structure and process in community organizations. In F. Cox, J. Erlich, J. Rothman, & J. Tropman (Eds.), *Strategies of community organization* (3d ed., pp. 112–37). Itasca, IL: Peacock.

Burghardt. S. (1987). Community-based social action. In A. Minahan (Ed.), *The encyclopedia of social work* (18th ed., Vol. 2, pp. 292–99). Silver Spring, MD: National Association of Social Workers.

Burghardt, S., & Fabricant, M. (1987). Radical social work. In A. Minahan (Ed.), *The encyclopedia of social work* (18th ed., Vol. 2, pp. 455–62). Silver Spring, MD: National Association of Social Workers.

Carley, M. (1997). Defining forms of successful state repression of social movement organizations. A case study of the FBI's Cointelpro and the American Indian Movement. *Research in Social Movements, Conflicts, and Change, 20,* 151–76.

Castelloe, P., & Watson, T. (1999). Participatory education as a community practice model: A case example from a comprehensive Head Start program. *Journal of Community Practice, 6*(1), 71–89.

Chonin, N., & Wildermuth, A. (2000, August 16). Mostly peaceful protests on day two. *San Francisco Chronicle,* p. A15.

Freire, P. (1970). *Pedagogy of the oppressed.* New York: Continuum.

Gutierrez, L., & Alvarez, A. (2000). Educating students for multicultural community practice. *Journal of Community Practice, 7*(1), 39–56.

Hardcastle, D., Wenocur, S., & Powers, P. (1997). *Community practice: Theories and skills for social workers.* New York: Oxford University Press.

Hardina, D. (1997). Empowering students for community organization practice: Teaching confrontation tactics. *Journal of Community Practice, 4*(2), 51–63.

Hardina, D. (2000). Models and tactics taught in community organization courses: Findings from a survey of practice instructors. *Journal of Community Practice, 7*(1), 5–18.

Hardina, D., & Malott, O. W. (1996). Strategies for the empowerment of low income consumers on community-based planning boards. *Journal of Progressive Human Services, 7*(2), 43–61.

Jasper, J., & Poulsen, J. (1995). Recruiting strangers and friends: Moral shocks and social networks in animal rights and anti-nuclear protests. *Social Problems, 42*(4), 493–512.

Jenness, V. (1995). Social movement growth, domain expansion, and framing processes: The gay/lesbian movement and violence against gays and lesbians as a social problem. *Social Problems, 42*(1), 145–170.

Kahn, S. (1991). *Organizing: A guide for grassroots leaders.* Washington, DC: National Association of Social Workers.

Lee, B. (1986). *Pragmatics of community organization.* Mississauga, Ontario: Commonact.

McNutt, J. (2000). Organizing cyberspace: Strategies for teaching about community practice and technology. *Journal of Community Practice, 7*(1), 95–109.

Mondros, J., & Wilson, S. (1994). *Organizing for power and empowerment.* New York: Columbia University Press.

Ndubisi, F. (1991). Variations in value orientations: Implications for guiding community decision behavior in cross cultural settings. *Journal of Planning Education and Research, 11*(1), 51–65.

Netting, E., Kettner, P., & McMurty, S. (1993). *Social work macro practice.* New York: Longman.

O'Donnell, S., & Karanja, S. (2000). Transformative community practice: Building a model for developing extremely low income African-American communities. *Journal of Community Practice, 7*(3), 67–84.

Pilisuk, M., McAllister, J., & Rothman, J. (1999). Social change professionals and grassroots organizing. In M. Minkler (Ed.), *Community organizing and community building for health* (pp. 103–99). New Brunswick, NJ: Rutgers University Press.

Reeser, L., & Epstein, I. (1990). *Professionalization and activism in social work.* New York: Columbia University Press.

Reisch, M., & Jarman-Rohde, L. (1999, March 11). *Using cultural activities to teach multicultural community practice.* Paper presented at the Annual Program Meeting of the Council on Social Work Education, San Francisco, CA.

Reisch, M., & Wenocur, S. (1986). The future of community organization in social work: Social activism and the politics of profession building. *Social Service Review, 60,* 70–93.

Rivera, F. (1990). The way of bushido in community organization teaching. *Administration in Social Work, 14,* 43–59.

Rivera, F., & Erlich, J. (1998). *Community organizing in a diverse society* (3d ed.). Boston: Allyn & Bacon.

Rothman, J. (1995). Approaches to community intervention. In F. Cox, J. Erlich, J. Rothman, & J. Tropman (Eds.), *Strategies of Community Organization* (4th ed., pp. 26–61). Itasca, IL: Peacock.

Rothman, J. (1996). The interweaving of community intervention approaches. *Journal of Community Practice, 3*(3/4), 69–99.

Schon, D., Sanyal, B., & Mitchell, W. (1999). *High technology and low-income communities.* Cambridge, MA: MIT Press.

Specht, H., & Courtney, M. (1994). *Unfaithful angels: How social work has abandoned its mission.* New York: Free Press.

Swerdlow, A. (1993). *Women strike for peace: Traditional motherhood and racial politics in the 1960s.* Chicago: University of Chicago Press.

Wagner, D. (1990). *The quest for a radical profession: Social service careers and political ideology.* Lanham, MD: University Press of America.

Warren, R. (1971). Types of purposive social change at the community level. In R. Warren (Ed.), *Truth, love, and social change* (pp. 134–49). Chicago: Rand McNally.

Weil, M. (1986). Women, community, and organizing. In N. Van Den Bergh & L. Cooper (Eds.), *Feminist visions for social work* (pp. 187–210). Silver Spring, MD: National Association of Social Workers.

Zachary, E. (2000). Grassroots leadership training: A case study of an effort to integrate theory and method. *Journal of Community Practice, 7*(1), 71–93.

Web Resources

Alliance for Justice—http://www.afj.org/

Applied Research Center—http://www.arc.org/

Association for Community Organization Reform Now (ACORN)—http://www.acorn.org/

Association for Community Organization and Social Administration—http://www.acosa.org/

Center for Third World Organizing—http://www.ctwo.org/

Civic Practices Network—http://www.cpn.org

COMM-ORG—http://comm-org.utoledo.edu/

Community Toolbox—http://ctb.lsi.ukans.edu/

HandsNet—http://www.handsnet-training.org/
Midwest Academy—http://www.midwestacademy.com/
National Organizers Alliance—http://www.noacentral.org
National Housing Institute—http://www.nhi.org/
Neighborhood Funders Group—http://www.nfg.org/
Neighborhoods On-line—http://www.neighborhoodsonline.net
Note: A number of these sites contain training manuals for community building and choosing strategies and tactics.

11 Planning Programs and Services

■ Community organizers often encounter situations in which they need to design programs or work with others collaboratively to construct service-delivery systems. In this chapter we examine theoretical approaches to planning and identify planning models. The role of citizen participation in the planning process is described; technical and political skills required for effective planning practice are examined. The reader is introduced to planning techniques that can be used to develop program plans and funding proposals. This chapter also describes computer applications that can be used to find information, analyze data, evaluate outcomes, and involve citizens in the planning process.

Planning as a Field of Practice

Social workers may be employed by public, nonprofit, and for-profit organizations that plan social services or health-related projects and programs. Although planning is considered a component of community organization practice—most social workers engage in planning when they write funding proposals, design programs, construct budgets, and work with coalitions to put together collaborative service-delivery systems—it is also a separate professional discipline that focuses on the development of technical skills necessary to gather information, analyze data, and make recommendations about the best options needed to address social problems. Planners also must develop political and interpersonal skills to interact with decision makers, influence decisions, and engage citizens in the decision-making process (Forester, 1989). In addition to social services planning, this field of practice can include national security planning, economic planning, environmental planning, city planning, regional development, and community economic development (Friedmann, 1987). Planning methods are also used in the design of health promotion, prevention, and primary care programs (Cornelius, Battle, Kryder-Coe, & Hu, 1999; Minkler, 1999).

Master's level graduate programs provide education for planners; the American Planning Association (http://planning.org) is the professional membership organization for this discipline. The terminal degree for this profession is a Ph.D. in policy analysis. Friedmann (1987) defines policy analysis as

a form of anticipatory decision-making, a cognitive process that uses technical reason to explore and evaluate possible courses of action. The client for this exercise is a "rational decision maker" who is implicitly regarded also as the executor of policy who will follow up his or her choice with the appropriate implementing actions. (p.181)

Rothman and Zald (1995) identify a number of technical skills needed by social workers who engage in social services planning: needs assessment, program development, ability to choose among alternative plans, political liaison, knowledge of how to draft legislation, program administration, proposal writing, fund-raising, and evaluation. All skills that are generic to the process of planning. In addition, both planning disciplines, social work and urban planning, require the planner to be committed to the promotion of citizen participation, the inclusion of program beneficiaries in the development and evaluation of plans and policies (Arnstein, 1969; Forester, 1989; Gilbert & Terrell, 1998). The urban planning and social work professions are also committed to social justice, fairness, and equity as basic practice principles and promote the implementation of public policies that reduce racial disparities and promote the equal distribution of resources across ethnic populations (Anthony, 1999; de Oliver & Dawson-Munoz, 1996; Giloth & Moe, 1999).

Theoretical Approaches to Planning

Planning involves making choices, clarifying options, and determining the benefits and risks of the various choices involved. Organizers use planning techniques to design programs, write funding proposals, coordinate services, lobby for funds, draft government policies, develop legislation, and produce intervention plans. Values are inherent in the planning process; interventions that support or uphold certain key values are proposed or implemented. Value assumptions often included in plans include access, adequacy, diversity, equality, equity, efficiency, representation, self-determination, self-sufficiency, and distribution (Patton & Sawicki, 1993).

Models of planning practice differ along two key dimensions (Gilbert & Terrell, 1998; Hudson, 1983):

1. The role of planning in society
2. Appropriate participants in the planning process

Planning is intended to serve the public interest. However, planners and other decision makers may not always define the public in the same way. Gilbert and Terrell (1998) identify three different views of the public interest: the organismic, communalistic, and individualistic approaches.

The organismic view is that the planner is the expert or technocrat. The planner views the public as a "unitary organism whose interests are greater or different than the sum of its parts" (p. 256). The public's best interests are served through using technological approaches to diagnose community problems and develop the solution that will create a healthy, well-balanced community. Though such planners may be employed by government or private agencies, their primary allegiance is to their profession and the appropriate use of technology, information sources, and logic to achieve the best outcome for the public.

The communalistic view holds that all members of the public have interests in common. These common interests are expressed in the political process by elected representatives and nonpartisan leaders in community institutions. Planning options are guided by the values and ideologies of these leaders. These values and planning preferences have priority over the preferences expressed by other, less powerful groups in society. The planner's role is that of a bureaucrat who is accountable to the elected officials he or she serves (Gilbert & Terrell, 1998).

The individualistic view is that a single, unified public interest cannot be defined. Groups express very different interests in the political process. As described in chapter 7, the public interest is defined through political negotiation and compromise among competing groups (Lindblom, 1959). In this view, the planner is primarily an advocate who represents the interest of a particular group in the planning process. Successful lobbying for legislation depends on the degree of power the interest group holds, the power resources associated with other groups, and the skill of the planner in promoting the group's interests.

Planners also disagree about who should be involved in planning. Some planners believe that only professional planners with appropriate technological expertise should be involved in the planning process. Others believe that politicians and interest groups, through lobbying, compromise and negotiation, should properly make planning decisions. A third view of planning is that planners and the people who will benefit from these plans should be equal partners in the planning process. Some approaches suggest that the planner has the responsibility for guiding beneficiaries in developing the best plan and choosing value preferences (to be incorporated into planning goals). Other approaches suggest that the "customer is always right," that the planner simply acts to represent the views of specific interest groups (Friedmann, 1987).

Forester (1989) argues that planners perform three primary tasks:

1. Technical problem-solving
2. Information processing
3. Establishing relationships with political decision makers and building coalitions to generate support for plans

Within these frameworks are a number of competing approaches to planning: rational, incremental, advocacy, transactive, and Marxist approaches. All of these approaches are organized using the five steps in the problem-solving model: problem identification, assessment, goal setting, implementation, and evaluation. Some problem-solving models add a sixth component: choosing among goals. As noted in chapter 1, Gilbert and Terrell (1998) add two additional components to be used in community organization practice: informing the public and building public support and legitimacy.

Rational Model

The rational model in planning is synonymous with the problem-solving model used in social work practice. The planner is to use rational logic, expert knowledge, and information to identify social problems, assess those problems, identify and choose among possible solutions or goals, implement the plan, and evaluate it. This model assumes that it is possible to collect sufficient knowledge so that the best plan will be chosen.

The model assumes that planning decisions should be made by the planner and that the planner is the best person to pass judgment on the most appropriate plan. The expert (by virtue of his or her technical skills and education) will always make the best decision to advance the well-being of society. The tasks that require expertise are problem analysis, data collection, priority ranking, program design, data analysis, and evaluation (Gilbert & Terrell, 1998).

The limitations of this model are that not all planners have enough money, time, and information to make the best decision in all situations (Forester, 1989). Planning decisions are not always made rationally; they may be influenced by politics, one's employer, and the planner's own values. The various participants in the planning process may have very different values that must be reconciled before a decision can be made (Rothman & Zald, 1995). In addition, these other participants (often program benefici- aries) may have information about the problem or the proposed solution that is not always available to the planner.

Incremental Approach

Incremental planning is the approach to decision making described by Lind- blom (1959). Policy and program plans are determined through negotiation among interest groups (see chapter 7). Compromises mediated by govern- ment (most often through legislative processes) allow powerful interest groups to obtain a measure of satisfaction when some of their preferences are incorporated into new legislation. This process is called satisficing. The role of the planner in this pluralist decision-making process is to "gather information by bridging organization boundaries, by using social networks, and by tapping sources of expertise" (Forester, 1989, p. 56).

The limitation of this model is that it gives the impression that no one group dominates the planning process, when in fact the most powerful groups dominate. The planner (often a government official) assumes a pas- sive role as the various interest groups compete to influence the final de- cision. The most politically expedient policy rather than the best plan is adopted and implemented.

Advocacy Planning

Advocacy planning also assumes that policy and plans are determined through the interaction of interest groups. All plans reflect the interests of specific groups. Advocacy planners work on behalf of specific groups in- volved in the planning process and utilize methods best suited to represent the views of these groups (Peattie, 1968). They reject the idea that there exists a single best solution to problems or that there is one unified public interest. Advocacy planners are employed by interest groups; often these groups are players in the political process who have fewer power resources than other participants (interest groups that represent the poor or members of oppressed groups). Consequently, the role of the planner is to develop strategies and tactics to equalize the decision-making playing field and to advocate for his or her constituency group (Forester, 1989). Davidoff (1973) describes advocacy planning as a pluralist approach that takes place in an atmosphere of competition:

> Where unitary planning prevails, advocacy is not of paramount im- portance, for there is little or no competition for the plan prepared

by the public agency. The concept of advocacy as taken from legal practice implies the opposition of at least two contending viewpoints in an adversary proceeding. (p. 282)

Forester (1989) argues that the involvement of multiple interest groups with varying ideologies and preferences makes the planning and decision-making process much more complex and often necessitates political bargaining to reconcile competing interests. The success of the planner in this process relies not on technical skill, but on the ability of participants to acquire and utilize power resources such as money, information, media connections, and members to influence the political process.

The major limitation of this model is that interest groups are perceived to be constantly fighting with one another. Few incentives exist to form coalitions around shared interests. The planner may adopt the values and perceptions of his or her employers, losing opportunities to find common ground with other groups. In addition, the advocacy planner who exclusively serves the employer's best interest may find that the employer's agenda conflicts with the planner's own values and interests.

Transactive Planning

The transactive model of planning, as described by Friedmann (1987), attempts to integrate the work of Freire (1970) into the planning process. Planning is carried out through face-to-face contact with the people affected by decisions (often those people who are least likely to have their voices heard in the planning process). Participants "acquire a critical consciousness of its [the community's] own conditions of oppression, but also learn to engage in direct action" (Friedmann, 1987, p. 302). Consequently, planners and constituents must engage in the process of mutual learning.

Both expert knowledge and the knowledge acquired through the experiences of constituency group members are central to the planning process. Planning is carried out through a process of dialogue and negotiation between constituents and planners. Consequently, planners and constituents are equal partners in the development of plans. Friedmann (1987) argues that planners who adopt this approach cannot be government employees because transactive planning is designed to oppose oppressive state practices.

The limitation of this model is that it may be cumbersome and time-consuming to incorporate the voices of many constituents in the planning process. Full participation may also be costly, forcing a number of delays and redirection of the planning process. It also requires cooperation among the people and organizations represented in the process. This may be difficult to achieve in real life.

Marxist Approach

The basic assumption of Marxist planning is that the state consists of institutions that act to promote social harmony and preserve economic arrangements that benefit corporate interests (Burghardt & Fabricant, 1987). The planning process focuses on social movements and grassroots community action. The purpose of Marxist approaches to planning is to try to understand how the economic system works and to increase the strength of the working classes. Traditional planning is viewed as serving the capitalist system. Consequently, new forms of social action and planning techniques are sought. Marxist planning is often associated with critical theory. Critical theory examines how existing social institutions foster oppression of the poor. The planner's role is to help members of oppressed groups understand restrictions imposed by the system. Such an understanding is believed to be essential for the success of taking action to foster social change. The critical perspective regards the current status quo as harmful and believes that action should be taken to address social problems (Friedman, 1987). According to Forester (1989), critical theory in planning "suggests how existing social and political-economic relations actually operate to distort communications, to obscure issues, to manipulate trust and consent, to twist facts and possibility" (p. 414).

Friedmann (1987) identifies tasks that planners who are committed to social change should conduct:

1. Critiquing the present situation
2. Mobilizing communities and working with them to search for solutions
3. Collecting information in order to develop change strategies
4. Working with groups to refine the technical details of their solutions
5. Using the transformative model to filter theoretical and ideological knowledge and values so that the group learns from its own experience
6. Developing experiential knowledge and disseminating it using methods appropriate for the project
7. Mediating communications between the group and the power structure
8. Ensuring participation by all group members
9. Helping the group develop ideology to support social action
10. Participating in the action so that the planner can link knowledge to action

The primary limitation of Marxist planning is that its short-term benefits may be sacrificed for long-term gain. Solutions proposed through this process may not be politically or economically feasible. A third problem with this approach is that members of oppressed groups may be unwilling to recognize their own oppression or to take action to change the system

(Minkler & Pies, 1999). This is especially true when planners from outside the community or group in question attempt to impose their own values and ideologies on the planning process (Rivera & Erlich, 1998).

Planning Activities

Basic planning activities include problem identification, assessment, goal development, techniques used to choose among alternative goals, implementation, and evaluation. There are two primary types of plans: strategic and tactical. Strategic planning focuses on identifying future situations that planning participants hope to achieve and establishing what the organization, coalition, network, or other systems need to do to achieve that outcome. Tactical planning is oriented toward developing a course of action to meet these future goals (Burch, 1996).

Problem Identification

Planners use a variety of data sources to identify problems to address during the planning process. Many of these techniques are described in chapter 6: informational interviews, ethnographic approaches, nominal group technique, and the Delphi approach. In addition, planners may conduct formal surveys and rely on information from agency or government records and the U.S. census. Planners also use population forecasting and estimation techniques to identify future problems and develop appropriate plans to address them (Klosterman, 1990). The approach the planner uses for problem identification can vary depending on his or her professional orientation and employer. Working alone, a rational planner makes use of available technology and data sources to identify problems. Advocacy and incremental planning approaches require that the planner rely on political processes for problem identification. The planner's role can be simply to advocate for the adoption of particular political perspectives on problems or to help politicians and the public recognize that the problem exists (Gilbert & Terrell, 1998). Planners using transactive, radical, or Marxist approaches will engage in dialogue with the intended program beneficiaries to identify problems and the ways in which these problems affect their lives (Forester, 1999; Friedmann, 1987).

Assessment: Gathering Information to Make Decisions

Assessment requires that the planner find information about the scope of the problem and why the problem exists. The planner should also try to find information about the best remedies to alleviate the problem (see goal development). Literature reviews (library or Web based) should be the starting point for any effort to generate theories about social problems (Patton

& Sawicki, 1993). Census data and other social indicators are a useful source of information about the scope of the problem. Assessment tools that can be used to rate community or program attributes are also available to planners. You can find some of these materials on the Internet or in library resources such as research reports or professional journals. Note, however, that the development of standardized instruments for community programs has lagged behind that of clinical practice. One of the advantages of using standardized tools is that you can make comparisons across communities or organizations. You can also use these standardized instruments to measure the outcome of planning efforts. For example, Israel, Checkoway, Schulz, and Zimmerman (1999) designed a scale to measure perceptions of individual, organizational, and community control. Hardina and Malott (1996) constructed a standardized instrument to determine the degree of consumer empowerment on community planning boards (see box, "Assessment Tool: Consumer Empowerment on Planning Boards").

Goal Development

Goals are intended to address specific social problems. They are written in broad and ambiguous terms and are intended to represent an ideal state. For example, program goals could include ending hunger, reducing homelessness, or "increasing employment. Mondros and Wilson (1994) identify four general goal categories associated with community organization practice:

1. Developing leadership skills so that constituency group members can produce social change
2. Enhancing organization capacity
3. Influencing social change
4. Educating the public about social problems and needs of specific populations

Objectives are steps that must be taken to achieve these goals. Objectives should be time limited and measurable and must incorporate information on specific actions and target groups. For each objective, the planner must state "who will be affected, what is going to occur, when, how, and what will be the indicator of the desired outcome" (Hummel, 1996, p. 46). Objectives must also include criteria for evaluating whether the objective has been achieved. The criteria associated with objectives can be absolute or relative. Absolute objectives specify that undesirable conditions are to be eliminated or a desirable state be attained. Relative objectives specify that a specific proportion of the desirable condition be attained or a proportion of an undesirable state can be eliminated (Rossi & Freeman, 1982). For example, an absolute objective might be "to provide an emergency food

Assessment Tool: Consumer Empowerment on Planning Boards

Organization Structure and Cohesion

1. Do all participants (government officials, organization staff, and board members) agree on planning goals? **YES** No
2. Are roles of board members, staff, and government sponsors in the planning process clearly specified? **YES** No
3. Is government the planning organization's sole funding source? Yes **NO**
4. Does the board have a specific government mandate to develop and implement local service-delivery plans? **YES** No

Types of Decisions Made

5. Are the decisions to be made highly technical in nature? Yes **NO**
6. Is the role of the board to approve community plans developed by staff or community experts? Yes **NO**
7. Is the intent of the planning effort to increase access to and improve the quality of service? **YES** No
8. Is the intent of the planning effort to reduce government expenditures through the rationalization of resources? Yes **NO**

Board Membership and Selection Processes

9. Are mandatory seats on the board reserved for consumers? **YES** No
10. Do consumer representatives on the board have the support of or access to local constituency groups? **YES** No
11. Is the board representative of the community in terms of
    Gender? **YES** No
    Ethnicity? **YES** No
    Class? **YES** No
12. Are consumer board members selected through election or nomination by appropriate neighborhood constituency groups rather than through general election or nomination by government agencies, the board's nominating committee, or planning board staff? **YES** No

Staff/Consumer Relationships

13. Is training in technical language and board decision
    making available for staff, board members, and
    consumer participants?   **YES**   No
14. Are organization staff committed to fostering the ability
    of board members to make technical decisions?   **YES**   No
15. Are staff members willing to share knowledge and
    information and technical expertise with board
    members?   **YES**   No

Note: Responses in boldface indicate conditions that promote consumer empowerment.

Source: Hardina & Malott 1996.

---

basket to every low-income family in Fairtown." Alternatively, a relative objective might be "to provide an emergency food basket to 50 percent of the low-income families in Fairtown."

Objectives may be either task or process oriented. Task objectives identify a specific action to be taken or achieved (Netting, Kettner, & McMurty, 1993). Often task objectives simply specify the quantity of tasks to be accomplished or the number of people served. Process objectives specify how a task will be accomplished. In some cases, goals and objectives also include a third level of program steps: activities needed to accomplish each of the objectives (see box, "Goals and Objectives for a Medicaid Outreach Program").

Choosing among Alternative Goals

In addition to literature reviews, sources for program goals include existing projects or solutions, recommendations from experts, modifications in existing programs, using scientific methods (including experimentation), and examining parallel cases (Dunn, 1981; Patton & Sawicki, 1993). Quick surveys, the Delphi approach, nominal group technique, and bringing a group together to brainstorm are all valid methods that can be used to generate alternatives (Burch, 1996).

Planners can construct models to help them choose among the proposed plans. Models are temporary constructs that simplify ideas but that have a similar structure (Flynn, 1992). They can help us examine the probable outcomes of a plan. Sometimes these models may be mathematical, identifying the components (usually inputs and constraints) involved in each

Goals and Objectives for a Medicaid Outreach Program

Goal: Improve health care status among Fairtown residents
Program: Door-to-door outreach by peer community workers
Timeline: January 1, 2001, to December 31, 2001

Objective 1:	Recruit ten community residents for paid employment as peer health educators by February 1, 2001
Objective 2:	Provide a series of six training workshops on Medicaid eligibility, health issues, and community resources by April 1, 2001
Objective 3:	Inform the public about Medicaid eligibility through local media and community forums by June 1, 2001
Objective 4:	Contact at least 1,200 households and assess eligibility for Medicaid by September 1, 2001
Objective 5:	Increase the number of Medicaid enrollees by 20 percent by September 15, 2001
Objective 6:	Provide at least 600 referrals for health care and social services to households contacted during door-to-door outreach by October 1, 2001
Objective 7:	Increase utilization of health care services in the contacted households by 40 percent by November 1, 2001
Objective 8:	Conduct follow-up interviews with at least 75 percent of the households contacted in door-to-door outreach to determine whether enrollment in Medicaid was achieved and whether health care utilization improved by December 31, 2001
Evaluation Measures:	Follow-up interviews, number of households contacted, number of referrals, number of people enrolled in Medicaid, and number of referrals provided

model and producing outcomes that vary in relation to the inputs that compose each of the alternative plans (Stokey & Zeckhauser, 1978). Models can also involve the construction of charts and graphs to describe the distribution of resources among population groups or communities or illustrate key decision-making points and lines of authority in organizations (Patton & Sawicki, 1993; Stokey & Zeckhauser, 1978). Decision trees are models used to examine essential decision-making points in organizations and estimate

Figure 11.1. Decision tree for Medicaid outreach.

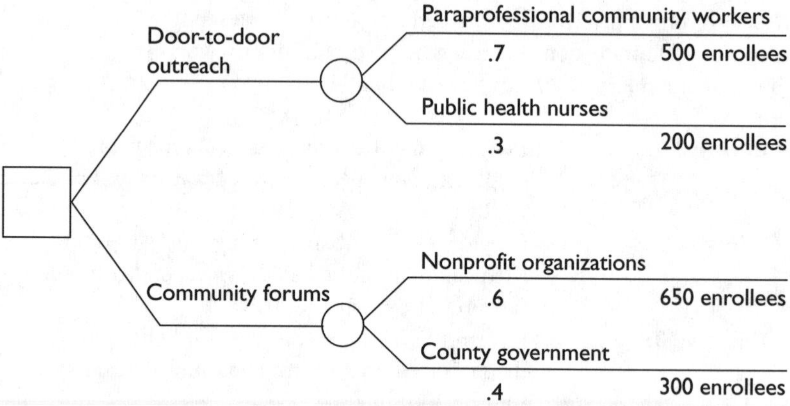

Note: The probabilities in the center of the figure refer to the probability of achieving the outcome in the last column. Circles indicate the point at which a decision must be made.

the odds of events or outcomes occurring that could influence our choice of options (see figure 11.1). Organizational charts are often constructed to examine or lines of authority or key decision makers in organizations (see figure 11.2). Models can also be constructed to illustrate the types and the logical order of decisions that must be made to put a program into operation (see figure 11.3).

Models can also help the planner rank order the value assumptions that he or she will use to determine what planning option to select for implementation (Burch, 1996). Models can include the values identified in the National Association of Social Workers code of ethics: self-determination, equality, empowerment, confidentiality, social justice, and cultural diversity (Flynn, 1992; Gilbert & Terrell, 1998). They can also include such concepts as equity, efficiency, access, distribution, and adequacy of service. One concept often used in conjunction with economic models is pareto optimality. Pareto optimal decisions are those that benefit the most people at the least cost. However, economic planners have modified this principle so that a project may be assessed as pareto optimal if benefits outweigh costs and are big enough to allow beneficiaries to compensate the losers. Projects may be assessed as appropriate if conditions exist to foster a potential pareto optimal condition, that is, the beneficiaries could potentially compensate the losers (Burch, 1999; Stokey & Zeckhauser, 1978). The concept of distribution is related to social justice: are goods and benefits distributed in such a way that disadvantaged groups attain their fair share of the benefits?

In addition to constructing models, planners use a number of techniques

Figure 11.2. Organizational flowchart: Lines of decision-making authority, Fairtown Community Organization.

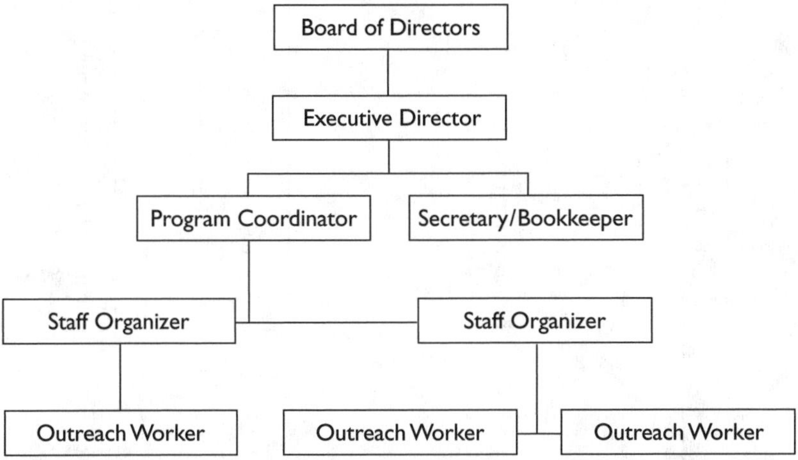

Note: Organizational charts are most typically constructed using the assumption that the organization functions as a hierarchy. Consequently, the decision makers with the most power are located at the top of the hierarchy (board of directors, executive director), followed by midlevel administrative staff. The lines connect supervisors with those people they are responsible for supervising.

to choose among different plans. In some situations, planners will construct decision trees that illustrate planning options, probable outcomes, and risks. Planners also use the principle of transitivity to choose among alternative plans. Transitivity involves making comparisons among pairs of statements or plans and making logical deductions (Patton & Sawicki, 1993; Stokey & Zeckhauser, 1978). For example, if

plan A is better than plan B, and

plan B is better than plan C,

then plan A must be better than plan C.

Planners also look for nondominated alternatives. Dominated alternatives are those in which at least one component is inferior to those of other alternatives. Planners sometimes make such an evaluation by graphing the location of the various ranks assigned to two components or criteria used to assess a project. The best plan is the one that is graphed to the north and east of all the other alternatives on the graph (see figure 11.4).

Linear programs or mathematical models that examine program constraints, resources, and probable outcomes can also be constructed. Sensitivity analysis, in which the effects of differing values of model components are examined, is typically used to compare the effects of each alternative

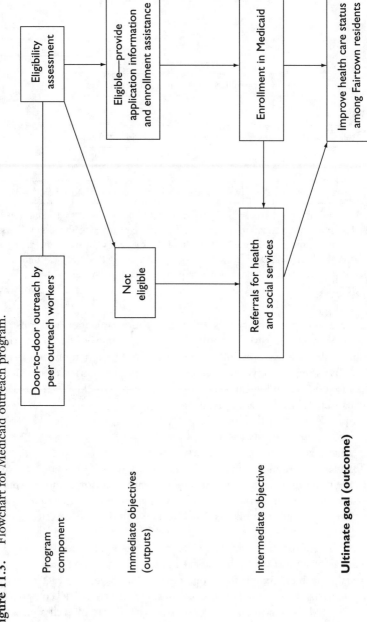

Figure 11.3. Flowchart for Medicaid outreach program.

Program
component

Door-to-door outreach by
peer outreach workers

Immediate objectives
(outputs)

Eligibility
assessment

Eligible—provide
application information
and enrollment assistance

Not
eligible

Intermediate objective

Enrollment in Medicaid

Referrals for health
and social services

Ultimate goal (outcome)

Improve health care status
among Fairtown residents

Figure 11.4. Nondominated alternatives.

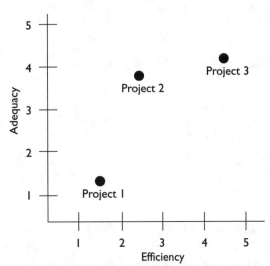

Note: Project 3 is the preferred nondominated alternative.

(Patton & Sawicki, 1993). Some mathematical models examine cost-effectiveness of program options. Cost-benefit models look at whether program costs outweigh anticipated benefits.

Both cost-benefit and cost-effectiveness analysis focuses on the combination of program resources that produces the best results at the least cost. It is therefore possible for program analysts to specify programmatic resources, the dollar costs associated with them, and the anticipated outcomes associated with each program option (Patton & Sawicki, 1993; Stokey & Zeckhauser, 1978). In cost-effectiveness analysis, it is assumed that the type of outcomes associated with each option will be the same but that the quantity (degree of effectiveness) will differ. The planner can also specify cost constraints (maximum dollars that can be spent). Consequently, it is possible to estimate the average or unit cost per outcome for alternative plans. If cost-effectiveness is the only criterion used to make a decision, the option with the lowest unit cost will be chosen (see table 11.1).

Corporations and government agencies often use cost-benefit analysis to choose among several alternative programs. Planners and community organizers often criticize this method because of the difficulties related to assigning dollar values to benefits (Burch, 1999; Stokey & Zeckhauser, 1978). For example, can we assess the dollar value of a person's life or the worth of increasing an individual's self-esteem? Other concerns about this method have to do with the planner's inability to anticipate unintended consequences, spillover effects (the program's impact on other segments of

Table 11.1 Using Linear Program Methods to Examine the Cost-Effectiveness of Medicaid Outreach Programs

	Number of Workers	Weeks of Work	Number Enrolled Each Week/ Worker (estimated)	Maximum Pay per Project $8.00/hour, 35 hours per week	Total Enrollees	Cost per Enrollment
Option 1	10	12	10	$33,600	1200	$28.00
Option 2	5	10	20	14,000	1000	$14.00
Option 3	20	6	15	33,600	1800	$19.00

Note: Constraints = minimum enrollment of 1,000, within a 12-week period, maximum cost = $35,000.

the economy, future generations, or individuals), discount rates (valuation of present or future benefits), and the difficulty involved in determining who should benefit (the public in general, taxpayers, low-income people, or members of the elite). Distributional effects are especially difficult to examine using mathematical approaches. Many economists agree that decisions related to how program benefits should be distributed should be left to the political process (Stokey & Zeckhauser, 1978). In table 11.2, two projects are examined. Project 1 produces a greater proportion of net benefits for society as a whole, but members of the elite, or landlords, receive the same amount of net benefits as tenants. Project 2 actually produces a monetary loss for society as a whole; however, net benefits are highest for members of a disadvantaged group, the tenants.

Table 11.2 Cost-Benefit Analysis

	Benefits	Costs	Net Benefits
Project 1			
Landlords	$100,000	$90,000	$10,000
Tenants	30,000	20,000	10,000
Whole Society	$130,000	$110,000	$20,000
Project 2			
Landlords	$40,000	$80,000	−$40,000
Tenants	40,000	10,000	30,000
Whole Society	$80,000	$90,000	−$10,000

Source: Adapted from Stokey & Zeckhauser, 1978.

The planner should also examine whether the recommended option is politically feasible (Patton & Sawicki, 1993). Would decision makers and potential beneficiaries support the plan? Would taxpayers agree that their money should be used to support this activity? Burch (1996) also recommends that the following criteria be used to examine whether the plan should be implemented: the potential success of the plan, the capability to carry it out, the availability and affordability of resources, the commitment of staff, and the acceptability of the plan to target groups. Some plans will not be culturally acceptable to all potential beneficiaries. Consequently, it is vital that the people who are to benefit (or who may be inconvenienced or harmed by the plan) be consulted or involved in final decision making before implementation (Friedmann, 1987).

Implementation

Implementation involves creating plans and carrying out the activities necessary to put the program into operation. Creating measurable objectives is not sufficient to actually make the program work. You must obtain resources and recruit staff. Hasenfeld (1979) identifies a number of activities that the planner must perform to effectively implement a program:

- Find a permanent source of funding
- Find consumers or beneficiaries for the service
- Obtain adequate resources to operate the program
- Set eligibility standards and benefit levels
- Identify local organizations that can be involved in collaboration and coordination
- Obtain legitimacy and public support for the program
- Assign appropriate roles to staff and delineate lines of authority and responsibilities
- Schedule activities necessary to deliver program services
- Establish a system for program monitoring, evaluation, and feedback
- Ensure that staff people perform their jobs adequately

Rein (1983) argues that in most organizations, tensions exist between maximizing benefits (giving resources away to everyone who needs them) and minimizing costs (protecting the resources necessary for organization maintenance). Consequently, the most problematic issue for program designers is how much access to program services and decision-making processes should be given to service consumers. Gilbert and Terrell (1998) identify the following service-delivery elements that social service organizations use to control access to goods, services, and information: advocacy, citizen participation, hiring former clients to deliver services, coordination, and income-related restrictions on applicant eligibility for services. Self-help advocacy, citizen participation, and hiring nonprofessionals increase access to services. Coordination to eliminate duplication of services or to limit applicant choice of service agencies and cumbersome or intrusive applications that require applicants to verify income actually discourage potential consumers (Hardina, 1993).

Choices among these elements require the planner to put basic values (such as adequacy, empowerment, and equality) into action. Increasing the influence of consumers in the delivery of services will conflict with efforts to increase the autonomy and control of professional staff. Hardina (1990, 1993) examined these access structures in fifty-three community-based organizations in Chicago. She found that most organizations were not exclusively oriented to limiting or increasing access but used a combination of approaches to deliver services.

Evaluation

To determine if the best plan was adopted and was implemented appropriately, the planner should develop an evaluation plan before the program is actually implemented. Evaluations can be summative (conducted at the end of the project to assess whether the program was effective in meeting its goals) or formative (initiated during the early stages of program implementation) (Rossi & Freeman, 1982). Summative evaluations help planners, administrators, and funders to make "go" or "no-go" decisions about whether the program should be continued as is or terminated. Formative evaluations allow planners to recommend adjustments in the program during operation.

Summative evaluations are quantitative; they are used to determine whether the program produced the desired changes (Chambers, Wedel, & Rodwell, 1992). In other words, they establish whether a cause-and-effect relationship exists between the program and the outcome. Formative evaluations may be quantitative, oriented toward monitoring whether the program has operated in the manner intended to produce certain types of outputs: serving adequate numbers of eligible clients, generating appropriate amounts of revenues and expenditures, and producing a certain number of products or carrying out a specified number of activities. Formative evaluations also may be qualitative, examining program processes: How were program activities carried out? What type of interactions occurred among staff members or between staff members and program consumers?

Process evaluations are primarily intended to look at implementation. Was the program actually implemented in the manner intended? If activities were not carried out in the prescribed manner, why did this occur? What barriers prevented successful implementation? Were appropriate resources (money, staff, clients, facilities) available to carry out the project? Chambers et al. (1992) identify four common reasons that programs may not be properly implemented:

- Program delivery was insufficient.
- The program was not delivered at all.
- The program was not delivered in a standardized manner to all participants.
- The wrong program was delivered.

Evaluations can be conducted internally by program staff, or outside paid consultants can be hired to conduct external evaluations (Royce & Thyer, 1996). External consultants often start by making an assessment as to whether the program is evaluable: Does the program contain clear goals? Do staff members recognize that they are working toward these agreed-upon goals? If such conditions do not exist, the external evaluator may work with staff and other key constituents to identify and implement appropriate goals. The evaluator should also clarify the purpose of the evaluation and determine how the information gathered will be utilized (Patton, 1997).

Computer Applications for Planning

Spreadsheet software programs (such as Excel, Lotus, and Access) can be used to set up linear programs that identify program constraints and resources and produce different outcomes when inputs vary. A number of more specialized software packages are available to help planners make population projections, examine economic trends, design maps, plan transportation systems, and conduct statistical analysis (Klosterman, 1998). The most prevalent use of computer technology for planning involves the use of geographic information systems (GIS) and the analysis of population data (McNutt, 2000).

Government and nonprofit organizations have also begun to make municipal and land-use plans as well as statistical reports available on the Web. Some local governments have also created systems that allow the public to provide direct feedback on these plans via E-mail (O'Mara, 2000). In addition, some local governments have made GIS maps pertaining to problems residents experience available through city-maintained Web sites. For example, the City of Oakland, California, makes maps available on its Web site that help citizens identify trends in local crime and geographic areas that are considered crime "hot spots" (DeFao, 1999).

The Internet also provides a valuable source of information about programs and policies adopted to address specific social problems. For example, a program planner who is interested in techniques for increasing Medicaid utilization among low-income women can find information on Web sites maintained by Children Now (http://www.childrennow.org) or the Children's Defense Fund (http://www.childrensdefense.org). Research on planning techniques can be found at the Web site maintained by the University of Buffalo's School of Architecture and Planning (http://cyburbia.org).

Planning information can also be found on a University of California–Berkeley Web site, http://www.lib.berkeley.edu/ENVI/. Information on neighborhood planning and links to a number of community development sites can be found on the COMM-ORG Web site (http://comm-org.utoledo.edu).

Computers can also help student urban planners examine choices and constraints. The computer game "SIM City" allows student planners to examine different land-use and service options available to city planners. Researchers have also experimented with techniques that allow three-dimensional representations of cities to be developed on the Internet (O'Mara, 2000).

Summary

Planning requires both technical skills and the ability to negotiate with employers, government officials, and constituents to facilitate agreement among the key decision makers and beneficiaries. Planners need political and administrative skills to ensure that plans are actually implemented. They must use all the steps in the problem-solving model—problem identification, assessment, goal setting, implementation, and evaluation—to create appropriate plans. In addition, planners must employ a variety of techniques to choose among appropriate goals. Computer technology can be used to gather information, inform the public about plans and decision-making processes, analyze the impact of alternative plans, and evaluate outcomes. Planners must also find appropriate resources to carry out the plan and monitor how these resources are used. Chapter 12 will describe proposal writing and techniques for finding foundation and government funding.

■ QUESTIONS FOR CLASS DISCUSSION

1. How would you define the public good? Who do you think should benefit from plans produced by government agencies, community planning boards, or nonprofit organizations?
2. Which of the planning models described in chapter 11 do you think are most appropriate for social work practice? Can you think of different situations or practice settings where the various models are best used?
3. Why is citizen participation critical for the construction of effective plans?
4. Which of the three planning options in table 11.1 is the best? Should cost-effectiveness analysis be the only criterion? If not, what other criteria should be used?
5. Which of the outcomes described in table 11.2 is better? Should net benefit to society or distributional effects be the most important criterion

in choosing a program? Which of these criteria do you think are used in government decision-making processes?

■ SAMPLE ASSIGNMENTS AND EXERCISES

1. Develop a decision tree related to a decision that must be made that affects your place of employment or field agency.
2. Identify a community problem, conduct a literature review to determine the best program to address the problem, and write a set of measurable goals and objectives with a specific timeline and an evaluation mechanism.
3. Apply Hardina and Malott's (1996) assessment tool, "Consumer Empowerment on Planning Boards," to the board decision-making process in the organization in your place of employment or field agency. Write a three- to five-page paper describing how your organization meets or fails to meet the criteria described in the scale. Is the scale adequate to measure consumer empowerment in organizations? Why or why not? How could it be improved? Also, address the limitations of using a standardized scale to assess interactional patterns and organization structure.
4. Construct an organizational flowchart to describe organizational lines of authority and decision makers (figure 11.2) or decision-making processes that pertain to one program your organization offers (see figure 11.3).

References

Anthony, C. (1999). Race, justice, and sprawl. *Forum for Applied Research and Public Policy, 14*(4), 97–101.

Arnstein, S. (1969). Ladder of citizen participation. *Journal of the American Institute of Planners, 35*, 216–34.

Burch, H. (1996). *Basic social policy and planning*. New York: Haworth.

Burch, H. (1999). *Social welfare policy analysis and choice*. New York: Haworth.

Burghardt, S., & Fabricant, M. (1987). Radical social work. In A. Minihan (Ed.), *The encyclopedia of social work* (18th ed., Vol. 2). Silver Spring, MD: National Association of Social Workers.

Chambers, D., Wedel, K., & Rodwell, M. (1992). *Evaluating social programs*. Boston: Allyn & Bacon.

Cornelius, L., Battle, M., Kryder-Coe, J., & Hu, D. (1999). Interventions to developing community partnerships for HIV planning: Successful macro applications of social work principles. *Journal of Community Practice, 6*(1), 15–32.

Davidoff, P. (1973). Advocacy and pluralism in planning. In A. Faludi (Ed.), *A reader in planning theory* (pp. 277–96). New York: Pergamon.

DeFao, J. (1999, December 27). Oakland's crime data available on the net. *San Francisco Chronicle*, pp. A17, A19.

de Oliver, M., & Dawson-Munoz, T. (1996). The inadequacy of geography to address racial disparities. *Review of Black Political Economy, 25*(2), 37–161.

Dunn, W. (1981). *Public policy analysis: An introduction.* Englewood Cliffs, NJ: Prentice-Hall.

Flynn, J. (1992). *Social agency policy* (2d ed.). Chicago: Nelson-Hall.

Forester, J. (1989). *Planning in the face of power.* Berkeley: University of California Press.

Forester, J. (1999). *The deliberative practitioner: Encouraging participatory planning processes.* Cambridge, MA: MIT Press.

Freire, P. (1970). *Pedagogy of the oppressed .* New York: Continuum.

Friedmann, J. (1987). *Planning in the public domain: From knowledge to action.* Princeton: Princeton University Press.

Gilbert, N., & Terrell, P. (1998). *Dimensions of social welfare policy* (4th ed.). Boston: Allyn & Bacon.

Giloth, R., & Moe, K. (1999). Jobs, equity, and the mayoral administration of Harold Washington in Chicago (1983–87). *Policy Studies Journal, 27*(1), 129–56.

Hardina, D. (1990). The effect of funding sources on client access to services. *Administration in Social Work, 14*(3), 33–46.

Hardina, D. (1993). The impact of funding sources and board representation on consumer control in organizations serving three low income communities. *Nonprofit Management and Leadership, 4,* 69–84.

Hardina, D., & Malott, O. (1996). Strategies for the empowerment of low income consumers on community-based planning boards. *Journal of Progressive Human Services, 7*(2), 43–61.

Hasenfeld, Y. (1979). Program development. In F. Cox, J. Erlich, J. Rothman, & J. Tropman (Eds.), *Strategies of community organization* (3d ed., pp. 13–159).

Hudson, B. (1983). Comparison of current planning theories: counterparts and contradictions. In R. Kramer & H. Specht (Eds.), *Readings in community organization practice* (3d ed., pp. 246–63). Englewood Cliffs, NJ: Prentice-Hall.

Hummel, J. (1996). *Starting and running a nonprofit organization* (2d ed.). Minneapolis: University of Minnesota Press.

Israel, B., Checkoway, B., Schulz, A., & Zimmerman, M. (1999). Scale for measuring perceptions of individual, organizational, and community control. In M. Minkler (Ed.), *Community organization and community building for health* (pp. 378–80). New Brunswick, NJ: Rutgers University Press.

Klosterman, R. (1990). *Community analysis and planning techniques.* Savage, MD: Rowman & Littlefield.

Klosterman, R. (1998). Farewell to the computer reports. *Journal of the American Planning Association, 64*(4), 47–56.

Lindblom, C. (1959). The science of muddling through. *Public Administration Review, 19,* 79–88.

McNutt, J. (2000). Organizing cyberspace: Strategies for teaching about community practice and technology. *Journal of Community Practice, 7*(1), 95–109.

Minkler, M. (1999). Community organizing among the elderly poor in San Francisco's Tenderloin District. In M. Minkler (Ed.), *Community organization and community building for health* (pp. 244–77). New Brunswick, NJ: Rutgers University Press.

Minkler, M., & Pies, C. (1999). Ethical issues in community organization and community participation. In M. Minkler (Ed.), *Community organization and community building for health* (pp. 120–36). New Brunswick, NJ: Rutgers University Press.

Mondros, J., & Wilson, S. (1994). *Organizing for power and empowerment.* New York: Columbia University Press.

Netting, E., Kettner, P., & McMurty, S. (1993). *Social work macro practice.* New York: Longman.

O'Mara, W. (2000). *Catching up with the Net: How computers are being used on the job* [On-line]. Available: http://planning.org

Patton, C., & Sawicki, D. (1993). *Basic methods of policy analysis and planning* (2d ed.). Englewood Cliffs, NJ: Prentice-Hall.

Patton, M. (1997). *Utilization-focused evaluation: The new century text.* Thousand Oaks, CA: Sage.

Peattie, L. (1968). Reflections on advocacy planning. *Journal of the American Institute of Planners, 34*(2), 80–87.

Rein, M. (1983). *From policy to practice.* Armonk, NY: M. E. Sharpe.

Riveira, F., & Erlich, J. (1998). *Community organizing in a diverse society.* Boston: Allyn & Bacon.

Rossi, P., & Freeman, H. (1982). *Evaluation: A systematic approach.* Beverly Hills, CA: Sage.

Royce, D., & Thyer, B. (1996). *Program evaluation: An introduction.* Chicago: Nelson-Hall.

Rothman, J., & Zald, M. (1995). Planning and policy practice. In J. Rothman, J. Erlich, & J. Tropman (Eds.), *Strategies of community organization* (5th ed., pp. 283–96). Itasca, IL: Peacock.

Stokey, E., & Zeckhauser, R. (1978). *A primer for policy analysis.* New York: Norton.

12 Resource Development and Grant Writing

■ Most community organization work is conducted through nonprofit organizations. Although some funding for community and social action organizations is derived from membership dues, nonprofits must rely on government grants and contracts as well as donations from individuals, foundations, and corporations to survive. It is therefore essential that community organizers obtain funding for their organizations and start-up money for new programs. Organizers must understand that the use of external funds will limit the activities in which the organization can participate. This chapter examines the impact of various sources of funds on nonprofit organizations. Federal restrictions on nonprofit organizations that lobby government are also examined.

Methods that organizers can use to conduct research on funding sources and the guidelines and restrictions these funders impose are described. Steps in the funding proposal–writing process are also examined. Components of funding proposals are problem identification, goals and objectives, a needs assessment, methods of program delivery, budgeting, and an evaluation plan.

Theoretical Perspectives on the Impact of Funding Sources on Community Organizations and Social Movements

Power dependency and resource mobilization theories indicate that nonprofit organizations that accept funding from sources outside the organization (grants and contracts) will be obligated to the funder (Blau, 1964; Priven & Cloward, 1979). This obligation often requires that the organization comply with regulations and restrictions on the use of funds as determined by the donor. The mission and goals of social action organizations that receive government funds or donations from members of the elite will be displaced as the organization undergoes a transformation, engaging in only those activities that are acceptable to the funder (Berg & Wright, 1981).

Researchers have documented a number of specific changes experienced by nonprofit organizations that accept external funding: reductions in client advocacy and lobbying activities, funding shortfalls as a consequence of grant cycles and delays in reimbursement, and adoption of service-oriented goals in lieu of a social action–oriented agenda (Gronbjerg, 1993; Hardina, 1993; Holmes & Grieco, 1991; Morrill & McKee, 1993). Some types of government funding arrangements promote standardization of service-delivery and eligibility determinations. Consequently, acceptance of such finds may require that the organization monitor the behavior of recipients, enforce government sanctions for noncompliance, and limit discretion in eligibility determinations (Smith & Lipsky, 1993). Snowden (1993) argues that restrictions on the use of government funds for service delivery disproportionately hurt people of color and those individuals with incomes below the poverty line.

Another problem facing administrators is the possible loss of autonomy, Most nonprofit organizations engage in lobbying government for funds or for better services for their client populations. Nonprofit organizations that depend on the government for funds (and must be reassessed on a yearly basis for contract renewal) can choose not to lobby against government policies. Kramer (1981) argues that the dependency of nonprofit organizations on government funding is mitigated by the diversity of income sources available to organizations, the low level of accountability expected by government funders, and the organizations' ability to lobby government. According to Smith and Lipsky (1993), the relationship between government and private contractors is often one of mutual dependence due to the limited availability of some types of specialized services and the difficulties government agencies face in determining what organizations can best provide services.

Large, well-funded organizations (as well as organizations that have expertise in a particular service area) have a competitive advantage in obtaining contracts (Gronbjerg, Chen, & Stagner, 1995). Many of these organizations use their political contacts to capture contract dollars. Consequently, smaller organizations may be at a competitive disadvantage, especially if they fear the consequences of lobbying on behalf of unpopular issues or client groups. These organizations may also have trouble obtaining alternative sources of funds, particularly if they serve low-income communities; little in the way of donations may be generated locally (Hardina, 1993; Schorr, 1997).[1] Alexander (2000) states that these organizations have low autonomy and few options but to meet the demands of funders. Social action–oriented organizations also have trouble finding external funds. The National Committee for Responsive Philanthropy (2000) estimates that only 3 percent of the $13.8 billion in contributions that are provided by private foundations go to organizations concerned with social or economic justice.

The impact of funding sources on social change organizations requires that administrators and organizers carefully select funding sources that set priorities and guidelines that are consistent with the organization's mission and goals (Hall, 1995; "Working Assets," 1999). When this is not possible, organizations must be able to control the proportion of funds provided by donors. Overreliance on one or two funders places the organization in a dependency situation—they have limited room to bargain to maintain autonomy or retain flexibility in how funds are used. There are at least three strategies organizations can use to retain autonomy:

- Raise all funds locally through membership fees, fees for service, and donations from individuals.
- Offer a unique service not provided by other organizations. Funders may be eager to support this service and consequently allow the organization flexibility in service delivery.
- Develop power resources such as a board of directors with prominent and powerful members, or network with legislators and other government officials to protect organization resources and obtain more funds for the organization (Froelich, 1999; Gronbjerg, 1993; Hardina, 1993; Smith & Lipsky, 1993).

Note, however, that external funding does have some positive effects on organizations. Foundation and government support allows for the creation of new services, fosters collaboration among organizations, and helps subsidize some nonfunded activities in community-based organizations (Lipsky & Thibodeau, 1988; Rundall et al., 1993).

Types of Funding Sources for Community Organizations and Advocacy Groups

Primary sources of funding for community-based organizations are federal, state, and local governments. The Independent Sector estimates that in

1990, total expenditures of nonprofit organizations in the United States were $327 billion, just 14 percent of all federal, state, and local government expenditures (O'Connell, 1996). Among those nonprofit organizations that provide health and human services, 40 percent of all income came from government contracts, grants, and fees for service. Foundation funds, corporate grants, and individual donations comprised about 30 percent of non-profit revenue (Froelich, 1999). Foundation grants to nonprofits totaled $10.4 billion in 1995 while corporations donated $7.4 billion (Edwards, Benefield, Edwards, & Yankey, 1997). Over 38,000 foundations provide funds to nonprofits each year (Henry, 1998). Primary types of foundations include:

- Independent foundations (often family run or, if larger, governed by a board of trustees)
- Private industry–sponsored foundations that support research or social service programs (but may not grant funds to outside organizations)
- Community foundations (such as the United Way or Community Trust) that obtain funding form individual donations or payroll deductions (Gitlin & Lyons, 1996)

Many nonprofits use commercial activities to supplement other funding streams. Such activities involve selling goods and services at market rates. Commercial activity gives nonprofits flexibility to supplement their budgets with funds that do not restrict spending to certain types of activities (Froelich, 1999). The only constraints on spending involve supply and demand (costs must be congruent with what consumers will pay). Note also that low-income consumers often cannot pay for services. Consequently, some types of nonprofit services that operate on a fee-for-service basis (nursing facilities, day care centers, and arts organizations) are targeted to middle- or upper-income populations.

Nonprofit organizations that engage in social action may find that government funding is available primarily for the delivery of health and social services. Though some organizations find that this is a valuable source of revenue, others feel that government funding for this purpose detracts from the organization's primary mission. Many organizations seek funds from a variety of sources: foundations, corporations, and donations from a few wealthy individuals. Organizations may also choose to engage in grassroots fund-raising: holding special events or soliciting contributions of "not so large" donations from many individuals. They may also use direct mail campaigns to solicit funds from individual donors. The typical response rate for direct mail campaigns is 1 percent, with donations averaging $5 to $50 per response (Edwards et al., 1997). The high cost of postage may result in direct mail appeals just breaking even; however, organizations often attempt to maintain their donor base and make repeated appeals to those individuals who are likely to donate. Many nonprofit organizations use E-mail to send requests for donations to prospective donors.

Products sold by nonprofit social action organizations to support the cause have also become an important source of revenue. In some instances, the nonprofit may partner with a for-profit company to promote services or products, with a portion of the revenues going to the nonprofit organization. For example, the Sierra Club, in partnership with the First Bank of Rochester, New York, issues a credit card to its members, generating over $225,000 a year in revenue (Edwards et al., 1997).

Organizations can also solicit in-kind donations from individuals and other organizations. In-kind donations may include furniture, food, printing, facilities, and other concrete goods and services. In-kind donations often pass through the organization and are provided to third parties (for example, a local caterer may donate leftover dinners for distributions by a shelter). Some in-kind donations are used to defray expenses related to fund-raising events or direct mail campaigns (the local copy center might donate the cost of printing tickets for the organization's annual casino night). Such donations, properly documented by the organization, can provide tax deductions for the contributor. The tax code also allows entertainers to receive tax deductions for the value of their services. Many nonprofit social action organizations and foundations use these in-kind benefits to generate resources.

Grants from the entertainment and professional sports industries can provide an unrestricted source of funding for social action–oriented organizations. Less entrenched than family foundations, these organizations' grant priorities may be set by the celebrities themselves. In the rock music industry, this type of donation makes good business sense, especially for '60s-era musicians who wish to be associated with progressive causes that their fans support (Goldman, 1997). For example, Farm Aid (founded by Willie Nelson, Neil Young, and John Mellencamp) provides grants to rural organizations that provide emergency food and counseling services to low-income farmers (see http://www.farmaid.org). Farm Aid also lobbies for legislation that will benefit small farmers. Artists such as Carlos Santana and Wyclef Jean also fund foundations that provide assistance to children's programs and social justice organizations.

Restrictions on the Use of Grants and Contracts

Organizations that employ community organizers engage in advocacy activities, political action, and lobbying. Much of this activity is oriented toward changing government policies or putting pressure on political leaders. Consequently, government may decline to fund such activities. The Internal Revenue Code contains specific restrictions that prohibit nonprofit organizations from engaging in most types of political activities (see chapter 9) and spending a substantial amount of their annual budgets on lobbying (see box, "IRS Restrictions on Nonprofit 501(c)(3) Organizations' Use of Funds for Lobbying Expenditures"). For this reason, organizations that invest "a substantial" amount of resources to lobbying and social action cannot qualify for 501(c)(3) status.[2] They are covered by section 501(c)(4) of the tax code. However, such organizations cannot provide donors with a tax deduction. As Hopkins (1989) notes, IRS rules are ambiguous; there is no formal definition of "substantial" or "insubstantial" amounts of lobbying activities or expenditures for such activities. Lobbying activities can be direct actions taken by organization staff or board members to influence individual legislators or grassroot, urging members of the public to contact legislators for the purpose of influencing legislation (Arons, 1999; Hopkins, 1989). Certain types of lobbying activities are exempt from IRS expenditure limits (see box, "Lobbying Expenditure Exclusions").

The ways in which donors deliver funding to nonprofit organizations also create difficulties in terms of service delivery. Short (one-year) foundation grant cycles negatively affect the stability of nonprofits. In addition, foundation boards set priorities for funding that can vary on a year-to-year basis. Changing the organization's priorities to qualify for funds often results in goal displacement (Froelich, 1999). Partnerships between nonprofits and corporations may also detract from the organization's mission. For example, recent controversies involve partnerships between companies that market beer or cigarettes and health or anti–drunk driving organizations (Minkler & Pies, 1999).

IRS Restrictions on Nonprofit 501(c)(3) Organizations' Use of Funds for Lobbying Expenditures

Expenditure Thresholds for Direct Lobbying

20% of the organization's first $500,000
15% of the organization's second $500,000
10% of the organization's third $500,000
5% of any remaining funds
   An organization may not spend more than $1,000,000 total for lobbying expenditures on an annual basis.

Expenditure Thresholds for Grassroots Lobbying

25% of the total spent for direct lobbying activities

Source: Hopkins, 1989.

Note: Penalties for exceeding IRS spending ceilings include repayment of 25 percent of the excess expenditure or loss of 501(c)(3) status.

Lobbying Expenditure Exclusions

- Lobbying government (executive branch) employees for changes in regulations
- Lobbying by volunteers, unless the organization spends its own money on these activities
- Any communication (for example, a newsletter or E-mail) that simply informs members about a legislative issue, unless the member is urged to lobby
- An organization's response to a legislator for technical information regarding pending legislation
- Self-defense activity or any lobbying that is intended to protect the organization's funding, programs, or tax-exempt status
- Dissemination of the results of a nonpartisan analysis or research study on a legislative issue if the report presents a balanced portrait of the issue and does not urge readers to contact legislators
- Urging the public to support or oppose a ballot initiative or a referendum is an allowable activity, but expenditures cannot exceed the organization's expenditure limit for direct lobbying.

Source: Arons, 1999.

Another funding-related dilemma for community organizations involves purchase-of-service contracts. Government has used purchase-of-service contracts to finance the delivery of public services by private, nonprofit, and for-profit organizations. Until the mid-1970s, most government-funded social services were delivered by government agencies or nonprofit organizations (Salamon, 1995). Nonprofits were given yearly grants to provide specific types of services to low-income consumers. Grant money could be used for a variety of program expenditures and were not contingent on the success of the program. Concerns about holding down the cost of services and ensuring that government funds were used effectively resulted in the use of purchase-of-service contracts rather than grants by federal, state, and local governments. Cuts in federal grant funding during the Reagan administration made purchase-of-service contracts an attractive source of new revenue for many nonprofit organizations (Fabricant & Burghardt, 1992).

Purchase-of-service contracts are intended to hold organizations accountable for the services they provide. They are also intended to reduce the cost of service delivery; government agencies reimburse the contractor only when services have been effective. These contracts typically reimburse social service organizations for services rendered using performance-based criteria. In performance-based contracting, the organization must provide evidence that it has produced certain measurable outcomes as specified in the contract (Kettner & Martin, 1995).

One of the advantages of purchase-of-service contracts for government is that they are generally award based on a competitive bidding process. This means that the winning contractor may be the one that provides a service at the lowest cost. Most state agencies, however, use additional criteria such as past experience and expertise in providing the service in determining which organizations receive the contract. For yearly contracts to be renewed, the contractor must provide evidence that the outcomes specified in the previous contract have been achieved (Smith & Lipsky, 1993).

One of the main reasons government agencies contract for service delivery is that both nonprofit and for-profit organizations are viewed as able to deliver comparable services at competitive rates due to lower staff costs (Starr, 1989). Generally, these organizations pay their workers less than government agencies. Workers in nonprofits tend to be non-unionized (most government workers belong to unions); some staff may be volunteers. Purchase-of-service contracts are intended to help government contain the cost of delivering a service. Consequently, the rates at which organizations are reimbursed for services are often set below actual costs. Government payments may be delayed, and the organization could find itself in financial trouble. As a result, the organization must find ways to cut costs. Even if reimbursements for services are made in a timely manner, purchase-of-service contracts can still have a negative financial impact on the organization. In performance-based contracting, the organization is reimbursed only for producing successful outcomes. If the outcome is not successful, the contractor then loses money and may not be able to recover expenses (Kramer & Grossman, 1987).

Reimbursement for only successful outcomes creates an incentive for the organization not to help difficult-to-serve consumers with complex needs. Some organizations may develop processes to screen out these service consumers (Hardina, 1990; Kramer & Grossman, 1987). Such a service-delivery process is at odds with the social work value of individualization, the idea that services should be flexible enough to respond to individual needs (Smith & Lipsky, 1993).

Purchase-of-service contracts restrict the use of funds in a number of ways:

- Funds may be used only for activities specified by the funders; organizations that are to receive reimbursement through purchase-of-service contracts may qualify for reimbursement for these specified activities.
- Eligibility for service is determined using guidelines developed by the funder; no other people may be served using these funds.
- Transfers of funds between budget expenditure categories must be approved by the funders.

- The organization must use specific guidelines related to staff qualifications when hiring staff members with program funds.
- The organization might undergo an audit if the funder has questions about expenditures.
- The organization will be expected to compensate for funding shortfalls or unauthorized activities by generating additional funds from other sources or providing in-kind matching support (Dropkin & La Touche, 1998; Kramer & Grossman, 1987; Smith & Lipsky, 1993).
- Social change–oriented organizations may be forced to abandon organizing activities in favor of providing services to individuals in order to qualify for contract funds (Delgado, 1997).

Alexander (2000) identifies a number of management strategies nonprofit organizations use to cope with problems associated with purchase-of-service contracts and increased competition for foundation grants, corporate support, and individual donations. These strategies include the adoption of business approaches and technologies, computer-assisted fund-raising, creation of marketing plans, and the use of interorganizational networks to generate funding (grants are submitted cooperatively by a group of organizations rather than a single bidder).

Using the Internet to Find Funding Sources

Organizations must do research to find which funding sources have goals and priorities that are congruent with their primary missions. Government agencies post announcements regarding grants and contracts on the Web. For example, see the Department of Health and Human Services Web site (http://ww.os.dhhs.gov/). It contains a list of grants and contracts available to nonprofit organizations and educational institutions. Funding announcements, also known as requests for proposals (RFPs), are also posted in the *Federal Register* at http://www.access.gpo.gov/su_docs/aces/aces140html and in the *Catalog of Federal Domestic Assistance* (http://aspe.hhs.gov/cfda).

Information on past awardees is essential for determining whether your organization's plans fit within guidelines established by the funder (New & Quick, 1998). Many foundations have their own Web sites that feature information about the foundation's goals, previous grants funded, applications, and grant guidelines. A number of sites on the Web contain foundation directories. One such site is the Foundation Center (http://fdncenter.org/). Annual reports published by foundations and corporations list those organizations and programs funded. Such reports can provide the researcher with valuable information about the foundations' funding priorities and the types of organizations they are likely to fund (Gitlin & Lyons, 1996). You can also gain access to information about foundations by completing a topic search on the Web. For example, searching for information on welfare reform will give you a list of sites offering both background information and links to potential funding sources.

It is also possible for an organization to raise funds and recruit members on the Internet. Johnston (1999) describes how Web sites can be constructed to attract donors. Organizations can ask prospective contributors to complete membership forms and send credit card information so that donations can be processed via a secure on-line reply device (nonprofits can contract with financial institutions and other security firms to ensure the confidentiality of credit card information). Nonprofits that wish to raise funds can also conduct merchandise sales and auctions over the Web. According to Johnston, on-line donors tend to be younger and have more money than individuals using traditional methods to make contributions. They also are more likely to be male and are almost exclusively Caucasian.

Developing Funding Proposals

To survive financially, nonprofit organizations must develop well-written proposals that will persuade funders to provide resources. Eighty to 95 percent of all proposals are rejected for such reasons as being outside foundation priorities or having unclear goals and objectives, unreasonable costs, or ideas that do not seem worth exploring (Henry, 1998). Foundations may also have insufficient funds to provide grants to all organizations that apply.

Government agencies and many foundations regularly issue RFPs that contain specific proposal guidelines and time frames.

These are three basic types of proposals:

1. A proposal letter—three pages describing project purpose, goals and objectives, and the monetary request.
2. A letter of intent—a short summary sent to the foundation or corporation that informs the funder of the organization's intent to submit a longer proposal. Many funders will use the letter of intent as a screening device to determine if they wish to request a longer proposal from the organization.
3. A long proposal—formatted to contain comprehensive information about the project, including a statement of need, background information about the organization, goals and objectives, time frames, and budget (Carlson, 1995).

Components of Funding Proposals

Although each foundation or government agency establishes its own guidelines and application processes for proposals, most successful proposals have the following components: problem statements, statements of need, background and significance of the host organization, goals and objectives, description of methods, budget, dissemination plan, evaluation mechanism, and attachments (see box, "Proposal Components"). Proposal packets also contain a cover letter that introduces the organization, briefly describes the proposed project, and summarizes the organization's qualifications to carry out the plan. A title page and executive summary for the proposal should also be included in the proposal packet. The content of the full proposal should be logically written and link the proposed project with clear goals and objectives and a plan to evaluate program outcomes and processes.

Statement of Need

The needs statement should include a description of the problem, information from needs assessments conducted by the organization or other local sources, some historical background about the problem, and the impact of the problem on the target community or specific subpopulations (New & Quick, 1998). Statistical information on the scope of the problem is also important. Census data is a good source of information; other government agencies and federal, state, or local advocacy groups also can provide information about prevalence or incidence rates. The needs statement should also include detailed information about how the needs assessment was con-

---

Proposal Components

- Cover letter
- Title page
- Executive summary
- Problem statement
- Needs statement
- Background and significance of applicant organization
- Goals and objectives
- Methods
- Time frame
- Budget
- Budget justification
- Dissemination plan
- Continuation plan
- Reference list
- Appendices
- Staff qualifications: vitae or brief biographies
- Proof of 501(c)(3) status
- Organization chart
- Letters of support

---

ducted and how data for secondary sources were obtained (Hummel, 1996).

The need described in the proposal should be directly related to the mission of the organization (Carlson, 1995). If the need described is outside the scope of the organization's mission, the grantee should take special care in describing why the organization should address this problem, what other organizations may or may not be doing to address it, and the grantee's qualifications for addressing it. New and Quick (1998) suggest that the grantee quote directly from funder guidelines to substantiate the need for programs likely to receive funding.

Information about the Applicant Organization

The proposal should include information about why your organization is qualified to provide the specified services. Include in this section of the proposal information on the organization's mission, its target population, the total annual budget, and the geographic areas it serves (Hummel, 1996). Describe any unique characteristics of the organization. Also include historical information about how the organization was founded and the services it has provided to the community. It is appropriate to describe current and past leadership (board members and administrators) in this section and the roles that these leaders have played in the community. Staff qualifications to deliver the specific services identified in the proposal should also be included. In addition, describe in detail data from previous evaluations of the identified program or programs similar to the one described in the proposal.

Goals and Objectives

As described in chapter 11, each program should be associated with a goal or a proposed solution for the problem identified in the statement of need. Some programs will contain multiple goals. Follow each goal with a list of objectives or steps that should be undertaken to achieve it. Each objective should be quantifiable and measurable so that the activities involved can be evaluated. Objectives should also include words such as "increase, describe, enable, and enhance" (Gitlin & Lyons, 1996). Goals and objectives should be directly tied to the statement of need. The proposal should include both process and outcome objectives. Outcome objectives identify expected results (Carlson, 1995). Process objectives describe how you will achieve those results.

Objectives should identify the area to be changed, the target population, the direction of the change (increase or decrease), the amount of change required, and a time frame or deadline (Carlson, 1995; Hummel, 1996). Some proposals also list specific activities needed to accomplish each objective. Activities are different from objectives in that objectives are a list of program-specific actions (for example, organize six block clubs, recruit twenty volunteers), whereas activities are actions that will be taken by administrators or individual staff to construct the program, maintain operations, or deliver services (see box, "Goals and Objectives for an Antihunger Program"). Methods used to evaluate outcomes objectives should be included in any task objective. Process objectives should include a description of methods to assess program quality, client satisfaction, or the process of service delivery.

Goals and Objectives for an Antihunger Program

Ultimate Goal: To reduce hunger in the Fairtown community

Program: Food Pantry Development
Time frame: January 1 to December 31, 2002

Immediate Objectives:

Objective 1 (Process):   Improve service quality in the five food pantries currently operating in the Fairtown community through the establishment of consumer advisory boards for each pantry. Establish advisory boards by March 31, 2002. **Evaluation Measures:** Client satisfaction survey; advisory board meeting minutes.

Objective 2 (Task):   Increase service delivery (number of food baskets provided to families) in the five pantries by 20 percent. The increase in service delivery will be implemented by April 30, 2002. **Evaluation Measures:** Use agency records to document the amount of service provided.

Intermediate Objectives:

Objective 3 (Process):   Improve the nutritional status of residents by offering training on food preparation and bargain shopping to 200 residents by August 31, 2002. **Evaluation Measures:** Goal attainment: number of people trained. Participant evaluation of training seminars.

Objective 4 (Task):   Reduce by 10 percent the number of families that involuntarily miss at least two meals a week by December 31, 2002. **Evaluation Measures:** Pre- and post-door-to-door survey of neighborhood residents.

The Methods Section

The methods section of the proposal should describe those concrete activities that must be undertaken for objective accomplishment. Activities should be tied to a specific time frame. This section should include information on how participants are selected and provide justification for the use of specific methods to accomplish the identified tasks (Carlson, 1995). Consequently, it should include a theory of action, specific assumptions made about why certain activities should lead to goal achievement (Rossi & Freeman, 1982). The theory of action should also be clearly evident in the goals and objectives section of the proposal. While the proposal writer should examine theories about the causes of the social problem identified in the needs section of the proposal, the theory of action should link the proposed program with the solution of the problem (Chambers, Wedel, & Rodwell, 1992). In other words, the theory of action should specify the program designer's assumptions about how the program (the independent variable or cause) will produce program outcomes (dependent variable or effect). Program theories are generated from empirical research, practitioner experience, available program models, and evaluations of similar programs disseminated by successful organizations (Patton & Sawicki, 1993).

According to Patton (1997), the theory of action can best be described by linking immediate, intermediate, and ultimate program objectives. Immediate objectives (specific program activities) must be accomplished for intermediate objectives (program outputs) to be attained. The accomplishment of intermediate objectives leads to the attainment of ultimate objectives (program goals). Specifying cause and effect helps the program designer articulate why the program should have an impact on the target group and what outcomes are expected (see figure 12.1). Cause-and-effect linkages also help identify those factors (outputs and outcomes) that should be examined in the program evaluation.

Budget

The budget of the proposal should be organized to list major line items or cost centers for the program described in the proposal. Personnel (salaries and benefits), office supplies, travel, insurance, rent, and other major expenditures should be identified. Indirect costs should also be specified in the proposal. Many funders limit the percentage of indirect funds that can be awarded to applicant organizations; some funders refuse to pay any indirect costs at all. Consequently, the percentage of indirect costs specified in a proposal should be kept to a minimum (usually below 15 percent). The proposal writer should also specify those in-kind funds or services (for example, printing or office space) the organization will pay or absorb into its own operating budget. Assign dollar amounts to the in-kind resources if possible. The proposal writer must make sure that the requested funds are

Figure 12.1.   Theory of action for hunger program.

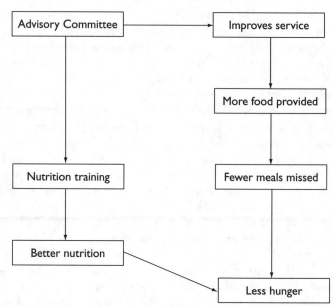

Note: Also see figure 11.5, flowchart for Medicaid outreach program, which describes the theory of action for the outreach program.

reasonable and can be linked with identified goals and objectives. A specific dollar amount of funds should be requested in the proposal. However, most funders will not provide 100 percent of the funding for individual programs. It is usually anticipated that funding will come from multiple sources (Hummel, 1996).

Proposals should also contain a brief statement that explains how costs identified in the budget were estimated and how the funds will be used. This section of the proposal is the budget narrative (Carlson, 1995). Specific details should be provided about anticipated expenditures and how expenditures will be utilized to meet program goals. The proposal writer should also specify how dollar amounts in major expenditure categories are estimated.

Evaluation Plan

The evaluation component should be clearly linked to goals and objectives. Many funders prefer that the evaluation mechanism be clearly identified in each statement of objectives (New & Quick, 1998). A number of evaluation methods can be used to evaluate the program. The easiest way to evaluate program outcomes is simply to look at whether the program attained its goals (see chapter 14). Compare actual outcomes (in terms of either absolute or relative numbers) to the outcomes specified in the program's list of objectives. Other types of quantitative methods can be used to evaluate outcomes for task objectives, including survey research, social indicator analysis, and quasi or experimental designs. Process objectives require that qualitative methods be used to assess program quality or participant perceptions about the program. Such methods can include individual interviews, focus groups, consumer satisfaction surveys, or content analysis of program documents and meeting minutes (see box, "Goals and Objectives for an Antihunger Program"). Some funders also require that an overall process evaluation be conducted that focuses on project implementation (Catalog of Federal Domestic Assistance, 2000). Program evaluation is described in more detail in chapter 14.

Dissemination Plan

Many funders require that the proposal contain a dissemination plan, a description of how the program will distribute information about the effectiveness of the program and the results of the evaluation (New & Quick, 1998). Dissemination plans should include a description of any reports that are to be mailed to other organizations or funding sources and any plans for informing the media about the effectiveness of the proposed intervention. Findings can also be disseminated at community forums and conferences or through formal presentations and lectures. Many funding sources will provide money specifically for dissemination. Consequently, money for this activity should be included in the budget, and planned expenditures should be described in the budget narrative.

Appendices and Attachments

Appendices are often included with the proposal. These attachments can include letters of support, proof of tax-exempt status, biographies or resumes of key staff, newspaper articles or other information about program accomplishments, charts that illustrate project activities and timelines, and plans for project continuation (Catalog of Federal Domestic Assistance, 2000; New & Quick, 1998). Many organizations include letters of support or formal endorsements from key community groups or individuals. Some funders request that such information be provided in the proposal, especially in instances when the success of the proposal requires collaboration with these organizations. Formal endorsements, especially from individuals with a high degree of name recognition and legitimacy in the community, provide the funder with critical information about the organization's capacity to perform the task indicated in the proposal.

Many funders require that the organization provide proof of nonprofit status. In some instances, coalitions or other nonincorporated groups ask another organization with tax-exempt status to function as the project's fiscal agent. This information should be included in the proposal. Other attachments that can be used to verify that the organization can get the job done include resumes of key project staff and newspaper accounts that highlight the organization's accomplishments. Although not required by all funders, proposals should contain information about how the program will be continued. If the grant-making agency provides start-up funds only for a one-year cycle, it will want to know how the grantee plans to keep the program going after the start-up funding is exhausted (New & Quick, 1998). Identify other potential funding sources and describe any plans to raise funding for the project locally.

Proposals should also include a chart that illustrates the activities that must be undertaken to operate and maintain individual programs (for example, hiring staff, obtaining licensing approval, finding appropriate facilities, recruiting clients, and conducting an evaluation). These charts are also used to provide information on the timeline during which each of these activities should take place (Netting, Kettner, & McMurty, 1993). A detailed written description of these activities should be included in the methods section of the proposal. A chart with the timeline (also called a GANNT) chart should be located in the proposal attachment or appendix (see figure 12.2). Each activity should be entered into the chart in time sequence. Some activities must logically precede others if the identified tasks are to be successfully completed.

Completed Proposal Package

The completed proposal with a cover letter should be mailed to the funder. Proposal guidelines specify the number of copies to be mailed. Hand delivery or express mail is generally the best way to ensure that the proposal is

Figure 12.2. GANNT chart for a neighborhood watch program.

	January	February	March	April	May	June
Hire staff	———→					
Print flyers		———→				
Recruit volunteers		————→				
Meet with local police to form collaborative effort			———→			
Hold meetings with neighborhood residents				———→		
Provide training to residents					———→	
Implement watch program						———→

received by the due date. All copies should be collated and stapled or bound with the appropriate attachments. Include in the package a table of contents that identifies each section of the proposal. The funder will evaluate the proposal in terms of the inclusion of all required information and documents and whether the proposal is well written and makes logical sense. The project described should be feasible and justified by the information in the proposal. Funders use a number of criteria to screen proposals (see box, "Proposal Screening Guide").

Summary

To survive, nonprofit organizations must secure monetary resources. Because most nonprofits provide free or low-cost services to low-income people, they must obtain funds from sources outside the target community. Foundations, corporate donors, and government grants or contracts are primary sources of funds for social action, community development, and social planning organizations. Community organizations also rely on membership fees, sales of products, special events, and gifts from individuals to raise funds. However, many of these funding sources come with strings attached. All nonprofits face restrictions on lobbying and political activities because of their tax-free status with the IRS. In addition, most large funders (foundations, corporations, and government) can request that donated funds be used for only certain purposes and specific activities or that this money can benefit only those groups the donor has designated as eligible. The methods used to allocate or distribute funds also create difficulties for many organizations; reimbursement delays or lack of start-up funds can put a financial strain on organizations. The best way to deal with these problems is to generate a mix of funding sources to support the organization and start new programs.

The Internet provides a good low-cost method for finding prospective donors. It is important, however, that nonprofit organizations develop very clear, concise, and logically written funding proposals for submission to prospective donors. A proposal should contain information on the qualifications of the organization, a list of measurable goals and objectives, a reasonable budget, and an evaluation plan. Chapter 13 describes methods to analyze and construct program budgets.

■ SAMPLE ASSIGNMENTS AND EXERCISES

1. Identify sources of funding for your field agency or employer. Describe the process your organization uses to raise funds. What are the dollar amounts provided? How would you assess your organization's reliance on individual funding sources? Is the mix optimal, or do funding arrangements place restrictions on the organization?
2. Working with a team of your classmates, identify a problem or need in

Proposal Screening Guide

1. Eligibility
   - Information on tax-exempt status and annual budget
   - Executive summary indicating how the proposal meets the foundation's interest
2. Organization Strengths
   - Credibility of organization
   - Mission
   - Track record
   - Population served
   - Services are not duplicated by other organizations
   - Services provided are distinctive
3. People
   - Qualifications of key personnel
   - Diversity (skills and backgrounds) of board members
4. Financial Condition
   - Sufficient funds of ongoing expenditures
   - Reasonable budget
5. Problem Proposal Addresses
   - Importance of issue
   - Evidence to substantiate the problem
   - Involvement of beneficiaries in the needs assessment process and identification of solutions
6. Program objectives
   - Clear, measurable objectives
   - Feasibility of the project
   - Objectives that relate to the need
   - Information that explains how the program compares to similar projects
7. Methods
   - Detailed plans
   - Clear theory of action
   - Clear time frame
   - Adequate staff to carry out the plan
8. Evaluation
   - Plan for measuring the program's progress
   - Dissemination plan for major findings
9. Future funding
   - Identification of additional sources of funds for the project
   - Plans for ongoing financial support beyond the grant period
10. Language and form
    - Proposal logically written
    - Facts and assumptions are supported

Source: Henry, 1999.

the community that should be addressed. Use the Web to identify at least five prospective funding sources.

3. Develop a funding proposal that contains all the elements listed in the "Proposal Screening Guide" box. After your instructor or a third party reviews the proposal, submit it to the funding sources identified in sample assignment 2. (Note: Funding proposals need to be linked to an existing organization or program. Do not proceed to this step unless such an arrangement is feasible and appropriate arrangements have been made.)

■ SAMPLE ASSIGNMENT ON FUNDING ALLOCATIONS

Members of your work team have been appointed to the board of the Fairtown Community Trust. You have been asked to review funding proposals and, if the proposals are approved, allocate funds. Which of the following organizations should receive funding, and how much will you give them? You have $100,000 to allocate.

Organization 1: Chief Joseph Youth Group. Native American organization that provides recreational activities for urban Indian children. Its annual budget is $750,000. Most of its current funding comes from nearby tribes that raise funds through casino gambling. Request: $40,000 to upgrade playground equipment.

Organization 2: The Hernandez Immigrant Rights Organization requests $100,000 to fight legislation that would prevent children who are not legal citizens from attending public schools and universities. This organization currently has an operating budget of $80,000. These funds were obtained from a number of unions and wealthy individuals. HIRO has used these funds to engage in a variety of direct action–related activities, including picketing the homes of legislators and burning the American flag.

Organization 3: The Sunriver Neighborhood Organization requests $55,000 to start a neighborhood watch program. The money would be used to hire a part-time coordinator and buy two-way radios for citizens who patrol the community each night. The neighborhood contains residents from diverse backgrounds with incomes ranging from working class to middle class. Burglary and vandalism have been a problem in this neighborhood. However, the organization was formed two years ago specifically to oppose the location of low-income housing in this community.

Organization 4: Save Our Pets (SOP). Recently incorporated group that seeks to build a no-kill shelter for cats and dogs. The group requests $75,000 to pay an architect to design the shelter. It currently has $10,000 in donations on deposit in a local bank.

Organization 5: Beautify Fairtown. Established organization (ten years old—annual budget of $50,000) that plants trees downtown and along major thoroughfares. Beautify Fairtown has requested a $60,000 grant to buy trees.

Notes

1. Kretzmann and McKnight (1993) argue that in-kind services, labor, physical facilities, institutional resources, and ingenuity are sources of economic capital in low-income communities. However, Delgado (1997) argues that there are limited external funds allocated by government or foundations for organization operating support, making many community organizations focus on projects rather than organizational maintenance.
2. According to Hopkins (1989), the IRS decisions related to the "substantial test" rules may vary among organizations, but is often set at 15 percent of the organization's annual budget.

References

Alexander, J. (2000). Adaptive strategies of nonprofit human service organizations in an era of devolution and new public management. *Nonprofit Leadership and Management, 10*(3), 287–303.

Arons, D. (1999, November). *Teaching nonprofit advocacy: A resource guide.* Washington, DC: Independent Sector.

Berg, W., and Wright, R. (1981). Goal displacement in social work programs. *Administration in Social Work, 4,* 29–39.

Blau, P. (1964). *Exchange and power in social life.* New York: Wiley.

Carlson, M. (1995). *Winning grants step by step.* San Francisco: Jossey-Bass.

Catalog of Federal Domestic Assistance. (2000). Appendix VI: Developing and writing grant proposals [On-line]. Available: http://www.aspe.os.dhhs.gov/cfda/index.htm.

Chambers, D., Wedel, K., & Rodwell, M. (1992). *Evaluating social programs.* Boston: Allyn & Bacon.

Delgado, G. (1997). *Beyond the politics of place: New directions in community organization.* Berkeley, CA: Chardon.

Dropkin, M., & La Touche, B. (1998). *The budget-building book for nonprofits.* San Francisco: Jossey-Bass.

Edwards, R., Benefield, E., Edwards, J., & Yankey, J. (1997). *Building a strong foundation: Fundraising for nonprofits.* Washington, DC: National Association of Social Workers.

Fabricant, M., & Burghardt, S. (1992). *The welfare crisis and the transformation of social service work.* New York: Sharpe.

Froelich, K. (1999). Diversification of revenue strategies: Evolving resource dependence in nonprofit organizations. *Nonprofit Sector Quarterly, 23*(3), 246–58.

Gitlin, L., & Lyons, K. (1996). *Successful grant writing: Strategies for health and human service professionals.* New York: Springer.

Goldman, F. (1997). *The mansion on the hill: Dylan, Young, Geffen, Springsteen, and the head-on collision of rock and commerce.* New York: Random House.

Gronbjerg, K. (1993). *Understanding nonprofit funding.* San Francisco: Jossey-Bass.

Gronbjerg, K., Chen, T., & Stagner, M. (1995). Child welfare contracting: Market forces and leverage. *Social Service Review, 69,* 583–613.

Hall, M. (1995). *Poor peoples' social movement organizations.* Westport, CT: Prager.

Hardina, D. (1990). *Solution or illusion? Purchasing job services in Wayne County*. Detroit, MI: Wayne State University, Center for Urban Studies.

Hardina, D. (1993). The impact of funding sources and board representation on consumer control in organizations serving three low income communities. *Nonprofit Management and Leadership, 4*, 69–84.

Henry, C. (1998). Effective proposal writing. In R. Edwards, J. Yankey, & M. Altpeter (Eds.), *Skills for effective management of nonprofit organizations* (pp. 45–58). Washington, DC: National Association of Social Workers.

Holmes, L., & Grieco, M. (1991). Overt funding, buried goals, and moral turnover: The organizational transformation of radical experiments. *Human Relations, 44*(7), 643–64.

Hopkins, B. (1989). *Starting and managing a nonprofit organization*. New York: Wiley.

Hummel, J. (1996). *Starting and running a nonprofit organization* (2d ed.). Minneapolis: University of Minnesota Press.

Johnston, M. (1999). *The fundraiser's guide to the Internet*. New York: Wiley.

Kettner, P., & Martin, L. (1995). Performance contracting in the human services: An initial assessment. *Administration in Social Work, 19*, 47–61.

Kramer , R. (1981). *Voluntary agencies in the welfare state*. Berkeley: University of California Press.

Kramer, R., & Grossman, B. (1987). Contracting for social services: Process management and resource dependencies. *Social Service Review, 61*, 32–55.

Kretzmann, J., & McKnight, J. (1993). *Building communities from the inside out*. Chicago: ACTA.

Lipsky, M., & Thibodeau, M. (1988). Feeding the hungry with surplus commodities. *Political Science Quarterly, 103*(2), 223–44.

Minkler, M., & Pies, C. (1999). Ethical issues in community organization and community participation. In M. Minkler (Ed.), *Community organization and community building for health* (pp. 120–36). New Brunswick, NJ: Rutgers University Press.

Morrill, C., & McKee, C. (1993). Institutional isomorphism and informal social control: Evidence from a community mediation center. *Social Problems, 49*(4), 445–63.

National Committee for Responsive Philanthropy (2000). Payout factsheet: An NNG & NCRP campaign [On-line]. Available: http://www.ncrp.org.

Netting, E., Kettner, P., & McMurty, S. (1993). *Social work macro practice*. New York: Longman.

New, C., & Quick, J. (1998). *Grantseeker's toolkit: A comprehensive guide to finding funding*. New York: Wiley.

O'Connell, B. (1996). A major transfer of government responsibility to voluntary organizations. *Public Administration Review, 56*, 222–25.

Patton, C., & Sawicki, D. (1993). *Basic methods of policy analysis and planning* (2d ed.). Englewood Cliffs, NJ: Prentice-Hall.

Patton, M. (1997). *Utilization-focused evaluation: The new century text*. Thousand Oaks, CA: Sage.

Rossi, P., & Freeman, H. (1982). *Evaluation: A systematic approach*. Beverly Hills, CA: Sage.

Rundall, T., Celetano, D., Marconi, K., Bender-Kitz, S., Kwait, J., & Gentry, D. (1994). *The impact of the Ryan White CARE act on the organization and availability of HIV-related services in Baltimore and Oakland.* Paper presented at the Annual Meeting of the Association for Research on Nonprofit Organizations and Voluntary Action, Berkeley, CA.

Salamon, L. (1995). *Partners in public service.* Baltimore: Johns Hopkins University Press.

Schorr, L. (1997). *Common purpose: Strengthening families and neighborhoods to rebuild America.* New York: Anchor.

Smith, S. R., & Lipsky, M. (1993). *Nonprofits for hire.* Cambridge, MA: Harvard University Press.

Snowden, L. (1993). Emerging trends in organizing and financing human services: Unexamined consequences for ethnic minority populations. *American Journal of Community Psychology, 21*(1), 1–14.

Starr, P. (1989). The meaning of privatization. In A. Kahn & S. Kamerman (Eds.), *Privatization and the welfare state* (pp. 15–48). Princeton: Princeton University Press.

Working assets launches Web site for donors to progressive causes. (1999, October 19). *Philanthropy News Digest, 5*(42), 10.

Web Resources

Information on Grants

Catalog of Federal Domestic Assistance—http://aspe.hhs.gov/cfda/
Chronicle of Philanthropy (subscription fee required)—http://www.philanthropy.com/
Federal Register—http://www.access.gpo.gov/su_docs/aces/aces140.html
Foundation Center (includes database on foundations and prospective funding sources; subscription fee required for use)—http://fdncenter.org/

Information on Nonprofit Organizations and Restrictions on Lobbying

American Institute of Philanthropy (rates national charities using a quality assessment scale)—http://www.charitywatch.org/
Independent Sector—http://www.indepsec.org/
Internet Nonprofit Center—http://www.nonprofits.org/
National Center for Charitable Statistics (data on the nonprofit sector)—http://www.nccs.urban.org/
National Charities Information Bureau—http://give.org
National Committee for Responsive Philanthropy—http://www.ncrp.org/
OMBWatch (provides information to nonprofit organizations about federal expenditures and legislation; focuses primarily on the work of the White House Office of Management and Budget)—http://ombwatch.org/

Note: Many Web sites related to fund-raising are designed for commercial purposes; there is either a charge for utilization or the site is designed to sell a product. Before using such sites, do your research. Is the product or service of use to your organization? Will it actually increase your organization's fund-raising potential? You can also access information on grants by going directly to foundation Web sites and by conducting Web searches related to specific topics (for example, welfare reform, health insurance outreach, or homelessness).

13 Fiscal Analysis

■ Money is power. Consequently, budget analysis is an essential component of community organization practice. This chapter examines the role of budget analysis in community practice and discusses the components of organization and program budgets. Techniques for analyzing budgets, identifying revenue resources, and monitoring expenditures in nonprofit organizations are examined. Computer applications for budget construction, monitoring, and analysis are described. This chapter also provides information about government budgets and techniques for examining government budget priorities.

The Role of Budgeting in Community Practice

A community organizer should know how to construct a budget, monitor spending, and identify funding priorities set by government and other key decision-making bodies. Organizers engaged in social planning must be able to create program plans and gather resources to address unmet community needs. Organizers engaged in community development must bring together resources from diverse organizations to collaborate on community projects (Wasserman, Goodman, & Butterfoss, 1999). Often such activity involves negotiating contracts among organization partners in the community-development process. Organizers engaged in social action must make sure that sufficient resources (money, volunteers, facilities, and office supplies) are available to carry out the plan (Mondros & Wilson, 1994).

Organizers also need information about the budgets of nonprofit, public, and for-profit organizations to gain information about their agendas, activities, and priorities. We may want to know whether these organizations will provide funding for our cause. If so, we may plan a fund-raising campaign to solicit money from these organizations (Edwards, Benefield, Edwards, & Yankey, 1997). We may also want to know something about the budgets of our opponents when we undertake social action organizing: what resources do these organizations have that they can use to undermine our cause? Organizers often examine the budgets of government agencies to find out what funds are allocated for programs that benefit the poor and the percentage of funds that benefit members of special interest groups (Kahn, 1991).

Program and Organization Budgets

A budget is a statement that describes the costs associated with organizational or program plans (Feit & Li, 1998; Lewis, Lewis, & Souflee, 1991). Budgets must be designed to meet predetermined goals within a specific time frame (Dropkin & La Touche, 1998). Budgets also allow administrators to control the distribution of resources, develop fund-raising campaigns and marketing plans, make decisions about hiring and termination of staff, acquire resources, and evaluate the effectiveness and efficiency of programs (Chambers, Wedel, & Rodwell, 1992).

Budget periods for organizations are typically one year—although budgets for specific projects may be shorter or spread over a number of years. Organizations must decide when the budget period or fiscal year begins and when it ends (Dropkin & La Touche, 1998). Budget cycles are typically January 1 through December 31 or July 1 through June 30.

There are two primary types of budgets: line item and program budgets. A line item budget contains a list of major spending categories: personnel, rent, office supplies, phones, travel, training expenses, and other resources needed to operate the program. Program budgets also contain line items listing major expenditures, but these expenses are broken down to represent the costs of running individual programs within the organization. Administrative expenditures (for example, the salary of the executive director and clerical support staff) can be listed as a separate program or distributed among the various programs in the organization (see table 13.1).

Accounting Procedures

Most community organizers work for nonprofit organizations. Nonprofit accounting and budget systems are significantly different from those used

Table 13.1 Program Budget for the Fairtown Community Organization

	Anti-Alcohol Initiative	Neighborhood Beautification	Welfare Reform Coalition	Total
Personnel				
Salaries	$120,000	$75,000	$55,000	$250,000
Fringe benefits				
@ 20% of salary	$24,000	$15,000	$11,000	$50,000
Operating expenses				
Office supplies	$9,600	$6,000	$4,400	$20,000
Phone	$4,320	$2,700	$1,980	$9,000
Printing	$7,200	$4,500	$3,300	$15,000
Postage	$2,400	$1,500	$1,100	$5,000
Rent	$14,400	$9,000	$6,600	$30,000
Equipment	$5,760	$3,600	$2,640	$13,000
Insurance	$960	$600	$440	$2,000
Travel	$3,360	$2,100	$1,540	$7,000
Training	$2,400	$1,500	$1,100	$5,000
Subscriptions	$576	$360	$264	$1,200
Professional				
Memberships	$480	$300	$220	$1,000
Total expenditures	$195,456	$122,160	$89,584	$407,200

by for-profit organizations because of the unique tax status of nonprofits. All funds are to be used for organization expenses; any profits are to be rolled back into the organization and are not to be used to benefit owners or board members. Most nonprofits that employ organizers are incorporated by the IRS as 501(c)(3) or 501(c)(4) organizations. These organizations are not taxed on the money they earn, and funds contributed to 501(c)(3) organizations qualify the donor for a tax deduction. In return, these organizations are required to submit annual reports to the IRS that verify that funds are used properly. Government monitoring requires, however, that nonprofits keep careful records of income and expenses (Smith, 1999). So that accounting information is interpreted consistently, most nonprofits use accounting standards established by the Financial Accounting Standards Board (FASB) and the Government Accounting Standards Board (GASB).

Nonprofit organizations may use two general types of accounting procedures: cash and accrual accounting. In cash accounting, transactions are recorded only when money flows into and out of the organization (Smith, 1999). Accrual accounting requires that income be recorded in the organization's account book or computerized record system during the time period in which it is earned. Expenses are recorded when they occur rather than when the bills are paid. Accrual accounting also requires that an asset be logged into the account books when it is earned. Consequently, pledges made during fund-raising drives and any other funds owed to the organization are considered assets in accrual accounting. Most small nonprofit organizations use cash accounting. However, in large organizations failure to record expenditures when they are incurred may overstate the amount of funds available for spending. This is particularly problematic when bills are not paid during the budget year in which the expense occurs.

Another concept important in understanding the budget process in nonprofit organizations is fund accounting. Many foundations, corporate donors, and government funding sources restrict the use of grants and contracts to specific purposes (Edwards et al., 1997). Consequently, organizations must establish accounting systems that can verify that the funds obtained were used only for these purposes. Monies that are limited to predesignated uses are called restricted funds (Dropkin & LaTouche, 1998). Operating statements and other financial documents are organized to indicate whether funds are restricted or unrestricted. Fund accounting is used to differentiate money from different sources, especially in cases where funds can be used only for certain purposes (Smith, 1999). Generally, the easiest method for doing this is to set up separate columns in the account book for each funding source. Organizations with unsophisticated accounting systems often go to the extreme of setting up separate checking accounts for programs funded through restricted sources. Though this is a good method of keeping funds separate, the organization's bookkeeper or accountant would still need to record expenditures and bill them to the appropriate program and funding source. Fund accounting is simply a device that allows the organization to track funds and expenses separately and to obtain starting and ending balances, even in cases where funds are commingled in the same bank account. Organizations often organize their budget statements to reflect separate totals for restricted and unrestricted funds (see table 13.2).

Developing a Budget

One of the most problematic situations for new program planners is how to estimate budget expenditures. Administrators typically monitor yearly expenditures and calculate what proportion of the budget has been used each month as well as on a cumulative basis (for example, what proportion of the yearly budget was used between January and October). Often budgets for ongoing programs are constructed based on whether the program was over or under budget during the year. The new budget is generally based on these previous expenditures, with a small adjustment added to represent the current rate of inflation (usually 3 to 5 percent). Anticipated changes in

Table 13.2   Operating Statement for the Fairtown Community
Organization: Identifying Restricted Funds

	Unrestricted	*Restricted*	*Total*
Support and Revenue			
Foundation grants	$175,000	50,000	$225,000
Membership dues	30,000		30,000
United Way	25,000		25,000
Government contracts		47,000	47,000
Individual donations	40,000		40,000
Special events	24,000		24,000
Union contributions	17,000		17,000
Total Support and Revenue	$311,000	$97,000	$408,000
Operating Expenses			
Salaries	$187,000	$63,000	$250,000
Fringe benefits	37,400	12,600	50,000
Supplies and maintenance	71,000	20,000	91,000
Insurance	2,000	0	2,000
Travel	5,600	1,400	7,000
Professional development	7,200	0	7,200
Total Expenses	$310,200	$97,000	$407,200
Operating Excess (Deficiency)	$800	$0	$800

organization operating plans are also factored into the revised budget. For
example, plans to terminate a program should decrease the amount the
organization spends on most types of operating expenses such as office supplies, travel, or salaries (Dropkin & La Touche, 1998).

Budget estimates for new programs are more difficult. Often the budget
planner must examine the amount of funds the program used during the
first year of operation. Sources of information can include funding proposals
or program budgets constructed for programs that are similar to yours. If
this information is not available, you must make an estimate of costs for
each line item. Most vendors who work with nonprofit organizations provide free cost estimates for many items.

There are a number of rules of thumb for constructing a budget. The
budget planner can assume that personnel costs should approximate about
80 percent of the program's total budget. Personnel costs include both salaries and fringe benefits. Fringe benefits include a number of components—
the employer's portion of Social Security, unemployment, and worker's
compensation taxes as well as benefits provided at the employer's option:
medical, dental, and eye care insurance and pension benefits (New & Quick,
1998). Most small nonprofit organizations seldom provide more than basic

medical coverage, although organizations that are more progressive have started to recognize these benefits (in addition to a living wage) as a basic right for all employees. Fringe benefits typically range between 15 and 25 percent of the worker's salary. Rather than costing out these expenses for each employee, budget planners simply estimate the proportion of the average worker's salary that is represented by the fringe benefits and use that in budget calculations. For example, if the average worker's fringe benefits total 20 percent of salary, to estimate fringe benefits for all five of our agency's workers, we take the salary total and multiply it by 20 percent:

$$\$150,000 \times 20\% = \$30,000 \text{ (fringe benefits)}$$

$$\$150,000 + \$30,000 = \$180,000 \text{ (total personnel costs)}$$

Fixed and Variable Costs

Nonprofit programs also incur a number of other expenditures: rent, utilities, office supplies, purchase or maintenance of office equipment, telephone service, postage, travel, professional development (subscriptions and training), and printing (Dropkin & La Touche, 1998). Almost all organizations carry some form of insurance for theft or other damage to the office or injury to employees and clients, as well as liability insurance (Strachan, 1998). Workers may be legally liable for harm to clients. Board members are legally liable for fiscal decisions and other potentially damaging administrative actions made by the organization. Some of these costs are not billed directly to specific programs but are absorbed in the cost of administering the organization. Costs that are directly associated with the program are called direct costs (New & Quick, 1998). Costs that the organization may accrue in the administration of that program (such as accounting services, a proportion of the organization's overall rent budget used to support the program, or a proportion of the agency administrator's salary used to supervise program activities) are considered to be indirect costs. Indirect costs are also called overhead, the cost of administering the program (Carlson, 1995).

Most program budgets include a line item for indirect costs. Indirect costs are usually estimated as an average and may range from 8 to 20 percent of the program or total budget of the organization. Other methods used to calculate the proportion of indirect costs allocated per program are based on per-unit costs (people served; amount of service produced) of program activities and the proportion of total organization space (facilities) used by the program (Dropkin & La Touche, 1998).

Some of these expenditures can be easily estimated in advance; others cannot. Those costs that we know in advance are called fixed costs. Costs that we cannot estimate accurately or that may vary substantially by situation are called variable costs. It is easy to determine the amount of fixed costs for certain items in your budget. Most programs obtain long-term leases

for office space or negotiate contracts in advance for office cleaning or maintenance of office equipment. The date of contract initiation is usually the
first day of the program's budget year.

Often organizations implement procedures that limit the use of resources
to reduce expenditures or convert variable costs to fixed costs. For example,
organizations may limit employee access to the photocopying machine, assign a code number to each employee to track the number of copies made,
or limit employees to a certain number of copies per month. Some organizations keep detailed records to indicate how certain variable costs (such
as telephone, postage, and travel) are accrued in the organization or devise
ways to attribute these costs to the work of individual employees or staff
positions (Dropkin & La Touche, 1998). The predictability of these expenditures helps the organization allocate appropriate amounts of funds for
anticipated expenditures during the budget year.

Revenue

Sources of revenue for most social action and community organizations are
foundation grants, government contracts, membership dues, and donations
from individuals (Hardina, 1993). Community organizations may also receive contributions from unions and corporations and fees for services and
sales of products. Most community organizations raise funds from grassroots, or local, sources: direct mail campaigns to community residents and
special fund-raising events (for example, bingo games, raffles, spaghetti dinners, awards ceremonies, and concerts). Organizations also generate revenue with interest-bearing bank accounts and assets (such as property or
businesses) donated to the organization (Strachan, 1998). As noted in chapter 3, the source of funds and the priorities of the funding agency may
restrict an organization's ability to fight for a cause (Blau, 1964; Piven &
Cloward, 1979). Consequently, organizations generally attempt to limit the
funder's capacity to control service provision by combining a variety of funding sources rather than relying on a single donor (Froelich, 1999).

In-kind Resources

Organizations can also contribute in-kind resources to help fund a new
program (New & Quick, 1998). In-kind support can include staff time (typically administrative or clerical work) or use of equipment, office supplies,
and facilities. These resources are paid for with money from other sources
(for example, the organization may have a foundation grant to pay basic
operating costs). In some cases, an external funding source may require that
the organization provide matching funds generated internally in return for
a grant (Dropkin & La Touche, 1998). Matches of 100 percent of the value
of the grant are seldom required. However, the organization may be required to make a match of 25 to 50 percent of the value of the grant.

Monitoring Expenditures

Financial statements are used to monitor how organizations use funds. Board members and administrators review budget information on a periodic basis to make adjustments in how funds are used and to determine if action must be taken to either conserve organization resources or raise additional funding (Dropkin & La Touche, 1998). Four basic types of reports are used: operating statements, balance sheets, cash flow statements, and annual reports. The operating statement contains information about funding generated directly by the organization (fees for service, sales of products) and support provided by grants and contracts (Strachan, 1998). It also lists expenditures in line item categories and indicates whether the organization is in a surplus or deficit situation (see table 13.3).

Balance sheets are also used to examine an organization's expenditures.

Table 13.3 Operating Statement for the Fairtown Community Organization

Operating Support and Revenue	
Foundation grants	$225,000
Membership dues	30,000
United Way	25,000
Government contracts	47,000
Individual donations	40,000
Special events	24,000
Union contributions	17,000
Total Support and Revenue	$408,000
Operating Expenses	
Personnel	
Salaries	$250,000
Fringe benefits @ 20% of salary	50,000
Office supplies	20,000
Phone	9,000
Printing	15,000
Postage	5,000
Rent	30,000
Equipment	12,000
Insurance	2,000
Travel	7,000
Training	5,000
Subscriptions	1,200
Professional memberships	1,000
Total expenses	$407,200
Operating Excess (Deficiency)	$800

Typically, managers and organization boards use balance sheets to examine the organization's net worth. Both organization assets and liabilities are listed. Assets are any resource the organization owns that can be used to benefit the organization. Liabilities include debts or obligations to deliver goods and services (Strachan, 1998). Assets can include cash in checking and savings accounts, investments, accounts receivable (money owed to the organization for services), and pledges. Liabilities are accounts payable (money owed to individuals and vendors) and loans.

The fund balance (assets minus liabilities) is also included in the balance sheet (see table 13.4). The observer should be able to use the information on the balance sheet to determine the organization's net worth and future prospects. Generally, balance sheets also contain information from one or more previous years so that net worth can be tracked over time. Is the organization growing or declining? Is the source of monetary problems debts, or does the organization have difficulty raising funds?

Organizations also keep records of their cash flow. Grants and contracts do not always arrive at the organization on a regular basis. Funds received on a reimbursement-only basis may not arrive when bills need to be paid. Government agencies are notoriously slow in processing reimbursements; organizations that receive contracts seldom are granted start-up funds and often do not know in advance how many services will have successful outcomes. Consequently, these organizations may experience cash shortfalls. Organizations often cope with such problems by deferring bill payments, laying off staff, asking staff to work temporarily without pay, or taking out short-term loans (Kramer & Grossman, 1987). Keeping track of the cash is essential for the organization's survival and allows the administrator to plan

Table 13.4 Balance sheet for the Fairtown Community Organization: Fiscal Year Ending June 30, 2001

	2000	2001	Difference	Percent Difference
Assets				
Cash and equivalent	$14,000.00	$10,000.00	($4,000)	− 28.6%
Accounts receivable	0	1,000	1,000	100.0%
Grants receivable	100,000	125,000	25,000	25.0%
Total assets	114,000	136,000	22,000	19.3%
Liabilities				
Accounts payable	22,000	0	(22,000)	− 100.0%
Loans and notes	0	27,000	27,000	100.0%
Total liabilities	$22,000.00	$27,000.00	($5,000)	− 22.7%
Fund Balance	$92,000	$109,000	$17,000	18.0%

Note: Figures in parentheses indicate a deficit.

for fiscal crises. Cash flow statements allow for the comparison of funds received each month with bills received. If funds received each month exceed bills, that money is used to offset bills during the succeeding month (see table 13.5).

All tax-exempt organizations are required to undergo a yearly audit by an outside firm and the results are to be submitted to the IRS (Strachan, 1998). In addition to the professionally certified auditor's statement about the organization's fiscal integrity, each organization must file a Form 990 with the IRS that contains information about program expenditures and revenues as well as assets and liability. The IRS also requires that nonprofit organizations publish an annual report that includes this financial information. The annual report must be released to the public on request. In addition to the required financial information, annual reports generally include information about the organization's program, key administrative staff, board members, and major donors.

Analyzing a Program or Organization Budget

At the most basic level, a budget analysis is used to compare funds allocated for specific purposes in the line item budget to those funds actually used (Feit & Li, 1998). Though organizations may be slightly over or under budget in some categories during the budget year, three situations may be problematic:

1. The organization is over budget in a number of expenditure categories. This indicates inability to control organizational expenditures or unanticipated events (for example, high rates of local unemployment due to bad weather in an agricultural area could substantially increase demand for food from an emergency food provider). It could also indicate that the organization did not receive all funds anticipated at the budget year or could not obtain additional support when faced with unanticipated costs.
2. The organization is under budget for some types of expenditures. This indicates that the organization has not been able to spend funds in the manner indicated. It can also indicate lack of work effort or failure to implement funded programs (Chambers et al., 1992; Rossi & Freeman, 1982).
3. The organization is under budget in some categories and over budget in others. Many of the funds are restricted for certain uses and cannot be transferred among budget categories (Feit & Li, 1998).

One technique used for analyzing expenditures involves the calculation of year-to-date budget totals. Analysts should examine whether actual yearly expenditures match, exceed, or are significantly below the amounts the or-

Table 13.5 Cash Flow Budget

		July	August	Sept.	Oct.	Nov.	Dec.	Total
Foundation grants	$225,000	25,000		40,000		10,000	40,000	$115,000
Membership dues	30,000	1,000	500	3,000	2,500	$100	5,000	$12,100
United Way	25,000	10,000						$10,000
Government contracts	47,000		7,500			10,000		$17,500
Individual donations	40,000	500	1,200	1,000	3,400	1,400	6,000	$13,500
Special events	24,000	11,500			3,000			$14,500
Union contributions	17,000			8500				$8,500
Total Support and Revenue	$408,000	48,000	9,200	52,500	8,900	21,500	51,000	$191,100
Operating Expenses								
Personnel								
Salaries	$250,000	20,830	20,830	20,830	20,830	20,830	20,830	$124,980
Fringe benefits	50,000	4,166	4,166	4,166	4,166	4,166	4,166	24,996
Supplies and maintenance	91,000	6,000	9,000	7,000	9,000	8,000	6,500	45,500
Insurance	2,000	1,000						1,000
Travel	7,000	1,200	800	900	1,500	1,000	600	6,000
Professional development	7,200	500	800	100	1,200	400	300	3,300
Total Expenses	$407,200	$33,696	$35,596	$32,996	$36,696	$34,396	$32,396	$205,776
Cash surplus (deficit)		14,304	(26,396)	19,504	(27,796)	(12,896)	18,604	(14,676)
Cash balance at the end of month		14,304	(12,092)	7,412	(20,384)	(33,280)	(14,676)	(14,676)

ganization budgeted. If the funds do not balance, management has not been successful in meeting organizational goals and controlling costs (Strachan, 1998). A month-to-month analysis of budget expenditures can also be used to indicate how quickly the organization is using resources in the various budget categories. Monthly service-delivery patterns usually do not vary substantially except in exceptional situations. Consequently, the organization should use only about one-twelfth of its resources each month, or about 50 percent of its resources in a 6-month period. Doing this type of analysis on a regular basis allows the organization to transfer funds between budget categories, take steps to control costs, and develop a plan to raise additional funding (see table 13.6). Using the year-to-date totals, the analysts can also recognize specific patterns in the organization's use of funds: incoming revenue, expenditures as a proportion of the total budget, and the efficient use of agency resources.

Revenue Analysis

Organizations also conduct revenue analysis to assess whether the organization is maximizing its use of resources. A revenue analysis can address the following questions:

1. What proportion of revenue comes from grants, contracts, and donations? What proportion of revenue is generated from specific sources?
2. Does the proportion of funds generated from these sources help the organization balance its accounts? Are some revenue sources more

Table 13.6 Year-to-Date Budget for the Fairtown Community Organization: First Six Months of Operation: 2001 Fiscal Year

	Annual Budget	Year-to-Date Budget July–Dec. 2001	Year-to-Date Actual	Year-to-Date Difference	Percentage Difference Year to Date
Salaries	$250,000	$125,000	$124,980	$20	0.0%
Fringe benefits	50,000	25,000	24,996	4	0.0%
Supplies and maintenance	91,000	45,500	49,500	(4,000)	−8.8%
Insurance	2,000	1,000	1,000	0	0.0%
Travel	7,000	3,500	6,000	(2,500)	−71.4%
Professional development	7,200	3,600	3,300	300	8.3%
Total Expenses	$407,200	$203,600	$201,766	($6,176)	−3.0%

influential in determining organization programs and services than others due to organizational dependence on this source?

3. How reliable is the revenue base? Did the organization experience a shortage of funds during the budget year? Can the organization count on funding from the various foundations and from government, individual, and other donors to continue on a regular basis?

4. How can new revenues be generated? Are any of the current sources of funds underutilized? (Dropkin & La Touche, 1998; Strachan, 1998)

Expenditure Analysis

To examine whether an organization is using funds effectively, an analysis of the proportion of expenditures in major line items categories should be conducted. One method used to evaluate nonprofit program administration and fund-raising efforts is to examine indirect costs as a proportion of the overall budget. The lower the amount of indirect expenditures, the more confidence the analyst has that the program is run efficiently (National Charities Information Bureau, 2000). The amount of funds spent on fund-raising (through either internally conducted activities or the employment of an external fund-raising consultant) is also a concern. Because direct mail, telephone solicitation, and special-event fund-raising often have high overhead costs, such efforts are wasted if monies collected do not exceed costs. One method to assess whether a particular charity is worthy of your contribution is to determine how much of the money the organization raises actually goes to charity rather than to fund-raising expenses. High indirect costs (of almost 100 percent) are usually an indication that the purpose of the fund-raising effort is to pay the fundraiser rather than to provide services to people in need or support a cause (National Charities Information Bureau, 2000).

Efficiency Analysis

A budget analysis can also examine how efficiently the organization has used its resources. You can easily determine the unit cost of providing the service by dividing program costs by the number of services provided. This might prove a little bit tricky in community organization work as opposed to social work with individual clients. For work with individuals, we would simply divide the cost per program by the number of individuals served (Chambers et al., 1992; White, 1981). For example, if total expenditures for a food program were $10,000 and 200 families were served, the unit cost would be $50. We may not always be able to break down community practice into such precise numbers because our clients include the entire community. However, we may be able to calculate the unit cost for organizing twenty block clubs or recruiting 100 volunteers.

We could also calculate the amount of work effort used to perform certain tasks. For example, if an organizer works 235 days per year and spends the entire year organizing fifty block clubs at an average rate of thirty hours per block club, we could calculate the actual percentage of the worker's time used for that purpose.

$$\frac{50 \text{ block clubs} \times 30 \text{ hours per block club} = 1{,}500 \text{ hours}}{235 \text{ work days} \times 8\text{-hour days} = 1{,}880}$$

$$= 71\% \text{ of worker time}$$

Unit cost and workload analysis are generally used to make comparisons among programs operated by one organization or to make comparisons between two organizations with similar programs. Such an analysis allows the budget planner to examine whether resources can be used appropriately and whether unrestricted funds should be transferred among programs. For example, the budget analyst may recommend changes if the unit cost for recruiting volunteers in program A is $200 and the unit cost per volunteer in program B is $50 ($10,000 ÷ 2,000). Obviously, the methods or staff time used in program B represents a more efficient use of resources, and the analyst could conceivably recommend that program A adopt similar procedures or that staffing arrangements be changed (Kettner, Daley, & Nichols, 1985). However, the analyst should also incorporate indicators of program quality and consumer satisfaction into his or her final recommendation (Chambers et al., 1992).

Using Computer Technology for Budgeting

Some software packages have been developed exclusively to assist with the budgeting process. Spreadsheet programs, available with most office-oriented software, also can easily be used in lieu of traditional account books to track expenditures and revenues. They also can be used to produce monthly and annual reports. Programs such as Excel, Lotus, and Quicken, among others, are good choices for the budget analyst. Once column headings and budget categories are entered into the spreadsheet, the analyst can simply enter formulas into the various spreadsheet cells and calculations are automatically performed. In addition, the analyst can use the budget information to produce graphs and charts that illustrate budget trends and that can be easily understood by board members and other constituents (see figure 13.1).

Analyzing Government Budgets

Federal and state governments have similar processes for developing annual budgets. The chief executive recommends budget allocations, but members

Figure 13.1.   Revenue sources as a proportion of the annual budget for
the Fairtown Community Organization.

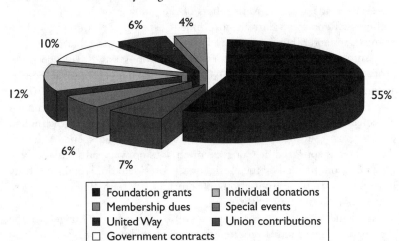

of the legislative branch actually set budget priorities and approve allocations. Lobbyists and members of interest groups advocate for specific dollar
allocations for programs and services. Community organizers are often involved in the budget process as analysts (what impact will proposed allocations have on organizations, special populations, and individuals?) and as
advocates.

Federal Budget

Government budget cycles are different from those of most nonprofit organizations. The federal fiscal year runs from October 1 to September 30.
By law, the president must send his budget recommendation to Congress
by February 1. Through the Office of Management and Budget (OMB),
the president receives budget requests from the various federal agencies and
then sets priorities (OMB, 2000a). The president, however, does not have
constitutional authority to set the budget, authorize expenditures, or levy
taxes. Consequently, the president can only recommend that his budget be
accepted.

Both House and Senate committees work with the Congressional Budget
Office (CBO) to review the president's budget and establish parameters for
the budget that is actually approved by Congress (Dye, 1998). The CBO is
nonpartisan. Its duties also include helping Congress assess the fiscal impact
of new legislation that includes federal mandates (with which states must
comply in return for federal funding). The CBO also develops economic

forecasts and projections that are used to make decisions about how federal funds will be used in the future (CBO, 2000a). These projections and estimates are made available to members of the public as well as members of Congress. Reports on current government expenditures (outlays) and receipts (taxes and other income) are also disseminated (see table 13.7).

Congress reviews the president's budget proposal and may reject, approve, or modify it (OMB, 2000a). Congressional budget approval requires action on thirteen separate appropriation bills, initiated in the House (Dye, 1998; OMB, 2000a). These bills provide money that the federal government can spend; additional legislation is required to authorize new government programs and set limits on the amount of money it can spend. Although the budget as approved by Congress often does not vary substantially from the one recommended by the president, the president does retain authority to veto the various appropriation bills outright or use the line item veto to cancel some of the expenditures.

Key issues of concern for organizers in relation to the budget are the total percentage of funds allocated to means-tested programs (such as food stamps, school lunch and Supplemental Security Income programs). For example, in President Clinton's 2000 budget, 6 percent of all funds were allocated for these means-tested programs for low-income people. An additional 6 percent of the budget was allocated for Medicaid (OMB, 2000b). A budget analyst would compare these budget allocations to the 15 percent allocated for defense, nondefense discretionary spending (18 percent) and interest payments on the federal debt (12 percent). Six percent of the 2000 budget was also held in reserve and applied toward paying down the debt (see table 13.8).

The debt represents accumulated yearly deficits (outlays exceed receipts); the interest paid is the cost of borrowing from private individuals and lending institutions (through notes and bond offerings) to cover the deficit. Although much of recent political rhetoric has focused on paying down the debt and reducing taxes, note that in the United States government spending represents a much lower proportion of the gross domestic product (total economic activity) than in six other industrialized nations (see figure 13.2).

Table 13.7 Monthly Treasury Statement for April 2000 (in Billions of Dollars)

	Preliminary Estimate	Actual	Difference
Receipts	295	295	0.5
Outlays	132	136	3
Surplus	163	159	−3

Note: Figures in column four are rounded to the nearest billion.
Source: Congressional Budget Office, 2000.

State Budgets

State government budget cycles usually start on July 1 and end on June 30. This concurs with the end of the state legislative session. Although most states require that all budget negotiations be finalized by the end of the fiscal year, some states do not meet this deadline (Lucas & Gledhill, 2000). Appropriations for some state programs and employees may be put on hold until all budget decisions are finalized. Though some nonprofits operate on a July through June fiscal year, concurrence with the state budget cycle is not enough to ensure that state funds will be available to nonprofit organizations on a timely basis. Decisions about dollar amounts and procedures for distributing funds allocated by the legislature may require a great deal of time (two to three months) to pass before the nonprofit actually receives grants or contract reimbursement. Analysis and tracking of the state budget helps the nonprofit plan for funding shortfalls that may occur due to delays in the state decision-making process. In addition, the organization can respond to events in the legislature to prevent cuts in funds allocated for specific programs or lobby for increased or new program funds.

Techniques for Government Budget Analysis

Budget analysts examine trends in government funding for specific programs. Are funds increasing or decreasing? What proportion of funds is allocated for programs for the poor versus funds allocated to programs that will benefit special-interest groups or members of the economic elite? Most government budgets and secondary analyses of budget information will contain information about the funds allocated during previous years. The analyst can simply examine increases, decreases, and changes in the proportion of overall funds allocated for certain purposes. The analyst will want to bear in mind, however, that some small increases are actually just inflation-adjusted amounts. In some instances, these increases actually represent decreases in real dollars after adjusting for inflation. The analyst can use several techniques to examine whether dollar amounts have actually increased:

1. Look at federal expenditures in terms of the proportion of the gross domestic product represented by those expenditures.
2. Look at average year-to-year increases or decreases in specific budget items.
3. When comparing two time periods, adjust the value of the dollar expenditures in the earliest category to normalize or hold constant dollar amounts (Klosterman, 1990; Palm & Qayum, 1985). For example, an analyst could compare two sets of expenditures:

    Neighborhood outreach   1970 $1,000,000
    Neighborhood outreach   2000 $12,000,000

Table 13.8 Federal Expenditures (in Billions of Dollars)

Budget Policy with Social Security Reform	1998 Actual	1999	2000	2001	2002	2003	2004
				Estimate			
Outlays							
Discretionary							
Department of Defense	258	265	262	269	279	291	301
Non-DOD discretionary	297	317	330	341	339	338	338
Priority initiatives				2	4	7	10
Subtotal discretionary	555	581	592	612	623	636	649
Mandatory							
Social Security	376	389	405	424	444	465	487
Medicare and Medicaid	291	311	328	350	363	391	416
Means-tested entitlements	99	107	112	118	124	129	134
Deposit insurance	−4	−5	−2	−2	−1	*	1
Other	92	117	116	118	115	125	131
Subtotal mandatory	855	919	959	1,007	1,044	1,110	1,170
Net interest	243	227	215	207	197	188	179
Subtotal mandatory and net interest	1,098	1,146	1,174	1,214	1,241	1,297	1,998
Total outlays	1,653	1,727	1,766	1,826	1,863	1,934	1,998

Receipts	1,722	1,806	1,883	1,933	2,007	2,075	2,166
Resources contingent upon Social Security reform							
Department of Defense				-10	-17	-13	-15
Non-DOD discretionary				-15	-20	-16	-9
Priority initiatives				-2	-4	-7	-10
Related debt service				-1	-2	-4	-6
Total							
Reserve pending Social Security Reform	69	79	117	134	187	182	208
Surplus	0	0	0	0	0	0	0

* $500 million or less

Source: Office of Management and Budget, 2000.

Figure 13.2. Government spending as a proportion of gross domestic product in seven industrialized nations.

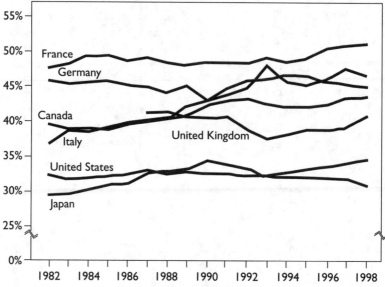

Source: Office of Management and Budget, 2000.

To convert expenditures for the year 2000 into 1970 dollars (using an average estimated inflation rate of 5 percent over a period of 30 years), a formula is used to calculate the 1970 value of the dollars allocated in the earlier time period:

$$\text{Present value} = \frac{1}{(1 + .05)^{30}} = \$780,640$$

In this example, it is clear that funds allocated for outreach services have not kept pace with inflation, and current allocations actually represent a substantial decrease from 1970 expenditures.[1]

Using Computer Resources for Analysis of Government and Nonprofit Expenditures

Budget information about other nonprofit organizations is available through the organization's annual report (the IRS requires that annual reports be made available to the public on request). In addition, the Urban Institute and the Kellogg Foundation have begun to post information from Form 990 on the Web site maintained by the National Center for Charitable Statistics at http://www.guidestar.org (*Philanthropy News Digest*, 1999). Information included on this Web site includes components of the organization's annual report: the actual operating budget (revenue and expenditures) and the year-end balance statement (assets and liabilities) for the organization. Information from the organization's previous balance statement is also included so that the analyst can examine whether the organization's financial status has improved or declined.

Information about government budgets is available from university and local libraries and on the Web. You can find information about the federal budget on Web sites maintained by the Office of Management and Budget (http://www.whitehouse.gov/OMB) and the Congressional Budget Office (http://www.cbo.gov). The General Accounting Office (GAO) also produces regular reports on the use of federal government funds (http://www.gao.gov). National advocacy organizations such as the Center on Budget and Policy Priorities (http://www.cbpp.org) and OMB Watch (http://ombwatch.org) publish regular reports about government expenditures and the annual budget. Interest groups and advocacy organizations also issue regular reports about programs of concern to their members and the status of congressional allocations for these organizations (see, for example, the Web site maintained by the Children's Defense Fund, http://www.childrensdefense.org). In addition, a Web site maintained by the Economic Democracy Network contains the National Budget Simulation Project. This Web site allows the user to "balance" the federal budget by making choices about program cuts and increases and tax rates (http://socrates.berkeley.edu.333/budget). Most state legislatures have offices that are the state equivalent of the CBO. They are designed to analyze and critique the governor's proposed budget and its implications for taxpayers and program beneficiaries. Often the Legislative Analyst's Office (LAO) issues reports on the use of funds for specific programs of public concern. Much of this information is posted on the Web and can be easily downloaded.

Summary

To operate programs successfully, community organizations must obtain funds and monitor revenues and expenditures. Information about how these organizations spend funds must be made available to board members, the IRS, and the public. A number of accounting devices can be used to display and analyze this information: operating statements, balance sheets, cash flow statements, annual reports, and year-to-date analyses. It is also important for organizers to be able to obtain budget information from nonprofit organizations and government to plan lobbying campaigns and requests for funding. Organizers must be able to review government budgets and examine funding priorities that affect programs for marginalized groups. Budget or efficiency analysis is often one of the primary components involved in program evaluation. Chapter 14 describes methods used for program evaluation.

1. Would you donate money to the organization described in table 13.4? Why or why not? What circumstances could contribute to the organization's budget deficit? Is this a big problem for the organization? Has the organization's financial status improved or deteriorated?
2. What steps would you take to control the costs described in table 13.5? What budget categories are most problematic?
3. The federal budget for fiscal year 2000 was $1.8 trillion. Does the dollar amount of the budget or the appropriations for the various programs surprise you? Why or why not? How would you change budget priorities?

■ SAMPLE ASSIGNMENTS AND EXERCISES

1. Find out how your employer, social work field agency, or social work program pays for printing, photocopying, phone, or postage costs. Are these costs easily estimated in advance or are they variable? What measures does the organization take to monitor these expenditures? Can these costs be easily linked to the work of individual employees? What procedures are in place to control expenditures or ration these resources?
2. Use the National Budget Simulation (http://socrates.berkeley.edu.333/ budget) to balance the federal budget. Choose tax rates and increases or deficits until the budget is balanced. How difficult was it to complete this task? Did you have all the information you needed to do this? What obstacles do you think members of Congress face in allocating funds and setting tax rates? Were you surprised by the size of the budget? Why or why not?
3. Analyze the budget for your field agency or place of employment. Did you have difficulty finding this information? What are the major expenditure categories? What steps could be taken to minimize costs? Are revenues sufficient? Create a fund-raising plan for your organization.
4. Using a computer spreadsheet package (for example, Excel or Lotus), create a program budget for the Neighborhood Community Organization using the following information. Assume that the director and bookkeeper/secretary split their time between programs in the manner indicated. Their salaries can be allocated among these programs as a portion of the regular salary expenditures or calculated as indirect costs. Using the information presented in this chapter, you must decide how to distribute funds in the organization's line item budget among the three programs. Assume that you are the new executive director. Write a memo to the board of directors describing how you have chosen to allocate funds across the three programs. Use the information available to you (time allocation, number of staff per program, number of people served) to justify your decision. You may also develop your own quantifiable

Table 13.9 Budget for the Neighborhood Community Organization

	Salaries			Time Allocation		
Position	# of positions	Annual salary	Medicaid outreach	Immigration reform	Antiviolence initiative
Executive director	1	$60,000	20%	50%	30%
Bookkeeper/Secretary	1	$25,000	20%	50%	30%
Program coordinator	1	$35,000			100%
Staff organizer	2	$30,000		50%	50%
Outreach workers	3	$18,000	100%		
Fringe benefits	18% of salary					
Office space allocation (square feet)			600	2,200	1,200

Program objectives

Number who receive service			500	100	0
Number who receive training			100	200	400
Public service announcements made			10	20	30
Contacts with public officials			0	20	30

Budget	Medicaid Outreach	Immigration Reform	Antiviolence Initiative
Personnel			
Salaries	$168,000		
Fringe benefits	$30,240		
Operating Expenses			
Rent	7,200		
Equipment	10,000		
Office supplies	5,500		
Printing	7,700		
Postage	2,000		
Insurance	1,500		
Travel	3,600		
Total	$235,740		

decision rules (such as equal division of resources among programs), but be sure you fully describe in your memo how the decision was made (see table 13.9).

References

Blau, P. (1964). *Exchange and power in social life.* New York: Wiley.

Carlson, M. (1995). *Winning grants step by step.* San Francisco: Jossey-Bass.

Chambers, D., Wedel, K., & Rodwell, M. (1992). *Evaluating social programs.* Boston: Allyn & Bacon.

Congressional Budget Office. (2000a, June 18). *About CBO* [On-line]. Available: http://www.cbo.gov/about.shtm/.

Congressional Budget Office (2000b, June 18). *Monthly budget review: Fiscal year 2000* [On-line]. Available: http://www.cbo.gov/show.doc.cfm?index/.

Dropkin, M., & La Touche, B. (1998). *The budget-building book for nonprofits.* San Francisco: Jossey-Bass.

Dye, T. (1998). *Understanding public policy* (9th ed.). Upper Saddle River, NJ: Prentice-Hall.

Edwards, R., Benefield, E., Edwards, J., & Yankey, J. (1997). *Building a strong foundation: Fundraising for nonprofits.* Washington, DC: National Association of Social Workers.

Feit, M., & Li, P. (1998). *Financial management in human services.* New York: Haworth.

Froelich, K. (1999). Diversification of revenue strategies: Evolving resource dependence in nonprofit organizations. *Nonprofit Sector Quarterly, 23*(3), 246–58.

Hardina, D. (1993). The impact of funding sources and board representation on consumer control in organizations serving three low income communities. *Nonprofit Management and Leadership, 4,* 69–84.

Kahn, S. (1991). *Organizing: A guide for grass-roots leaders.* Washington, DC: National Association of Social Workers.

Kettner, P., Daley, J., & Nichols, A. (1985). *Initiating change in organizations and communities.* Monterey, CA: Brooks/Cole.

Klosterman, R. (1990). *Community analysis and planning techniques.* Savage, MA: Rowman & Littlefield.

Kramer, R., & Grossman, B. (1987). Contracting for social services: Process management and resource dependencies. *Social Service Review, 61,* 32–55.

Lewis, J., Lewis, M., & Souflee, F. (1991). *Management of human service programs.* Pacific Grove, CA: Brooks/Cole.

Lucas, G., & Gledhill, L. (2000, June 23). Legislature breaks budget gridlock. *San Francisco Chronicle,* pp. A1, A9.

Mondros, J., & Wilson, S. (1994). *Organizing for power and empowerment.* New York: Columbia University Press.

National Charities Information Bureau. (2000). *Standards in philanthropy* [On-line]. Available: http://give.org.

New, C., & Quick, J. (1998). *Grantseeker's toolkit: A comprehensive guide to finding funding.* New York: Wiley.

Office of Management and Budget. (2000a). *The budget system and concepts* [On-line]. Available: http://www.whitehouse.gov/OMB.

Office of Management and Budget. (2000b). *A citizen's guide to the federal budget* [On-line]. Available: http://www.whitehouse.gov/OMB.

Palm, T., & Qayum, A. (1985). *Private and public investment analysis*. Cincinnati, OH: South-Western.

Philanthropy News Digest. (1999, October 19). Nonprofit tax returns now available online. 5(42), 1.

Piven, F. F., & Cloward, R. (1979). *Poor people's movements: Why they succeed, how they fail*. New York: Vintage.

Rossi, P., & Freeman, H. (1982). *Evaluation: A systematic approach*. Beverly Hills, CA: Sage.

Smith, G. (1999). *Accounting for libraries and other not-for-profit organizations*. Chicago: American Library Association.

Strachan, J. (1998). Understanding nonprofit financial management. In R. Edwards, J. Yankey, & M. Altpeter (Eds.), *Skills for effective management of nonprofit orga-nizations* (pp. 343–70). Washington, DC: National Association of Social Workers.

Wasserman, A., Goodman, R., & Butterfoss, F. (1999). Understanding coalitions and how they operate. In M. Minkler (Ed.), *Community organization and community building for health* (pp. 261–77). New Brunswick, NJ: Rutgers University Press.

White, S. (1981). *Managing health and human service programs: A guide for managers*. New York: Free Press.

Web Resources

Center for Budget and Policy Priorities—http://www.cbpp.org
Congressional Budget Office—http://www.cbo.gov/
Economic Policy Institute—http://www.epinet.org/
General Accounting Office—http://www.gao.gov/
Office of Management and Budget—http://www.whitehouse.gov/OMB
OMB Watch—http://ombwatch.org/
National Budget Simulation—http://garnet.berkeley.edu.3333/budget/budget.html
National Center for Charitable Statistics (information from IRS 990 forms)—http://www.guidestar.org

■ PART FOUR

Evaluation

14 Outcome and Process Evaluation

■ This chapter describes evaluation approaches that allow for the examination of program outcome and processes. Most of the methods presented here are associated with the concept of program evaluation. Program evaluation can be defined as a "process that generates the information used to describe what a program is doing and how well it does it" (Krause, 1996, p. 1). Evaluation approaches that pertain solely to the examination of community intervention–oriented processes and outcomes are also described in this chapter. Quantitative, qualitative, and mixed approaches to evaluation practice are identified; factors that should be taken into consideration when choosing a measurement approach are described. Procedures for choosing a research design, data collection methods, sampling, the protection of human subjects, data analysis, and report writing are also examined.

Evaluation is an inherently political process rather than a method that is entirely scientific or value free (Bisman & Hardcastle, 1999; Meier & Usher, 1998). Evaluations often incorporate the values and perceptions of the researchers, program funders, constituents, program beneficiaries, key informants from the community, and elected officials. Consequently, in the last two sections of this chapter, methods are described for the involvement of constituents in the evaluation process and working with coalitions to conduct evaluations of community projects.

Paradigms for Evaluation Research

As with other types of research, evaluations may be either quantitative or qualitative. In quantitative research, hypotheses and research questions are generated from the theoretical and empirical literature in the field. Quantitative researchers argue that this method is scientific and is intended to be objective or value free. The reasoning employed in quantitative research is deductive, that is, general theories are applied to explain cause-and-effect relationships that occur in specific situations (Patton, 1997; Rodwell, 1998).

Qualitative research requires inductive reasoning (Cummerton, 1986). The researcher conducts a very detailed examination of a specific situation. This may involve repeated observations over a long period or lengthy, open-ended interviews with a variety of individuals or groups. The information collected is used to generate theories about what has happened in these specific situations. As a result, inductive thought involves reasoning from specific situations and applying these concepts to general situations. Qualitative research is used when the researcher can find little in the way of theoretical literature that applies to the problem at hand. It is also used when the previous research cannot be applied to specific subpopulations (for example, women, people of color, lesbians, or low-income communities). In program or practice evaluation, qualitative research is also used to answer how and why questions about the intervention: How or why does the intervention work? What actually happens in the program to produce or inhibit its effects (Chambers, Wedel, & Rodwell, 1992; Rossi & Freeman, 1982)?

Qualitative evaluation is intentionally not value free. It is assumed that the values of both the researcher and the participants are to be an inherent part of the evaluation process. Consequently, this type of research is considered subjective rather than objective. Qualitative researchers argue that the traditional quantitative paradigm also contains biases. Quantitative researchers impose their own values and perspectives on the research process. The researcher's choice of variables, research questions, data collection methods, research design, and data analysis reflect his or her values (Patton, 1997).

Two primary subtypes of qualitative research are ethnographic and feminist approaches. Ethnographic research assumes that traditional quantitative approaches are insufficient to conduct research that will allow us to document the values, behaviors, meanings, and perspectives of cultures other than that of the dominant group. According to Fetterman (1998), ethnography looks at the daily lives of specific cultural groups. While the researcher is expected to keep an open mind about what he or she encounters, it is recognized that the researcher often comes to the process with built-in biases and explicit values. The challenge with this process is to minimize how these biases influence research findings and to make explicit the researcher's own values in instances where such biases cannot be adequately controlled (Bell, Sloan, & Strickling, 1998). Feminist research assumes that women are oppressed by the male patriarchy. Such oppression is inherent in traditional scientific approaches to research in which the expert researcher imposes his or her agenda on research subjects (Harding, 1997; Lindsey, 1997; Reinharz, 1992).[1]

Quantitative researchers also integrate into the research design their own ideas about the appropriate social distance between the researcher and the subjects. Quantitative researchers prefer to keep their distance from subjects. There is unlikely to be any contact between the researcher and participants except when the intervention and measurement instruments are administered. Qualitative researchers argue that the research process should bridge the social distance between experts and participants. Consequently, participants should be included in the process of problem identification, research design, data collection, and analysis. Research methods should be developed using dialogue among equal participants in the process (Sohng, 1998).

Perkins (1983) identifies three dimensions that pertain to one's choice of evaluation design:

- Intensity of measurement
- Degree of structure imposed on respondents
- Degree of manipulation (of intervention or respondents)

Intensity refers to the number of measurements. Qualitative methods require observations made repeatedly over time. Quantitative measures involve observations or surveys administered on one, two, or three occasions, requiring very brief intervals. Exceptions to this rule are longitudinal or time series analyses with multiple measures. However, the actual intensity of measurement during observation periods in quantitative longitudinal or time series analysis is often of short duration or occurs during prespecified periods.

Degree of structure refers to whether allowable response categories are constructed before measurements are taken. Standardized instruments or surveys constructed expressly for the study provide the researcher with a list of questions and predeveloped response categories. Limited deviation from these categories is allowed in most quantitative studies (the use of a category designated "other" is generally recommended to generate answers that may be different from those identified by the researcher).

Ideally in quantitative studies, the researcher has identified those response categories respondents are most likely to utilize based on a review of the literature, personal knowledge and experience, or consultation with peers or members of the target population. In qualitative studies, limited structure if any is imposed on responses. Most responses are open-ended (the exception is often limited to personal demographic indicators or yes/no questions), with respondents encouraged to describe feelings, reactions, and perceptions about the questions posed in the research instrument. Consequently, the researcher has imposed no structure on these responses and has not solicited certain types of responses. Qualitative researchers argue that this method is preferable to quantitative, structured approaches because the researcher will not have imposed his or her own perceptions about the "correct" responses on the participants (Patton, 1997; Rodwell, 1998).

Manipulation refers to the introduction of an intervention to the research setting. In classical experimental design the researcher assigns respondents to experimental and control groups (Campbell & Stanley, 1963). In control groups, no intervention is introduced. Experimental group members will receive an intervention that is intended to change their behavior, feelings, or attitudes. Consequently, the impact of the intervention also can involve some degree of actual manipulation of research subjects (obviously this requires that subjects be informed about possible risks inherent in the intervention).

In some quantitative studies, the researcher creates two or more different experimental groups. In each of these groups, a slightly different type of intervention is used. Effects are compared between these groups and the no-intervention control group. In qualitative research, no intervention will be introduced. No attempt will be made to alter the behaviors, feelings, and perceptions of respondents. One term often used to describe the application of qualitative methods to evaluation of practice is naturalistic observation, meaning that research is to take place in settings that naturally occur without the manipulation of subjects or the imposition of structure and meaning (Guba, 1987).

Measurement: Validity and Reliability in Evaluation Research

The concepts of validity and reliability in evaluation research also differ by research paradigm (Patton, 1997). Quantitative evaluators concern themselves with whether instruments used to collect data accurately measure the concept under study, whether the concept measures can be correlated with other measurement techniques for assessing that concept, and whether the interrelationship between the variable measured and other related concepts can be substantiated (validity). Quantitative researchers also examine whether the measure consistently provides the same assessment using repeated measures of that concept (reliability). Procedures commonly used to establish validity and reliability include the following:

1. Administration of a pretest of the instrument to several members of the intended target group to determine whether participants will recognize the concepts and can respond to each question.

2. Review of the instrument by experts in the field to assess whether the intended concept is measured accurately.

3. Correlation of the test results with other instruments that measure the same concept or with instruments that measure concepts that are theoretically related to the first variable.

4. Using multiple measures of the same concept and assessing whether responses to these items are consistent with one another (internal consistency).

5. Repeated testing of the instrument using the same participants or replicating the study to examine similar problems or research settings (Bisman & Hardcastle, 1999; Rubin & Babbie, 1997).

In qualitative evaluation, the researcher is most interested in establishing the trustworthiness of the data collected and the manner in which the evaluator has interpreted the data (Reinharz, 1992). Consequently, most qualitative evaluations contain a feedback component in which the researcher consults with the research subjects to ensure that the findings are consistent with the participants' perceptions. One additional method used to establish trustworthiness is to include research subjects and beneficiaries in the identification of the research problem, research design, data collection, data analysis, and report writing phases of the study (Smith, 1997; Telfair & Mulvihill, 2000). Another method evaluators use to establish the validity and reliability of measures and results data is to collect both quantitative and qualitative data. As noted in chapter 6, this is known as the process of triangulation. If both types of data produce similar results, the evaluator can establish that the data collected is both trustworthy and reliable (Cherry, 2000).

Evaluation of Community Interventions

Although the methodology used to examine community interventions is not as well defined as that of program evaluation, practitioners commonly use a number of techniques to examine outcomes and processes:

- Goal attainment
- Social indicator analysis
- Field interviews
- Critical incidence analysis

As used in this chapter, the concept of evaluation of community intervention pertains to the outcomes and processes associated with the actual implementation of strategies and tactics used to facilitate community change: community development, planning processes, social action, and transformative models of practice. It does not pertain to evaluations of outcomes and processes associated with the delivery of a specific program or service to community residents.

Goal Attainment

As described in chapters 10 and 11, evaluation of intervention outcomes can be conducted at the most basic level through the assessment of whether goals and objectives have been achieved. As described in chapter 12, the evaluator and program participants must have a clear understanding (and be able to communicate verbally and in writing) about how programmatic needs are linked to the program's theory of action (or interventions used to address the problem). Components of this intervention plan should include specification of participant and programmatic needs, constituent expectations, activities required to implement the program, resources needed for operation, and identification of programmatic stages of development.

Evaluators must also be able to specify the logic behind program operation. A set of specific program activities must be linked to outcomes. In other words, the evaluator must be able to describe what happens in the program and to link these activities to programmatic outputs and long-term outcomes associated with the program. A relationship between the program (independent variable) and outcomes (dependent variables) must be made explicit (Chambers et al., 1992; Royse & Thyer, 1996). Sources of information about these relationships can be found in the theoretical, empirical, and best-practices literature.

Specification of a theory of action requires the identification of immediate objectives, intermediate objectives, and ultimate program goals (Meier & Usher, 1998; Patton, 1997). The theory of action must also be clearly linked to evaluation criteria. These criteria should also be linked to the identified problems to be addressed by the program or project (see figure 14.1). In addition, the data collected should make it possible for the evaluators to derive clear information about how the program should be modified in response to the research findings. Consequently, an effective evaluation should contain a feedback loop, allowing the organization to engage in continuous efforts at formative as well as summative evaluation.

Chambers et al. (1992) report that correlations between goal attainment scores and other outcome measures are low. Consequently, goal attainment alone may be insufficient to address whether the intervention itself (exclusive of factors in the external environment) has actually produced the outcome intended. As Krause (1996) points out, program designers often forget to include important components of the program in lists of goals and objectives compiled for funding proposals. Consequently, evaluations conducted by external reviewers may be essential in helping organizations identify primary program goals. Sometimes these goals may be implicit, evolving through the interaction among staff and other par-

Figure 14.1.   Linking problems, outcomes, and evaluation criteria to the program's theory of action.

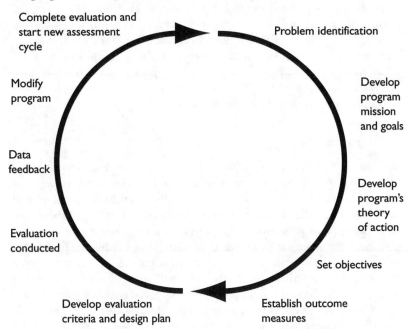

ticipants, or attempts to make do with resources and guidelines provided by funders (Patton, 1997).

Social Indicator Analysis

In addition to goals outlined in intervention plans and program proposals, an evaluation can focus on social indicators (see chapter 6), data collected from records compiled by public and nonprofit social service organizations or health care providers. For example, if our intervention is intended to reduce crime in the Fairtown community, we would at a minimum obtain data from local policing agencies about crime rates in this area both before and after the implementation of the intervention. You can also use case record data from your own organization to establish benchmarks for goal attainment (Royse & Thyer, 1996). If the intervention's goal is to reduce hunger in Fairtown by increasing enrollment in the food stamp program, one indicator could be the decrease in demand for emergency food from people who are served by the Fairtown Community Organization. It is critical, however, that organization participants establish levels of desirability for increases or decreases in these measures before the implementation of the intervention (Patton, 1997).

If available, secondary data (case record information and social indicators) can be obtained at regular intervals throughout the implementation stage of the project. Statistical techniques described in chapter 6 can be used to control for random error in time series data. As noted previously, social indicators are only as reliable as the concepts and tools used to obtain measurement. Hence, evaluators using these standardized indicators to measure community health, safety, hunger, or unemployment should note any limitations associated with the measure and supplement the data with information from other sources (Royse & Thyer, 1996).

Field Interview

MacNair (1996) describes two methods that can be utilized to obtain information about the organizing process: field interviews and critical incidence analysis. Field interviews are used to gather information about how participants view the organizing process. Information is collected about how these participants have constructed meaning about their experiences, actions, and the outcomes produced. The purpose of conducting field interviews is to help the organizer develop practice knowledge that can be used in the future. Sometimes these interviews will be conducted with key informants, or leaders who have been highly involved in the organizing process. Sometimes, key informants may include observers who are in the know about particular issues: members of the media, experienced organizers, local clergy, politicians, or businesspeople. Obviously, including the perspectives of intended beneficiaries and constituents is very important as well. Interviews may be conducted using standardized questionnaires or ethnographic approaches described in chapter 6.

Critical Incident Analysis

Critical incident analysis requires that the organizer record observations that pertain to specific events or confrontations that are intended to produce social change–related outcomes (MacNair, 1996). These observations are used to assess the process of organizing. Characteristics of the incident measured include specific strategies, tactics, reactions to strategic maneuvers, targets, constituency group members, the feelings or values expressed by participants, group behavior, leadership qualities, the strength of collaborative relationships, and outcomes. Such observational studies require that the evaluator/researcher take detailed field notes (Fetterman, 1998). Field notes include the following components: observations of nonverbal behavior, physical traces or residues that indicate patterns of human behavior (for example, garbage and other evidence that people attended a picnic or a rock concert), and a written journal used to record the researcher's feelings and perceptions about what he or she saw and heard (Chambers et al., 1992).

Program Evaluation

The term program evaluation is generally used to describe outcomes and processes associated with the delivery of a tangible good or service to a specific target population. Evaluation criteria are typically integrated into program plans and funding proposals; successful evaluations make it necessary to prespecify measurable goals and objectives before rather than after project implementation. However, as described in chapter 11, it is not uncommon for evaluators to conduct formative evaluations that are used to make changes in the program during the implementation process. Program evaluation techniques may be quantitative or qualitative (Chambers et al., 1992; Patton, 1997). In many cases, the evaluator will use measurement tools that combine qualitative and quantitative methods or choose to conduct an evaluation that examines both outcome (using quantitative measures) and program processes (using qualitative data) (see table 14.1).

Quantitative Approaches

Traditional types of program evaluation focus on goal attainment as well as outcome evaluation using group designs. It is critical, as in community intervention evaluation, that the evaluators understand the program's theory of action and be able to link programmatic activities to objectives and evaluation criteria. Social indicators and case record information may also be used as outcome measures in program evaluation.

The use of experimental and control groups or pre- and posttest measures help the evaluator establish whether the program, rather than confounding or extraneous variables, has produced changes in individuals or groups. Quantitative research designs (as feasible) should control for threats to internal and external validity. Internal validity refers to extraneous variables that limit the degree to which we can determine whether the independent variable (program) influences the dependent variable. These variables may be either confounding (variables such as demographic indicators that may co-vary with the intervention) or completely spurious—that is, while their value can seem to co-vary with that of the outcome measure, there is no direct relationship between the variables. Threats to internal validity include history, maturation, testing, instrumentation, mortality (study dropout rate), bias in the selection of participants, and statistical regression (the degree to which extreme pretest scores move closer to the mean upon repeated testing). Also of concern are situations in which the evaluator has failed to identify which of the measured variables has produced a direct impact on the other (Bisman & Hardcastle, 1999; Campbell & Stanley, 1963).

External validity refers to whether findings from the study can be generalized from the sample to the larger population from which the sample was selected. Specific threats to external validity include interaction between

Table 14.1 Evaluation Methods: Quantitative and Qualitative Approaches

	Quantitative	*Qualitative*
Role of values	Objective	Subjective
Type of logic	Deductive	Inductive
Degree of structure	High	Low
Degree of manipulation	High	Low
Amount of time required for observations	Low	High
Social distance between researcher and subject	High	Low
Role of researcher	Expert	Partner with subjects
Types of evaluation approaches	Experimental	Ethnographic study
	Quasi-experimental	Feminist research
	One group, pre- and posttest	Constructivist evaluation
	Time series	Process analysis
	Social indicator analysis	Implementation analysis
	Longitudinal study	Focus groups
	Social indicator analysis	Community forums
	Cross-sectional survey	Critical incidence analysis
	Consumer satisfaction survey	Key informant interviews
	Goal attainment	Field interviews
	Program monitoring	Personal narratives and life stories

participant reaction to the pretest and the treatment, the interaction between selection bias and the treatment (some participants have unique characteristics that influence how they respond to the intervention), and the reaction of participants to their involvement in the study (William, Unrau, & Grinnell, 1998). Ideally, we can be confident about our ability to both generalize findings and control for extraneous variables only if we have drawn our sample randomly. However, this is not always possible in community-based research due to considerations about time and resources. A number of quasi-experimental designs can be used instead to conduct community-based or program evaluations (Chambers et al., 1992; Royse & Thyer, 1996).

The evaluator must establish specific outcome measures and set expectations for change desired to indicate whether the program is actually working. Although strict adherence to the quantitative paradigm does not require that the evaluator include staff and program participants in preparing the evaluation, many evaluators believe that such involvement helps to ensure cooperation from participants and the accuracy of results (Patton, 1997).

Process Evaluation

In addition to outcomes, information can also be collected to answer how and why questions about the program. Process analysis is used to look at how organizations deliver programs. It is sometimes assumed that cause-and-effect relationships (or the relationship between the program and outcomes) take place in a black box (Patton, 1997; Rossi & Freeman, 1982). Although we may be able to give a written description of the activities that constitute the program or intervention, we may be unclear about what actually happens in the program to produce both intended and unexpected results. Process analyses typically examine some of the following program attributes:

- Interactions between supervisors and workers
- Interactions among workers
- Interactions between workers and clients or consumers of the service, or (in community practice) between workers and constituents, beneficiaries and decision makers
- Resources used to deliver the intervention
- Staff effort needed to deliver the intervention
- The fit between the intervention and the intended outcome
- The degree to which the intervention has actually been delivered
- Whether clients, consumers, or other intended beneficiaries can easily obtain access to the program
- Ability to coordinate programs and share resources with other organizations (see figure 14.2)

As described in chapter 6, two additional types of process analysis are program monitoring and implementation analysis. In program monitoring, questions about resources and intended beneficiaries are addressed on an ongoing basis as the policy is put into operation. Types of information examined include budgets, resource utilization, staff qualifications., recruitment of clients, the number of eligible clients served, the number of ineligible clients served, program dropouts, and appropriate application of laws and other legal requirements (Rossi & Freeman, 1982). Much of this information will be found in the organization's files; some social service organizations establish computerized information systems so that this data can be easily examined. If in the evaluator's opinion the program is not functioning appropriately, it may be altered to meet its intended goals.

Figure 14.2. Organization as a "black box" for evaluation.

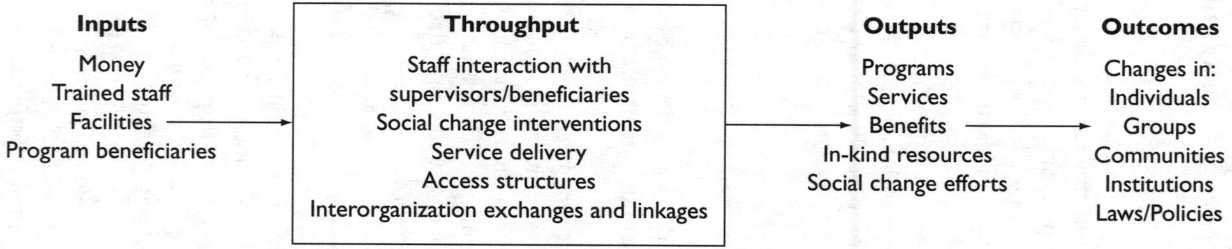

Inputs

Money
Trained staff
Facilities
Program beneficiaries

Throughput

Staff interaction with
supervisors/beneficiaries
Social change interventions
Service delivery
Access structures
Interorganization exchanges and linkages

Outputs

Programs
Services
Benefits
In-kind resources
Social change efforts

Outcomes

Changes in:
Individuals
Groups
Communities
Institutions
Laws/Policies

Note: Program outputs differ from outcomes in that outcomes represent the net effects of changing individuals, institutions, communities, and laws. For example, providing self-help advocacy training to food stamp recipients changes the immediate situation (gain access to food, self-empowerment) for those individuals (output or immediate outcome), but also helps the program reach its ultimate goal (reducing hunger in the community).

In implementation analysis, the evaluator examines whether the program or policy has actually been implemented in the manner intended (Patton, 1997). Such analyses are generally conducted after the policy has been in operation for a number of years. Qualitative research is often used to assess implementation. Data collection methods include interviews with decision makers, administrators, frontline staff, clients, or a combination of these. Observation can be used to examine interaction among staff members or interaction between frontline staff and clients.

Implementation studies of government programs often focus on the congruence between the goals of state or federal policy makers and the goals of local administrators (Handler & Sosin, 1983; Hardina, 1990) or discretionary decision making by frontline workers in public bureaucracies (Hagen & Wang, 1994; Solomon, 1994). Implementation analysis can also involve analysis of how institutions work with one another to develop policies. Existing institutional structures (decision making, administrative procedures, and paperwork) may impede full implementation of the policy or shape it in ways not intended by the decision maker. For example, DeHoog (1984), in a study of job training programs, found that among the organizations that provided these services, completing the paperwork became more important than placing people in jobs. Evaluators who use such an approach are using an institutional model (Haynes & Mickelson, 1991; Pierce, 1984). Evaluators can also use a systems model in which policy is examined in terms of inputs, throughputs, and outputs of organizations, institutions, and systems (Flynn, 1992).

Data Collection

You can use a number of quantitative and qualitative approaches to collect data for process and outcome evaluation. These approaches include narrative, grounded theory, focus group interviews, and consumer satisfaction surveys. Generic research approaches such as development of interview guides, surveys, and community forum approaches were described in detail in chapter 6.

Using Personal Narratives

One qualitative approach to data collection is a process called narrative. The narrative approach requires that participants describe their own experiences and the meanings they associate with these experiences. Often narrative is used to gather information about culture, the process of acculturation into the dominant culture, and barriers to participation in social and economic life encountered by new immigrants or members of traditionally marginalized groups. The meanings associated with these experiences vary not only by culture, but also by gender and social class (Bachay & Cingel, 1999). According to Riessmann (1994):

Creating a narrative about one's life is an imaginative enterprise, too, in which an individual links disruptive events in a biography to heal discontinuities—what should have been with what was. Stories are a kind of cultural envelope into which we pour our experience and signify its importance to others, and the world of the story requires protagonists, inciting conditions, and culminating events. A near universal form for ordering our worlds, narrative allows us to make connections and this meaning by linking past and present, self and society. (p. 114)

While narrative has most often been used as a device for gaining knowledge that can be utilized in clinical practice, it also has applications for evaluation of programs and institutions. For example, individual narratives can help us gain insight into the experiences of single mothers in the welfare system or the encounters Southeast Asian immigrants may have with relief agencies. Fetterman (1998) describes gathering life stories as an essential component of ethnographic research (supplemented with data from other sources). These stories are used to document cultural practices and meanings as well as to evaluate program impacts within cultural groups.

Grounded Theory

Grounded theory is an approach to conducting qualitative research. Using this approach, the evaluator rejects much of the previous theoretical literature in the field and relies on practice as well as tacit knowledge (feelings and perceptions of the researcher and the participants) to develop evaluation methods and basic assumptions. Data is collected primarily from observation and interviews. Previous theories are not as significant to the development of the evaluation plan as tacit knowledge, or the feelings and perceptions of all evaluation participants (researchers, administrators, staff, and beneficiaries). Consequently, the approach to evaluation emerges during the data collection process, brought about by negotiations among participants and through the ongoing collection of data. As noted in chapter 3, this approach is also called constructivist, in that the social-environmental context (culture, history, social, and physical) provides a framework for data analysis (Chambers et al., 1992; Harding, 1997; Reinharz, 1992). The basic assumption in this approach is that all knowledge is socially constructed (Rodwell, 1998).

Focus Group Interviews

Focus group interviews also provide a rich source of data about program implementation (Denning & Verschelden, 1993). Focus groups involve six to eight respondents who are asked a small number of questions about how they have experienced the intervention. The emphasis is often on what works and what doesn't in terms of individual program components, policies, and interactions among program participants during the delivery of services. Such techniques can provide information about service gaps and generate ideas for improvement in program performance. Focus group interviews can also be used to assess the degree to which the program is accessible to intended beneficiaries (see table 14.2). Consequently, the collection of qualitative data from participants offers the evaluator detailed information about how key informants, staff members, and beneficiaries experience the program and how the program actually operates.

Consumer Satisfaction Surveys

Consumer satisfaction surveys are also used to collect data about program effectiveness. Traditionally such surveys have employed quantitative indicators; some standardized assessment tools for measuring satisfaction have been constructed. However, this type of methodology has been criticized for a number of reasons. One of the primary concerns is that low-income consumers, who seldom pay a fee for service, may fear losing benefits if they provide negative information about the program (Stipak, 1982). In fact, most studies conducted on the reliability of consumer satisfaction surveys have found satisfaction levels of over 70 percent for most of these studies (Royse & Thyer, 1996). This suggests that some of these studies fail to measure dissatisfaction with agency performance.

Several additional reliability concerns are related to satisfaction studies. For example, agencies may request that only people who have successfully completed the service participate in the survey. As a result, people who had negative experiences, found that the service did not work for them, or dropped out of the program may not be contacted. Consumer satisfaction instruments have also been criticized because of imprecision in the definition of the term satisfaction and the fact that most assessment tools are constructed in-house, with little attempt to establish validity or reliability of the measure.

A number of methods are typically used to increase the validity and reliability of these measures. One method requires that the evaluator survey program dropouts as well as successful cases. A second method involves recognition that the concept of satisfaction is multidimensional (Lebow, 1983). Rather than employing one or two questions with a five-point scale to measure overall satisfaction with the program, the evaluator should construct a series of questions to examine individual program components (for example, intake, delivery of service, follow-up) or attributes (such as quality of interaction with staff, wait time for service, cleanliness of facilities). Evaluators can also use questionnaires that supplement quantitative indicators with several open-ended questions about consumer feelings and perceptions

Table 14.2 Elements of Program Access

Organization Attribute	High Access	Low Access
Referrals	Makes referrals if the organization lacks the resources to provide the services	Makes limited referrals; uses the referral process to limit client access to additional resources
Intake and eligibility procedures	Simple	Complex
Application (length, language, and complexity)	Short	Long
	In appropriate languages	English-only
	Simple	Complex
	Easy to read	Difficult to understand
Length of wait time for service	1–2 hours, maximum	Days or weeks
Conditions in waiting room	Comfortable	Uncomfortable
	Well-lit	Dark
	Clean	Dirty
	Safe	Hazardous
	Welcoming	Discouraging
Hours of operation	When people are likely to be available	Nine to five, Weekdays
	Evenings and weekends	Limits on daily hours of operation
Day care	Organization provides on-site day care	Organization does not provide on-site day care
Availability of public transportation and parking	Parking	No parking
	Located near public transportation	Not accessible by public transportation

Factor		
Transportation assistance	Organization provides rides or reimbursement for travel	Organization provides no transportation assistance
Geographic location	In community of need	Located outside community Highways or other geographic barriers separate the community from the agency
Degree of stigmatization of recipients	Everyone is welcome	Staff may be rude or unpleasant to members of certain groups
Physical accessibility of facilities	Ramps and other features make the building accessible to people with disabilities	Not accessible to people with disabilities
Coverage/bias	Provides services to all in need	Does not serve everyone who needs the service or serves only members of specific demographic groups
Monetary costs	Free or low-cost	Charges fees to all recipients
Quality of interaction among supervisors, staff, and consumers	Good; recipients treated as colleagues or peers	Bad; social distance maintained between workers and clients
Transactions and exchanges with the organization's external environment (coordination, shared resources, information exchange, case-management procedures, and ability to obtain funds)	Organization shares resources with others	Organization does not coordinate resources with others

about the program (Gutek, 1978). Royse and Thyer (1996) recommend that consumer representatives be involved in planning and constructing the survey. Questions about the reliability of the data can also be addressed by using consumer satisfaction surveys only in conjunction with a number of additional measures of program effectiveness (Stipak, 1982).

A final approach can involve the use of open-ended telephone, in-person, or focus group interviews to assess satisfaction levels. Note, however, that in some instances, face-to-face interaction with agency staff might increase consumer fears about confidentiality of information and how it will be used. One way to deal with this is to hire a neutral party such as a consultant or outside evaluator to conduct the evaluation (Stipak, 1982). Bush and Gordon (1978) argue that it is critical for the success of a program to understand what is happening from the consumer's perspective rather than that of staff members; often an understanding of the problem at hand, the meaning of the problem, the experience of actually receiving the service, and the outcomes produced will be quite different among members of these two constituency groups.

Sampling Methods

Sampling requires choosing a representative group of people to include in your study. However, qualitative and quantitative evaluators define representative differently. In quantitative research, a sample is representative if participant characteristics are essentially the same as those of members of the population group studied. The best way to assure this is by using scientific techniques for selection. Using qualitative methods, the researcher uses his or her best judgment, recommendations from other participants, and existing groups to find subjects.

Quantitative Sampling Methods

Within the quantitative paradigm, researchers ideally want to select participants using probability sampling methods involving random selection (Marlow, 1998). Random selection requires assignment of a number to every possible participant and the random selection of those numbers. Though the process can be visualized as randomly pulling slips with prewritten numbers from a hat, more sophisticated techniques can be used to simplify the process, such as the use of tables of random numbers in research textbooks or generating random sets of numbers using a statistical software package.

Random sampling allows the evaluator to select a group of people who are representative of a specific population or subpopulation group for inclusion in the study. By representative, we mean that members of the sample will be similar on some basic demographic characteristics (for example, gender, ethnicity, age) to members of the population group studied. Consequently, it is possible to take the findings generated from the sample and infer that our analysis will also hold true for the population group study. We can also conduct a stratified random sample in which we organize population members into specific subgroups and then randomly select from within each of these groups. This allows us, in advance, to control for the effects of these demographic characteristics in evaluation outcomes. For example, we might decide that political party affiliation will affect how community residents perceive an antipoverty program. Therefore, we would determine the percentage of registered voters who are members of Republican, Democratic, Reform, and Green parties or are unaffiliated with any political party. We would organize potential respondents into groups from each party and select respondents from each group in proportion to political party affiliation (see table 14.3).

It is also possible to draw random samples from pre-existing groups or clusters. Cluster sampling is often used in community research. For example, we can decide to randomly choose X number of people from specific blocks. However, we can actually start the process by randomly choosing blocks within a specific community or even by randomly choosing communities from a larger sample (see figure 14.3). Clusters can also include housing projects, dormitories, community groups, or geographic areas that contain specific projects or activities (for example, economic development zones).

An additional technique involves systematic sampling. In this type of sampling, it is necessary to have a predeveloped or assembled list of people and to select every Xth (for example, every fifth) person from the list for participation in the study (Williams et al., 1998). The difficulty with this process is that many existing lists (for example, the phone book or a list of National Association of Social Workers [NASW] members in your state) contain built-in or systematic biases. The phone book often excludes households with incomes below the poverty line (who are less likely to have phones) as well as wealthier people or single women, who are often unlisted. The NASW list could potentially overinclude private practitioners or clinicians; administrators and organizers are often underrepresented in pro-

Table 14.3 Stratified Random Sample: Political Party Affiliation (N = 200)

Party	Republicans	Democrats	Reform	Green	Independents
Proportion of registered voters	30%	30%	5%	10%	25%
Number of respondents (N = 200)	60	60	10	20	50

Figure 14.3. Cluster sampling by community, block, and household.

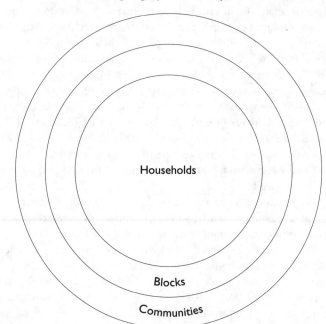

fessional social work organizations due to the profession's emphasis on clinical practice.

Qualitative Sampling Methods

Nonprobability-related sampling methods include convenience, purposive, quota, and snowball sampling (Marlow, 1998). These methods are most often associated with qualitative methods but can often be successfully employed with quantitative approaches. A convenience sample requires that the researcher simply recruit all possible subjects, most often members of an existing group of people who come together in one place at a particular point in time. Purposive samples are those in which participants are hand selected by the researcher to fit a particular demographic profile and consequently can be said to be representative of a particular population group. In quota sampling, people are selected from within preorganized groups (as in stratified random samples). However, their selection is made not at random but simply by the researcher in terms of whether they seem to have the desired characteristics. In snowball sampling, the researcher starts with a small group of people who may fit a particular demographic profile or who are members of a specific organization or group. Each member of this small group is interviewed and is asked to recommend friends, relatives, or neighbors who may fit the profile or who have the particular problem examined for participation in the study. Consequently, the group of people included in the study becomes bigger and bigger (like a snowball) as the research progresses. This method is preferred in instances when the researcher does not know who might be likely participants.

Selection of an appropriate sampling method should be made using the following criteria:

- Whether an inference will be made from the sample to the general population
- Whether qualitative or quantitative methods are utilized (qualitative research does not attempt to generalize findings to the general population using qualitative methods)
- The amount of funds, staff resources, and time the evaluator has available to conduct the study
- The size of the sample and whether it is necessary to minimize sampling error and control for the effects of confounding and extraneous variables
- The financial resources available to the researcher. Large random samples are much more expensive than small convenience samples, especially in terms of locating people for participation in the study.

Sample size also varies in terms of the type of evaluation approach and the amount of time and resources available to the researcher. Minimum sample size for each group in a quantitative study is $N = 30$. Consequently, if the evaluator establishes an experimental and control group, then sample size should, at a minimum, be 60 (30×2). If the evaluator employs a stratified random sample with five separate demographic categories, then total sample size should be 150 (30×5). If the evaluator wishes to use inferential statistics to establish whether cause-and-effect relationships exist within a predetermined confidence level (probability $\leq .10$), then the sample size will need to be large enough to minimize random error. Random error can be defined as an "error due to unknown or uncontrolled factors" that affect the variable being measured and the process of measurement in an inconsistent manner (Williams et al., 1998, pp. 375–76). Sources of random error include the characteristics of participants selected for the study, situational factors (such as the emotional state of individual participants, or environmental events that affect a participant's ability to respond), and the manner in which the research instrument is administered.

Maximum and minimum size for samples in qualitative studies have not been standardized. However, such samples are generally quite small ($N = 10$ to 30). This permits the evaluator to collect very detailed information from each respondent. Larger sample size in qualitative evaluations requires more resources, time, and labor to organize data into categories and narratives. An increase in the number of respondents also requires that data analysis become more complex and detailed (Williams et al., 1998).

Note also that in many quantitative and qualitative evaluations, the question of sample size is determined simply by the number of available respondents. Especially when the evaluation focuses on organizations within a limited geographic area, the number of individuals served by a particular program, or key informants knowledgeable about a specific issue, there will be few potential respondents. In such cases, the evaluator should simply attempt to include all available respondents in the study (Marlow, 1998).

Ethical Practices

The NASW code of ethics requires that practitioners take appropriate steps to protect the safety, confidentiality, and privacy of program participants in any evaluation (Reamer, 1998). Informed consent that fully describes the risks and benefits associated with evaluation study should be obtained from each participant. Preferably, informed consent should be obtained in writing from the participant or his or her proxy. In cases where informed consent is not possible (such as observational or archival research), social workers should ensure that the methodology has been subjected to a rigorous institutional review by peers, colleagues, and (when feasible) by the research participants.[2]

All participants should be protected from physical harm and emotional distress. Participants should also be advised that participation is entirely voluntary and they can withdraw from the research study at any time. According to Rubin and Babbie (1997), responses should be held anonymous (the researcher cannot match any given response to an individual informant) or confidential (the researcher does know from whom the response originated but will not release this information to anyone, especially to those people who might harm the respondent or withhold benefits as a consequence of the response). An ethical issue that may occur during an evaluation involves the use of deception to recruit or gain entry into the community (see table 14.4 for a list of human subjects criteria). Deception is likely to be used in situations where the researcher feels it is necessary to withhold his or her identity from members of the participant group. Such a circumstance should be used when it is the only way to obtain a reliable response from the subject and when adequate consultation has taken place with colleagues; supervisors; and, as possible, representatives of institutions or groups who are the subject of the study.

Also of concern are situations in which the use of an experimental and control group requires that the intervention be withheld from one group of subjects. This may involve unethical conduct on the part of the evaluator

Table 14.4 Human Subjects Checklist

		Minimal Risk	Participants at More than Minimal Risk
Amount of Risk	Pain or physical danger	No	Yes
	Emotional arousal or stress	No	Yes
	Intervention produces long-term behavior or attitude changes	No	Yes
	Intervention causes embarrassment or social distress	No	Yes
	Intervention involves misinformation or deceit	No	Yes
Cultural Competence	Project procedures are examined or modified in order to show respect for participants' cultural, religious, or personal values	Yes	No
Components of Consent	Accurate explanation of evaluation procedures is made	Yes	No
	Respondent is given an explanation of risks and benefits	Yes	No
	An offer is made to answer any additional questions about the project	Yes	No
	Participant is told that he or she can withdraw at any time	Yes	No
Confidentiality	Anonymous responses as feasible	Yes	No
	Information is kept confidential	Yes	No
	A coding system is kept in a secured location separate from the responses	Yes	No
	The responses are also kept in a secure location; only the evaluator will have access	Yes	No

Source: Adapted from Alter Evens, 1990. Interpretation: Any "no response" indicates that the project is more than minimum risk and that further precautions should be taken.

if withholding the treatment results in harm, deprivation, or loss of benefits for the participants (Cherry, 2000). Recent welfare reform experiments have been conducted in which control group members have been refused participation in jobs programs or employment. These evaluations are controversial; welfare advocates have generally argued that such practices are harmful to recipients (Cherry, 2000; Rubin & Babbie, 1997). Note that a number of methods can be utilized in lieu of withholding the intervention from the control group to establish that the intervention has actually produced the intended outcomes:

- Using people on the waiting list to serve as controls
- Using generic controls such as social indicators, changes in service demand, or recognized or established standards for remediation of social problems (for example, reducing infant mortality rates in inner-city communities to 9.0 or fewer per 1,000 births)
- Using a quasi-experimental design in which different levels of the intervention are compared
- Using statistical controls (such as cross-tabulations or regression analysis) to hold constant the effects of confounding variables)
- Simply comparing the pre- and posttest scores of participants on outcome measures (Chambers et al., 1992; Rossi & Freeman, 1982; Royse & Thyer, 1996).

Data Analysis Methods for Qualitative and Quantitative Research

Social workers with bachelor's degrees, MSWs, and Ph.D.s have access to a wide range of data analysis procedures, involving qualitative analysis or descriptive statistics and inferential statistics. However, effective community-based practice requires that researchers use data analysis methods that can easily convey both major findings and the implications of these findings to multiple audiences (Douglas, 1995)

For nonacademic audiences, quantitative data analysis should probably be limited to descriptive statistics such as means or frequencies. This information can be presented in tables or charts and graphs (see figure 14.4). Cross-tabulation is a good method for presenting the different effects of interventions or varying responses to survey questions across different subpopulations—for example, gender, age, or ethnicity (see table 14.5). Cross-tabs allow the researcher to control for the effects of confounding variables that can influence outcomes (Cherry, 2000; Reinharz, 1992). If inferential statistics are utilized to examine the impact of interventions, the authors should provide sufficient information that allows a general audience to understand the results. The use of charts and graphs is a good shorthand way to present key findings to the general public. Note, however, that the reproduction of color charts could substantially increase printing and copying costs.

Quantitative analysis requires that the researcher strive to accurately represent the thoughts, behaviors, perceptions, and feelings of respondents.

Figure 14.4. Pie Chart: How well do your neighbors know you?

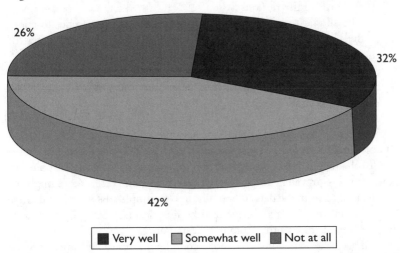

| ■ Very well | ▨ Somewhat well | ▨ Not at all |

Table 14.5 Cross-Tabulation: Source of Information about Medi-Cal by Ethnic Group Membership

	African American	Asian	Latino	White	Other
Outreach worker	10.6%	1.4%	11.4%	1.9%	7.7%
Media	14.9%	79.2%	7.4%	3.2%	5.8%
Word-of-mouth	40.4%	16.7%	39.4%	42.4%	46.2%
HSS	4.3%	0.0%	3.6%	2.5%	0.0%
Doctor	10.6%	2.8%	18.6%	17.7%	11.5%
Other	19.1%	0.0%	19.6%	32.3%	28.8%
Total	100.0%	100.0%	100.0%	100.0%	100.0%

Qualitative methods require that you simply observe the situation or conduct in an in-depth interview and describe in detail what occurred during the course of your observation. Because each respondent may make very different or unique statements or be observed in very distinctive behaviors, the researcher must find a way to communicate and summarize this information to his or her audience. Qualitative researchers employ a number of different steps to perform this task:

1. The researcher chooses a unit of analysis. Will the entire interview or response to individual questions, a sentence, or a phrase be used to compare responses?

2. The researcher identifies common themes, symbols, patterns, ideas, or words in the responses.
3. The simplest way to present this data is for the researcher to count the number of times comparable words, phrases, ideas, themes, or symbols occur in the data set analyzed.
4. A written narrative is developed that describes the patterns in the data using information from the frequency count (Strauss & Corbin, 1990; Williams et al., 1998).

The researcher can add detail and complexity to this narrative by using sample quotations from respondents. The researcher often presents examples of the majority response given and may present information about minority or less-prevalent responses. However, in some cases, there might be no clear patterns in the data. Generally, in very simple analyses of qualitative information, responses are organized by question (see box, "Using Qualitative Methods to Identify Common Data Patterns").

Some researchers construct more complex narratives to describe what they found through an analysis of the data. Such narratives can include the following:

1. A complex, detailed description of an individual, a group of people, or an interaction among individuals. Information should be included on the appearance, behaviors, body language, and speech (if possible) of the individuals involved.
2. Information on the surrounding environment. What is happening around the individual that could influence his or her behavior? Describe where the research is taking place.
3. The evaluator's interpretation of these results as they related to the evaluation question.
4. The evaluator's examination of relevant ethical, cultural, social justice, and empowerment issues raised in the data analysis and discussion of this in the data analysis and recommendations sections of the report.
5. Construction of a theory about why certain behaviors, feelings, perceptions, and so on occurred in this situation. To create grounded theory, the evaluator must identify concepts and link these concepts together in cause-and-effect relationships (Strauss & Corbin, 1990).

Report Writing

Those individuals and groups that will want to review the evaluation report include supervisors, constituency group members, research participants, government bureaucrats, politicians, and representatives from community institutions or groups. The organizations or government agencies that have funded the research study will have very clear expectations of how the data

Using Qualitative Methods to Identify Common Data Patterns

Question: Describe the most positive aspects of your previous advocacy experiences.

A sense of accomplishment—when signs of empowerment are seen in clients.

Clients developing skills for self-advocacy has become a positive aspect. The confidence in my professional skills and ability has increased as a result of advocacy. Advocacy in a true sense is a positive tool to ensure need fulfillment for all.

Being able to work a cumbersome closed system to client's advantage. Client empowerment and independence.

Enabling other people to realize that the system can change to suit them and increasing a sense of hopefulness.

Educating/empowering clients on how to use skills and resources to advocate for themselves—agency contacts, elected officials, etc.

Being able to help clients who are unable to work through all the bureaucratic red tape to get the benefits that they are entitled to.

Some clients received improved services. Some policies were developed or modified. Some legislation was implemented, amended or quashed.

Bringing about agency practice changes that will benefit large numbers of people over time. Empowering the disadvantaged.

Feeling involved and committed.

Analysis: 3 categories found:	Unit of Analysis: Phrase	Respondents
1) Empowerment of clients	4	4
2) Sense of accomplishment	3	3
3) Changing the system	7	5
4) Other	2	1
Total	14	9*

*Note: Four respondents gave more than one response.

Narrative: Seven respondents stated that the most positive aspect of advocacy was that it "changed the system." One of these respondents stated that the most positive aspect of advocacy was "being able to work a cumbersome closed system to client's advantage." Another respondent stated that advocacy enabled "other people to realize that the system can change to suit them." Four respondents felt that the most positive aspect of advocacy was that it helped to "empower" clients. Three respondents stated that advocacy increased their own sense of personal accomplishment.

should be reported to them. They may also require that you prepare a report on your findings that will be disseminated through key constituency groups. Findings should be presented in a manner that is respectful of the knowledge and experiences of the key beneficiaries and decision makers. Consequently, the research report should be sufficient to address the informational needs of a variety of groups.

Reports that list key findings, use graphs and tables to present results, and briefly summarize the implications of the results may be sufficient. In some cases, however, the evaluator may need to prepare different reports for different audiences. Another technique that can be utilized is to provide an executive summary that highlights important findings and recommendations while providing a more detailed report for scholars, funding sources, and advocacy organizations.

The structure of the report may vary with the intended audience, the types of data collection or approaches evaluation (research paradigm), and the purpose of the study. However, key components of evaluation reports include the following:

- A title and author credits
- An abstract (one-paragraph summary of the purpose of the study and major findings)
- A one- to five-page executive summary, usually in outline form that describes major findings and recommendations
- An introduction that includes the background and purpose of the study
- Identification of the problem addressed by the program intervention, its scope, and its impact on the target population or community
- A description of the organization or program, including history, leadership, members, target community served, mission of the organization, and the program examined
- The purpose of the evaluation study and the type of information needs the study addresses
- A review of the theoretical, empirical, or best-practice literature in relation to the type of program offered and its intended outcome (this section should be used to identify the program's theory of action)
- The program's goals, objectives, outcome measures, and evaluation criteria
- The evaluation methodology utilized: sampling, data collection, research design, and data analysis methods
- Primary evaluation questions addressed (and their links to outcome measures and objectives)
- Definitions of key concepts
- A description of measurement tools and steps used to preserve reliability and validity
- A description of how human subjects will be protected

- A description of how the evaluator will ensure that instruments, data collection, and analysis procedures will address cultural issues that are likely to affect the evaluation
- Primary findings; organized to address key evaluation questions
- Charts and graphs used to display data
- In qualitative studies, a deep description, or written narrative that summarizes the values and perspectives of respondents and/or conclusions drawn from the observations of the evaluation participants
- Recommendations for change, based on an analysis of the data
- A description of the limitations of the study
- Implementation plan for putting recommendations into action
- A dissemination plan for the report
- Appendices (for example, copies of research instruments, consent forms, a list of organizations or individuals who serve on the evaluation team, resumes of paid evaluation staff) (Bisman & Hardcastle; Williams et al., 1998).

Evaluation as a Political Process

Although adherents of the quantitative paradigm argue that research should be both value free and nonpolitical, the evaluator must often play a role in mediating conflicts among program participants and negotiating with them regarding the conduct of the study. Therefore, acting politically is an inherent part of any evaluation study (Forester, 1989; Meier & Usher, 1998). This applies to studies using both quantitative and qualitative paradigms. However, the following principles associated with constructivist evaluation can be used as a guide for the more political aspects of evaluative work:

1. The program evaluated is to be understood from the point of view of the people involved in the process.
2. The evaluator is the primary data collection instrument, using observations, interviews, and perceptions to construct an accurate understanding of the program's environmental context and the program participants.
3. The evaluator is both a student of the stakeholders' perceptions about the program and a teacher, informing participants about the research process and giving new insights about the program.
4. Conflict rather than consensus is expected during the evaluation process. Different constituency groups and individuals will assign different meanings to program processes and outcomes.
5. Constituents (clients, staff, beneficiaries, board members, funders, or neighborhood residents) should be involved in the planning, research design, data collection, analysis, and report writing process.
6. The evaluator should collect information relevant to all stakeholders.

7. Generalizability of the findings is not a primary concern. Negotiations among the program's constituency groups will determine evaluation findings (Chambers et al., 1992, pp. 305–6).

Hence, the involvement of program stakeholders in the evaluation is key for conducting an effective evaluation (Patton, 1997). The last two sections in this chapter examine common structures used to conduct evaluations that involve participants as collaborators in the research process: involvement of constituency groups in agency self-evaluations and working with coalitions to evaluate collaborative programs and services.

Working with Constituency Groups to Conduct Evaluations

Constituency group members are most often involved in projects that involve participatory action research or agency-specific self-evaluations. Approaches that involve constituents in evaluation serve to fulfill basic social work principles related to empowerment, social justice, and cultural diversity (see chapters 4 and 5). They also require a commitment on the part of the evaluator to using social learning or transformative approaches to research (Freire, 1970; Harding, 1997; Reinharz, 1992). According to Telfair and Mulvihill (2000):

> The evaluator who serves community stakeholders has a responsibility to facilitate, support, and engage in the problem-solving aspects of these activities, rather than accept a definition of activities, objectives, or criteria that were developed by outside funders and other stakeholders. In this regard, the evaluator becomes a collaborator in the enabling process of capacity building and empowerment ideally leading to skill development and self-determination. (p. 40)

Participatory Action Research

According to Sohng (1998), participatory action research (PAR) "attempts to decentralize knowledge, as well as the power it confers, through the participation of ordinary people in gaining knowledge" (p. 191). Reinharz (1992) defines participatory action research as a "model used to create social and individual change by altering the role relations of people involved in the project . . . to achieve an egalitarian relation, the researcher abandons control and adopts an approach of openness, reciprocity, mutual disclosure, and shared risk" (p. 181).

To address this goal in community-based evaluation projects, Johnson (1994) recommends that research partnerships be established between academics and community residents. She identifies two approaches for conducting participatory action research:

- Parallel process model. The researcher simply acts as a consultant for the group and provides knowledge about research methodology, data collection, design, and analysis.
- Deep entry model. The researcher becomes part of the evaluation team. However, constituents provide leadership to the group, set the agenda, and participate in data collection and analysis. The data is utilized for the purpose intended by the community.

Smith (1997) identifies a number of steps in the PAR process that should be used by the outside consultant or expert to enhance the validity and reliability of the data collection process. These techniques also enhance the capacity of participants to problem solve. The evaluator should do the following:

- Assess his or her own value assumptions and biases.
- Be prepared to learn from participants.
- Get to know all aspects of the setting: individuals, groups, and the surrounding environment.
- Establish trusting relationships with participants.
- Facilitate the group's understanding and analysis of their life experiences and the root causes of their needs.
- Help people to organize to take appropriate actions to facilitate social change; link actions to data analysis.
- Act in a manner that continually validates the work of the group.
- Work in partnership with the group to identify internal leaders and facilitators. (pp. 235–40)

Self-Evaluation

Meier and Usher (1998) define self-evaluation as derived from the participatory research approach used to evaluate specific programs. The procedure explicitly links program design and management procedures to evaluation. This allows for constant monitoring and modifications in program design that flow from the data. This process generally requires that the organization hire an outside consultant to work with task groups of staff, managers, service users, residents, and representatives from other organizations in the community. The consultant helps these groups identify the program's theory of change. Once this task has been accomplished, the program participants and the consultant work together on the research design and data collection.

In the final stages of self-evaluation, the consultant works with the task group to develop the capacity to analyze data, interpret findings, and make recommendations for program change. The result is that the program (and its parent organization) makes improvements in program design that enhance both quality and program effectiveness. Self-evaluation procedures produce other intended results, including leadership development, feelings of empowerment among participants, internal capacity to conduct evaluations, utilization of findings, and acceptance of program improvements by staff, management, and clients (Meier & Usher, 1998).

Working with Coalitions to Conduct Evaluations

Some practitioners of participatory research use the term empowerment evaluation to describe processes in which organization and coalition members are involved in the assessment of outcomes associated with community planning (Fetterman, 1996). Empowerment evaluation is used to conduct both internal self-evaluations and structure and assessment projects that involve community-based collaboration. This method is believed to be preferable to the more traditional evaluation model for the following reasons:

- The use of expert knowledge may sustain and even enhance traditional power imbalances between the haves and the have-nots.
- The information produced will be relevant to the needs of participants.
- The findings are more likely to be used in a manner that is beneficial to the community.
- Participants are empowered with technical skills, knowledge, and access to data.
- Culturally competent programs and approaches to evaluation are developed (Coombe, 1999; Padilla, Lein, & Cruz, 1999; Rapp, Shera, & Kisthardt, 1993; Schulz, Israel, Selig, & Bayer, 1998).

Fetterman (1996) defines empowerment evaluation as "a collaborative group activity, not an individual pursuit. An evaluator does not and cannot empower anyone; people empower themselves, often with assistance and coaching" (p. 5). In addition to capacity-building and program-evaluation activities, its explicit intent is to engage participants in advocacy and social change. Consequently, while it employs a combination of quantitative and qualitative research approaches, this method is not intended to be objective or strictly scientific in intent but serves a political purpose.

Consequently, the role of facilitators is to bring about agreements and common perspectives about how the evaluation should proceed and how the data should be utilized. Schmuck (1997) identifies ten components of group structure that make all types of participatory evaluation processes successful:

1. Establish feelings of inclusion and trust.
2. Develop a shared leadership process.
3. Emphasize friendliness and group cohesion.

4. Deal directly with differences in social class, ethnicity, gender, and other relevant demographic characteristics.
5. Develop appropriate group processes and a structure to conduct meetings.
6. Develop good communication skills; deal with group problems explicitly and directly.
7. Develop operation agreements with full participation of group members.
8. Try to make decisions by consensus.
9. Discuss group processes and outcomes with members.
10. Assess whether group members have followed through on task assignment. (p. 107)

Urwin and Haynes (1998) describe how a focus group structure can be utilized to develop partnerships among members of a collaborative (see table 14.6). This framework can also be used to conduct an evaluation, using collaborative members as research subjects, or to establish the collaborative as a steering committee to collaboratively evaluate a program or intervention. According to Urwin and Haynes, effective collaboratives contain three dimensions: preconditions for operation, group process, and intended outcomes. These groups also move through three developmental stages:

Table 14.6 Using Focus Groups to Establish Collaborative Research Partnerships

THEORETICAL FRAMEWORK		APPLICATION
Dimensions of Collaboration	*Developmental Stages*	*Focus Group Processes*
Preconditions	Problem setting	Relationship building
		Gathering information
		Ventilating concerns
Process	Direction setting	Planning
		Exploring challenges
		Generating solutions
		Constructing research design
Outcomes	Structuring	Implementing evaluation
		Establishing a structure
		Data collection
		Analysis
		Feedback from group
		Members and other participants

Source: Adapted from Urwin & Haynes, 1998.

- Problem setting. In this stage, participants begin to build relationships with one another, gather information about common problems, and vent their concerns.
- Direction setting. During this stage, members plan how the evaluation will be conducted.
- Structuring. During the final stage, the evaluation plan is implemented, the data is collected and analyzed, and the final report is written. Group members and other research participants are asked to give feedback regarding the perceived accuracy of the findings and recommendations generated from the findings.

Summary

Effective community organization and program evaluation require that the organizer employ technical, analytical, and interpersonal skills to examine processes and outcomes. The organizer must be able to work with participants to identify the program's theory of change, set goals, plan data collection and research design strategies, select participants, and analyze data. Writing the research report in a clear way that can communicate major findings and recommendations is also required. The organizer/evaluator must be prepared to think strategically, using the most resource-efficient techniques to answer research questions, but must also act politically, responding to the demands of diverse constituency groups involved in the evaluation: funders, board members, beneficiaries, clients, and other concerned citizens.

Recent innovations in evaluation practice—participatory action research, self-evaluation, and empowerment evaluation—require that the evaluator take on the role of a consultant and mediator, helping participants gain a common understanding of program goals, information needs, and evaluation techniques. Consequently, the evaluator must be prepared to work as an equal partner, recognizing that participants in program and social efforts bring strength, values, perceptions, experiences, and expertise that are critical for the development of culturally competent and effective services.

■ QUESTIONS FOR CLASS DISCUSSION

1. How could such factors as maturation or repeating testing affect outcomes from quasi-experimental designs? What precautions can be taken to preserve internal validity?
2. Is it important that the evaluator be able to generalize research findings to other programs, individuals, or settings? What are the barriers associated with establishing the external validity of program evaluations?
3. What objections would a quantitative researcher use in opposing participatory action research or empowerment evaluation? Are such studies consistent with qualitative approaches to research? Why or why not?

4. How could narrative be used in the program evaluation? How could it best be used to evaluate social change efforts?
5. What are the strengths and weaknesses of consumer satisfaction studies? Why, and in what circumstances, should they be conducted?
6. Describe circumstances when a grounded theory approach could best be used in program evaluation.
7. How would you anticipate that evaluations could become political? Whose values and preferences are likely to be incorporated into the evaluation process?
8. What precautions could be taken to facilitate consensus among program participants involved in empowerment evaluation?
9. What are the advantages and limitations of using a classical experimental design to conduct an evaluation? What modifications can be made in this approach to allow for the collection of sufficient data in an affordable manner?

■ SAMPLE ASSIGNMENTS AND EXERCISES

1. Use the available theoretical and empirical literature to identify problems and barriers associated with collaborative program development and evaluation. Write a four- to five-page paper that reviews this literature and identifies strategies for surmounting these barriers.
2. Conduct a minimum of five "life story" interviews that document participant reactions to a community change effort. Construct an appropriate open-ended interview guide. Write a brief narrative paper (five to seven pages) that describes your findings.
3. Conduct an observation of a demonstration or protest-related activity. Note your observations in a journal either during or immediately after the event. Components of the field notes should include number of participants, number of visible opponents, interactions between proponents and opponents, demographic composition, appearance, verbal behavior, relevant nonverbal behavior, the surrounding environment, nonparticipant reactions to the event, and the outcome of the activity. Also, state whether you believe the event produced the desired impact and any unanticipated consequences. Summarize your observations in a three- to five-page paper (include your field notes as an attachment).
4. Conduct a minimum of three ethnographic interviews using an interview guide you have constructed. Participants should be of an ethnic group that is culturally different from your own or who share a cultural affiliation outside the dominant culture. Write a three- to five-page paper that identifies cultural symbols, norms, music, art, behaviors, or beliefs that are common among the three participants.
5. Identify a problem in your place of employment or field agency. Construct a brief (five to eight pages) question focus group interview guide.

Select representative participants who are likely to have information about the problem, using an appropriate sampling method. Use qualitative data analysis methods to analyze your results among respondents. Write up your findings in a three- to five-page paper that identifies common ideas and themes as well as minority responses.

6. Identify a community of interest to you. Find census data for this community for 1970, 1980, 1990, and 2000 (using techniques identified in chapter 6). Look at indicators related to income, poverty rates, housing status, ethnicity, and gender. What recent trends can you identify? What does this information tell you about current needs in the community? What do these trends suggest about the impact of social problems in this community in the future? Construct an appropriate pie or bar chart to illustrate recent trends using at least one of the identified variables.

7. Construct a ten- to twenty-page consumer satisfaction survey that can be administered in your field agency or place of employment. Take appropriate steps to prevent problems with reliability and validity. Select potential respondents and choose an appropriate approach for administering the instrument that protects the confidentiality of participants. Make sure that your instrument can assess specific program components and document the demographic composition of respondents. Administer the instrument to a minimum of ten participants. Analyze the results. Present your data in a report using frequencies, means, and cross-tabulations (attach your instrument to your final paper).

■ ASSIGNMENT: SPECIFYING THE PROGRAM'S THEORY OF ACTION

1. Choose a program in which you are employed or completing a field placement. Write a two- to five-page description of the program's theory of action. Specify the following program components: needs addressed, goals and objectives, timelines, resources, and the current stage(s) of program development.

2. Write a brief (one- to two-page) narrative that gives a logical rationale for the program model. What are specific program models intended to do? What outputs (short-term objectives, immediate objectives, and long-range goals) should be produced using this intervention?

3. In your narrative, incorporate references to the available theoretical and empirical literature and information from interviews with program participants. It is also appropriate to use references from the best-practices literature found on many government and advocacy organization Web sites as well as existing program proposals and other organization literature.

4. Identify program objectives, desired outcomes, and evaluation criteria. In your opinion, are these elements consistent with the theoretical assumptions associated with the program?

Notes

1. Lindsey (1997) notes that feminist research differs from the more generic qualitative approach in that (1) it is possible to conduct "feminist" quantitative research, integrating feminist values into structured measurement tools, and (2) feminist research is inherently "political" or an "applied" research approach in that its primary intent is to change social conditions experienced by women. In some cases, ethnography and other forms of qualitative research can also be conducted to facilitate social change (Fetterman, 1998).

2. In some types of ethnographic research, written consent may not be pursued because the target community is made up of people who do not read, write, or speak the same language as the researcher. Ethnographers may seek written or verbal consent from community leaders or representatives. In some cases, the researcher may expect to be engaged by prospective subjects in a prolonged, sustained "entry" process by community leaders. This process is used to establish whether the researcher can be trusted by the community (Berg, 1995; Fetterman, 1998).

References

Alter, C., & Evens, W. (1990). *Evaluating your practice*. New York: Springer.

Bachay, J., & Cingel, P. (1999). Restructuring resilience: Emerging voices. *Affilia, 14*(2), 162–75.

Bell, H., Sloan, L., & Strickling, C. (1998). Exploiter or exploited: Topless dancers reflect on their experiences. *Affilia, 13*, 352–68.

Berg, B. (1995). *Qualitative methods for the social sciences* (3d ed.). Boston: Allyn & Bacon.

Bisman, C., & Hardcastle, D. (1999). *Integrating research into practice*. Belmont, CA: Brooks/Cole.

Bush, M., & Gordon, A. (1978). The advantages of client involvement in evaluation research. In T. Cook (Ed.), *Evaluation studies review annual* (pp. 767–83). Sage: Beverly Hills.

Campbell, D., & Stanley, J. (1963). *Experimental and quasi-experimental designs for research*. Chicago: Rand McNally.

Chambers, D., Wedel, K., & Rodwell, M. (1992). *Evaluating social programs*. Boston: Allyn & Bacon.

Cherry, A. (2000). *A research primer for the helping professions: Methods, statistics, and writing*. Belmont, CA: Brooks/Cole.

Coombe, C. (1999). Using empowerment evaluation in community organizing and community-based health initiatives. In M. Minkler (Ed.), *Community organization and community building for health* (pp. 291–307). New Brunswick, NJ: Rutgers University Press.

Cummerton, J. (1986). A feminist perspective on research. What does it help us see? In N. Van Den Bergh & L. Cooper (Eds.), *Feminist visions for social work* (pp. 80–100). Silver Spring, MD: National Association of Social Workers.

DeHoog, R. (1984). *Contracting out for human services*. Albany: State University of New York.

Denning, J., & Verschelden, C. (1993). Using the focus group in assessing training needs. *Child Welfare, 72*, 569–79.

Douglas, R. (1995). How to use and present community data. In J. Rothman, H. Erlich, & J. Tropman (Eds.), *Tactics and techniques of community intervention* (3d ed., pp. 427–38). Itasca, IL: Peacock.

Fetterman, D. (1996). Empowerment evaluation: An introduction to theory and practice. In D. Fetterman, S. Kaftarian, & A. Wandersman (Eds.), *Empowerment evaluation: Knowledge and tools for self-assessment and accountability* (pp. 3–46). Thousand Oaks, CA: Sage.

Fetterman, D. (1998). *Ethnography: Step by step.* Thousand Oaks, CA: Sage.

Flynn, J. (1992). *Social agency policy: Analysis and presentation for community practice.* Chicago: Nelson-Hall.

Forester, J. (1989). *Planning in the face of power.* Berkeley: University of California Press.

Freire, P. (1970). *Pedagogy of the oppressed.* New York: Continuum.

Guba, E. (1987). *Naturalistic evaluation: New directions for program evaluation.* San Francisco: Jossey-Bass.

Gutek, B. (1978). Strategies for studying client satisfaction. *Journal of Social Issues, 34*(4), 44–56.

Hagen, J., & Wang, L. (1994). Implementing jobs: The functions of front-line workers. *Social Service Review, 68,* 369–85.

Handler, J., & Sosin, M. (1983). *Last resorts.* New York: Academic Press.

Hardina, D. (1990*). Solution or illusion: Purchasing job services for welfare recipients in Wayne County.* Detroit, MI: Center for Urban Studies.

Harding, S. (1997). *Is science multicultural: Postcolonialisms, feminisms, and epistemologies.* Bloomington: Indiana University Press.

Haynes, K., & Mickelson, J. (1991). *Affecting change: Social workers in the political arena.* New York: Longman.

Johnson, A. (1994). Linking professionalism and community organization: A scholar/advocate approach. *Journal of Community Practice, 1*(2), 65–86.

Krause, D. (1996). *Effective program evaluation.* Chicago: Nelson-Hall.

Lebow, J. (1983). Research assessing consumer satisfaction with mental health treatment: A review of the findings. *Evaluation and Program Planning, 6,* 211–36.

Lindsey, E. (1997). Feminist issues in qualitative research with formerly homeless mothers. *Affilia, 12*(1), 57–76.

MacNair, R. (1996). A research methodology for community practice. *Journal of Community Practice, 3*(2), 1–19.

Marlow, C. (1998). *Research methods for generalist social work* (2d ed.). Pacific Grove, CA: Brooks/Cole.

Meier, A., & Usher, C. (1998). New approaches to program evaluation. In R. Edwards, J. Yankey, & M. Altpeter (Eds.), *Skills for the effective management of nonprofit organizations.* Washington, DC: National Association of Social Workers.

Padilla, Y., Lein, L., & Cruz, M. (1999). Community-based research in policy planning: A case study—addressing poverty in the Texas-Mexico border region. *Journal of Community Practice, 6*(3), 1–22.

Patton, M. (1997). *Utilization-focused evaluation: The new century text.* Thousand Oaks, CA: Sage.

Perkins, D. (1983). Evaluating social interventions: A conceptual schema. In R. Kramer & H. Specht (Eds.), *Community organization practice.* Englewood Cliffs: NJ: Prentice-Hall.

Pierce, D. (1984). *Policy for the social work practitioner.* New York: Longman.

Rapp, C., Shera, W., & Kisthardt, W. (1993). Research strategies for consumer empowerment of people with severe mental illness. *Social Work, 38,* 727–35.

Reamer, F. (1998). *Ethical standards in social work.* Washington, DC: National Association of Social Workers Press.

Reinharz, S. (1992). *Feminist methods in social research.* New York: Oxford University Press.

Riessmann, C. (1994). Making sense of marital violence: One woman's narrative. In C. Riessmann (Ed.), *Qualitative studies in social work* (pp. 113–32). Thousand Oaks, CA: Sage.

Rodwell, M. (1998). *Social work constructivist research.* New York: Garland.

Rossi, P., & Freeman, H. (1982). *Evaluation: A systematic approach.* Beverly Hills, CA: Sage.

Royse, D., & Thyer, B. (1996). *Program evaluation: An introduction.* Chicago: Nelson-Hall.

Rubin, A., & Babbie, E. (1997). *Research methods for social work.* Pacific Grove, CA: Brooks/Cole.

Schmuck, R. (1997). *Practical action research for change.* Arlington Heights, IL: SkyLight Professional Development.

Schulz, A., Israel, B., Selig, S., & Bayer, I. (1998). *Development and implementation of principles for community-based research in public health.* In R. MacNair (Ed.), Research strategies for community practice (pp. 83–110). New York: Haworth.

Smith, S. (1997). Deepening participatory action research. In S. Smith, D. Wilms, & N. Johnson (Eds.), *Nurtured by knowledge.* New York: Apex.

Sohng, S. (1998). Research as an empowerment strategy. In L. Gutierrez, R. Parsons, & E. O. Cox (Eds.), *Empowerment in social work practice: A source book* (pp. 187–201). Pacific Grove, CA: Brooks/Cole.

Solomon, C. (1994). Welfare worker's response to homeless applicants. In C. Kohler Riessman (Ed.), *Qualitative studies in social work research* (pp. 153–68). Thousand Oaks, CA: Sage.

Stipak, B. (1982). Using clients to evaluate programs. In E. House, S. Mathison, J. Pearsol, & Preskill, H. (Eds.), *Evaluation Studies Review Annual, 7,* 585–602.

Strauss, A., & Corbin, J. (1990). *Basics of qualitative research.* Newbury Park, CA: Sage Publications.

Telfair, J., & Mulvihill, B. (2000). Bridging science and practice: The integrated model of community-based evaluation (IMCBE). *Journal of Community Practice,* 7(3), 37–65.

Urwin, C., & Haynes, D. (1998). A reflexive model for collaboration: Empowering partnerships through focus groups. *Administration in Social Work,* 22(2), 23–39.

Williams, M., Unrau, Y., & Grinnell, R. (1998). *Introduction to social work research.* Itasca, IL: Peacock.

Web Resources

Ann E. Casey Foundation—http://www.aecf.org/

American Evaluation Association (AEA)—http://www.eval.org

AEA Topical Interest Group on Collaborative, Participatory, and Empowerment Evaluation—http://stanford.edu/~davidf/empowermenteval.html

Community Tool Box—http://ctb.lsi.ukans.edu

East St. Louis Action Research Project (University of Illinois at Urbana-Champaign)—http://www.eslarp.uiuc/

PARNET (Participatory Action Research, Cornell University)—http://www.parnet.org

15 Technological Approaches and Techniques

The Implications of the Internet for Community Organization Practice

■ This textbook has focused on skill development for community organizers. Many of the skills identified in the book involve tasks that can be conducted using the Internet. Community organizers can conduct research on the World Wide Web. They can locate legislation and find out who has contributed to political campaigns. Organizers can use E-mail to recruit constituents and mobilize them to take action. E-mail can also be used to lobby decision makers. In addition, organizers can construct Web pages to inform the public about a variety of social problems, coordinate service delivery, and raise funds. The Internet can also be used to form virtual communities; E-mail, bulletin boards, and chat rooms provide opportunities for constituents to exchange information, network, or simply get to know one another (McNutt, 2000; Shiffer, 1999). Consequently, the Internet provides organizers with an important tool for carrying out our work. However, this technology also contains access structures that may limit participation by some social and cultural groups.

This chapter discusses advantages of the Internet, including increased access to information, constituency groups, and decision makers; development of a sense of community among members of constituency groups; and using the Web for voting and fostering participation in government. Possible negative consequences of Internet technology are also examined, especially the implications of this technology for increasing income disparity and limiting access to members of the dominant culture.

Access to Constituency Groups and Decision Makers

Before the Internet, much of community organization practice involved legwork. Organizers traveled to public or university libraries to obtain published information about members of the elite. (The *Social Register* and *Who's Who* were often important sources of information for the organizer.) University libraries generally provided access to census data and copies of legislation or the *Congressional Record*. Organizers also visited small libraries maintained by city government to obtain maps and copies of regional plans. Additional trips were made to foundation centers to identify sources of funding for grants.

Now all this information can be obtained using the Internet. Not only does this save time for the organizer, it also increases access to this information for all citizens. Consequently, open access to information can be used to empower members of marginalized groups. In the past, government sometimes functioned to limit access to information for some groups of people. For example, it has often been difficult for low-income people to find out what benefits are public agencies provide and how to apply for these benefits (Lipsky, 1980). Now public agencies often post this information directly on the Internet. However, as we shall discuss in later sections of this chapter, such information may still be inaccessible to low-income people and other marginalized groups.

Provision of Services, Support, and Technical Assistance on the Internet

Community-based organizations have begun to explore how to use the Internet to deliver and coordinate services. For example, the HIV Cybermall, serving southern California, links eighteen partner agencies that provide information, referral, medical care and drug treatment, and counseling (Henrickson & Mayo, 2000). The Cybermall involves a computer network and a linked transportation system. At the Cybermall Web site, agencies have access to information, provide case-management services, and link the participant agencies to one another.

Many social action organizations have begun to establish structures, using the Internet to provide technical assistance, employment-related information, information on strategies, and emotional support. A number of organizations such as HandsNet, COMM-ORG, and the Community Tool Box have developed extensive curriculum packages that are posted on their Web sites (Schultz et al., 2000). Some organizations also publicize curriculum projects or continuing education workshops using Internet technology, while others offer opportunities via electronic bulletin boards, discussion groups, chat rooms, and LISTSERVs for organizers to exchange information and offer social support to one other (Meier, 2000).

Organizing on the Web

The organizer can use a variety of vehicles on the Internet to link people and organizations. Nartz and Schoech (2000) identify four models of community practice on the Internet: information dissemination, community building, constituent mobilization, and community planning. LISTSERVs, chat rooms, and bulletin boards can be used to form on-line communities (Cart, 1999). They provide a mechanism for developing relationships that can transcend physical, economic, cultural, and social distances. The obvious disadvantage is that participants cannot actually see one another unless specific arrangements are made to do so off-line. According to Schopler, Abell, and Galinksy (1998), groups organized on-line have some obvious advantages:

> In computer groups, members share feelings, exchange information, develop skills, solve problems, work on tasks, and make decisions through messages they post simultaneously or asynchronously, at their convenience, at any time of the day or night. Membership in technology-based groups may be as few as three people . . . . But hundreds of people conceivably may participate in a computer group. (p. 255)

Relationship building on-line does work, helping people to exchange ideas and information. On-line groups also allow people to remain anonymous and choose whether to divulge personal information. Consequently, issues of power and status may not be relevant in the group. However, Schopler et al. (1998) note that anonymity and the lack of personal contact may make it difficult to impose social norms and regulate group behavior. It is important for group members to make rules of decorum explicit or to utilize a facilitator to enforce the rules. As Cart (1999) notes, "Another challenge for organizers is that of being alert to and working to prevent sexism, racism, homophobia, and other forms of prejudice and domination online" (p. 336).

E-mail, LISTSERVs, and other mechanisms have been used successfully to recruit participants and bring them into the organization. As mentioned previously, MoveOn is a prototype for organizational formation on the Web. Once people were recruited to sign a petition to oppose the conviction of President Bill Clinton on impeachment charges, the LISTSERV was used to contact progressive individuals to support a variety of legislative initiatives. Advocacy organizations have been successful in using LISTSERVs, bulletin boards, newsgroups, and chat rooms to inform members and the general public about legislative issues and to identify serious social problems. Announcements about protests and demonstrations can also be posted on Web sites or discussed on LISTSERVs and chat rooms. However, one potential problem with this tactic is that such plans seldom can be kept confidential: discussion on the Internet can allow opponents the opportunity to design countertactics.

As described in chapter 13, this technology has been used successfully to solicit funds from members. Web page construction, although not discussed explicitly in this text, is a skill that is critical for organizers. In addition to recruitment and fund-raising, an organization can achieve a number of its primary goals with the development of a good, eye-catching Web page: retention of volunteers; publicity; public information; issue analysis; and the maintenance of links with coalition members, similar organizations, and decision makers.

Participatory Democracy

Political parties have begun to master the art of recruiting and maintaining their membership based on the Internet. Some observers believe that the use of the Internet to deliver information to likely voters offers a unique opportunity to engage the public in the political process (Associated Press, 1999). A number of organizations involved in the political process (National Organization of Women; the American Association of Retired Persons) have built up their membership bases by offering on-line services (E-mail, Internet access services) at a discount to members. The AFL-CIO also provides low-cost computers to their members (Lazurus, 2000).

Instant news coverage has become available from sources that broadcast over the Web. One major advantage of the Internet is that it allows organizers to examine multiple sources of broadcast and print media. Certain information or types of news stories are often given regional rather than national coverage. The Internet allows activists to have access on a daily basis to major print media sources or alternative news coverage that is not available from other sources. For example, a number of newspapers and wire services posted reports on their Web sites that challenged mainstream press reports naming George W. Bush the victor in Florida after a media-sponsored recount ("So Gore Really Won," 2001).

Though some of the news coverage on the Web involves merely posting brief news stories just after they occur, the more powerful (and expensive) personal computers allow for the display of live pictures and sound on Web pages. Mainstream news organizations maintain some of these sites. Others are sponsored by small organizations that seek to provide the public with alternative news sources (Taylor, 2000). Some of these organizations are designed explicitly for progressive activists, providing information that news organizations associated with the corporate sector are not likely to provide. One example of this type of service is Speakout.com. Another is Wired News, which provided coverage of the demonstrations at the World Trade Organization conference in Seattle in 1999 and at the 2000 Democratic and Republican national conventions. One good source of information for organizers is the LISTSERV maintained by COMM-ORG. Reports sent by individual members have featured eyewitness accounts of the WTO demonstrations and the police response and included reports and information that was the major networks and newspapers did not provide.

The availability of government services and planning information on the Web can potentially help consumers design personal service systems and make decisions that will ensure their safety and quality of life. The Internet also helps to break down barriers that may limit participation within organizations or the political process. For example, computer technology has allowed persons with disabilities to transcend barriers related to mobility, transportation, and ability to communicate verbally. People who cannot talk can use computers to communicate with others (see http://www.bridgeschool.org).

Using the Internet to Vote

Some states have started to allow citizens to vote using the Internet. In March 2000, members of the Arizona Democratic party were given the option of voting on-line for candidates in the presidential primary. Participants without computers were able to find terminals at predesignated sites or vote by paper ballots (Thomsen, 1999). Voters in Washington state and Iowa have participated in test elections to assess the feasibility of on-line voting. Internet voting would seem to have potential for increasing voter participation. Voting at home is more convenient and private than traveling to polling places. The Internet would also seem to have great potential for increasing voting registration.

However, there are significant negative aspects to Internet voting as well as the use of the Internet to transmit information about politics. Not all citizens have access to computers or the Internet. As discussed in chapter 9, poor people currently are less likely to vote than middle- or upper-income individuals. Telephone polls conducted to predict the likely outcomes of political campaigns often contain bias simply because poor people are the least likely to have phones. Internet-conducted polls are likely to contain the same type of bias. Consequently, the use of computer technology to increase voter participation may increase participation from white, well-educated individuals but have limited utility for members of oppressed and marginalized groups unless specific mechanisms are established to ensure equal access for everyone.

An additional concern in relation to online voting is how to ensure that voter registrations are accurate and whether it is the registered voter who actually votes. Many organizers have been actively involved in both registering poor people to vote and ensuring that their vote actually counts. Some political machines have ensured election victory by controlling access to the polls or stuffing ballot boxes in poor communities (Joyce, 1997). Procedures that ensure one vote for each citizen are an essential component of ensuring equity in participation in the voting process.

Negative Effects: Potential for Increasing Income Disparities

Although more than 40 percent of all U.S. households contain computers, only 8 percent of families with annual incomes of less than $5,000 per year own this type of equipment (U.S. Department of Commerce, 1999). Among those low-income households who do own computers, only 3 percent are connected to the Internet. Income severely restricts parental ability to purchase computer equipment and maintain Internet access. As any working organizer knows, many low-income families will forgo payment of monthly phone bills in order to buy food or pay rent. Consequently, they will not have consistent phone service from month to month. Low-income people also move frequently. Because most Internet access occurs over phone lines, it is unreasonable that low-income and working-class parents will be able to purchase and maintain Internet services for their children.

Elementary and high schools in low-income neighborhoods often do not have sufficient computer and instructional resources to provide Internet access to all students. Most local school districts receive the bulk of their funding from property taxes. As a result, schools in wealthy geographic areas are much more likely to invest in computers and Internet connections than schools serving low-income children in the inner city or rural neighborhoods. This exacerbates the digital divide between the wealthy and the poor (Bolt & Crawford, 2000). Low-income children seldom have parity with children from middle-income or upper-class families in terms of textbooks, school facilities, and the quality of instruction. Hence, lack of access to computers will put these children even farther behind their peers in terms of educational content, learning, and knowledge of instruction. An additional issue is that children with parents who are computer literate will have greater access to technology along with parental encouragement and assistance in learning these new skills. Many low-income parents will not have been exposed to computers in their jobs, limiting transmission of these new vehicles for knowledge as well as parental access to well-paying jobs in the dot.com economy.

Federal grants and donations of equipment from computer hardware manufacturers have been used successfully to obtain computers for schools serving low-income communities (Bolt & Crawford, 2000; May, 2000). In addition, government and corporate partnerships have been proposed to help parents purchase equipment and obtain Internet connections for a small monthly fee. However, corporate donations and subsidies have been criticized as not particularly helpful for educational or economic development in low-income communities. The manufacturer's primary goal in pursuing this type of philanthropy may be primarily to increase brand-name recognition and open new consumer markets. Given the nature of marketing and software agreements among manufacturers, corporate partnerships may serve to help larger computer companies maintain a monopoly in the market.

Potential for Fostering or Limiting Diversity

According to a study conducted by the U.S. Department of Commerce (1999), African American and Latino households are one-third as likely to have access to the Internet as Asian/Pacific Islander households and two-fifths as likely to have access as European American households (see figure 15.1). Among Latinos and other new immigrants, the digital divide may be increased due to language access. Most well "traveled" Web sites in the United States offer services exclusively in English, although some organizations maintain sites in Spanish and other languages or offer culturally specific services.

E-mail technology does permit the inclusion of software that automatically translates text into the computer owner's preferred language. Consequently, E-mail can transcend ethnic as well as geographic boundaries. Another advantage of the Internet is that immigrants can easily link up with organizations from their country of origin or form computer networks with other immigrants from that country to provide them with support and alleviate feelings of isolation after arrival in the United States. For this reason, the Internet does increase the potential for organizing within ethnic communities and interacting across ethnic boundaries to form multicultural coalitions (Cox News Service, 1999; Delgado, 1997). It can also be used to conduct research on voter preferences and participation patterns within ethnic groups that have historically been underrepresented in the political process (Jesuit, Nirchi, de Haymes, & Sanchez, 2000). This information can be used effectively to increase the participation of ethnic groups in mainstream politics. Bolt and Crawford (2000) argue that the degree to which computer technology fosters diversity or promotes exclusion is a matter of social choice:

> Ideas, innovation, and advances that help all of society know no specific language or skin color. What a true embodiment of diversity means is that segments of our society have the ability to share points of view, to discuss differences, to agree to be in accord or to disagree, to develop a tolerance for ideas and influences different from our own,

Figure 15.1. Households using the Internet in 1998 by ethnicity.

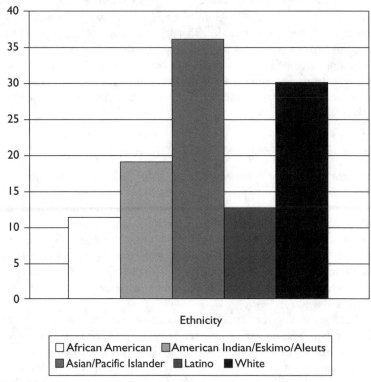

Ethnicity

☐ African American ▨ American Indian/Eskimo/Aleuts
■ Asian/Pacific Islander ▨ Latino ■ White

Source: U.S. Department of Commerce, 1999.

and to celebrate both our differences and our similarities. The true digital revolution rests in this movement towards each other and to acceptance and inclusiveness. (p. 120)

An Organizer's Responsibility to Reduce the Digital Divide

Organizers should be at the forefront of trying to reduce the digital divide between the haves and the have-nots. Community organizations and educational institutions have begun to establish community-based programs to educate the public about computer utilization and Internet access. One of these organizations, Plugged In in East Palo Alto, California, operates a community technology center available to all residents. Plugged In also includes an after-school program to teach computer skills and a teen enterprise program that constructs Web pages and performs desktop publishing functions for local businesses (Bolt & Crawford, 2000). A similar program, Logo Lab, was established through a partnership between a local elementary school in Cambridge, Massachusetts, and faculty at the Massachusetts Institute of Technology. University faculty designed a computer lab, provided computers, and trained students to successfully use the computers in instruction. The students were encouraged to design computer programs and conduct experiments using the equipment (Bamberger, 1999).

Another method for reducing the digital divide is to increase access to employment for people of color in the computer industry. Bolt and Crawford (2000) note that only 4 percent of the Silicon Valley computer workforce is African American and only 7 percent is Latino. Yet these employers have actively lobbied the federal government for visas for technical workers from overseas.

At minimum, community organizers should do the following:

- Make sure they educate themselves so that they can use appropriate computer technology for research, analysis, organizational maintenance, lobbying, and membership recruitment. However, individual organizers need not specialize in all aspects of computer applications.
- Be prepared to transmit computer skills and knowledge to members of constituency groups. Acquisition of skills will help ensure that constituents have access to the Internet and develop their skills in gathering information, publicizing a cause, lobbying, and building organizations (Blundo, Mele, Hairston, & Watson, 1999). Hence, participatory democracy is promoted.
- Pursue opportunities to equalize access to computers and other educational resources among elementary and high schools serving low-, middle-, and upper-income communities.
- Explore options to develop alternative educational structures (after-school programs, adult education, and vocational training) to supplement existing institutions.
- Work for the adoption of economic-development strategies that stimulate well-paying jobs in the dot.com economy for low-income groups and people of color.

Summary

The computer revolution offers unique opportunities and challenges for the organizer. Access to information, money, technical knowledge, decision makers, and constituents allows communities to build sustainable community organizations and social, cultural, professional, and economic networks. It offers a low-cost method for bringing people together across social boundaries, provided that computer technology and Internet access is made available across all social and economic groups. It also provides a mechanism for skill development and knowledge transmission that can be used to generate opportunities for individual entrepreneurship and the acquisition of new jobs in the computer technology. Computers can also be used proactively to involve individuals and groups in the political process and in volunteer activities and social activism. As organizers, we must make a commitment to ensure that technology will be used not to further marginalize some members of society but to ensure empowerment, respect for cultural diversity, and social justice for all.

■ QUESTIONS FOR CLASS DISCUSSION

1. Identify the types of information government agencies should put on the Internet. How realistic are current government proposals to make services accessible to citizens on the Internet? Will all citizens be likely to have access? Why or why not?
2. How realistic are current proposals by government to form partnerships with computer and software manufacturers to make computers with Internet connections affordable for low-income families?
3. How realistic are proposals to allow citizens to vote using the Internet? What are some of the possible problems and barriers that might limit the success of these efforts?
4. How should computer manufacturers and other businesses related to the "dot.com" economy use their technical expertise and new wealth to benefit members of marginalized groups?
5. Identify at least five ways in which a community organization can use Internet technology to recruit members, raise funds, contact decision makers, establish community, or conduct research.

■ SAMPLE ASSIGNMENTS AND EXERCISES

1. Subscribe to a LISTSERV or visit a chat room. You may choose a community organization, fund-raising group, or interest group LISTSERV or choose a LISTSERV that focuses on a topic of personal interest to you (entertainment, popular culture, hobbies). Stay on the list for a week or two. Examine the type of interaction among members and any explicit or implicit rules of conduct as well as inclusion or exclusion. Note: Academic discussion lists and chat rooms are fairly safe, although some do not receive many messages from individuals. On personal interest–related lists, you may choose whether to reveal your real identity or use an alias. It is advisable to use an alias until you feel comfortable. It is also advisable to use discretion in returning messages "off-list."
2. Subscribe to a LISTSERV used by an organization that actively uses E-mail to inform members about pending legislation (for example, the Children's Defense Fund or the United Farm Workers). How useful is the information you receive?

3. Use this information to contact a politician or other decision maker using E-mail or "snail mail." Did you receive a response? Was it a form letter or did you receive a personal response? How likely do you think it was that your letter helped to influence a decision maker? Would multiple letters, similar to the one you wrote, be likely to influence decision makers?

4. Create a proposal for a new community organization to alleviate a social problem. Include a mission statement and a list of goals and objectives. Include in your list of objectives at least four activities that can be conducted using computer technology. Describe in your prospectus the manner in which computer and Internet technology will be used to enhance organization maintenance, implement intervention plans, or deliver services.

References

Associated Press. (1999, September 11). Internet may draw young folks to politics. *San Francisco Chronicle*, p. A2.

Bamberger, J. (1999). Action knowledge and symbolic knowledge. The computer as mediator. In D. Schon, B. Sanyal, & W. Mitchell (Eds.), *High technology and low-income communities*. Cambridge: MIT Press.

Blundo, R., Mele, C., Hairston, R., & Watson, J. (1999). The Internet and demystifying power differentials: A few women on-line and the housing authority. *Journal of Community Practice*, 6(2), 11–26.

Bolt, D., & Crawford, R. (2000). *Digital divide: Computers and our children's future*. New York: TV Books.

Cart, C. (1999). Online computer networks: Potential challenges for community organizing and community building now and in the future. In M. Minkler (Ed.), *Community organization and community building for health* (pp. 325–38). New Brunswick, NJ: Rutgers University Press.

Cox News Service. (1999). Latino Web site aims to boost voter registration. *San Francisco Chronicle*, p. A16.

Delgado, G. (1997). *Beyond the politics of place: New directions in community organization*. Berkeley, CA: Chardon.

Henrickson, M., & Mayo, J. (2000). The HIV Cybermall: A regional cybernetwork of HIV services. In J. Finn & G. Holden (Eds.), *Human services online: A new arena for service delivery* (pp. 7–26). New York: Haworth.

Jesuit, D., Nirchi, A., de Haymes, M., & Sanchez, P. (2000). The 1996 Chicago Latino registered voter political survey: Political participation and public polity positions. *Journal of Poverty*, 4(1/2), 151–65.

Joyce, P. (1997). A reversal of fortunes: Black empowerment, political machines, and city jobs in New York City and Chicago. *Urban Affairs Review*, 32(3), 29–57.

Lazarus, D. (2000, January 13). Political groups wire up faithful. *San Francisco Chronicle*, pp. A1, A4.

Lipsky, M. (1980). *Street-level bureaucracy*. New York: Sage Foundation.

May, M. (2000, January 19). Digital divide: Students without home computers getting left behind. *San Francisco Chronicle*, pp. A17, A20.

McNutt, J. (2000). Organizing cyberspace: Strategies for teaching about community practice and technology. *Journal of Community Practice*, 7(1), 95–109.

Meier, A. (2000). Offering social support via the Internet: A case study of an online support group for social workers. In J. Finn & G. Holden (Eds.), *Human services online: A new arena for service delivery* (pp. 237–66). New York: Haworth.

Nartz, M., & Schoech, D. (2000). Use of the Internet for community practice: A Delphi study. *Journal of Community Practice*, 8(1), 37–59.

Schopler, J., Abell, M., & Galinsky, M. (1998). Technology-based groups: A review and conceptual framework for practice. *Social Work*, 43(3), 254–67.

Shiffer, M. (1999). Planning support systems for low-income communities. In D. Schon, B. Sanyal, & W. Mitchell (Eds.), *High technology and low-income communities*. Cambridge: MIT Press.

Schultz, J., Fawcett, S., Francisco, V., Wolff, T., Berkowitz, B., & Nagy, G. (2000). The community tool box: Using the Internet to support the work of community health and development. In J. Finn & G. Holden (Eds.), *Human services online: A new arena for service delivery* (pp. 193–216). New York: Haworth.

So Gore really won. (2001, April 6). *Consortium News* [On-line]. Available: http://www.consortiumnews.com.

Taylor, M. (2000, July 30). Caught in a political web. *San Francisco Chronicle*, pp. A10, A11.

Thomsen, S. (1999, December 5). Click and choose: Arizona Democrats plan online voting for their presidential primary in March. *Fresno Bee*, p. A8.

U.S. Department of Commerce, National Telecommunications and Information Administration. (1999). Falling through the Net [On-line]. Available: http://www.ntia.doc.gov/ntiahome/fttn99.

Index